PAPERS OF THE 12TH WORLD SANSKRIT CONFERENCE VOL. 5

Themes and Tasks in Old and Middle Indo-Aryan Linguistics

Edited by

BERTIL TIKKANEN
HEINRICH HETTRICH

MOTILAL BANARSIDASS PUBLISHERS
PRIVATE LIMITED • DELHI

First Edition: Delhi, 2006

ISBN: 81-208-3062-8

**PAPERS OF THE 12TH WORLD SANSKRIT CONFERENCE
HELD IN HELSINKI, FINLAND, 13-18 JULY 2003
VOL. 5**

MOTILAL BANARSIDASS
41 U.A. Bungalow Road, Jawahar Nagar, Delhi 110 007
8 Mahalaxmi Chamber, 22 Bhulabhai Desai Road, Mumbai 400 026
203 Royapettah High Road, Mylapore, Chennai 600 004
236, 9th Main III Block, Jayanagar, Bangalore 560 011
Sanas Plaza, 1302 Baji Rao Road, Pune 411 002
8 Camac Street, Kolkata 700 017
Ashok Rajpath, Patna 800 004
Chowk, Varanasi 221 001

General Editors
PETTERI KOSKIKALLIO & ASKO PARPOLA

Printed in India
BY JAINENDRA PRAKASH JAIN AT SHRI JAINENDRA PRESS,
A-45 NARAINA, PHASE-I, NEW DELHI 110 028
AND PUBLISHED BY NARENDRA PRAKASH JAIN FOR
MOTILAL BANARSIDASS PUBLISHERS PRIVATE LIMITED,
BUNGALOW ROAD, DELHI 110 007

Preface

Considering the vast extant Vedic, classical and post-classical Sanskrit literature, the continuing use of Sanskrit as a spoken language, and the importance of Sanskrit to historical-comparative linguistics, it is but natural that this language has attracted and still attracts so much attention among philologists and linguists the world over. Thanks to the efforts of countless scholars, starting with the native Indian grammarians, the actual description of the language is drawing nearer and nearer to perfection. Yet there are lingering synchronic and diachronic problems; and new questions emerge as new documents are found, the analysis goes deeper, and the linguistic and historical sciences progress.

The present volume contains twelve of the sixteen papers presented at the Linguistics section of the 12th World Sanskrit Conference (Helsinki, Finland, 13-18 July, 2003). The papers span a wide range of topics and time depth, extending from Common Indo-Iranian all the way to Modern Indo-Aryan. The general focus is, nevertheless, on Old and (early) Middle Indo-Iranian.

The papers have been arranged thematically as follows: historical phonology of Old Indo-Aryan (Kobayashi), Vedic morphosyntax (Hock, Kulikov), evolutionary aspects of Indo-Aryan morpho-syntax (Bubenik, Oguibénine), Old Indo-Aryan etymology (Seldeslachts), loanwords and substrata/convergence at various stages of Indo-Aryan/-Iranian (Baghbidi, Pinault, Scharfe), Sanskrit translation of Avestan (Sheldon), Gāndhārī lexicography (Glass), and computer processing of Sanskrit (Huet).

At the end of the volume there is a brief index giving selected technical terms, proper names, and Sanskrit words of particular interest treated at length in one or several articles.

A trend which can be discerned in some of these papers, as well as in present-day Sanskrit studies in general, is the ever-increasing impact of modern linguistic theories of, in particular, both phonology and syntax. In these areas Sanskrit offers interesting challenges and data. Another strong trend is the study of languages in contact, as eminently exemplified by Scharfe's enlarged paper on the complex and much debated issue of linguistic convergence in South Asia. This field is particularly demanding in that it requires first-hand knowledge of the non-Aryan languages of the subcontinent. Computational linguistics is a new-comer in Sanskrit studies. As seen in Huet's paper, a program for processing Sanskrit texts by computer not only has a utilitarian value for the student and the researcher, but it puts descriptive formalism to the most rigorous test.

We wish to thank Jouna Pyysalo, who assisted in proof-reading the manuscripts and suggesting corrections. The financial support of the Finnish Cultural Foundation to the Conference is duly and gratefully acknowledged.

Helsinki, 27.5.2005

Bertil Tikkanen
Heinrich Hettrich

Contents

Preface v

Contents vii

Contributors ix

MASATO KOBAYASHI
The development of Proto-Indo-Iranian **sć* into Sanskrit /(c)c^h/ 1

HANS HENRICH HOCK
Reflexivization in the Rig-Veda (and beyond) 19

LEONID KULIKOV
The Vedic medio-passive aorists, statives and their participles: reconsidering the paradigm 45

VIT BUBENIK
On the evolutionary changes in the Old and Middle Indo-Aryan systems of case and adpositions 65

BORIS OGUIBÉNINE
Notes on the instrumental case of the subject/agent vs. other cases in Buddhist Sanskrit 89

ERIK SELDESLACHTS
Prākrit-like developments in Old Indo-Aryan: testing the 'Kölver-principle' 121

HASSAN REZAI BAGHBIDI
Iranian elements in Sanskrit 143

GEORGES-JEAN PINAULT
Further links between the Indo-Iranian substratum
and the BMAC language 167

HARTMUT SCHARFE
Indo-Aryan and Dravidian convergence:
gerunds and noun composition 197

JOHN S. SHELDON
The Sanskrit translation of the Avestan Haoma Liturgy
in the light of recent research 255

ANDREW GLASS
A preliminary study of Gāndhārī lexicography 273

GÉRARD HUET
Lexicon-directed segmentation and tagging in Sanskrit 305

Index 325

Contributors

HASSAN REZAI BAGHBIDI
Department of Ancient Iranian Languages, Tehran University, Engelab Avenue, Tehran, Iran

VIT BUBENIK
Department of Linguistics, Memorial University of Newfoundland, St. John's, A1B 3X9, Canada

ANDREW GLASS
Department of Asian Languages and Literature, University of Washington, Box 353521, Seattle WA 98195-3521, U.S.A.

HANS HENRICH HOCK
Department of Linguistics, University of Illinois, 4088 FLB, MC-168, 707 S. Mathews, Urbana, IL 61801-3652, U.S.A.

GÉRARD HUET
Institut National de Recherche en Informatique et en Automatique, Le Chesnay Cedex, France

MASATO KOBAYASHI
School of Business Management, Hakuoh University, 1117 Daigyoji, Oyama 323-8585, Japan

LEONID KULIKOV
Faculty of Arts, Department of Comparative Linguistics, Leiden University, P.O. Box 9515, NL-2300 RA Leiden, The Netherlands

Boris Oguibénine
Institut de Sanskrit, Université Marc Bloch de Strasbourg, 14, rue Descartes, F-67084 Strasbourg Cedex, France

Georges-Jean Pinault
École Pratique des Hautes Études, Section des Sciences historiques et philologiques, Sorbonne, 45-47, rue des Écoles, F-75005 Paris, France

Hartmut Scharfe
Asian Languages and Cultures, University of California, Box 951540, 290 RH, Los Angeles, CA 90095-1540, U.S.A.

Erik Seldeslachts
Department of Languages and Cultures of South and East Asia, Ghent University, Blandijnberg 2, B-9000 Gent Belgium

John S. Sheldon
Macquarie University, Sydney NSW 2109, Australia

The development of Proto-Indo-Iranian **sć* into Sanskrit /(c)c^h/*

MASATO KOBAYASHI

1. INTRODUCTION AND PROBLEM

In a theory to explain phonological changes, the result of the change should ideally be generated by a limited set of cross-linguistic principles. And if a certain part of the theory makes a wrong prediction or overgenerates a spurious output, its use should be limited to a restrictive condition. When judged by this criterion, historical phonology has a few explanatory devices which could compromise its theoretical rigour, such as dissimilation and metathesis, which are often employed rather freely. Generative phonologists have developed understanding of the relationship of interdependency between distinctive features, and now phonological representation has become possible for many sub-phonemic entities and phenomena which could formerly be captured only by phonetic description. In this article, we revisit the old puzzle of the change

---

* I thank Dr. George Cardona and Dr. Werner Knobl for their valuable comments. Throughout this paper, aspiration is written with a superscript h as t^h, and a syllabic sonorant is written with a vertical stroke as *r̩*. The following are other special notations and abbreviations. *: A reconstructed form; ˟: An unattested form; √: A root; +: "Or later"; /t/ etc.: Phonemic representation; T: Stop; P: Plosive (i.e. plosive or affricate); S: Sibilant; AV: Atharvaveda; Kāṭh.: Kāṭhaka-Saṃhitā, R̩V: R̩gveda; TS: Taittirīya-Saṃhitā, VS: Vājasaneyi-Saṃhitā; PIE: Proto-Indo-European; PIIr.: Proto-Indo-Iranian; Skt.: Sanskrit; Av.: Avestan; OAv.: Old Avestan; YAv.: Younger Avestan.

of the Proto-Indo-Iranian cluster **sć* < PIE **sḱ* into Sanskrit /(c)c^{h}/, and seek the possibility to explain what appears to be unarguably discontinuous development as a result of the accumulation of common and regular phonological changes.

Although Sanskrit /c^{h}/ is traditionally arranged as an aspirated counterpart of /c/, it is actually a unit phoneme and behaves as a cluster /cc^{h}/ unless it is utterance-initial or is preceded by a long vowel; it is thus written /(c)c^{h}/ in this paper. Its prosodic status as a consonant cluster is explained by its reconstruction as **sḱ* or **sk* in Proto-Indo-European; more importantly, this sequence must still have been a solid cluster in Proto-Indo-Iranian, probably **sć* according to the general development of PIE **ḱ* into PIIr. **ć*, for Proto-Indo-European clusters simplified earlier do not usually maintain two timing slots, as in Sanskrit *áśi* pres.2sg. of √*as* 'be' < PIE **és-si*, or even PIE **th*$_2$ in, e.g., *rát*^{h}*a-* 'carriage', which is considered to have still been a cluster in Proto-Indo-Iranian (PIE **róth*$_2$*o-* > PIIr. **rátHa-*). Preservation of the original cluster status in Proto-Indo-Iranian is found not only in /(c)c^{h}/ < PIIr. **sć*, but also in /ḍ^{h}/ < PIIr. **žd*^{h} and /ḍ/ < PIIr. **žd*; for example, it can be taken as making position in ṚV 10.121.5a *yéna dyáur ugrā́ pṛt*^{h}*ivī́ ca dṛḷ*^{h}*ā́*/, and in 2.27.14a *ádite mítra váruṇota mṛḷa*/ (ṚV *ḷ*^{h} = /ḍ^{h}/, *ḷ* = /ḍ/).

Among the Sanskrit morphemes with /(c)c^{h}/ which are traceable back to Proto-Indo-European, the one most widely attested in other Indo-European languages is the verbal suffix **-s{k/ḱ}{é/ó}-*. Its reflexes, or at least its traces, are proposed for almost all subgroups; Hittite *atskantsi* 'they devour', Tocharian B class IX verbs like *pāskau* 'I keep', Latin *poscere* 'to ask' < **pṛ(k)-sḱé-*, Old Irish *arcu, arco* 'I ask' < **pṛ(k)-sḱó-h*$_2$, Armenian *e-harc'* aor.3sg. 'asked' < **é-pṛ(k)sḱet*, Homeric Greek *báske* 'go', *érk*^{h}*omai* 'I go' < **h*$_1$*ér-sḱo-*, Old High German *wascan* 'to wash', Old Church Slavonic *iskati, ištetĭ* 'seeks' < **h*$_2$*is-sḱé/ó-*, Albanian *nieh/nief* 'to count, consider' < Proto-Albanian **nem-ska-* (Orel 1998: 100).

The reconstruction of the second consonant not as velar **k* but as palatal **ḱ* is based on Avestan *-s-*, as in *jasaiti* 'goes', to which Vedic *-cc^{h}-*, as in *gácc^{h}ati* 'goes', corresponds: Avestan *s* is the regular outcome of Proto-Indo-European palatal **ḱ* before vowels (Hoffmann & Forssman 1996: 102, 188), e.g. YAv. *satəm* 'hundred' < PIIr. **ćatám* < PIE **(d)ḱm̥tó-m*, and the last of a cluster of sibilants (*s* < PIIr. **ć* of **sć* in this case) survives.[1]

Of the Early Vedic words containing *c^{h}*, those deriving from the **-sḱé/ó-* suffix are: √*gam* : *gácc^{h}a-* 'go', √*yam* : *yácc^{h}a-* 'hold', √*yav* : *yúcc^{h}a-* 'keep away', √*hvar* : Kāṭh.+ *hū́rc^{h}a-* 'waver, go astray' with secondary initial accent, √*eṣ* : *icc^{h}á-* 'seek', √*vas* : *ucc^{h}á-* 'shine', √*ar* : *r̥cc^{h}á-* 'come across', √*praś* : *pr̥cc^{h}á-* 'ask', √*mūrc^{h}* : AV+ *mūrc^{h}a-* 'thicken'. A few verbal roots have initial *c^{h}*: √*c^{h}ad* 'cover': *c^{h}ādáya-*, *c^{h}adíṣ-*, √*c^{h}and* 'appear, please': *c^{h}adáya-*, YAv. *saδaiieiti*, √*c^{h}ed* 'cut': *c^{h}idrá-* adj., Av. √*sid*, Greek *sk^{h}ízō*, Latin *scindō* < **sḱ$^{(h)}$id*, √*c^{h}ard* 'vomit': *c^{h}r̥nátti*, √*c^{h}ā*: AV+ *c^{h}yáti* 'cut (the skin)'. There are several other cases of *c^{h}*, some of which do not have transparent etymology: *ácc^{h}ā* 'toward' < PIIr. **a-sćā* according to Lubotsky (2001: 42), AV+ *r̥cc^{h}árā-* 'fetlock' : R̥V *an-r̥kṣará-* 'spineless' (?), *ducc^{h}únā* f. 'calamity' < *duṣ-* 'ill-' + *śuná-* n. 'felicity', AV+ *púcc^{h}a-* 'tail', TS+ *párucc^{h}epa-* prop.n. < *parut* + *śepa-* (Hoffmann 1975: 332), *c^{h}úbuka-* n. 'chin', *c^{h}aví́-* f. 'skin, hide', *c^{h}āyā́-* f. 'shadow' : Greek *skiā́*, Albanian *hijē* 'shadow', *c^{h}ā́ga-* m. 'goat', *tuc^{h}yá-* a. 'empty, vain' (Examples from EWA and Lubotsky 2001).

The compound *ducc^{h}únā-* from /dus-śuná-/ or PIIr. **duš-ćuná-*, compared with another, more general type of R̥gvedic compounds such as *duḥśáṃsa-* < /dus-śáṃsa-/, shows that the change of PIIr. **sć* into Sanskrit *cc^{h}* stopped at some point in pre-Vedic Indo-

---

[1] Pointing out the fact that inherited /(c)c^{h}/ is limited to postvocalic contexts, Lubotsky 2001 argues that there is no problem with reconstructing **sk* instead of **sḱ* in Proto-Indo-European, and that Sanskrit /(c)c^{h}/ and Avestan /s/ are explainable by levelling from palatalizing contexts. As Proto-Indo-European **sk* in an intervocalic context is levelled to palatal **sć* in Proto-Indo-Iranian in his theory (Lubotsky 2001: 37), however, it does not affect our discussion of the development of Proto-Indo-Iranian **sć* after Indo-Aryan branched off.

Aryan. The compound *ā́sat-* 'nothingness', for example, is considered to date back to a period when the verb PIE **$h_1$es* 'be' > PIIr. **Has* > Sanskrit √*as* still had an initial laryngeal, because the compensatory lengthening of *a-* 'un-' < PIE **n̥-* would not have taken place once the root-initial laryngeal had disappeared. In a similar way, the irregular sandhi found in a few compounds in Vedic with *dus-* 'ill-', i.e. R̥V *dūḍáb^{h}a-* instead of ˣ*dur-dáb^{h}a-*, AV *dūḍā́ś-* instead of ˣ*dur-dā́ś-*, R̥V *dūḍ^{h}ī́* instead of ˣ*dur-d^{h}ī́*, R̥V *dūṇáśa-* instead of ˣ*dur-ṇáśa-*, or R̥V *dūṇā́śa-* instead of ˣ*dur-ṇā́śa-*, indicates that they are old enough to be established as lexical units and thus are exempt from application of external sandhi rules.

This is the philological evidence we have at hand. From the viewpoint of historical phonology the development of PIIr. **sć* < PIE **s{k/ḱ}* into Vedic /(c)c^h/ involves two developments which cannot be explained merely by adding up gradual sound changes. In the first place, why is only the **s* in the cluster **sć* lost, unlike the **s* before other voiceless plosives, which are not lost until Middle Indo-Aryan? Secondly, where does the aspiration of /(c)c^h/ come from, although the original Proto-Indo-Iranian sequence **sć* contains no aspiration?

2. PREVIOUS EXPLANATIONS

a) Place assimilation **sć* > **ść* + occlusion

Wackernagel (1896: 156) considers that the **s* in PIE **sḱ* had already undergone place assimilation to *ś* in Proto-Indo-Iranian; i.e. PIE **sḱ* > PIIr. **śś* > Av. *s*, Ved. *cc^h*. Wackernagel (1896: 179) points out parallelism between this change of **śś* to *cc^h* and the occlusion of *ss* to *ts* as in √*vas* 'dwell' : fut. *vat-sya-ti*.

It is more likely, however, that PIE **ḱ* had occlusion in Proto-Indo-Iranian, according to the Nuristani evidence such as Waigali *čūnə-* 'empty' (*č*: [ts]) < PIIr. **ćuHna-* and Kati *duč* 'ten' : PIE **deḱm̥t-*, and hence the Proto-Indo-Iranian reflex of PIE **sḱ* with place assimilation would better be written as **ść* rather than **śś* (Hoffmann & Forssman 1996: 103). Burrow (1965: 92-93), Hock

(1987: 151) and Jamison (1991: 83) give essentially the same explanation with occlusion.

A problem with this explanation is pointed out by Bartholomae (1896: 710) and Leumann (1941: 12-13), regarding the occlusion of a sibilant before */ś/ < PIIr. **ć*; according to them, this theory overestimates the regularity and antiquity of the occlusion of **s*~**š* in a cluster of two sibilants. The occlusion of the first of two contiguous sibilants, as in √*vas* 'dwell' : *avātsīḥ* (AV+) s-aor.2sg. act., *vatsyati* fut.3sg.act. (Brāhmaṇa+), is probably not a phonological phenomenon but an alteration which gradually emerges in Vedic in certain morphological contexts such as the aorist and the future tense, while the occlusion of a sibilant before *ś* < PIIr. **ć* should have been a regular development.

b) Transfer of **s* to aspiration

Zubatý (1892) and Wackernagel (1896: 157) suggest that the development of PIE **sḱ* into Sanskrit /(c)c^{h}/ is essentially the same as the change of the Old Indo-Aryan clusters /sp/, /st/, /ṣṭ/, /sc/, /sk/ into /pp^{h}/, /tt^{h}/, /ṭṭ^{h}/, /cc^{h}/, /kk^{h}/ in many Middle Indo-Aryan languages, e.g.

Skt. *púṣpa-* 'flower' : Mahārāṣṭrī etc. *pupp*^{h}*a*
Skt. *ásti* 'is' : Pāli *att*^{h}*i*
Skt. *dr̥ṣṭí-* 'look' : Mahārāṣṭrī etc. *diṭṭ*^{h}*i*
Skt. *paścā́(t)* 'afterwards' : Gāndhārī Dharmapada *pac*^{h}*a*
Skt. *śúṣka-* 'dry' : Ardhamāgadhī *sukk*^{h}*a-*

In featural terms, the transfer of /s/ into aspiration in Middle Indo-Aryan can be represented as follows.[2] The sequence /sP/, of which /P/ covers /k, c, ṭ, t, p/, is a legitimate cluster in Old Indo-

[2] This is not the only explanation given by the proponents of this theory. See, for example, Bubenik 2003: 217 for an explanation with metathesis of /sC/ into /Cs/. In this paper, we try to do without metathesis unless the phenomenon is otherwise unexplainable.

Aryan. Then in Middle Indo-Aryan, an /s/ in coda position is treated as ill-formed and becomes fricative, losing its segmental status, something like /ʰP/.

> Then in the third stage, any coda or coda-like element is eliminated unless it is multiply linked to an onset. Floating aspiration relinks to the onset /P/.
>
> ⌴ P^h
ǂ
[asp.]

> Finally, the empty consonant slot is filled in by a voiceless counterpart of /P^h/, which is the only possible plosive coda before a plosive.
>
> [P] ← P^h
| |
C C

The problem with using transfer of aspiration to explain the origin of /(c)c^h/ is the centuries of chronological gap between the change from PIIr. **sć* into Sanskrit /(c)c^h/, which was completed already in the pre-Vedic period, and the change from Old Indo-Aryan clusters of the same shape, /SP/, into Middle Indo-Aryan /PP^h/ clusters. In other words, this theory fails to explain Proto-Indo-Iranian /SP/ clusters other than **sć* not becoming /PP^h/. Vedic shows, in fact, a few precursors of the transfer of /s/ to aspiration, such as the doublet root √*kʰyā* ~ √*kśā* 'see', or the historically unexplainable aspiration of initial /sP-/ cluster as in Ved. *spʰíj-* 'loin' : Old High German *spec* 'fat', and it is not inconceivable that an /SP/ cluster became /PP^h/ already in pre-Vedic. However, in Old Indo-Aryan, where /SP/ clusters are perfectly well-formed, transfer of /s/ to aspiration occurs only sporadically (Wackernagel 1896: 122-123), and this is different from the sweeping elimination of coda sibilants in most of the non-northwestern Middle Indo-Aryan languages.

The explanations by Bloomfield (1911: 44), Leumann (1941: 17, 19) and Lubotsky (2001: 48) are also based on the transfer of a sibilant to aspiration. Instead of a rather *ad hoc* use of the term Prākritism, however, Leumann and Lubotsky explain the transfer by sensibly pointing out the aspirational nature of a sibilant in Old Indo-Aryan. And instead of comparing the abrupt loss of the cluster-initial **s* of **sć* with Middle Indo-Aryan, Bloomfield explains it as analogous to the simplification of obstruent clusters, as in /vṛśc-si/ > *vṛkṣi*, s-aor.1sg.mid. of √*vraśc* 'hew'. In sections 4 and 5, we will examine this possibility in more detail.

3. ESTIMATED PRONUNCIATION OF PALATAL PLOSIVES

The phonemic inventory of Proto-Indo-Iranian is reconstructed with two series of palatal plosives, primary and secondary. Primary palatal plosives **ć*, **ȷ́* and **ȷ́ʰ* come from PIE palatalized velars **ḱ*, **ǵ* and **ǵʰ*. On the other hand, secondary palatals **č*, **ǰ* and **ǰʰ* come from other velars in palatalizing contexts, i.e. before front vowels, e.g. *śúci-* adj. 'bright' : *śóka-* m. 'light'.

The phonetic values of the primary and secondary palatal plosives in Proto-Indo-Iranian are estimated as follows. For the Proto-Indo-Iranian primary palatal voiceless plosive **ć*, both Sanskrit and Avestan have sibilants, but this is reconstructed as an affricate in Proto-Indo-Iranian, primarily based on its reflex as a dental affricate /t^s/ (*c*) in the Nuristani languages. The primary palatal voiced plosives **ȷ́* and **ȷ́ʰ* are similarly reconstructed as affricates. From the reflexes of PIIr. **ć* in a pre-vocalic context, i.e. the dental fricative *s* in Iranian, the dental affricate /t^s/ in Nuristani, and the palatal fricative *ś* in Indo-Aryan, the place of articulation of the primary palatals can be reconstructed either as dental or as palatal (Degener 2002: 109-110); the Proto-Indo-Iranian development of **ć* into anterior **š* in a cluster, such as PIIr. **nać-tá-* 'perished' > **naš-tá-* > Skt. *naṣṭá-*, YAv. *našta-* (Hoffmann & Forssman 1996: 102), however, is better explained by assuming that primary palatal plosives were not yet depalatalized in Proto-Indo-Iranian as in Iranian or Nuristani.

In the case of the secondary palatal plosives, palatalization of the original Proto-Indo-European velars or labio-velars is more recent than that of the primary palatals, and if they were already affricated in Proto-Indo-Iranian, they would have merged with, or at least have been confused with, primary palatals, and hence I assume them to be palatalized velars or palatal stops (i.e. non-affricative plosives).

	primary palatals (palatal/palato-alveolar affricates)			secondary palatals (palatal/palatalized velar stops)		
PIIr.	*ć [ʧ]	*j́ [ʤ]	*j́^{h} [ʤ^{h}]	*č [k^{j}/c]	*ǰ [g^{j}/ɟ]	*ǰ^{h} [g^{hj}/ɟ^{h}]
Sanskrit	/ś/ [ɕ/ʃ]	/j/ [ɟ/ʤ]	/h/ [ɦ]	/c/ [c/ʧ]	/j/ [ɟ/ʤ]	/h/ [ɦ]
Avestan	/s/ [s]	/z/ [z]	/z/ [z]	/c/ [ʧ]	/j/ [ʤ]	/j/ [ʤ]

Based on their Sanskrit reflexes as fricatives, the first occlusive parts of the Proto-Indo-Iranian primary palatals **ć*, **j́* and **j́^{h}* are lost in pre-Vedic Indo-Aryan as well as in Iranian. Although Sanskrit /j/ is a plosive, forms such as *iṣ-ṭá-*, vb.adj. of √*yaj/ij* 'worship', must have gone through an intermediate form **iʒ-tá-*, unlike *tik-tá-*, vb.adj. of *tej/tij* 'sharpen' with a /j/ from secondary **ǰ*. The same intermediate stage is assumed for the voiced aspirate **j́^{h}*, for *rīḍ^{h}á-*, a verbal adjective of √*rih* 'lick', is considered to have developed from PIIr. **rij́^{h}-tá-* > **riʒ^{h}-d^{h}á-* > **riʒ-d^{h}á-* by BARTHOLOMAE'S LAW, deletion of **ʒ* and compensatory lengthening, closely parallel to the development of an actual sibilant in PIE **misd^{h}-u̯ós-* > PIIr. **miž-d^{h}vás-* (*ž: [ʒ]) > Sanskrit *mīḍ^{h}vás-* 'bountiful'.

All three primary palatal plosives are thus considered to have been sibilants in one period in pre-Vedic Indo-Aryan, and their development from affricates into sibilants is generalized as a change of contour segments[3] into simple segments. Since primary palatals are the only contour segments in Proto-Indo-Iranian, this

[3] A contour segment is a segment with one timing slot and two root nodes, which roughly correspond to articulatory gestures or acoustic phases in phonetic terms.

amounts to saying that Indo-Aryan, shortly after it branched off from Proto-Indo-Iranian, came to have a restriction with respect to contour segments. As a contour segment is a segment with two root nodes under one timing slot, this restriction is formulated in the following way:

> AFFRICATE FILTER: In early pre-Vedic Indo-Aryan, one timing slot can have only one root node (i.e. only one phase such as occlusion or frication).

Let us call this restriction the AFFRICATE FILTER in the following part of this paper, for an affricate, which has stop and fricative phases under one timing slot, is ruled out by this filter. Proto-Indo-Iranian secondary palatals were probably not yet affricated at this point, and they passed this filter. As a filter, an AFFRICATE FILTER merely checks how well-formed a segment is, and the actual repair process is taken care of by a separate rule of delinking, which is tentatively formulated as follows:

> When there is more than one root node under one timing slot, the furthest left is delinked.

It would be more cogent, however, if we could view this delinking phenomenon in a wider context of cluster simplification, than setting up an *ad hoc* rule merely to explain the deocclusion of primary palatals.

4. SIMPLIFICATION OF CLUSTERED OBSTRUENTS

Simplification of a consonant cluster is an issue too complicated to cover exhaustively in this paper; instead, let us limit our discussion to the simplification of clustered obstruents (i.e. plosives and fricatives), and start with easily generalizable phenomena.

In the first place, it is widely accepted as a peculiarity of Indo-Aryan that an /s/ trapped between two plosives is deleted (Wackernagel 1896: 269, Reichelt 1909: 36, Mayrhofer 1986: 110-111).

*$P_{[den]}sP_{[den]}$: PIIr. **sad-s-tá-* > R̥V *sattá-* vb.adj. of √*sad* 'sit', Av. *sasta-*. In Proto-Indo-European, an **s* is inserted between a heteromorphemic cluster of dental stops.

*$P_{[2pal]}sP_{[den]}$: PIIr. **b^haǰ-s-ta* > Sanskrit *áb^hakta* 3sg.s-aor. of √*b^haj* 'share'. **s* is not lost in Old Avestan *baxštā* (Hoffmann & Forssman 1996: 231).

*$P_{[vel]}sP_{[den]}$: PIIr. **(a-)g^hs-ta* ipf.mid.3sg. > *gd^ha*, PIIr. **n̥-g^hs-ta-* > Sanskrit *a-gd^ha-* vb.adj. of √*g^has* 'eat' (Leumann 1952: 33).

*$P_{[1pal]}sP_{[den]}$: PIIr. **čaćs-tai̯* becomes Sanskrit *cáṣṭe*, pres.3sg.act. of √*cakṣ* 'see'. If the medial sibilant of the cluster **ćst* dropped out already in Proto-Indo-Iranian, it would further become **št* in Proto-Indo-Iranian (PIIr. **ćt* > PIIr. **št* according to Hoffmann & Forssman 1996: 102), and then **čaštai̯* would develop into Sanskrit *cáṣṭe* and YAv. *cašte*. This is the view of Reichelt (1909: 51 §83.3) and Wiedenmann (1992: 244). Deletion of a medial sibilant, however, does not occur in other Avestan forms such as *sasta-* < PIIr. **sad-s-tá-*. If a primary palatal plosive triggers the "RUKI" rule and changes the following **s* into anterior **š*, PIIr. **čaćs-tai̯* should have become **čaćš-tai̯* already in Proto-Indo-Iranian; if so, it is simpler to consider that the cluster-initial **ć* was lost already in Proto-Indo-Iranian (> **čaštá-*).

As far as heteromorphemic dental contexts such as PIIr. **sad-s-tá-* are concerned, this phenomenon has no exception, and probably between other stops as well, although we are uncertain about the simplification process when the first plosive is a primary palatal, which is not a stop but an affricate.

ERASURE OF STRAY /*s*/ in Pre-Vedic Indo-Aryan:
PIIr. **s* → ∅ / T___T (T: stop), or possibly P___P (P: plosive).

There is a case, however, where this rule does not seem to apply. ṚV *viśvá-psnya-* 'alle Milch(labung) habend' (KEWA) is explained to come from PIIr. **-pstnya-*, a derivative of PIIr. **pstana-* 'breast', with deletion of **t* instead of **s*. Younger Avestan also has *ərᵊdva-fšnī-* 'with protruding breasts', and the simplification might have taken place already in Proto-Indo-Iranian.[4] In Iranian, there are at least two more cases of the loss of a cluster-internal dental (Reichelt 1909: 36): PIE **nept-sú*, loc.pl. of **népt-/népōt-* 'grand-son', for which no Indo-Aryan form is attested, becomes *nafšu* in Old Avestan. Although not a cluster of three obstruents, YAv. *ā-sna-* adj. 'successful' is explained by Bartholomae (1904: 341) as coming from PIIr. **ā-zd^h-na*, with the same root as Sanskrit √*sād^h* 'succeed'. In these three cases, **t* stands next to **s*, and next to **n* in two of them; a cluster-internal **t* might be deleted when it stands next to another coronal.

In order to make further generalizations, let us examine forms with simplified obstruent clusters other than the type /PsP/. Some are already simplified in Proto-Indo-European or Proto-Indo-Iranian.

PIE **pṛḱ-sḱé-ti* 'asks', Sanskrit *pṛcc^{h}áti*: Since no Indo-European language preserves the cluster-initial **ḱ*, it is considered to have been deleted already in Proto-Indo-European.

PIE *$P_{[pal]}P_{[den]}$ > PIIr. **št*: PIIr. **naćtá-* > YAv. *našta-*, Sanskrit *naṣṭá-*. The first occlusive constriction of the cluster PIIr. **ćt* [tʃt] was lost before the split between Iranian and Indo-Aryan (Hoffmann & Forssman 1996: 102); this sound change must be reconstructed in Proto-Indo-Iranian in order to explain the difference between it and the Indo-Aryan rule **PsP > PP*. This is not a case of cluster simplification in the traditional sense, but I cite it here because the occlusive part of **ć* is lost outside the usual context of the deocclusion of the primary palatals before

[4] Outside Indo-Iranian, Latin has a similar loss of a dental stop in a coronal context, e.g. **postne* > **posne* > *pōne* 'behind' (Leumann 1926–1928: 209).

sonorants. Also worth noting are Sanskrit _dāśvā̃ṁs-_ < PIE _*de-dḱ-u̯ós-_ (Klingenshmitt 1982: 129) and _pañcāśát_ 'fifty' < PIE _*pen_k^w_e-dḱm̥t_ with the early loss of _*d_ and compensatory lengthening.

PIIr. _*pstána-_: > _stána-_ 'breast', by the loss of the initial _*p_.

PIIr. _*vr̥ćk_ + _-tvī́_ > _vr̥ktvī́_, gerund of √_vraśc_ 'hew', and _vr̥kṣi_ s-aor.1sg.mid.

PIIr. _*nápt-b_^{h}_yas_ > _nád-b_^{h}_yaḥ_ (R̥V 10.60.6a), dat.pl. of _nápt(r)-/nápāt-_ 'grandson': Which of the cluster consonants _*p_ and _*t_ is lost remains an unresolved question, for the loss of the cluster-initial _*p_ would create _nád-b_^{h}_yaḥ_, but _*náp-b_^{h}_yas_ could also end up as _nád-b_^{h}_yaḥ_ by place dissimilation, as in _ad-b_^{h}_yáḥ_, ← _*ap-b_^{h}_yás_, dat.pl. of _áp-_ 'water'.

PIIr. _*ći-ćk-š-_: While Sanskrit _śíkṣati_ 'help', desid. of √_śak_ 'be able', can come from both _*śi-ś[k]-ṣá-_ and _*śi-[ś]k-ṣá-_, Av. _sixš-_ shows that _*ć_ is lost in the cluster _*ćkš_, for _*ćš_ would develop into _š_ in Avestan. Cf. Pāṇini, Aṣṭ. 8.2.29 _skoḥ saṃyogādyor ante ca_.

PIIr. _*di-db_^{h}_-sa-ti_: > _dípsati_ desid. of √_dab_^{h} 'deceive'. There are other cases of this formation, such as √_pat_ or √_pad_ : _pitsati_, but as Leumann (1952: 47) points out, not all of them result from a purely phonological process of simplification.

An obvious fact in these examples is that there is no demonstrable case of deletion of a cluster-final obstruent; on the contrary, it is possible in almost all cases to argue that the cluster-initial obstruent is deleted. A general rule of obstruent cluster simplification from Proto-Indo-Iranian to Indo-Aryan and Iranian seems to be to drop the initial one. Wackernagel (1896: 127 and 1905: 213), furthermore, gives _ád_^{h}_a kṣarantī́r_ (R̥V 7.34.2) and the compound _divá-kṣāḥ_ nom.sg. 'Himmelsherr' (Geldner) as examples of exceptional sandhi *-s kṣ-* > *-∅ kṣ-*, but they might actually reflect an older rule of obstruent cluster simplification, as we discuss here.[5]

Against this general rule, Indo-Aryan independently developed the ERASURE OF STRAY **s*, which has priority over the former rule, as the following chart illustrates. Deletion of the middle one in a medial cluster of three obstruents seems to be limited to PIIr. **t* followed or preceded by an **s*.

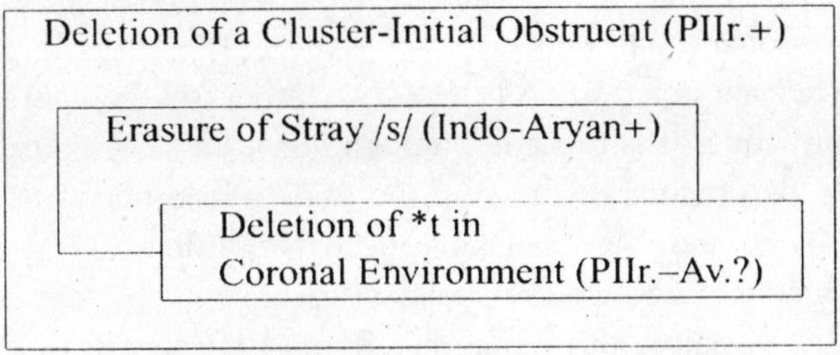

5. REGULAR DEVELOPMENT OF **sć* INTO /(c)c^h/

In section 3, we argued that primary palatal plosives are ruled out by the AFFRICATE FILTER and lose occlusion by delinking of the first root node or phase, without considering primary palatals in consonant clusters. And in the preceding section, we tried to generalize cluster simplification of mainly three obstruents. There we saw that cluster simplification seems to occur not only in a cluster of three obstruents but also in a cluster of two obstruents when one of them is a primary palatal plosive. Primary palatal plosives are affricates already in Proto-Indo-Iranian, and as they had stop and fricative phases, a two-obstruent cluster with a primary palatal might have been ill-formed in the same manner as clusters of three or more obstruents, and this might be the reason why Proto-Indo-Iranian **sć*, unlike other /ST/ clusters, was subject to simplification.

---

[5] Oldenberg 1912 considers that the emendation from *ád*^{h}*a* to $^{\times}$*ad*^{h}*á(s)* is unnecessary.

Now, if a cluster of three obstruents, including a cluster of two obstruents of which one is a primary palatal, is ill-formed in early pre-Vedic Indo-Aryan, and so is a singleton primary palatal because of the AFFRICATE FILTER, the question arises as to which was repaired first. Both delinking of the first of two phases and deletion of the first of three obstruents are phonologically motivated by a universal tendency called the Onset First Principle, i.e., an onset consonant is incorporated into a syllable with higher priority than a coda consonant, and hence is more resistant to phonological processes such as deletion. As these two processes are based on the same principle, it is possible, though not necessary, that they were actually two results of one and the same phenomenon; if this was the case, **ć* and **sć* must have been simplified to *[ʃ] and *[tʃ] simultaneously.[6] Since the skeletal structure of the two consonant slots still remains, the remaining [t] and [ʃ] spread to these two consonant slots. If, as I assume, */tʃ/ preserved the two timing slots of the original sequence PIIr. **sć*, its actual pronunciation was probably not [tʃ] but rather [ttʃ], just as plosives are doubled in other plosive-continuant clusters such as *patra-* 'leaf', which is pronounced *pattra-* with unoriginal gemination of the /t/.

The realization of [tʃ] as aspirated /(c)cʰ/ is due to the feature [aspirated] (or [spread glottis]) which Sanskrit sibilants seem to have. Firstly, the external sandhi rule *-t ś- > ccʰ* suggests that /ś/ was treated as aspirated. Secondly, the emergence of the so-called Aspiration Throwback in the new layer of Vedic as in ṚV *dipsa-* : VS *dʰipsa-*, desid. of √*dabʰ* 'deceive', makes sense if we assume that the feature [aspirated] began to be redundantly specified for the underlying representation of Indo-Aryan sibilants in the late pre-Vedic period. Given Old Avestan cognates such as *diβža-*,

---

[6] Alternatively, we could argue that PIIr. **ć* underwent deocclusion before a vowel but **ć* in the cluster **sć* remained an affricate, for a plosive in an **sC* cluster sometimes develops differently from a singleton, as the failure of GRIMM'S LAW in applying to a voiceless stop after voiceless fricatives as Gothic *ahtau* 'eight' shows. In that case, Indo-Aryan would be different from Avestan, where both a singleton **ć* and a **ć* in the **sć* cluster seem to have become sibilant *s*. I thank George Cardona for pointing out this possibility to me.

BARTHOLOMAE'S LAW must have originally worked for a **T^{h}s* cluster (the first diagram), until an **s* gained a preset value for the feature [aspirated] in Indo-Aryan. The same feature of the root-final aspirate then fails to link to the suffix-initial **s*, to which [aspirated] is prespecified, and spreads inside the root domain, backward to the root-initial stop (the second diagram).

$_{root}$[d i p] s a-

[asp.] Ø

$_{root}$[d^h i p] s a-

[asp.] [asp.]

(Two [asp]'s side by side are ill-formed by the Obligatory Contour Principle.)

If Sanskrit palatal plosives were affricates, the AFFRICATE FILTER might have ceased to be active sometime after the deocclusion of the primary palatal plosives, for it would otherwise block affrication of the secondary palatal plosives. On the other hand, a new restriction on voiced fricatives must have emerged sometime after the AFFRICATE FILTER, for **z* and **ź* (< PIIr. **ǰ*) are completely eliminated from the surface forms of Sanskrit. While the former was lost with compensatory lengthening or rhotacized if it is in a "RUKI" context, the latter regained occlusion and merged with the affricate *j* < PIIr. **ǰ*.

SIBILANT VOICING FILTER: A voiced oral obstruent must be a non-continuant, i.e. a voiced fricative is not allowed. Arranged after the AFFRICATE FILTER.

The development of the Proto-Indo-Iranian primary palatal plosives and the cluster **sć* are summarized as follows:

PIIr.		early Pre-Vedic	late Pre-Vedic	Vedic
		Affricate Filter ↓	Sibil. Voicing Filter	
Obstr. Cluster			Asp. of Sibilants →	
Simplification		→	→	→
		Stray /s/ Erasure →	→	→
*sć	*[sʧ]	*[ṭʃ̣]	*[ṭʃ̣$_{[asp.]}$]	/(c)c^h/
*ć	*[ʧ]	*[ʃ̣]	*[ʃ̣$_{[asp.]}$]	/ś/
*j́	*[ʤ]	*[ʒ]	*[ɟ/ʤ]	/j/
*j́^{h}	*[ʤ^h]	*[ʒ^h]	*[ɦ]	/h/

To sum up briefly, PIIr. **sć* violates the criteria of phonological well-formedness in pre-Vedic Indo-Aryan with respect to contour segments, for PIIr. **ć* is considered to have been an affricate with stop and fricative phases, and PIIr. **sć* has three obstruent phases in two consonant slots. Just as a cluster of three obstruents loses the first one by the most general rule of simplification, PIIr. **sć* [stʃ] first became [tʃ], which spread to the two consonant slots. Then the feature [aspirated] was redundantly specified for all sibilants in late pre-Vedic phonology, as the sandhi *-t ś-* > *cc^h* reflects. Finally, [tʃ] was phonemicized as an aspirate /(c)c^h/ and filled in the empty place of an aspirated voiceless palatal plosive in the consonant inventory of Old Indo-Aryan.

NOTE: A full version of this paper is in my revised dissertation, *Historical Phonology of Old Indo-Aryan Consonants*, published by the Research Institute for Languages and Cultures of Asia and Africa, Tokyo University of Foreign Studies, 2004.

REFERENCES

BARTHOLOMAE, Christian 1904. *Altiranisches Wörterbuch*. Strassburg: Trübner.

------ 1896. Beiträge zur altindischen Grammatik. *Zeitschrift der Deutschen Morgenländischen Gesellschaft* 50: 674–735.

BLOOMFIELD, Leonard 1911. The Indo-European palatals in Sanskrit. *American Journal of Philology* 32: 36–57.

BUBENIK, Vit 2003. Prākrits and Apabhraṃśa. In: George Cardona & Dh. Jain (eds.), *The Indo-Aryan Languages*: 204–249. London / New York: Routledge.

BUDDRUSS, Georg 1977. Nochmals zur Stellung der Nuristan-Sprachen des afghanischen Hindukusch. *Münchener Studien zur Sprachwissenschaft* 36: 19–38.

BURROW, Thomas 1965. *The Sanskrit Language*. 2nd ed. London: Faber and Faber.

DEGENER, Almuth 2002. The Nuristani Languages. In: Nicholas Sims-Williams (ed.), *Indo-Iranian Languages and Peoples*: 103–117. (Proceedings of the British Academy, 116.) Oxford: Oxford University Press.

EWA = MAYRHOFER, Manfred 1986–2001. *Etymologisches Wörterbuch des Altindoarischen*. Heidelberg: Carl Winter.

HOCK, Hans Henrich 1987. Regular contact dissimilation. In: George Cardona & Norman Zide (eds.), *Festschrift for Henry Hoenigswald*: 143–153. Tübingen: G. Narr.

HOFFMANN, Karl 1975. *Kleine Schriften*, I. Wiesbaden: L. Reichelt.

HOFFMANN, Karl & Bernhard FORSSMAN 1996. *Avestische Laut- und Formenlehre*. Innsbruck: Institut für Sprachwissenschaft der Universität Innsbruck.

JAMISON, Stephanie W. 1991. A Cart, an Ox, and the Perfect Participle in Vedic. *Münchener Studien zur Sprachwissenschaft* 52: 77–100.

KEWA = MAYRHOFER, Manfred 1953-1976. *Kurzgefasstes etymologisches Wörterbuch des Altindischen*. Heidelberg: Carl Winter.

KLINGENSHMITT, Gert 1982. *Das altarmenische Verbum*. Wiesbaden: L. Reichelt.

LEUMANN, Manu 1926–1928. *Lateinische Laut- und Formenlehre*. München: C. H. Beck.

------ 1941. Idg. *sk* im Altindischen und im Litauischen. *Indogermanische Forschungen* 58: 1–26.

------ 1952. *Morphologische Neuerungen im altindischen Verbalsystem*. Mededelingen der Koninklijke Nederlandse Akademie van Wetenschappen, Afd. letterkunde. Nieuwe reeks; deel 15, no. 3. Amsterdam: Noord-Hollandsche Uitgevers Maatschappij.

LUBOTSKY, Alexander 2001. Reflexes of Proto-Indo-European *sk in Indo-Iranian. *Incontri Linguistici* 24: 24–57.

MAYRHOFER, Manfred 1986. *Indogermanische Grammatik*: I-2 *Lautlehre*. Heidelberg: Carl Winter.

OLDENBERG, Hermann 1912. *Rgveda. Textkritische und exegetische Noten. Siebentes bis zehntes Buch.* Berlin: Weidmann.

OREL, Vladimir E. 1998. *Albanian Etymological Dictionary.* Leiden / Boston: E.J. Brill.

REICHELT, Hans 1909. *Awestisches Elementarbuch.* Heidelberg: Carl Winter.

WACKERNAGEL, Jacob 1896. *Altindische Grammatik,* I: *Lautlehre.* Göttingen: Vandenhoeck & Ruprecht.

------ 1905. *Altindische Grammatik,* II, 1: *Einleitung zur Wortlehre, Nominalkomposition.* Göttingen: Vandenhoeck & Ruprecht.

WIEDENMANN, Frank 1992. Uridg. Palatal vor *s/t/st* im Altindischen und der Nom. sg. der Stämme auf *-ś*. *Münchener Studien zur Sprachwissenschaft* 53: 241–249.

ZUBATÝ, Josef 1892. Die altindische tenuis aspirata palatalis. *Zeitschrift für vergleichende Sprachforschung auf dem Gebiete der indogermanischen Sprachen* 11: 9–22.

Reflexivization in the Rig-Veda (and beyond)[*]

HANS HENRICH HOCK

Sanskrit offers three different means of marking reflexivization. One of these is middle voice marking on the verb[1], contrasting with active marking, as in (1a) vs. (1b). A second pattern consists of the use of the possessive reflexive pronoun *svá* (2). The third marking strategy employs a "full" reflexive pronoun based on a noun. In the Rig-Veda this is *tanū́*, literally 'body' (3a). The later language offers *ātmán*, literally 'body, Self', which perhaps occurs as a reflexive pronoun once in the Rig-Veda (3b). In addition, the Rig-Veda offers forms based on *tmán* which have been taken to be reflexive (3c).

(1) Middle voice:

a. *śíśīte áti* [1.36.16c]
'makes himself sharp'

vs. b. *tvā́m ... sáṁ śiśīmasy* [1.102.10c]
'we make you sharp'

An earlier version of this paper was read at the 2003 Annual Meeting of the American Oriental Society. I am grateful for feedback from various colleagues, especially George Cardona, Tatyana Elizarenkova, Arlo Griffiths, Jan Houben, Paul Kiparsky, Leonid Kulikov, and Georges Pinault. Although some of them may still disagree with my findings, they have helped me in further developing my argument.

[1] Middle voice inflection, of course, has functions other than reflexive (and the closely related reciprocal) marking. Some of these other functions are addressed in Kulikov's contribution to the Conference, as well as in Kulikov 2003.

(2) *svá*:[2]

a. *svá ā́ dáme sudúghā yásya dhenúḥ* [2.35.7a]
'whose [is] in his own house a well-milked cow'

b. *svéna yuktā́saḥ krátunā* [7.90.5b]
'yoked by your own power'

(3) *tanū́, ātmán, tmán*:

a. *evā́ yajasva tanvàṁ* [10.7.6d]
'so sacrifice to yourself [contrast with the Gods]'

b. *bálaṁ dádhāna ātmáni* [9.113.1c]
'putting power in himself [or in his body?]'

c. i. *tmánā tánā sanuyāma tvótāḥ* [10.148.1d]
'may we be victorious with your help, for ourselves and with our offspring [or just: we, ourselves?]'
Graßmann: 'für uns selbst und unsere Kinder'
Geldner: 'Selbst wollen wir dauernd mit deiner Hilfe Gewinn haben.'

ii. *tmáne tokā́ya tánayāya mṛ̥la* [1.114.6d]
'have mercy on us ourselves, on (our) semen, on (our) offspring'
(Graßmann's interpretation is similar to that of (3c.i).)
Geldner: 'hab mit uns selbst, mit dem leiblichen Samen Erbarmen!'

(Similarly 1.183.3cd = 4.49.5cd, 1.184.5c[3])

Of these different formations, the middle voice is clearly inherited from Proto-Indo-European. Most scholars would reconstruct

---

[2] I ignore *svayám* which, as in the later language, is simply an emphatic "reflexive" (as in Engl. *she herself*), albeit, in the Rig-Veda, generally construed with a middle voice verb (see Graßmann).

[3] Elsewhere Graßmann generally gives readings such as 'nach seiner Art, aus freien Stücken, aus eigener Kraft', or even "weaker" ones (similar to *svayám*).

the possessive reflexive too (e.g. Delbrück, see (4)), but Lehmann (see (5)) rejects the reconstruction and considers the possessive reflexive a late innovation. The nominally derived, full reflexive pronoun type is considered an innovation by all scholars. Of these nominal forms, RV *ātmán* and *tmán* must be excluded from the discussion. The former occurs just once in the Rig-Veda, in a passage that I would consider to be of ambiguous interpretation – with *ātmáni* interpretable either as reflexive, or in its more literal meaning as 'body' (see the gloss on example (3b)). The passages with *tmán* that Graßmann interprets as reflexive (see (3c)) are problematic on two counts: The only forms that are attested are the instrumental and the locative, a fact which suggests that these are not used as pronouns, but as some kind of adverbials. Second, in examples such as (3c.ii), the form *tmáne* does not refer to the subject or agent of the sentence. Geldner's translations with the emphatic "reflexive" (as in Engl. *we ourselves*) therefore seem more appropriate. (See Kulikov 2001 for a similar conclusion.) This paper therefore focuses on *svá, tanū́*, and middle voice marking, and their historical and synchronic relation to each other.

(4) Delbrück 1893: Only the possessive reflexive pronoun, Skt. *sva-*, continues a PIE pattern. PIE had no full-fledged reflexive pronoun.[4]

(5) Lehmann 1974: PIE had no reflexive pronouns at all. Being SOV, it marked reflexivization on the verb, as middle voice. Skt. *sva-* reflects an original adjective, simply meaning 'own', derived from an earlier meaning 'dear'. (Essentially the same view is still found in Lehmann 1993: 184, 207, where Skt. *priyá* is added as a parallel for the development 'dear' ⇒ 'own'.)

---

[4] This view, then, requires the assumption that the occurrence of full reflexive-pronoun paradigms based on **s(w)e-* in various Indo-European languages (such as Latin, Germanic, and Slavic) is an innovation. This issue is beyond the scope of the present paper.

Specifically, I propose to demonstrate the following two points:

a. the reflexive possessive is complementary to middle voice verb inflection, marking the one constituent that cannot be expressed on the verb, namely the nominal genitive relation (as distinct from possible genitive marking on the complements of verbs that are subcategorized for genitive complements)

b. the full reflexive (RV *tanū́*) is indeed a very recent innovation, whose development can still be traced in the Rig-Veda.[5]

I am fully aware that neither of these two points is completely novel. In fact, they probably constitute the communis opinio, at least for Sanskrit.[6] Curiously, however, the evidence to support this view has, to my knowledge, never been presented in sufficient detail. I therefore hope that the evidence that I provide will be useful, and I am confident that my argument will help to refute Lehmann's extreme view.

For point a. – the complementarity of reflexive possessive and middle voice – I present two arguments.

One is the general one that the nominal genitive relation is fundamentally different from that of the case relations of verbal complements, a fact accounted for by Pāṇini's *ṣaṣṭhī śeṣe* and, in

[5] Kulikov 2000, 2001 argues that some uses of *tanū* are emphatic "reflexive", similar to *tmán*, and that in this function the form can even occur in the vocative. This argument deserves fuller investigation in its own right. – The occurrence of (apparently) reflexive *tanū* in Avestan raises the interesting question that this innovation may have been shared with ancient Iranian. The fact that examples seem to come from Late Avestan (Reichelt 1909: 292) may cause difficulties; but since the clearly inherited (possessive) reflexive *hva/x^{v}a* also is found only in Late Avestan, the lack of examples for either formation in Gatha Avestan may either be an accident or a matter of different genre (see Hock 1997a on the question of chronology vs. genre vis-à-vis (Vedic) Sanskrit). This issue, too, deserves fuller investigation.

[6] For point b., see most recently Pinault 2001.

modern syntactic theory, by stating that the adnominal genitive relation is not subcategorized on the verb. A near-parallel formal distinction can be found in English, where verbal-complement reflexivization takes the form *themselves*, while the adnominal, possessive variant is of the form *their/their (own)*, but not *their-selves** or the like.

The second argument is based on the specific evidence of the Rig-Veda. While the middle voice can encode reflexivity on all the various complements for which verbs are subcategorized, there are no unambiguous Rig-Vedic examples of nominal genitive relations expressed by middle voice verb endings – the few putative examples are open to alternative, non-possessive analyses. See (6), where the examples under i.-iii. illustrate the use of middle voice with direct objects, indirect objects/beneficiaries, and causees; but the rare examples for which a possessive interpretation would be possible are amenable to alternative interpretations, as in (6.iv).[7]

(6) Verbal reflexivization/middle voice in the Rig-Veda:

i. Accusative/DO:

a. *śiśīte áti* [1.36.16c]
'makes himself sharp'

vs. b. *tvā́m ... sáṁ śiśīmasy* [1.102.10c]
'we make you sharp'

ii. Dative/IO/Beneficiary:

a. *ā́ tvā́m r̥jiśvā sakhyā́ya cakre* [5.29.11c]
'R̥. made you for himself for friendship'

vs. b. *r̥jrā́śvam...pitā́ndháṁ cakāra* [1.116.16b]
'(his) father made R̥. blind'

---

[7] Here as elsewhere it would have been desirable to follow George Cardona's suggestion to give the larger contexts in which the cited passages occur; but to do so would increase the size of this paper beyond acceptable limits. I hope that by citing all relevant passages and by clearly indicating my interpretations, I have made my paper sufficiently transparent for readers to evaluate my conclusions and, in case of doubt, to locate the passages in the Rig-Vedic text.

iii. With causative:

a. Acc./DO

dhāpáyete śíśum ékam [1.96.5b]

'the two make one child nurse them(selves)'

b. Acc. = Causee:

yád góbhir vāsayiṣyáse [9.2.4c = 9.66.13c]

'when you cause yourself to put on/be clothed with cows'

iv. Genitive/Possessive (??):

stríyo hí dāsá ā́yudhāni cakré [5.30.9a]

'for the dāsa made women his own weapons' (?)

OR: 'for the dāsa made women weapons for himself'

Before turning to point b., let me briefly comment on the question whether *svá* is, in fact, a reflexive pronoun. The issue has been recently revived by Vine (1997). As Vine observes, "the possessor indicated with *svá-* need not correspond with the grammatical subject." (203-204) Moreover, while in some cases it may be considered a "topic", as suggested by Watkins (1976), this analysis will not do for others. Vine concludes that the pronoun is "not, strictly speaking, a "reflexive possessive" at all", but rather has the meaning 'own'. At the same time, Vine demonstrates that in many cases where *svá* does not refer to the grammatical (or surface) subject, it can be construed as referring to the logical subject of an embedded participial construction or to an explicit or implicit possessor noun phrase.

It is these findings which turn out to actually support the idea that *svá* is reflexive, not only in the classical language (for which Vine accepts that value), but also in the Rig-Veda.

As noted in Hock 1986 and 1991, reflexive *svá* and *ātmán*, as well as absolutives in *-tvā/ya* exhibit a similar behavior, referring to (or being controlled by) not only agents (in the Pāṇinian sense) – in both finite and non-finite (participial etc.) structures, but also by explicit or implicit genitive possessor noun phrases, which therefore should be considered "possessive agent" NPs. Since the participle of the verb 'be' is commonly omitted, it is possible to consider genitive noun phrases in examples such as (7a) to be the head of a reduced clause with possessor NP plus participle of the verb 'to be' (as in (7b)), but with the participle deleted.

(7) Possessor-NP control of reflexive in post-Rig-Vedic

a. *pāpīyasy asya* ∩ *ātmanaḥ prajā syād* [TS 5.6.8.2]

b. ≈ [*pāpīyasy asya* ∩ [*ātmanaḥ satī*]$_{\text{pple.}}$ *prajā syād*]$_{\text{MC}}$
'His (own) offspring would be worse off.'

It is true, there are occasional examples of "sloppy" reflexives – at all stages of the language, just as there are examples of "sloppy" absolutives (see again Hock 1986, 1991). But these remain a relatively small and "manageable" residue, once we recognize genitive possessor NPs as agents. To sum up, then, *svá* is as much a reflexive possessive pronoun in the Rig-Veda as it is in the later language.

Let me now turn to point b. – the claim that the development of *tanū́* as a reflexive pronoun is a recent innovation.

To support this claim I examine the passages that Graßmann lists as examples of reflexive usage of this form. Graßmann's list was compared with Pinault's (2001) list of passages that he considers to contain reflexive uses of *tanū́*, a list which contained a number of examples that Graßmann had not considered reflexive. The resulting list, of course, constitutes only a part of the total number of passages containing *tanū́*; no significance should therefore be attached to the relatively small number of passages in which I consider *tanū́* not to be reflexive.

As it turns out, only 17 passages thus examined are likely to be reflexive, see example (8); 24 are ambiguous, (9); and 8 are not likely to be reflexive, (10). Note in this regard that I have tried to be as conservative as possible in assigning reflexive readings. The ease with which it is possible to read a reflexive usage into a particular passage can be illustrated with the case of (9.ii.a). Taken by itself, this passage seems to call for a reflexive interpretation. But once the continuation of this verse (9.ii.a') is considered, with its focus on the physical body of Indra, a literal interpretation becomes at least equally likely for (9.ii.a).

(8) *tanū́* likely to be reflexive

i. With verb in middle voice:

a. *vandā́rus te tanvàṁ vande agne* [1.147.2d]
Ge.: 'Als dein Lobredner lobe ich mich selbst, o Agni.'
(Graßmann suggest a literal reading, but this is not a likely interpretation.)

b. *sū́ra upāké tanvàṁ dádhāno* [4.16.14a†[8]]
'Placing yourself [your body?] next to the sun' (said of Indra)

c. *... vatsáṁ ... svayáṁ gātúṁ tanvà icchámānam* [4.18.10cd]
'the calf ... looking itself for a path for itself'
(Contrastive; hardly 'for its body')

d. *(á)gne yájasva tanvàṁ táva svā́m* [6.11.2d]
Ge.: '... opfere dir selbst, o Agni!'

e. *utá sváyā tanvā̀ sáṁ vade* [7.86.2a]
'and I consult with myself' (redundant; but better than 'with my own body')

f. *svā́ṁ cāgne tanvàṁ pipráyasv(a)* [8.11.10c]
'satisfy yourself (your own body?)'

g. *ā́ [vr̥ṇīmahe] sucetúnam ... tanū́ṣu ā́* [9.65.30b†]
'we request ... good recognition for our bodies (??)/ourselves'

---

[8] The symbol † indicates passages not listed as reflexive by Pinault 2001.

h. *evā́ yajasva tanvàṁ* [10.7.6d]
'so sacrifice to yourself [contrast with the Gods]'

i. *ádevayūn tanvā̀ śū́śujānān* [10.27.2b†]
Ge.: 'die ... mit ihrem Leib sich breitmachenden Gottlosen'
Or rather: 'die ... sich breitmachenden ...' (see k. below)

j. *yé hinviré tanvàḥ soma ukthaíḥ* [10.28.12b]
Ge.: '... die sich bei Soma mit ihren Lobliedern beeilt haben.'

k. *tanvā̀ śū́śujānaḥ* [10.34.6b]
Ge.: 'sich breit machend' [i. and k. are near-hapax legomena]

l. *mithó hinvānā́ tanvā̀* [10.65.2b]
Ge.: 'sich gegenseitig selbst anspornend'

ii. With verb in the active and possessive/genitive of *tanū́*:
yó agníṁ tanvò dáme ... saparyáti [8.44.15ab]
'He who worships Agni in his own home'
[Agni's or the sacrificer's?]

iii. With active verb, likely to be reflexive

a. *káro yátra várivo bādhitā́ya divé jánāya tanvè gṛṇānáḥ* [6.18.14d]
Ge.: '... in dem du gepriesen dem bedrängten Himmel, dem Volke, dir selbst einen Ausweg schufest.'

b. *janáyan mitráṁ tanvè svā́yai* [10.8.4d]
'creating a friend for yourself (your body???)'

c. *yajñáṁ janitvī́ tanvī́ ní māmṛjuḥ* [10.65.7d][9]

[9] Kulikov 2001 takes this example to be reflexive, since the singular is used; but note that the singular could simply be distributive, with the literal meaning of *tanū́*, 'each God into his own body'. What persuades me to nevertheless include this example in the list of likely reflexives is the parallelism with 10.66.9d (next example), where a literal interpretation seems unlikely (pace Graßmann).

'creating the sacrifice (the Gods) rubbed it into themselves'

d. *váśaṁ devā́sas tanvı̀ ní māmr̥juḥ* [10.66.9d][10]
Ge.: 'Die Götter eigneten sich die Herrschaft an.'

(9) *tanū́* ambiguous

i. With verb in the middle voice:

a. *áṣāḷhaṁ sáhas tanvì śrutó dadhe* [1.55.8b]
'the famous one places insurmountable power in his body/in himself' (Ge.: 'besitzt … am Leibe')

b. *nā́māni cid dadhire yajñíyāny ásūdayanta tanvàḥ* [1.72.3cd]
Ge.: 'haben sie sich selbst opferwürdige Namen erworben und ihre Leiber vervollkommt'
(Could also be reflexive.)

c. *ánu mr̥kṣīṣṭa tanvàṁ duruktaiḥ* [1.147.4d‡[11]]
Ge.: 'Es soll sich hernach selbst durch seine bösen Reden Abbruch tun.'
(Could also be literal, following Graßmann: 'seinem Leib'.)

d. *tanvàḥ śúmbhamānāḥ* [1.165.5b = 7.59.7a]
Ge.: 'unsere Leiber … schmückend'
(Could also be reflexive.)

e. *tanvàṁ parivyáta* [2.17.2c]
'girded himself/his body'

f. *méne iva tanvā̀ śúmbhamāne* [2.39.2c]
Ge.: 'wie Frauen mit ihrem Leibe prunkend'.
Or: 'like women ornamenting themselves/their bodies'

g. *agne tanvàṁ juṣasva* [3.1.1d‡]

---

[10] This example comes from Pinault 2001, who evidently did not restrict himself to passages labeled reflexive by Graßmann. I agree with Pinault's assessment of this passage.

[11] The symbol ‡ indicates passages that Pinault 2001 considers reflexive.

'O Agni, find pleasure in yourself/your body'
(Similarly, in plural, 10.8.3d‡)

h. *stómaṁ me agne tanvā̀ juṣasva* [3.15.2d]
'Enjoy my praise, Agni, with your body/yourself'

i. *sá mandasvā ... tànvā̀ ...* [3.41.6b]
'Enjoy with your body/yourself'

j. *punā́ne tanvā̀ mitháḥ* [4.56.6a‡]
Ge.: 'Wechselseitig euch selbst reinigend'
(Could also be 'mutually cleaning your bodies' [ref. to heaven and earth].)

k. *váyaḥ kr̥ṇvānás tanvè svā́yai* [5.4.6b]
'producing strength for his own body/ himself'

l. *tásya te śarmann upadadyámāne rāyā́ madema tanvā̀ tánā ca* [6.49.13cd‡]
Ge.: '… wollen wir in deiner dargebotenen Zuflucht am Reichtum uns ergötzen, wir selbst mit den Kindern.'
(Graßmann, too, interprets this as reflexive; but an alternative interpretation is possible: 'Under this offered protection of yours may we rejoice with wealth, our body, and our offspring.')

m. *svayáṁ ripús tanvàm rīriṣīṣṭa* [6.51.7d‡]
'may the traitor hurt his body/himself'

n. *svayáṁ vr̥dhasva tanvàṁ* [7.8.5d]
Ge.: 'mehre … selbst deinen Leib'
(Could also be reflexive.)

o. *hávanta u tvā hávyaṁ vívāci tanū́ṣu …* [7.30.2ab]
'They call upon you, the praiseworthy, in the dispute/battle about their bodies/themselves'

p. *prá yā́ jigā́ti khargáleva náktam ápa druhā́ tanvàṁ gū́hamānā* [7.104.17ab‡]

Ge. '(Die Unholdin), die wie eine Eule des Nachts zum Vorschein kommt, sich hinter einer Truggestalt verbergend.'
(Could also be: 'ihren Körper'; this is Graßmann's interpretation.)

q. *agníḥ ... śúmbhānas tanvàṁ svā́m* [8.44.12ab]
Ge.: 'Agni, der seinen Leib ... herausputzt'
(Similarly 7.56.11b with *svayám*)
(Could be reflexive, in both cases.)

r. *yán mātáraṁ ca pitáraṁ ca sākáṁ ájanayathās tanvàḥ svā́yāḥ* [10.54.3cd]
'when you created both father and mother from yourself/from your own body'

s. *utó tvasmai tanvàṁ ví sasre jāyéva pátya uśatī́ suvā́sāḥ* [10.71.4cd‡]
Ge.: 'Und dem einen hat sie sich aufgetan wie eine verliebte, schöngekleidete Frau dem Gatten.'
(Could also be literal, following Graßmann: '… she has opened = displayed her body'.)

t. *yā́ devéṣu tanvàm aírayanta* [10.169.3a‡]
Ge.: 'Die sich selbst den Göttern (zum Opfer) darbrachten …'
(Said of the cows. Could also be literal: 'ihren Leib'.)

ii. With verb in the active voice:

a. *yás te ánu svadhā́m ásat suté ní yaccha tanvàm* [3.51.11ab‡]
Ge.: 'Halte dich bei dem Soma auf, der deiner Natur entsprechen möge!'
(But a literal interpretation, following Graßmann, is possible, too; compare the next verse in the same hymn, which clearly refers to the physical body of Indra:

a'. *prá te aśnotu kukṣyóḥ préndra bráhmaṇā śíraḥ |*
prá bāhū́ śūra rā́dhase [3.51.12]
Ge.: 'Er soll in deine Seiten dringen, in dein Haupt mit Erbauung, o Indra, deine Arme zum Schenken, o Held!')

b. *yā́ vayáṁ cakr̥mā́ tanū́bhiḥ* [7.86.5b]
'which we have done by ourselves/with our bodies'

c. *ádha drapsó aṁśumátyā upásthé 'dhārayat tanvàṁ titviṣāṇáḥ* [8.96.15ab‡]
Ge.: Da behauptete sich Drapsa im Schoße der Aṁśumatī (zorn)funkelnd.'
(A literal reading, following Graßmann, would also be possible: 'D. maintained his body/life …'.)

d. *áyaṁ ta emi tanvā̀ purástād* [8.100.1a
'I here go in front of you, myself/with my body'

(10) *tanū́* not likely to be reflexive:

i. With verb in the middle voice:

a. *ririkvā́ṁsas tanvàḥ kr̥ṇvata svā́ḥ* [1.72.5c]
'abandoning their own (old) bodies they made (new bodies) for themselves.'

b. *utá smayete tanvā̀ vírūpe* [3.4.6b]
'and they smile (at us, at each other), different in form' (Hardly reflexive)

c. *śúśrūṣamāṇas tanvā̀ samaryé* [4.38.7b]
'being obedient in the contest with his body (by himself?)' (Reference to a prize horse)
(Repeated at 7.19.2b, said of Indra)

ii. With verb in the active voice:

a. ... *yán me ... śrútyam bráhma cakrá | índrāya ... máhyaṁ sákhye sákhāyas tanvè tanū́bhiḥ*
[1.165.10b-d]

'which invocation worthy to hear you made for me, for Indra, me, the friend, (you) the friends, for my person, with your persons'
(Hardly reflexive)

b. *turyā́ma dásyūn tanū́bhiḥ* [5.70.3c]
Ge.: 'Wir möchten mit unseren Leibern die Dasyu's überwinden'
(Compare next item)

c. *mā́ kásy(a) ... yakṣáṁ bhujemā tanū́bhiḥ | mā́ śéṣasā mā́ tánasā* [5.70.4ab]
'May we not experience the harm of/from anybody with/on our own bodies, on our offspring, on our children'

d. ... *gíra índrāya ... dhehí tanvè* [8.96.10cd]
Ge.: 'Bringe dem Indra für seine Person ... Lobesworte'

e. *evā́ ... ávocat svā́ṃ tanvàm índram evá* [10.120.9ab‡]
Ge.: 'Also ... hat ... zu ihm selbst, zu Indra gesprochen.'
(Unless one would want to read this as '... has declared himself (to be) Indra', this would not be a clear case of a reflexive; rather, an emphatic reading seems more appropriate, pace Graßmann.)

If we except possessive *tanvàḥ* in (8b) – which is adnominal, therefore does not bear any direct relation to the verb, and hence requires no verbal reflexive marking, only four passages have clearly reflexive *tanū́* with an active verb (8c). The remaining twelve passages with reflexive *tanū́* all have verbs in the middle voice.

Interestingly, middle voice predominates too for the ambiguous passages; see (9.i); only four passages have the active voice (9.ii). By contrast, passages in which *tanū́* is unlikely to be reflexive have a much higher ratio of active verbs; see (10).

These facts support the hypothesis that *tanū́* was reinterpreted in ambiguous passages of the type (9) as a reflexive pronoun redundantly co-indexed with the verbal middle voice in its reflexive value.

The first step in the grammaticalization of this usage is probably found in passages of the type (8.i), with relatively clear, unambiguous reflexive value for *tanū́* plus middle voice verb.

Of the four reflexive passages with **active** verbs (8.iii), only one occurs in a family book (in a hymn assigned to the "normal" stage by Arnold 1905); the remainder are found in the notoriously late Book 10.

This pattern of attestation suggests that the reflexive use of *tanū́* with active verbs is an innovation and that these passages represent the next step, the first attestation of the later Vedic and classical pattern in which a reflexive pronoun, nominal in origin (RV *tanū́*, later *ātmán*) has been reinterpreted as the major marker of reflexivization. At this stage, then, the verb no longer needs to be specifically marked for reflexivity and active marking becomes an optional alternative to the middle voice.

It is tempting to speculate that this process may have been helped by the fact that in some of the reflexive passages, *tanū́* is collocated with the inherited (possessive) reflexive *svá*: see examples (8.i.d, e, f, 8.iii.b). But such collocations also occur in ambiguous structures (9.i.k, q, r), as well as in the clearly non-reflexive examples (10.i.a, 10.ii.e), to which numerous other examples could be added (see Pinault 2001: 186-187 for a sampling).

Now, Tatyana Elizarenkova has reminded me that Lehmann claims that reflexive **swe* has the original meaning 'dear, beloved', as in Old High German *sṵ̄asat*, Greek *phílos*, Sanskrit *priyá*, and has referred me to collocations of Vedic *priyá* with *tanū́* in this regard. Bauer, too, in her recent (2000), sympathetic reexamination of Lehmann's claims, accepts this view, without however examining any specific Sanskrit evidence. Similarly, Pinault (2001: 186) refers approvingly to this interpretation, which seems to go back to

Scheller (1959). Moreover, he notes that RV *priyā́ tanū́* has an Avestan counterpart, *friiā tanū*, which to his mind shows that 'cette association … remonte à l'indo-iranien'. Perhaps significantly, there is also one Rig-Vedic attestation of the combination *priyá* + *ātmán*. These recent claims seem to support at least part of Lehmann's claims concerning the reflexive possessive **swe* and therefore justify closer textual examination.

Let me begin with an examination of the collocations of *priyá* with *tanū́*. Of the four passages found in the Rig-Veda, three are not likely to be reflexive (11a-c), the fourth one, (11d), could just possibly be reflexive, but neither Graßmann nor Geldner read it that way. At least in collocation with *tanū́*, then, there is no unambiguous evidence for a (proto-)reflexive value of RV *priyá*.

(11) Rig-Vedic collocations of *priyá* with *tanū́*:

a. *priyā́m índrasya tanvàm avīvr̥dhan* [9.73.2d]
'They have strengthened Indra's dear body (dear to them).'

b. *mā́ naḥ priyā́s tanvò rudra rīriṣaḥ* [1.114.7d]
'Do not, Rudra, injure our dear bodies (dear to us).'

c. *avór vā yád dhā́t tanū́ṣv ávaḥ priyā́su yajñíyāsv árvā* [10.132.5cd]
Ge.: 'oder wenn der Renner in seinen [für uns] lieben opferwürdigen Formen die Gnade der beiden Gnädigen erwirkt.'

d. *priyā́ṁ yamás tanvàṁ prárirecīt* [10.13.4d]
Ge.: 'Yama hat seinen lieben Leib fortgepflanzt'
(Geldner refers to the (near-)parallel *dadī́ réknas tanvè* [8.46.15a] '(you are) a giver (of) an heir for (**our**) body', in which *tanū́* must be read in the literal senses. Graßmann, too, does not take this as a reflexive.)

What about other contexts? Let us first examine the combination with *ātmán* (12). The context for this passage is the physical cutting up of the sacrificial horse's body in the ritual. The reference to *ātmán*, as well as to *tanū́*, therefore, must no doubt be taken in a literal, rather than a reflexive sense. And as in the case of (11a-c), *priyá* can be interpreted literally as 'dear (to the horse)'.

(12) Rig-Vedic *priyá* with *ātmán*:

mā́ tvā tapat priyá ātmā́piyántaṁ mā́ svádhitis tanvà ā́ tiṣṭhipat te [1.162.20ab]

'May not your dear/own body/life-breath hurt you dying; may the axe not do injury to your body.'

Spot checks on other occurrences of *priyá* in the Rig-Veda, focusing on collocations that could favor reflexive interpretations, yield similar results. Most examples are either ambiguous (e.g. RV 1.75.4, 10.123.7) or at most barely possible as reflexives (e.g. RV 1.25.17, 1.47.10, 1.143.1); others are most likely or clearly to be taken in the literal meaning 'dear (to)' (e.g. 1.71.9 (?), 1.26.7, 7.56.10, 10.84.5). The following passage may illustrate how easy it is to read a possessive or reflexive function into *priyá* – if only the first part of the verse (13a) is considered; but the last line (13b), with its parallel/reciprocal *priyá*, suggests a literal interpretation.

(13) *priyá* possessive/reflexive?

a. *priyó no astu ... viśpátir ...* [1.26.7a]

'May he be our own lord/May he be a dear lord for us ...'

b. *priyā́ḥ svagnáyo vayám* [1.26.7c

'... (may) we (be) dear (to him)/own to him (??), in possession of good fires.'

As far as I can tell, there is only one passage that, at least on first sight, seems to call for a possessive (reflexive?) interpretation, even though Geldner chooses the literal reading:

(14) Unambiguous possessive/reflexive use of *priyá* (?):

sá ha śrutá índro nā́ma devá ūrdhvó bhuvan mánuṣe dasmátamaḥ | áva priyám arśasānásya sāhvā́ñ chíro bharad dāsásya svadhā́vān [2.20.6]

Ge: 'Dieser unter dem Namen Indra berühmte Gott erhob sich für Manu, der größte Meister. Als Sieger trennte er den lieben Kopf des Dāsa Arśasāna ab, der Eigenmächtige.'

Here an interpretation 'den eigenen Kopf' seems to be more appropriate. Graßmann, to be sure, to judge by his question mark, seems to have had doubts as to whether *priyám* should be construed with *śíras*. And in fact a different, literal interpretation is possible:

(14') '... He bore down on the dāsa Arśasāna, winning (what was) dear (to him = A., Indra, or Manu?) ...'

Justification for this interpretation comes from the larger context. The next verse talks about Indra's destruction of the "black-yoni" forts of the dāsas and the consequent creation of land and the waters for Manu. The defeat of the dāsa Arśasāna in verse 20, thus, anticipates the defeat of all the dāsas in verse 21; the winning of the *priyá* in 20 similarly anticipates the winning of land and the waters (dear to Manu) in 21; and in both verses Manu is the lucky recipient of Indra's action.

All in all, then, I do not see any textual evidence that would require the assumption that *priyá* has clearly possessive/reflexive value in the Rig-Veda. This element of Lehmann's claims, therefore, must likewise be considered doubtful.

Let us then return to the effect of the innovated reflexive pronoun (RV *tanū́*, later *ātmán*) on verb marking, by briefly examining the later Sanskrit developments.

As noted earlier, the introduction of an (originally nominal) reflexive pronoun makes reflexive middle voice marking on the verb redundant and therefore permits active verb marking instead. The beginnings of this development are found in the Ṛig-Veda; but it is in the later language that its effects become more prevalent.

Delbrück, to be sure, finds a contrast in Vedic Prose for the distinction active : middle in constructions containing reflexive *ātmán*, with the active used when "die Gegenüberstellung von Subjekt und Objekt besonders deutlich empfunden wird" (see (15)). I am not sure, however, that I can see his point. Note especially the near-identical passages cited in (15). If anything, it is the parallelism in (15b) of the object *yajamānabhāgáṁ* with the object *ātmā́nam* that looks like a more plausible motivation for construing the verbs of both clauses in a parallel fashion, namely in the same voice. (Kulikov 2001 expresses similar doubts.) Unfortunately, I am not sure that this explanation will work for the other passages that Delbrück cites, on both sides of the divide. This issue clearly needs further detailed investigation.

(15) Delbrück (1888: 262-263) for Vedic Prose

a. *tā́bhir vaí sá ātmā́nam ā́prīṇīta* [TS 5.1.8.3]
'with these he pleased himself'

b. *yád yajamānabhāgáṁ prāśnā́ty ātmā́nam evá prīṇāti* [TS 1.7.5.2]
'In that he consumes the sacrificer's portion, (thereby) he pleases himself'

By Pāṇini's time, middle voice marking appears to have become clearly optional (16), assuming that *upapadena pratīyamāne* in (16b) can be interpreted as referring to the presence of a reflexive pronoun.

(16) Pāṇini

a. *svaritañitaḥ kartrabhiprāye kriyāphale* [1.3.72]
'[middle voice inflection] after a root marked by svarita or *ñ(it)*, if the result of the action benefits the agent'

b. *vibhāṣopapadena pratīyamāne* [1.3.77]
'optionally if marked by another word'

As is well known, by the time of the classical period, active vs. middle voice marking is either lexically determined ((17a) vs. (17b)) or (poetically) optional (17c). Middle voice marking no longer serves to indicate reflexivity.

(17) Classical Sanskrit

a. Always active: *asti*

b. Always middle: *āste* etc.

c. Some variation: *karoti, kurute*

To sum up, then, the Vedic evidence supports Delbrück's over Lehmann's position, namely that reflexive *svá* is inherited from PIE, but only adnominally, in genitival/possessive function. It was in complementary distribution with the use of the middle voice to mark reflexivization of verbal complements. The evidence of the Rig-Veda further suggests that the development of a pronominal reflexivization strategy for the latter category is indeed a recent innovation, whose initial stages can still be traced in the Rig-Veda. The eventual result of the introduction of this new strategy, in turn, leads to the demise of the inherited active : middle contrast.[12]

[12] For a very different, philosophical approach to the meaning and function of *tanū́* and *ātmán* see Gardner 1998. I am grateful to Arlo Griffiths for drawing my attention to this study, as well as to the papers by Kulikov 2000, 2001 and Vine 1997.

APPENDIX: Is *ātmán* a reflexive pronoun?

At the World Sanskrit Conference Paul Kiparsky disagreed with my using the term "reflexive pronoun" for (post-RV) *ātmán*. His most important arguments, presented in detail in Kiparsky (2003), are the following:

a. *ātmán* has nominal, not pronominal inflection and does not agree with its antecedent in gender, number, and person.
b. *ātmán* can be a nominative subject ("highly unusual for a reflexive")
c. Unlike pronouns, *ātmán* can be modified.

Let me first address point c. Kiparsky here is referring to structures such as *ātmanā katham ātmānam apraśasyaṁ praśaṃsasi* 'how can you yourself praise your unpraiseworthy self?' (R. 3.28.16; Kiparsky's example and translation); see also *tava ātmanaḥ* 'of yourself' (Kathas. 18.275, cited in Böhtlingk & Roth 1851-1875 s.v. *ātmán*). While such modification may indeed appear to be unusual from the English perspective, it is not at all anomalous for Sanskrit, which permits modification of personal pronouns, as in *so 'ham* "this I", *iyaṁ tvam* "this you" = 'you here' (see Hock 1997b with references). Even more pertinent are examples such as *yadi tvaṁ bhajamānāṁ māṁ pratyākhyāsyasi* ... (Nala 4.4) 'if you reject me (who is) devoted (to you)', where a participle modifies a personal pronoun. True, it could be argued that this is a case of apposition; but the same analysis would be available for Kiparsky's example, whose (negated) non-finite gerundive *apraśasyaṁ* is entirely comparable to the non-finite participle *bhajamānāṁ* of the Nala passage. (My own more literal translation of Kiparsky's passage would reflect this interpretation as follows: 'How do you, by yourself, praise yourself (who is) not to be praised.')

Point a. could be taken care of by opting for the terminology "reflexive noun", employed by Andersen (1993). But Andersen makes no attempt to distinguish "reflexive nouns" from "reflexive pronouns". Moreover, doing so would fail to account for the well-known fact that, with occasional (transitional) Vedic-Prose exceptions, *ātmán* does not behave like a normal noun, in that it is obligatorily used in the singular, even for dual and plural antecedents. A regular noun would at least optionally exhibit number agreement, as shown by *múkhaṁ tamáyanti* 'they deprive their mouth(s) of breath' (ŚB 3.8.1.15, Kiparsky's example and translation) beside the pattern ... *tato bhindanti nastakān* 'and then they perforate [their] septums' (MBh 12.15.51, Kiparsky's example and translation). Kiparsky acknowledges these facts, but fails to draw the appropriate conclusion.

In fact, it is precisely this reduction in syntactic variation which suggests that *ātmán* has become grammaticalized. More than that, unless we want to accept the radical scepticism of Andersen (1993), we have to recognize that lack of number, person, and gender agreement is a widespread phenomenon in reflexive pronouns, whether clearly derived from nouns (as in Skt. *ātmán*) or not (as in Skt. *svá*). Languages of this type include Japanese (*zibun*; Schachter 1985: 28 with references), as well as Indo-Iranian, Slavic, and Baltic; even Homeric Greek preserves traces of this pattern (Schwyzer 1950: 192).

A more common pattern in European members of the Indo-European stock is found in Classical Greek and Latin, with distinctive reflexive marking limited to third persons, but without gender and number agreement (see also Gothic, Old Norse, and traces in German reflexive accusative/dative marking).[13] One may speculate that the motivation for distinguishing reflexive and non-reflexive especially in the third persons is similar to that for the distinction "proximate" vs. "obviative" in many Native American languages (and elsewhere), namely that, in contrast to first and second persons, there may be more than one third-person actant per proposition, and devices such as reflexive or obviative marking

[13] See Geniušienė 1987 for a typological suvey of reflexive pronouns and their differences in behavior (and origins), including data from non-Indo-European languages.

help to distinguish these from each other. The consistent gender/number/person distinction of Modern English, thus, is by no means typical; and the fact that Skt. *ātmán* follows a different pattern is no grounds for denying its status as a reflexive pronoun. (Curiously, Old English exhibited an almost diametrically opposed pattern, namely no distinction at all between personal and reflexive pronouns, in any person, number, or gender.)

Finally, point b. simply is a consequence of the fact that just as the absolutive, reflexive formation is controlled, not by the surface subject, but by the underlying subject or "agent" in the sense of Pāṇini; see his *samānakartṛkayoḥ* as regards the use of the absolutive and see also Hock 1986 and 1991 with examples, discussion, and references.

The only argument that remains is that the inflection of *ātman* is nominal, not pronominal, and that even *sva* usually has nominal inflection.[14] But note that even among the words which I assume Kiparsky would consider true pronouns, there are considerable differences in inflection. Consider for instance the personal-pronoun ablative *mat, asmat* (with no number distinction on the suffix, and without the singular-oblique *-sm-* that is typical of the demonstratives) vs. the demonstrative *tasmāt, tebhyaḥ* etc. (with suffixal number distinction and with *-sm-* in the singular). Moreover, while the oblique singular of the demonstratives is markedly different from the nouns, this is not true for many of the plural

[14] In support of this assertion Kiparsky refers to Wackernagel 1930: 581. But this passage only tells part of the story. A closer reading of Wackernagel shows the following. In the Veda nominal inflection predominates (581), but in the classical language *sva* generally has pronominal inflection, along the lines of other pronominal adjectives, unless *sva* is used in secondary functions (588). The evidence of the Rig-Veda, with just three pronominal forms of *sva*, bears out Wackernagel's first observation. The post-Vedic evidence in Böthlingk & Roth (s.v. *sva*) yields a fair amount of pronominal forms, including *svasmāt, svasmin,* and *svasyāḥ*, but also a sizable number of examples with nominal *sve*, especially in āmreḍita. Note further Pāṇini 1.1.28-36 which provides for optional (vibhāṣā) pronominal inflection of all members of the gaṇa sarvādi (including *sva*), with sūtra 35 disallowing pronominal inflection for *sva* if it refers to relatives or possessions. The Sanskrit situation thus is considerably more complex than might be suggested by merely reading Wackernagel 1930: 581.

cases. Further, demonstratives differ from personal pronouns by marking gender, while the latter do not. Finally a number of adjectives, such as *sarva* 'every, all', exhibit pronominal inflection, even though they are not prototypical pronouns. Morphology, thus, is not an infallible guide to determining whether *ātman*, or any other word for that matter, is a pronoun or not.

There is, to be sure, a potential syntactic problem. Unlike the personal pronouns, which trigger different gender agreement on coreferential demonstratives, participles, etc., in accordance with the gender of the person that they refer to, *ātman* apparently does not. Renou (1984: 368) cites a passage, *ātmānaṁ paribhrāntam* (BKÇS 22.260), which in spite of the masculine gender on *paribhrāntam* refers to a female. This might suggest that *ātman* is, as Kiparsky claims, a regular noun and that its inherent masculine gender triggers masculine gender on *paribhrāntam* by the ordinary rules of agreement. However, a different approach is possible. As pointed out earlier, reflexive *ātman* is in the classical language always inflected in the singular, even with plural (or dual) antecedents. If the antecedent of *ātman*, thus, does not pass on its number features to *ātman*, it is likely that it also fails to pass on its gender features. As a consequence, the reflexive *ātman* has no number and gender features which it could pass on to its modifiers. At the same time, Sanskrit morphosyntax requires gender marking on modifying demonstratives, participles, or adjectives. In the case of impersonal constructions (such as passives from intransitives) we know that there is a default gender marking (neuter singular). We also know that a similar convention applies in cases of adjective, participle, etc. agreement with conjoint antecedents that differ in gender, except that here the default gender is masculine if all antecedents are human or animate (and neuter when there are non-human or non-animate antecedents); see Speyer (1886: 19-20). The masculine gender on modifiers of *ātman* thus can be accounted for as another instance of default marking, motivated by the fact that the antecedent of *ātman* usually is human or animate.

In light of these considerations I see no reason for abandoning the traditional term "reflexive pronoun" for *ātman*, for its Rig-Vedic predecessor *tanū́*, or for *svá* for that matter.

REFERENCES

ANDERSEN, Paul Kent 1993. Eine alternative Sprachtypologie für das Reflexiv. *Folia Linguistica* 27: 107-146.

ARNOLD, E. Vernon 1905. *Vedic Metre in its Historical Development.* Repr. Delhi: Motilal Banarsidass 1967.

BAUER, Brigitte 2000. *Archaic Syntax in Indo-European.* Berlin / New York: Mouton de Gruyter.

BÖHTLINGK, Otto & Rudolph ROTH 1851-1875. *Sanskrit-Wörterbuch.* St. Petersburg: Kaiserliche Akademie der Wissenschaften.

DELBRÜCK, Berthold 1888. *Altindische Syntax.* (Syntaktische Forschungen, 5.) Halle: Waisenhaus. Repr. Darmstadt: Wissenschaftliche Buchgesellschaft 1968.

------ 1893. *Vergleichende Syntax der indogermanischen Sprachen,* 1. (= Vol. 3 of K. Brugmann & B. Delbrück's Grundriß der vergleichenden Grammatik der indogermanischen Sprachen.) Straßburg: Trübner.

GARDNER, John Robert 1998. *The developing terminology of the Self in Vedic India.* University of Iowa Ph.D. dissertation.

GELDNER, Karl Friedrich 1951. *Der Rig-Veda* ..., 3 vols, posthumously edited by Charles R. Lanman. Cambridge, MA: Harvard University Press.

GENIUŠIENĖ, Emma 1987. *The Typology of Reflexives.* (Empirical Approaches to Language Typology, 2.) Berlin / New York / Amsterdam: Mouton de Gruyter.

GRASSMANN, Hermann 1872. *Wörterbuch zum Rig-Veda.* Repr. Wiesbaden: Harrassowitz1964.

HOCK, Hans Henrich 1986. "*P*-oriented" constructions in Sanskrit. In: Bh. Krishnamurti et al. (eds.), *South Asian Languages: Structure, Convergence, and Diglossia*: 15-26. Delhi: Motilal Banarsidass.

------ 1991. Possessive agents in Sanskrit. In: H. H. Hock (ed.), *Studies in Sanskrit Syntax*: 55-69. Delhi: Motilal Banarsidass.

------ 1997a. Chronology or genre? Problems in Vedic syntax. In: Michael Witzel (ed.), *Inside the Texts – Beyond the Texts: New Approaches to the Study of the Vedas*: 103-126. (Harvard Oriental Series, Opera Minora, 2.) Cambridge, MA: Harvard University

------ 1997b. Nexus and 'extraclausality' in Vedic, or '*sa*-figé' all over again: A historical (re)examination. In: H. H. Hock (ed.), *Historical, Indo-*

European, and Lexicographical Studies: A Festschrift for Ladislav Zgusta on the Occasion of his 70th Birthday: 49-78. Berlin / New York: Mouton de Gruyter.

KIPARSKY, Paul 2003. Morphological aspects of the passive-to-ergative shift. Paper presented at the October 2003 SALA meeting at Austin, TX.

KULIKOV, Leonid 2000. RV 1.120.11: A note on the Vedic reflexive. In: Michaela Ofitsch & Christian Zinko (eds.), *125 Jahre Indogermanistik in Graz*: 231-238. Graz: Leykam.

------ 2001. Typological notes on the Vedic reflexive. To appear in: *Proceedings of the International Conference "Reflexive and Middle"*, Tunis, 15-17 March 2001. Louvain: Peeters.

------ 2003. Valency-changing categories in Old Indo-Aryan in a diachronic perspective. Paper read at the Fifth International Conference on South Asian Linguistics, Moscow State University.

LEHMANN, Winfred P. 1974. *Proto-Indo-European Syntax*. Austin: University of Texas Press.

------ 1993. *Theoretical Bases of Indo-European Linguistics*. London / New York: Routledge.

PINAULT, Georges-Jean 2001. Védique *tanū́* et la notion de personne en indo-iranien. *Bulletin de la Société de Linguistique de Paris* 96 (1): 181-206.

REICHELT, Hans 1909. *Avestisches Elementarbuch*. Heidelberg: Winter.

RENOU, Louis 1984. *Grammaire sanscrite*. 2nd ed. Paris: Adrien Maisonneuve.

SCHACHTER, Paul 1985. Parts-of-speech systems. In: T. Shopen (ed.), *Language Typology and Syntactic Description*, 1: *Clause Structure*: 3-61. Cambridge etc.: Cambridge University Press.

SCHWYZER, Eduard 1950. *Griechische Grammatik*, 2: *Syntax und syntaktische Stilistik, vervollständigt und herausgegeben von Albert Debrunner*. (Handbuch der Alterumswissenschaft, 2:1:2.) München: Beck.

SPEYER, J. S. 1886. *Sanskrit Syntax*. Leiden: E. J. Brill. Repr. Delhi: Motilal Banarsidass 1973.

VINE, Brent 1997. On the expression of reflexive possession in the Rig-Veda: RV *svá*. In: E. Pirart (ed.), *Syntaxe des langues indo-iraniennes anciennes*: 203-214. Barcelona: Editorial Ausa.

WACKERNAGEL, Jacob 1930. *Altindische Grammatik*, III: *Nominalflexion, Zahlwort, Pronomen*. Göttingen: Vandenhoeck & Ruprecht.

WATKINS, Calvert 1976. Towards PIE syntax: Problems and pseudo-problems. In: S. Steever et al. (eds.), *Parasession on Diachronic Syntax*: 305-326. Chicago: Chicago Linguistic Society.

The Vedic medio-passive aorists, statives and their participles: reconsidering the paradigm*

LEONID KULIKOV

1. *-āna*-PARTICIPLES IN PASSIVE USAGES: PRELIMINARY REMARKS

The present paper deals with a group of athematic middle participles with the suffix *-āna-* which exhibit quite unusual syntactic properties in early Vedic, in the language of the Ṛgveda (RV). While the finite forms with which these participles are said to belong are employed only transitively, *-āna*-participles made from the same stem are attested in both transitive and intransitive (passive) constructions. This fact was noted already by Delbrück in his seminal *Altindische Syntax*.[1] Such asymmetry in the syntactic properties of finite and participial forms requires an explanation. To begin with, I shall focus on two typical examples, the participles *hinvāná-* and *yujāná-*.

---

* I should like to take this opportunity to express my thanks to the audience of the 12th World Sanskrit Conference (University of Helsinki, July 2003), in particular to St. Insler, W. Knobl and C. Watkins for their suggestions and critical remarks. I am also greatly indebted to A. Lubotsky for his criticism and valuable comments on earlier drafts of the paper. I acknowledge my debt to the Netherlands Organization for Scientific Research (NWO) for their financial support, grants no. 220-70-003 (PIONIER project) and 275-70-009 (VENI-project).

[1] "Verhältnissmässig häufig ist passivischer Gebrauch bei aus der Wurzel gebildeten Participien auf *āná*, die man zum Praesens oder Aorist ziehen kann" (Delbrück 1888: 264); see also Delbrück 1888: 379f.; Wackernagel & Debrunner 1954: 270.

hinvāná- (root *hi* 'impel') occurs 18 times in intransitive (passive) constructions (as in (1a)), and 10 times in transitive constructions (as in (1b)) in the R̥gveda (see e.g. Kümmel 1996: 141):

(1) a. RV 9.12.8b
sómo ***hinvānó*** *arṣati*
'Soma, **being impelled**, flows.'

b. RV 2.21.5
dhíyo ***hinvānā́*** *uśíjaḥ*
'Uśij's, **impelling** the (religious) thoughts...'

The syntactic properties of *hinvāná-* are in sharp contrast with those of the finite middle forms made from the nasal present (3pl. med. *hinváte* etc.), with which *hinvāná-* is supposed to belong. These forms can only be employed transitively, meaning 'impel', as in (2):

(2) RV 9.65.11c
hinvé *vā́jeṣu vājínam*
'I **spur** on this runner [in the race] for prizes.'

Similarly, the participle *yujāná-* (root *yuj* 'yoke') occurs 8 times in intransitive (passive) constructions (as in (3a)) and 14 times in transitive constructions (as in (3b)) in the R̥gveda (see Kümmel 1996: 90):

(3) a. RV 6.47.19a
yujānó *harítā ráthe*
'... (Tvaṣṭar,) **yoking** two fallow [horses] to the chariot.'

b. RV 6.34.2c
rátho ná mahé śávase ***yujānáḥ***
'... like a chariot **yoked** for the great power.'

Vedic grammars treat *yujānā-* as a middle participle of the root aorist (see, for instance, MacDonell 1910: 370). However, again, as in the case of *hinvānā-*, the corresponding finite forms (3sg.med. *áyukta* etc.) can only be employed in transitive usages, as in (4):

(4) RV 7.60.3
áyukta *saptá harítaḥ*
'He **yoked** (now) his seven dun (horses).'

Such remarkable syntactic behaviour of the middle participles requires an explanation: why do these participles show the syntactic features different from those of the corresponding finite forms?

Here it is in order to take a closer look at the syntactic properties of the other forms of the paradigms, where the participles *hinvānā-* and *yujānā-* belong. Apparently, in order to find a clue to our problem, we need to look for finite forms which are derived from the same stem as the participles in question (i.e. *hinv-* and *yuj-*) and can be employed as passives. Such forms indeed exist. In the case of *hinvānā-*, these are the statives 3sg. *hinvé* '(it) is impelled', 3pl. *hinviré* '(they) are impelled'. In the case of *yujānā-*, passive usages are attested for the passive aorist 3sg. *áyoji* '(it) was yoked', 3pl. *áyujran* '(they) were yoked'.[2]

To put it in morphological terms, the stem *hinu-/hinv-* is shared by the nasal present (3sg.act. *hinóti*, 3pl.med. *hinváte* etc.), which never occurs in passive constructions, and the stative (3sg. *hinvé*), which is employed in passive usages ('(it) is impelled'). Likewise, the stem *yuj-* (*yoj-*) is shared by the root aorist (3sg.med. *áyukta* etc.), never used in passive constructions (*áyukta* can only mean '(he) yoked', not 'was yoked'), and the passive aorist (3sg. *áyoji*, 3pl. *áyujran*), always employed as passive ('it was yoked', 'they were yoked').

---

[2] For statives and (medio-)passive aorists (*i*-aorists), two formations with defective paradigms (3sg. and 3pl. only), which are mainly employed in passive usages, see Kümmel 1996. For statives, see also Gotō 1997.

Thus, the passive syntax of the participles *hinvānā́-* and *yujānā́-* can readily be explained on the assumption that they belong with statives (3sg. *hinvé*, 3pl. *hinviré*) or passive aorists (3sg. *áyoji*, 3pl. *áyujran*).

This means that these participles are homonymous, or morphologically (grammatically) ambiguous, but their grammatical characteristics are distinguished by their syntax. *hinvānā́-* is a middle present participle when employed transitively, meaning 'impelling', and a stative participle when employed intransitively (passively), meaning 'impelled'. Likewise, *yujānā́-* is a middle root aorist participle when employed transitively ('yoking') and a passive aorist participle when employed in passive constructions ('yoked'):

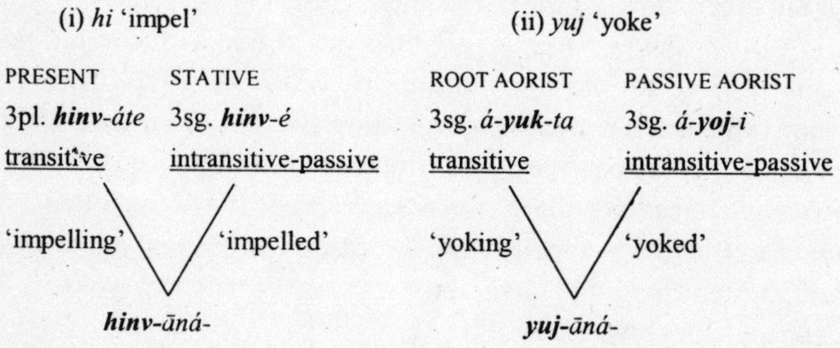

Despite the fact that participle forms are never listed in the standard Vedic grammars within the paradigms of statives and mediopassive aorists, the assumption that passive *-āna*-participles should be listed within these paradigms seems quite attractive, since it easily explains their abnormal syntax.

2. MEDIO-PASSIVE AORIST PARTICIPLES VS. MIDDLE ROOT AORIST PARTICIPLES

A similar account is appropriate for some other *-āna*-participles which display passive syntax. Particularly instructive is the case of the middle participles made from roots which do not have finite root aorist forms. Traditionally, such forms are treated as middle root aorist participles, but, assuming that they belong with the (medio-)passive *i*-aorists, we can more adequately explain the syntax and morphology of these formations. In this section I shall briefly discuss a few such participles.

2.1. *sṛj* 'set free, emit, create': *sṛjāná-*

The participle *sṛjāná-* is attested exclusively in passive constructions, as in (5):

(5) RV 9.76.1c
háriḥ ***sṛjānó*** *átyo ná sátvabhiḥ*
'The fallow [Soma], **set free**, like a horse, by warriors ...'

The only finite formation constructed directly on the root is the passive aorist (3sg. *ásarji*, 3pl. *ásṛgran / ásṛgram*; see Insler 1968a: 326f. with fn. 23; Kümmel 1996: 129ff.), as in (6):

(6) RV 1.190.2
sárgo ná yó ... ***ásarji***
'... like a discharge (= oblation) which **has been discharged** (in Agni = in the fire).' (see Insler 1968b: 5)

Since *sṛj* does not form root aorists properly speaking, *sṛjāná-* can only belong with this passive aorist.

2.2. *dṛś* 'see': *dṛśāná-*

The participle *dṛśāná-*[3] (RV 1.92.12, 10.45.8) 'visible' undoubtedly belongs with the passive aorist (3sg. *ádarśi*, 3pl. *adṛśran/ádṛśram*); the middle root aorist first appears in Vedic prose.

[3] For the hapax *dṛ́śāna-* (RV 2.10.4), with a different accentuation, see Section 5 below.

2.3. *ruc* 'shine': *rucāná-*

The participle *rucāná-* 'shining, bright' (6x in the RV) must belong with the medio-passive *i*-aorist (*(a)roci*, 3x in the RV);[4] the middle root aorist forms properly speaking are unattested.

3. STATIVE PARTICIPLES VS. MIDDLE PRESENT PARTICIPLES

As in the case of *hinvāná-*, the passive syntax of several middle participles can easily be accounted for on the assumption that they belong with statives made from present stems, not with these middle presents properly speaking.

3.1. *su* 'press (out)': *sunvāná-*

Unlike the finite middle forms of the nasal present *sunuté*, which are only employed in transitive usages, the middle participle *sunvāná-*, next to its transitive attestations, occurs once in a passive construction:

(7) RV 9.101.13
***sunvānásy**āndhasaḥ*
'...[speech ...] of the **pressed** sap.'
(see Gotō 1991: 689 fn. 79; Kümmel 1996: 126)

Most likely, this form belongs with the stative *sunvé*, *sunviré*, employed in passive usages (see Gotō 1991: 689 with fn. 78; Kümmel 1996: 123f.), as in (8):

(8) RV 7.29.1a = 9.88.1a
ayáṃ sóma indra túbhyaṃ ***sunve***
'This Soma **is pressed** for you, O Indra.'

---

4 Thus, although hesitantly, Wackernagel & Debrunner 1954: 273 ("*rucāná-* : 3. Sg. *aroci* ?").

3.2. *stu* 'praise, sing': *stávāna-, stavāná-, stuvāná-*

We find in the RV three athematic middle participles made from the bare root *stu* 'praise':[5] *stávāna-*, *stavāná-* and *stuvāná-*. Of these three formations, only the first, *stávāna-*, is fairly frequent in the RV (18x), while the others two are hapaxes. It occurs in passive constructions, as in (9):

(9) RV 1.130.10cd
divodāsébhir indra ***stávāno*** *' vāvr̥dhīthā́ áhobhir iva dyáuḥ*
'**Praised** by the Divodāsas, O Indra, increase, as the heaven [increases] through the days.'

By virtue of its root vocalism, *stávāna-* can only belong with the stative *stáve* (on which see, in particular, Oettinger 1976: 112, 120; Kümmel 1996: 131f.; Gotō 1997: 180ff.), that has apparently generalized the full grade in the root (cf. the class I present *stávati* formed from it[6]). By contrast, the participle *stuvāná-* (RV 7.96.3) is made in accordance with the rules of the derivation of the middle participles of the root aorist and therefore is likely to be a member of the paradigm of the *i*-aorist *ástāvi* (on which see Kümmel 1996: 132f.); its non-stative meaning ('being praised', rather than 'praised')[7] corroborates this assumption:

(10) RV 7.96.3
cetati vājínīvatī gr̥ṇānā́ jamadagnivát ***stuvānā́*** *ca vasiṣṭhavát*
'[Sarasvatī] appears as rich in horses when **being praised** in the Jamadagni style and sung in the Vasiṣṭha style.'

---

[5] For a synopsis of formations derived from this root, see Narten 1964: 276ff.; 1969: 12ff. [= *Kl. Schr.* I: 100ff.]; Gotō 1997: 180ff.; Kümmel 1996: 131ff.; 2000: 579f.

[6] For the secondary character and genesis of this formation, see Narten 1969; Gotō 1987: 331f. with fn. 807.

[7] For the non-stative usage of the participle *gr̥ṇānā́* in this passage, see Section 6.

The abnormal accentuation of the form *stavānā́-* (a hapax in the RV) may result from contamination of the stative and passive aorist participles, i.e. *stávāna-* and *stuvānā́-*.[8] The context does not help in determining its paradigmatic status:

(11) RV 6.46.2
sá tvám̥ naḥ ... mahā́ ***stavānó*** ...
gā́m áśvam̥ rathyàm indra sám̥ kira
'You, O Indra, ... bring us a cow and a horse for chariot together, when **being praised / praised** as the great one.'

3.3. *duh* 'milk, give milk': *dú(g)hāna- / duhānā́-*

As Kümmel (1996: 58) has demonstrated (see also Gotō 1991: 681ff.; 1997: 170ff.), the meaning and syntax of the middle participles *dú(g)hāna-* and *duhānā́-* depends on their accentuation: forms with the accent on the root give the meaning 'giving milk, milch(-cow)', whilst those with the suffix accentuation (2x in the RV) are employed in the sense 'milking (for oneself)'. This semantic contrast is perfectly parallel to that between the stative 3sg. *duhé*, 3pl. *duhré* 'give milk' and middle root present (3pl. *duhaté*) 'milk (for oneself)' (discussed at length by Kümmel 1996: 52ff.). Obviously, the difference in accentuation between these formations correlates with their grammatical characteristics: the root-accented participle *dú(g)hāna-* belongs with the stative 3sg. *duhé*, 3pl. *duhré* ('give milk, be a milch(-cow)'), whilst *duhānā́-* (with suffix accentuation) belongs to the paradigm of the middle root present, together with 3pl. *duhaté* etc. ('milk (for oneself)').

3.4. *idh* 'kindle': *índhāna-* and evidence from the Atharvaveda

The participle *índhāna-* occurs 5 times in transitive usages ('kindling'), as in (12a), and 3 times in passive usages ('kindled'), as in (12b), in the R̥gveda:

---

[8] Cf. Wackernagel & Debrunner 1954: 273: "*stavānā́-* (einmal; in *stuvānā́-* zu verbessern?)".

(12) a. RV 2.25.1a
índhāno agníṃ vanavad vanuṣyatáḥ
'The one who **kindles** Agni will overpower those who envy [us].'

b. RV 1.143.7
índhāno ... vidátheṣu dī́dyat ... úd u no yaṁsate dhíyam
'**Being kindled**, shining during the sacrifices, [Agni] will raise our prayer.'

The ratio of the transitive and passive usages is summarized in Table 1:

índhāna- in RV

transitive ('kindling')	intransitive-passive ('kindled')
5x RV 2.25.1, 8.102.22, 10.3.4, 10.45.1, 10.128.1	3x RV 1.143.7, 8.19.31, 8.23.11

Table 1

The usage of this participle nicely parallels the syntax of the finite forms derived from the stem *indh-*: middle present (3sg. *in(d)dhé,*[9] 3pl. *indháte/indhaté*, etc.) is used transitively, as in (13a); by contrast, the form *indhé*, attested at RV 7.8.1 in a passive construction (13b), must be a stative made from the present stem (see Kümmel 2000: 125f. fn. 80; Kulikov 2001: 46f.):

(13) a. RV 3.13.5c
ṛ́kvāṇo agním ***indhate***
'The singers **kindle** the fire.'

[9] With the secondary loss of gemination.

b. RV 7.8.1ab
indhé *rā́jā sám aryó námobhir* ' *yásya prátīkam ā́hutaṃ ghṛténa*
'With reverence the king, the noble [Lord] **is kindled**, whose face is anointed with ghee.'

Thus, the transitive ('kindling') and intransitive-passive ('kindled') occurrences of *índhāna-* belong with the transitive nasal present *in(d)dhé* and with the stative *indhé*, respectively.

Such an analysis of *índhāna-* is further supported by evidence from the Atharvaveda (Śaunakīya). Since the category of stative almost disappears after the RV (see Kümmel 1996: 11), we can expect that the *-āna-*participles which are grammatically ambiguous in the RV (i.e. belong either to stative or to some other formation with which stative shares the stem) will no longer be ambiguous in the Atharvaveda (AV). This assumption is corroborated by the ratio of usages of *indhāna-* in the AV, summarized in Table 2:

indhāna- in AV

transitive ('kindling')	intransitive-passive ('kindled')
2x AV 19.55.3, 19.55.4	

Table 2

4. RECONSTRUCTING STATIVES AND MEDIO-PASSIVE *i*-AORISTS

On the assumption that several *-āna-*participles with the 'unexpected' passive syntax belong with statives or *i*-aorists, we not only are able to account for their 'abnormal' syntax, but also to reconstruct some unattested statives and passive aorists.

4.1. *ad* 'eat': *adānā-* : **ā́di*

The middle participle *adānā-* (hapax in the RV) is employed in the passive usage ('being eaten'; cf. (14)), whilst finite forms of the root present (3sg.act. *átti* etc., middle forms are unattested and probably did not exist in the language of the RV), with which this participle is traditionally connected, never occur in passive constructions:

(14) RV 4.19.9
vamrī́bhiḥ putrám agrúvo ***adānám*** *... ā́ jabhartha*
'You [O Indra] have carried out [of a hole] the virgin's son, **being eaten** by ants.'

The passive syntax and the non-stative meaning ('being eaten', not 'eaten') of this RVic hapax are likely to point to the unattested passive aorist **ā́di* 'was eaten'.

4.2. *hū* 'call': *huvānā-* : **áhāvi*

The root aorist participle *huvānā-* (root *hū* 'call') is employed both in transitive (as in (15a)) and intransitive (passive) (as in (15b)) constructions:

(15) a. RV 7.30.3cd
ny àgníḥ sīdad ásuro ná hótā ' ***huvānó*** *átra subhágāya devā́n*
'Agni sits down, the Hotar, like the Asura, **calling** the gods hither for the fortunate [sacrificer].'

b. RV 10.112.3cd
asmā́bhir indra sákhibhir ***huvānáḥ*** *' sadhrīcīnó mādayasvā niṣádya*
'O Indra, **being called** by us, [your] friends, be exhilarated, having sat down together [with us].'

By contrast, the finite forms of the root aorist (*áhūmahi* RV 6.45.10 and a few other forms) are employed transitively. Thus, passive occurrences of *huvāná-* must belong with the unattested passive aorist **áhāvi* '(he) was called'.[10]

4.3. *hi* 'impel': *hiyāná-* : **áhāyi*

The participle *hiyāná-*, attested 8 times in the RV, is only employed in passive constructions ('being impelled') and has no corresponding finite root aorist forms (active root aorists, such as 1pl. *ahema*, 3pl. *ahyan*, are employed transitively). Most likely, this is the participle of the unattested passive aorist **áhāyi* 'was impelled'.

5. SOME FORMAL FEATURES OF THE PASSIVE *-āna*-PARTICIPLES

In general, the rules of derivation of (passive) *-āna*-participles do not differ from those for athematic middle participles made from other stems. There are, however, some cases of accent vacillation which have not yet received a satisfactory explanation. The majority of the participles in question have the zero grade in the root and, accordingly, bear the accent on the suffix (*-āná-*), not on the root. There are, however, a few participles made from the full grade root with root accentuation (*śáyāna-*, *stávāna-*). It seems that the grade of the root depends on its structure: *CaR* (*CaC*) roots display the full grade (*śī* / *śay*: *śáyāna-*, *stu* / *stav*: *stávāna-*), whilst *CaRC* / *CR̥C* roots have a zero grade (cf. *dr̥ś*: *dr̥śāná-*, *ruc*: *rucāná-*, etc.). Although we find only two examples of the former type (*śáyāna-*, *stávāna-*), active stative participles (see Section 7 below) seem further to corroborate this regularity, cf. *járant-* 'old' (not ***juránt-*) and *máhant-* 'great' (made from *CaR* / *CaC* roots), as opposed to *pŕ̥ṣant-* 'speckled' and *br̥hánt-* 'high' (*CaRC* / *CR̥C* roots).

---

[10] The morphologically unclear form *huvé* (RV 1.30.9) '(he) called' cannot represent a stative; see Kümmel 1996: 142 ("[e]s handelt sich um eine Augenblicksbildung nach 1. Sg. *huvé* in [pāda] b"); Lubotsky 1997: 1659 ("3sg., inf. or pf. w[ith]out red[uplication] (?)").

Perhaps, under the influence of the two very common stative participles, *śáyāna-* and *stávāna-*, some stative participles with the zero grade in the root have undergone secondary accent shift to the root (cf. *índhāna-*, *cítāna-*, *dú(g)hāna-*).[11] Thus, there may have been a weak tendency to **generalize the root accentuation for all stative participles**; cf. especially the root-accented participle *dú(g)hāna-* (see Section 3.3) opposed to the middle root present participle *duhāná-* with suffix accentuation.

6. PARTICIPLE OF STATIVES OR *i*-AORISTS?

The morphological identification of most passive *-āna*-participles poses no problem, but in some cases we may need additional criteria in order to determine which of these two passive formations (stative, passive aorist, or either of them) the participle in question may belong with. Below I shall briefly discuss the features which can disambiguate some unclear *-āna*-participles.

(i) *Stem*

Since passive *i*-aorists can only be made from root stems, those *-āna*-participles which are derived from the stems other than the bare root (i.e. from non-root present or intensive stems) can only belong with statives. In cases where a participle is formed directly from the root it may, theoretically, belong either with the medio-passive *i*-aorist or with the stative made from the root present stem.[12] Most often, however, only one of these two formations exists, which rules out the other option. Only in cases where either both or none are attested we are faced with a dilemma: the participle of statives or *i*-aorists?

[11] For the only example of a full grade root participle with suffix accentuation (*stavāná-*, RVic hapax), see Section 3.2.

[12] Statives derived from root aorist stems are almost unknown in Vedic, the only (possible) exception being *cité* (see Kümmel 1996: 10).

(ii) *Accentuation*

The accentuation of the passive *-āna*-participles, briefly discussed in Section 5, may provide an additional clue to the morphological identification of participles made from bare roots. Thus, the root accentuation of the participle *cítāna-* (RV 9.101.11) 'made perceivable' may support connecting this formation with the stative *cité* (RV 10.143.4) (as actually suggested by Kümmel 1996: 39 on semantic grounds), rather than with the passive aorist *áceti*.

Quite remarkable is the difference in accentuation between two *-āna*-participles made from the root *dr̥ś* 'see'. While *dr̥śāná-* (RV 1.92.12, 10.45.8) 'visible', discussed in Section 2.2, is a regular participial derivative of the passive aorist, the hapax *dŕ̥śāna-* (RV 2.10.4), judging from its abnormal root accentuation, might belong with the unattested stative **dr̥śé* 'is seen'. The context seems to support this analysis; note also the adjacent *br̥hánt-* 'high', which may represent a stative participle, too (see Section 7 below):

(16) RV 2.10.4
jígharmy agníṃ ... váyasā br̥hántaṃ vyáciṣṭham ánnai rabhasáṃ ***dŕ̥śānam***
'I besprinkle Agni, ... which is high by vital force, most expansive, appearing (lit. **seen**) as impetuous through food.'

(iii) *Temporal/aspectual semantics*

The temporal/aspectual meaning of the form in question may also hint at its grammatical characterization. Thus, for the participle *adāná-* (see Section 4.1), both the non-stative meaning ('being eaten', rather than 'eaten') and the suffix accentuation (*adāná-*, not **ádāna-*) seem to support the passive aorist analysis.

(iv) *Paradigmatic features*

There may also be some paradigmatic indications that favour one of the two interpretations. Thus, in the case of the passive participle *mṛjāná-* '(being) wiped, (being) cleansed' (*mṛj* 'wipe, cleanse'), we can probably rule out the stative analysis (stative **mṛjé*?) and reconstruct the passive aorist **ámarji*, since this root already has a stative participle, made from the intensive stem (*marmṛjāná-*).

To conclude this brief discussion of the features of the passive *-āna*-participles, a general methodological remark is in order. In some cases, evidence for the paradigmatic status (stative or passive aorist?) of *-āna*-participles is controversial. Thus, the well-attested participle *gṛṇāná-* (44x in the RV) can only belong with the stative *gṛṇé* 'is praised' (and the nasal present *gṛṇīté*), but some contexts rather point to the non-stative meaning, as in (10), where this form is coordinated with the passive aorist participle *stuvānā́* 'being praised'. Since the verb *gṝ* 'praise, sing' forms no aorists at all, one may assume that the participle *gṛṇāná-* could supply, where necessary, the participles of the non-existent passive aorist (**ágāri*, **girāṇá-*), thus being functionally shared by the two passive formations. This means that, even in cases where formal (morphological) features unambiguously determine the paradigmatic status of a participle, its actual usage can, in a sense, 'accommodate' both functional values, those of the passive aorist and stative.[13]

7. ACTIVE PARTICIPLES OF STATIVES?

Thus far, I have only discussed participles of statives and passive aorists formed with the suffix *-āna-*, thus presuming that only the middle morphology was possible for such participles (which, in general, meets our expectations with respect to the morphology of the forms employed in passive usages). Yet there seems to be evidence for the assumption that stative *-āna*-participles may have had active counterparts. It has frequently been noted (Renou 1966: 6 [= *Choix* I: 22]; Watkins 1969: 142ff.; Schaefer 1994: 45f.) that

[13] On the formal and functional overlapping of the stative and passive aorist, see Kümmel 1996: 20f.

the formation *stavánt-* (active participle?), which occurs three times in the family maṇḍalas of the RV (at 2.19.5, 2.20.5, 6.24.8, only in the nom. sg. form *stavā́n*), attests quite an unusual (for an active form) passive syntax, cf.:

(17) RV 2.20.5c
muṣṇánn uṣásaḥ sū́ryeṇa ***stavā́n***
'...while (he), the **praised** one, abducted the dawns with the sun.'

By virtue of its suffix accentuation and active morphology, this form cannot belong to the class I present *stávate*, which is only attested in the middle (see also section 3.2). On the other hand, its semantics and passive syntax plead for the connection of this formation with the stative *stáve*, as the active counterpart of the (middle) participle *stávāna-*.

The assumption of the existence of **active** stative participles may shed light on the paradigmatic status of some other formations in *-ant-* (most of which are traditionally taken to be adjectives). Watkins, who first drew attention to these formations (1969: 142ff.; see also Schaefer 1994: 45f.), assumed that they represent active participles with the secondary accent shift marking their passive (intransitive) syntax. These participles include, besides *stavánt-*:

(1) *járant-* 'old' (i.e. '(having) grown old'), treated by Gotō (1987: 153 with fn. 238) as an adjective outside the verbal paradigm because of its intransitive syntax ('(grown) old', not 'making old'), different from that of the class I present *járati* 'makes old';

(2) *pépiśat-* 'adorned' (RV 10.127.7; see Schaefer 1994: 45, 152f.), which may point to the unattested stative **pépiśe* 'is adorned' of the type *cékite* (on which see Schaefer 1994: 44);

(3) *pṛ́ṣant-* 'speckled' (see Wackernagel & Debrunner 1954: 165; Watkins 1969: 144);

(4) *br̥hánt-* 'high' may be the active stative participle of the verb *br̥h* 'be high, strong' (on which see, in particular, Narten 1959: 45f. [= *Kl. Schr.* I: 7ff.]; Jamison 1983: 97f.);

(5) *mahánt-* 'great' [whose parallelism with *stavánt-* was noted by Watkins (1969: 144)] may belong with the hapax stative *mahe* 'is able' (RV 7.97.2); see Kümmel 1996: 79ff.; Gotō 1997: 179f.

8. PARTICIPLES OF STATIVES AND *i*-AORISTS: A SUMMARY

The results of this preliminary sketch of the passive *-āna*-participles are summarized in tables 3 and 4, which bring together finite (3rd person singular and plural) and non-finite forms (participles) of the medio-passive aorists and statives attested in early Vedic, foremost in the RV:

Medio-passive *i*-aorists

Verb	3sg.	3pl.	participle
ad 'eat'	**ā́di*		*adāná-* RV 4.19.9
dr̥ś 'see'	*ádarśi* RV 15x, inj. *dárśi* RV 2x	*adr̥śran* RV 7x, *ádr̥śram* RV 2x	*dr̥śāná-* RV 1.92.12, 10.45.8
nid 'revile, blame'	**ánedi*		*nidāná-* RV 4.5.12
bhī 'fear'	**ábhāyi*		*bhiyāná-* RV 3x
mr̥j 'wipe, cleanse'	**ámarji*		*mr̥jāná-* RV 3x
yuj 'yoke'	*áyoji* RV 4x	*áyujran* RV 2x	*yujāná-* RV 8x
ruc 'shine'	*aroci* RV 2x, *roci* RV 1.121.6		*rucāná-* RV 6x
vr̥ 'cover'	*ávāri* RV 4.6.7		*vrāṇá-* RV 1.61.10
su 'press (out)'	*ásāvi* RV 7x		s^{u}*vāná-* RV 32x
sr̥j 'set free, emit'	*ásarji* RV 12x, inj. *sarji* RV 2x	*ásr̥gran/m* RV 19x, *ásasr̥gram* RV 2x	*sr̥jāná-* RV 11x
stu 'praise'	*ástāvi* RV 5x		*stuvāná-* RV 7.96.3 (*stavāná-* RV 6.46.2)
hi 'impel'	**áhāyi*		*hiyāná-* RV 7x
hū 'call'	**áhāvi*		*huvāná-* RV 10x

Table 3

Statives

Verb	3sg.	3pl.	participle
idh 'kindle'	*indhé* RV 7.8.1		*índhāna-* RV 3x
gr̥̄ 'praise'	*gr̥ṇé* RV 5x		*gr̥ṇāná-* RV 44x
cit 'appear, perceive'	*cité* RV 10.143.4		*citāna-* RV 9.101.11
duh 'give milk'	*duhé* RV (10x) +	*duhré* RV (7x[14]) +	*dú(g)hāna-* RV (12x[15]) +
dr̥ś 'see'	**dr̥śé* (?)		*dŕ̥śāna-* RV 2.10.4
brū 'say'	*bruve* RV 5.61.8		*bruvāṇá-* RV 3.59.1
mr̥j 'wipe, cleanse'	**marmr̥jé*		*marmr̥jāná-* RV 6x
śī 'lie'	*śáye* RV 11x	*śére* AV	*śáyāna-* RV 18x
śubh 'be beautiful'	*śóbhe* RV 1.120.5		*śubhāná-* RV 2x
su 'press (out)'	*sunvé* RV 3x	*sunviré* RV 4x	*sunvāná-* RV 9.101.13
stu 'praise'	*stáve* RV 5x		*stávāna-* RV 18x (*stavāná-* RV 6.46.2)
hi 'impel'	*hinvé* RV 2x	*hinviré* RV 8x[16]	*hinvāná-* RV 18x

Table 4

REFERENCES

DELBRÜCK, Berthold 1888. *Altindische Syntax*. Halle a.S.: Verlag der Buchhandlung des Waisenhauses.

GOTŌ, Toshifumi 1987. *Die "I. Präsensklasse" im Vedischen: Untersuchung der vollstufigen thematischen Wurzelpräsentia*. Wien: Verlag der Österreichischen Akademie der Wissenschaften.

------ 1991. Materialien zu einer Liste altindischer Verbalformen: 4. *dogh/dugh/doh/duh*, 5. *sav/su*, 6. ^{1}*sav*^{i}*/sū*, 7. ^{2}*(sav*^{i}*/)sū*. *Bulletin of the National Museum of Ethnology* (Osaka) 16 (3): 681-707.

------ 1997. Überlegungen zum urindogermanischen «Stativ». In: Emilio Crespo & José Luis García Ramón (eds.), *Berthold Delbrück y la sintaxis indoeuropea hoy. Actas del Coloquio de la Indogermanische Gesellschaft*: 165-192. Madrid: UAM; Wiesbaden: Reichert.

[14] 2x in transitive usages ('they milk the cow/udder').
[15] 1x or 2x in transitive usages ('milking'); see Kümmel 1996: 58.
[16] 6x in transitive usages.

INSLER, Stanley 1968a. The origin of the Sanskrit passive aorist. *Indogermanische Forschungen* 73: 312-346.

------ 1968b. Vedic *áñjasā, ṛñjasāná-* and the type *sahasāná-*. *Zeitschrift für vergleichende Sprachforschung auf dem Gebiete der indogermanischen Sprachen (KZ)* 82: 1-23.

JAMISON, Stephanie W. 1983. *Function and form in the* -áya-*formations of the Rig Veda and Atharva Veda*. (KZ, Ergänzungsheft 31.) Göttingen: Vandenhoeck & Ruprecht.

KULIKOV, Leonid 2001. *The Vedic* -ya-*presents*. PhD thesis. Leiden University.

KÜMMEL, Martin 1996. *Stativ und Passivaorist im Indoiranischen*. (Historische Sprachforschung, Ergänzungsheft 39.) Göttingen: Vandenhoeck & Ruprecht.

------ 2000. *Das Perfekt im Indoiranischen*. Wiesbaden: Reichert.

LUBOTSKY, Alexander M. 1997. *Ṛgvedic Word Concordance*. 2 parts. (American Oriental Society, 82/83.) New Haven: American Oriental Society.

MACDONELL, Arthur Anthony 1910. *Vedic Grammar*. (Grundriss der Indo-Arischen Philologie und Altertumskunde; Bd. I, Heft 4.) Strassburg: Trübner.

NARTEN, Johanna 1959. Formüberschneidungen bei ved. *vṛśc, vṛj, vṛh* (*bṛh*). *Münchener Studien zur Sprachwissenschaft* 14: 39-52. [= Narten 1995: 1-10.]

------ 1964. *Die sigmatischen Aoriste im Veda*. Wiesbaden: Harrassowitz.

------ 1969. Zum "proterodynamischen" Wurzelpräsens. In: J. C. Heesterman et al. (eds.), *Pratidānam: Indian, Iranian, and Indo-European studies presented to F.B.J. Kuiper on his sixtieth birthday*: 9-19. The Hague: Mouton. [= Narten 1995: 97-107.]

------ 1995. *Kleine Schriften*, I. Wiesbaden: Reichert.

OETTINGER, Norbert 1976. Der indogermanische Stativ. *Münchener Studien zur Sprachwissenschaft* 34: 109-149.

RENOU, Louis 1966. L'utilisation linguistique du Ṛgveda. *Bulletin de la Société de Linguistique de Paris* 61: 1-12. [= L. RENOU. *Choix des études indiennes*, I: 17-28. Paris: École française d'Extrême-Orient, 1997.]

SCHAEFER, Christiane 1994. *Das Intensivum im Vedischen*. (Historische Sprachforschung, Ergänzungsheft 37.) Göttingen: Vandenhoeck & Ruprecht.

WACKERNAGEL, Jacob & Albert DEBRUNNER 1954. *Altindische Grammatik*, II: 2. *Die Nominalsuffixe*. Göttingen: Vandenhoeck & Ruprecht.

WATKINS, Calvert 1969. *Indogermanische Grammatik*, III: *Formenlehre*. 1. Teil. *Geschichte der indogermanischen Verbalflexion*. Heidelberg: Winter.

On the evolutionary changes in the Old and Middle Indo-Aryan systems of case and adpositions

VIT BUBENIK

In this paper I want to demonstrate that the gradual erosion of the synthetic morphology of case during the Old Indo-Aryan and Middle Indo-Aryan periods was accompanied by a trade-off between the restructured nominal case system and the evolving system of postpositions. These matters will be discussed in a systemic fashion whereby the successive systems of local adverbs, postpositions and preverbs in Old Indo-Aryan and Middle Indo-Aryan will be presented in terms of 12 binary sets expressing basic topological and projective notions.

1. THE OLD INDO-ARYAN CASE SYSTEM

Vedic and Hittite athematic case endings are usually taken as reflecting the Late Proto-Indo-European state of affairs. In addition to the four grammatical cases (Nominative, Accusative, Genitive, Dative), there were three adverbial cases (Locative, Ablative and Instrumental) which we also reconstruct for Late Proto-Indo-European. Their morphology is surveyed in Table 1 (p. 66).

The reconstruction of the instrumental is problematic (notice the dental suffix *-(i)t*, *-ta* (?) in Hittite), and it could be that there was no formal difference between the instrumental and the ablative in Early Proto-Indo-European.

	Vedic	Hittite	Late PIE
Nom	*-s*	*-s*	**-s*
Acc	*-am*	*-an*	**-m*
Gen	*-as*	*-(a)s*	**-(o)s*
Dat	*-e*	} *-i/-ya*	**-(e)i*
Loc	*-i*		**-i*
Abl	(= Gen)	*-at*[s]	*(= Gen), *-(e)t*
Instr	*-ā*	*-(i)t, -ta*(?)	**-(e)h_1*

Table 1: *Vedic, Hittite and Late PIE (athematic) case endings*

Functionally, the instrumental could express not only the (inanimate) instrument but also the notion of movement through space ('perlative') as in the following Vedic example:

(1) *ā́* *kr̥ṣṇéna* *rájasā* *vártamāno* [RV i.35.2]
hither dark+INSTR darkness+INSTR rolling
'rolling hither through the dark space'

The instrumental case in this function is well documented in Balto-Slavic, e.g. Lithuanian *eĩti keliù* 'to walk along the road', Russian *idtí lesóm* 'to go through the forest'. In Ancient Greek the suffix *-ō* of certain adverbs such as ἄν-ω 'upward' is traceable back to the Late PIE instrumental suffix **-oh_1*.

When one matches the grammatical and adverbial cases, several notorious syncretisms appear. The accusative suffix expresses not only the direct object with transitive verbs but also the goal of movement with intransitive verbs (allative), e.g. *nagaraṃ gacchāmi* 'I go to the city'. In the singular, the genitive suffix expresses not only the possessor (adnominal function) but also the notion of spatial removal with intransitive verbs (ablative), e.g. *áditer ... ajāyata* 'he was born from Aditi'. Thematic nouns, however, distinguish these two cases (witness Gen *-asya* vs. Abl *-āt*, Late PIE **-os* vs. **-ōd*, respectively). But in the plural, the ablative is identical with the dative: *-bhyas*. It can be argued that PIE probably did not possess a separate suffix for the plural ablative; witness the situation in Vedic where the suffix *-ebhyas* (athematic *-bhyas*) performs the double duty of the dative and the ablative, and in Hittite where the ablative suffix *-at*ˢ is limited to inanimate nouns and is used without the distinction of number.

2. OIA LOCAL ADVERBS AND ADPOSITIONS

The basic topological notion of 'location' (in space and time) was expressed by the morphological locative; subtler distinctions of juxtaposition, inessive and location (with surface contact) were realized by various adverbial particles/adpositions accompanying the noun in the locative (*ā́* 'at, near' (Vedic), *mádhye* 'in (the middle), between, among', *ádhi* 'upon'). The pair expressing 'movement to(wards)' (allative) versus 'movement from' could be realized synthetically by the accusative (or dative) versus ablative; subtler distinctions such as unopposed movement ('unto', 'towards') and movement with opposing limit ('against') necessitated the use of various adpositions (such as *áccha* 'unto, to(wards)' and *práti* 'against). The notion of spatial removal realized by the ablative could be further specified by the distinction of surface contact (contrast *ápa* '(away) from' with *áva* 'down from, off'). The synthetic instrumental case was used, among others, to express the notions of accompaniment (comitative) and path (perlative); these meanings came to be reinforced by adpositions *sácā* 'with' and *tirás* 'by; through'.

No special cases were linked with other adverbial notions: inferiority/superiority (realized by preverbs *ní-/úd-* 'down'/'up' or adpositions *úpa/upári* 'under'/'over') and anteriority/posteriority (realized by adpositions *prá, purás/paścā* 'before'/'after'). Further specifications of the basic notion of location were achieved by the use of postpositions to express the distinction of two limits (*antár* 'between' / *parás* 'beyond') and circumference (*abhyantare* 'among' / *pári* 'about').

The genitive case (in its adnominal meaning of appurtenance 'of') was the only OIA case without any analytic (adpositional) counterpart. This state of affairs will change fundamentally during the Late MIA period (see below). Strictly speaking the same is true of the nominative case which will be replaced by the ergative postposition (=*ne* in Hindi) in the expressions of the perfect and past perfective events. (Since this change was fully realized during the NIA period, we will not consider it in this paper).

These salient pairings of OIA adverbial particles and adpositions are sketched in Table 2.

1. *ā́* 'near'	(N+GEN) 'of'	(juxtaposition)
2. *áccha* 'to(wards)'	*ápa* 'away from'	(movement 'to' vs 'from')
3. *ádhi* '(up) on'	*áva* 'down from, off'	(location)
4. *úd-* 'up'	*ní-* 'down'	(super/inferiority)
5. *mádhye* 'in(to)'	*bahís* 'outside, out (of)'	(inter/exteriority)
6. *abhí* 'for', *anu* 'towards, over'	*tirás* 'by'	(path)
7. *prá*, *purás* 'before'	*paścā* 'after'	(anter/posteriority)
8. *sácā* 'with'	*vinā́* 'without'	(relation)
9. *ánti*, *práti* 'against'	*tirás* 'through'	(opposing limit)
10. *antár* 'between'	*parás* 'beyond'	(two limits)
11. *abhyantare* 'among'	*pári* 'about'	(circumference)
12. *úpa*, *adhás*, *avás* 'under'	*upári*, *áti* 'over'	(infer/superiority)

Table 2: *Old Indo-Aryan local adverbial particles and adpositions*

The following are the salient features of the archaic Indo-Aryan system (I follow Beekes 1995 in the notation for PIE laryngeals):

In 2. & 3. it is the existence of the pair *ápa* '(away) from' vs. *áva* 'down from' (continuing PIE *h_2*épo* vs. *h_2*eu*). *h_2*eu* was lost in most IE languages (it is seen in Latin *au-*, Old Irish *ó*, *ua*, Gothic *u-s*(?), and Slavic *u-*).

In 4. it is the existence of the preverbal pair *úd-* 'up' vs. *ní-* 'down' (e.g. *ud-pat* 'fly upwards' vs. *ni-kr̥* 'bring down, humble') with cognates in 'northern' IE languages (Slavic *vy-*, Gothic *ūt*; Old Church Slavonic *ni-zъ*, Old High German *nidar*).

In 5. one notices the absence of the PIE pair *$h_1$en* 'in' vs. *h_1eǵh(s)* 'out' (a typical pair in Greek, Latin and Celtic). For 'in(to)' Sanskrit uses the adverb *mádhyam* (Acc) or *mádhye* (Loc) 'middle'; its counterpart *bahís* 'out(side)' has apparently cognates in Lithuanian *bè* and Old Church Slavonic *bez* 'without'.

In 6. one notices the absence of the PIE pair **$h_2$en* 'along in an upwards direction' vs. **ḱn̥t-* 'by, along' (ἀνά vs. κατά is a typical pair in Greek). Sanskrit adposition *ánu* 'along; towards; over' is obviously descended from **$h_2$en* but its *-u* makes it the only adposition with this vowel; its Avestan counterpart is *ana* (comparable with Greek ἀνά and Gothic *ana*).

It should be observed that the adverbial suffix *-as*, traceable back to the PIE genitive suffix **-os*, is used extensively for the formation of primary and secondary adpositions: **prh_2-ós* > *purás* 'before' (in 7.) and **trh_2-ós* > *tirás* 'through' (in 6. and 9.)

The adverb *avás* 'downwards' (in 12.) is derived from the shorter form *áva* 'off' (< **$h_2$eu*). The relationship of *adhás* 'under' to *ádhā/adha* 'now, then' and *ádhi* 'above, over, from, in' (cf. Old Persian *adiy* 'in') is moot. The latter form is best understood as derived by the locative postposition **=d^hi* (cf. Greek *=θι*) from the pronominal root *a-* (< **h_1e*). *Adhás*, in spite of its almost opposite meaning, would be based on reanalyzing **h_1é-d^hi* → **h_1éd^h-i* (Loc) leading to **$h_1$edh-ós* (Gen/Abl) > *adh-ás*. Mayrhofer (1956: 31) also mentions the possibility of deriving *á-dhi* from *n̥dhi*, with *n̥* representing the zero-grade of *en* 'in' (< **$h_1$en*). In view of the Old Persian cognate *adiy* 'in' and the gap for PIE **$h_1$en.* (replaced by *madhy-* 'middle' in Indo-Aryan), this would seem to be a viable option. (In 10.) *par-ás* 'further, beyond, away' (cf. also *par-é* (Loc) 'subsequently' and *par-ám* (Acc) 'over') can be understood as the old genitive form of the adjective *pár-as* 'ulterior, further'. The PIE etymon for 'beyond, across' was apparently **pér-i* (witness Hittite *pariy-an*); but **péri* is descended in the meaning 'around, about' in Sanskrit (and also in Hellenic πέρι).

Unlike their Classical Greek counterparts, all the Sanskrit adpositions in *-i* are paroxytones (*ánti*, *ápi*, *áti*, *ádhi*, *pári*, *práti*) with a sole exception of *abhí* (in *abhí-tas* 'around') cf. Greek ἀμφί, both from *h_2*m̥bhí* (*-i* survived also in Latin *ambi-*, Gaulish *ambi* and Old High German *umbi*). There is another (?) Vedic adposition, *abhí* 'to(wards); over; for' which is traced back to *h_3*eb*^{h}*i* with cognates in Old Slavonic *obъ* 'to(wards); (a)round', Latin *ob* 'before, for' and Gothic *bi* 'over, about' (cf. Beekes 1995: 221). In any case, these two adpositions would merge in Indic, and the notion of circumference limit is expressed by the primary adposition *pári* (cf. Gk πέρι), originally **péri* 'over') or the adverbial derivatives *parí-tas*, *abhí-tas* 'around'.

In 4. the pair *úd* 'up' vs. *ní* 'down' consists of adverbial particles which were univerbated quite early in Vedic and ended up as preverbs in Classical Sanskrit (*ut-tíṣṭhati* lit. up-stand 'get up, rise'; *ni-drā́ti* lit. down-sleep 'fall asleep'). In Vedic they are found separated from their verbs ('tmesis') and they host Wackernagel's clitics:

(2a)	*úd=u*	*eti*	*subhágo*	*viśvácakṣāḥ*	[RV vii.63.1]
	up=now	goes	charming	all-seeing	

'up rises the charming all-seeing [Sun]'

(2b)	*ní*	*pedáva*	*ūhathur*	
	down	Pedu+DAT	bring+PERF+2DU	
	āśúm	*áśvam*		[RV vii.71.5]
	swift+ACC	horse+ACC		

'you [two] brought a swift horse to Pedu'

In participial (subordinate) and imperative (main) clauses they are found univerbated (the verb in the subordinate clause has to be accented and the particles may function as phonological hosts for the imperative):

(3a) *sū́ra* *údite* [RV vii.63.5]
sun+LOC up-risen+ LOC
'when the sun has risen'

(3b) *mahā́ntam* *kóśam* *úd* *acā*
great+ACC bucket+ACC up draw
ní *siñca* [RV v.83.8]
down pour
'Draw up the great bucket, pour [it] down!'

Similarly the adverbial particle *prá* 'before, forward, forth' is found in the main clause with tmesis in (4), without tmesis but not univerbated in (5) and univerbated in (6):

(4) *prá=ṇa* *ā́yur* *jīváse* *soma* *tārīḥ* [RV viii.48.4]
forth=we+OBL years life+DAT S. prolong+AOR/INJ/2SG
'prolong our years that we may live, O Soma!'

(5) *prá* *tiranta* *ā́yuḥ* [RV vii.103.10]
forth extend+3PL/MED life
'they prolong [their own] life'

(6) *táṃ* *sā́mā́nu* *prā́vartata* [RV x.135.4]
that+ACC chant=along forth=roll+IMPF+MED+3SG
'after that there rolled forth a chant'

And finally *pra-* is univerbated in the subordinate clause and the verb is accented as shown in (7):

(7) *ágaṇma* *yátra*
go+AOR+1PL where
pratiránta *āyuḥ* [RV viii.48.11]
forth=extend+MED+3PL life
'we have gone to (where men prolong their years)'

Schematically, the grammaticalization of these particles as preverbs proceeded along the lines in (8):

(8) **From adverbial particles to preverbs in Vedic Sanskrit**

PŔT=CL		O	V	(main clause with tmesis)
O	PŔT		V	(main clause without tmesis)
O		PŔT=V		(univerbation)
O		Prev=V́		(in subordinate clause)

Univerbation was favored in contexts with augmented verbs preceded by adverbial particles in _-a_ such as _prá=avartata_ → _prā́vartata_ in (6), and in the subordinate clause where the verb was accented as in (7).

The PIE adposition *h_2_ed_, expressing the general notion of proximity/juxtaposition, 'to, by' is well-documented in Latin _ad_ and Gothic _at_, and it is seen in the Vedic adverb/postposition _áccha_ 'to, towards' (in the 2nd pair in Table 2) which is traceable back to *_ad-s-k_^{w}_e_ (cf. Latin _atque_ and _ab-s-que_). The notion of proximity ('on/in/at/(near) to') could also be expressed by _ā́_ 'hither, near to, towards' (cf. Old Persian _ā_). One notices two 'rhyming' pairs in the OIA system: _áccha_ 'to(wards)' vs. _ápa_ 'away from' / _áva_ 'down from, off'; and the relational pair _sácā_ 'with' vs. _vinā́_ 'without' (historically, however, their _-ā_ was of a different origin: _sac-ā_ < *_sok_^{w}_-eh_$_1$, the _o_-grade of the root *_sek_^{w}_-_ 'follow' with the instrumental suffix _-ā_ vs. _vi-nā_ with the suffix _-nā_). _satrā́_ '(together) with' (cf. Avestan _haθra_/_ā_) was another comitative adverb/adposition in Vedic; this one was derived by the adverbial suffix _-trā_ (whose _-ā_ is ultimately the instrumental suffix *_-eh_$_1$).

Long _-ā_ is also seen in _paś-cā́_ (but also _paścā́t_) 'after, behind', _párā_ 'away, off, backward, forth' and _tiraścā́_ (primary _tirás_) 'through'. Indo-Iranian *_pasča-_/*_paska-_ (cf. Avestan _pasča_ 'after', Old Persian *_pasča_ 'vice-') was etymologized as *_po-sk_^{w}_-o_, with *_po-_ (< _(a)pa_ < *h_2_pó_ 'from, as of') and the zero-grade of the root *sek*^{w}- 'follow' (cf. Mayrhofer 1963: 240). The adverbial *-ā* is apparently the instrumental suffix *-*eh*$_1$, and *-āt* the ablative suffix (< *-*ōd*). On the other hand, *tiraścā́* 'through' is an innovative form of Indo-Iranian (cf. Avestan *tarasca*) based on the adjectival compound *tiry-añc* 'transverse' (verbal root *a(ñ)c-* 'bend'), feminine form *tir-aśc-ī. Párā* 'away, off, forth' is apparently cognate with Greek πέρα 'across' and Hittite *parā* 'forward, farther'.

In 8. there was another relational pair comitative vs. privative, exploiting the suffix *-*ter* whose original meaning was 'excessive' (cf. *-*tero* in comparatives and *terh*$_2$ > OIA *tár/tir-* 'overcome'): *sa-trā́* 'with' (cf. Avestan *haθra*) vs. *sanu-tár* 'far from' / *sani-túr* 'without'. Its PIE ancestry could be **som* 'with' > *sa-* vs. **snh*$_1$*u-ter* > *sanu-tár/°sn̥-ter* (> Greek ἄτερ 'without', Middle High German *sunder* 'without, separately'). The suffix *-*ter* appears also in **hen*$_1$*-ter* 'between, inside' (Sanskrit *antár* 'within, inwards', Greek ἔντερον 'gut, entrails', Latin *inter*, Hittite *istarna* 'in the middle, among').

3. THE SYNTAX OF ADVERBS AND ADPOSITIONS

Vedic Sanskrit and Homeric Greek represent the state of affairs of PIE when the adverbial particles were used to indicate spatial and temporal locations in conjunction with nouns or verbs. Vedic grammars differentiate between (i) 'adnominal prepositions', which are never compounded with verbs and (ii) genuine preverbs, which are used to modify the meaning of the verb. Thus of the 29 adpositions (in Table 2) four are never used adnominally (*ápa* 'away from', *úd* 'up' vs. *ní* 'down', *prá* 'forth'; here belong also *níṣ* 'out', *pára* 'away', *ví* 'asunder', *sám* 'together'; then there are three adpositions which are used adnominally, but only with a highly restricted set of verbs: *áccha* 'towards', *tirás* 'across' and *purás* 'before'). This distinction goes all the way back to Pāṇini, who differentiated between such *nipāta*s 'particles' which are syntactically connected to verbs (*upasarga* 'verbal prefix' or 'preverb') and such particles which are syntactically connected to nouns (*karma-*

pravacanīya lit. determining the action 'pre/postpositions (used with nouns)'). The use of the term πρό-θεσις 'preposition' (designed by the Stoics for Ancient Greek) for what are mostly postpositions in Indo-Aryan is deplorable but it is well-established. For example, Whitney (1969 [1889]: 414–416), under the heading *Prepositions*, discusses "many of the adverbial words ... used with nouns in a way which approximates them to the more fully developed prepositions of other languages".

Adverbial particles in their 'action-determining' function (*karmapravacanīya*) could appear anywhere in the sentence; more specifically, as shown in (9).

(i) the adverbial particle in S-1 position could host Wackernagel's clitics;

(ii) the adverbial particle in preverbal position was exposed to univerbation and ended up as a preverb;

(iii) the noun phrase (of AN or NA typology) could be made discontinuous by the intervening adverbial particle:

(9) NP

##**PRT**=CL **PRT** ADJ **PRT** N **PRT** V##

(W'L clitic) adpositions preverb

These four positions were consequential for the later development of configurational syntax in MIA. Hand-in-hand with the increase of the OV and AN typology of OIA, the postposed particles were reanalyzed as 'postpositions'. Thus in (10) the adverbial particle *ā́* 'near, besides' appears after the noun in the ablative (= genitive) in the meaning of spatial removal:

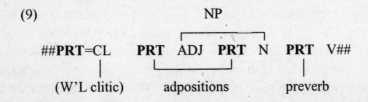

(10) *imáṃ sú asmai hr̥dá ā́*
this well he+DAT heart+GEN/ABL near
sútaṣṭaṃ mántraṃ vocema
well-fashioned hymn utter+AOR+1PL [RV ii.35.2]
'We would verily utter from our heart this well-fashioned hymn for him'

In (11) *ā́* hosts the pronominal clitic *te* (Gen/Dat) 'you' and has rather the meaning 'towards' (= allative):

(11) *áta ā́ ta*
thence near you+GEN/DAT
r̥taspŕ̥śo ní ṣeduḥ [RV iv.50.3]
rite-cherishers down sit+PERF+3PL
'from thence [coming] the rite-cherishers have seated themselves for you'

In (12), however, the meaning 'towards' is indicated by the preverb *prati-* 'towards' (= univerbated adverbial particle *práti* 'towards') in spite of *ā́* 'near' hosting the pronominal clitic *vaḥ* (oblique) 'you':

(12) *sionā́d ā́ vaḥ pratibúdhyamānāḥ* [RV iv.51.10]
couch+ABL near ye+OBL towards-awakening+PL
'awakening from our soft couch towards you'

It should be observed that in Classical Sanskrit *ā* could be preposed to the noun in the ablative and the meaning could paradoxically be that of allative or time limit '(up) to; till'; however, more 'logically' the accusative was also available):

(13) *ā pradānāt* ~ *ā pradānaṃ*
near marriage+ABL near marriage+ACC
'until [her] marriage' 'until [her] marriage'

In Vedic there are also instances where *ā́* would seem to function as an 'ambiposition', i.e. as a postposition linked with the notion of spatial removal and as a preposition linked with the notion of allative at the same time:

(14) *yatī́* *giríbhya* *ā́* *samudrā́t* [RV vii.95.2]
going+FEM mountains+ABL near ocean+ABL
'going from the mountains to the ocean'

In this example, the goal of the movement, 'the ocean', appears in the ablative. But there are also clear examples where *ā́* only belongs to a following ablative in an allative sense (as in *ā́ ántād* lit. near end+ABL 'to the end' [RV iii.61.4]). Therefore, also in (14) *ā́* may only belong to *samudrā́t* and this line cannot be taken as proof for the existence of an 'ambipositional' phrase.

Examples in (10) - (14) show the genuine indeterminacy in adjudicating the function of a preverb or that of an adposition to certain adverbial particles. The non-existence of the configurational postpositional phrase as known from Modern Indo-Aryan languages goes hand in hand with the non-existence of the configurational noun phrase. A logical consequence of the 'free' adverbial particle/adposition is the phenomenon of the 'discontinuous' NP as in the following example:

(15) *hiraṇyáyāt* *pári* *yóner* [RV ii.35.10]
golden+ABL around womb+GEN/ABL
'from the golden womb'

In terms of a fully functional system of morphological cases the notion of spatial removal derives from the ablative case of the head noun (in *i*-stems it happens to be identical with the genitive). The noun phrase is held together by agreement but the adjective marked appropriately by the ablative is not preposed to its head noun; the intervening adverbial particle/adposition *pári* 'around' makes the NP discontinuous: Adj[+Case] Adv/Adpo N[+Case].

Similarly, in (16) the local particle *pári* 'about' is not a postposition expressing the notion of spatial removal — this function is performed by the ablative case as in (15) above:

(16)	*áditer*	*dákṣo*	*ajāyata*		
	Aditi+GEN/ABL	Dakṣa	be-born+IMPF/3SG		
	dákṣād *u*	*áditiḥ*	*pári*		[RV x.72.4]
	Dákṣa+ABL=now	Áditi	about		
	'from Aditi Dakṣa was born, and from Dakṣa Aditi'				

Along the same lines in (17) the notion of spatial removal derives from the ablative suffix while *ádhi* only functions as the local particle expressing the notion of spatial proximity ('upon'):

(17)	*tásmād*	*virā́j*	*ajāyata*	
	he+ABL	Virāj	be-born+IMPF/3SG	
	virā́jŏ	*ádhi*	*pū́ruṣaḥ*	[RV x.90.5]
	Virāj+ABL	upon	Puruṣa	
	'From him Virāj was born, from Virāj Puruṣa'			

The locative function of the adposition *ádhi* '(up)on' is seen in instances such as *ádhi barhíṣi* 'upon the grass' and *pṛthivyā́m ádhi* 'upon the earth' with the noun in the locative. Here the notion of location is conveyed by the locative suffix on the noun but the adposition *ádhi* '(up)on' reinforces it in that its meaning coincides with the meaning of the locative suffix on the noun. In historical perspective, we are at the beginning of its development into the head of the postpositional phrase. We shall see in the next section that the coexistence of the postposition and the morphological case was typical of the MIA period. With the subsequent reduction of morphological case to the oblique during the Late MIA period it became practically impossible to 'disrupt' the noun phrase and the postpositional phrase became fully established. In terms of grammaticalization, the adverbial particle is reanalyzed as postposition. In more formal syntactic terms, as sketched in (18), we can portray this development from OIA to MIA as a recategorization from an adverbial to a postpositional phrase. Example (14) may serve as an example of a non-configurational Vedic adverbial phrase, to be contrasted with a MIA configurational postpositional phrase such as *uccaho Kailāsaho upari* 'on the high Kailāsa':

(18) **From non-configurational adverbial phrase in OIA > Configurational postpositional phrase in MIA**

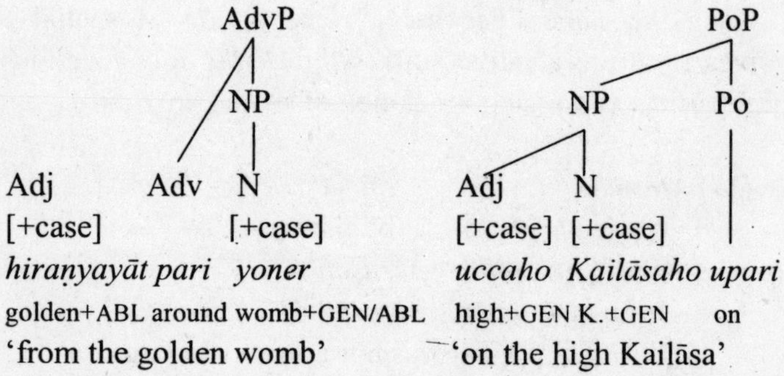

4. RESTRUCTURING OF THE NOMINAL SYSTEM AND THE EVOLUTION OF THE PHRASAL CASE

The nominal system of late MIA underwent a considerable erosion of case contrasts and Apabhraṃśa ended up with only one form for earlier Nom vs. Acc, Instr vs. Loc, and Gen vs. Abl. Table 3 (adopted from Bubenik 1996: 73) puts these matters into diachronic perspective of OIA and MIA (Old and Middle Prākrits represented by Pāli and Ardha-Māgadhī). Globally speaking, Old and Middle Prākrits created a new type of the opposition of the direct (Nom, Acc) to the oblique cases (Instr, Gen, Abl, Loc) in both numbers: a monosyllabic ending in the direct case vs. a disyllabic ending in the oblique case (trisyllabic in the Abl in AMg). In Apabhraṃśa, in addition, a new opposition of the singular to the plural in oblique cases based on the presence of the nasalized vowel started emerging: plain vs. nasalized ultima of the ending signalized the opposition between the singular vs. plural oblique case (here we are reaching an NIA state of affairs). In morphological terminology, the cumulative exponence of grammatical significates of OIA and earlier stages of MIA gave way gradually to new types of semi-agglutinative exponence in MIA. At the end, the nasalization of the ultima became more or less consistent in the plural cases in Apabhraṃśa, whereas it was only optional during the previous stages (as shown by AMg).

	OIA Sanskrit	Old Prākrits Pāli	Middle Prākrits AMg	Late Prākrits Apabhraṃśa
Sg Nom	*-aḥ*	*-o*	*-o*	*-u*
Acc	*-am*	*-ã*	*-ã*	*-ũ*
Instr	*-ena*	*-ena/ã*	*-eṇa*	*-ẽ*
Dat	*-āya*	*-assa/āya*	*-assa*	*-aho*
Gen	*-asya*	*-assa*	*-assa*	*-aho, -ahu*
Abl	*-āt*	*-asmā*	*-ā(o)*	*-ahe, -ahu*
Loc	*-e*	*-asmĩ*	*-ãsi*	*-i, -e*
Pl Nom	*-āḥ*	*-ā*	*-ā*	*-a*
Acc	*-an*	*-e*	*-a,e*	*-a*
Instr	*-ebhiḥ*	*-ehi*	*-ehĩ*	*-a/ehĩ*
Dat	*-ebhyaḥ*	*-ānã*	*-āṇã*	*-ahã*
Gen	*-ānām*	*-ānã*	*-āṇã*	*-ahã*
Abl	*-ebhyaḥ*	*-ehi*	*-ehinto*	*-ahũ*
Loc	*-eṣu*	*-esu*	*-esũ*	*-ahĩ*

Table 3: *The nominal system (*a*-stems) of Old and Middle Indo-Aryan*

Given the drastic reduction from the seven fusional cases of OIA to four by the end of the MIA period, the postpositions grew steadily in importance in denoting relational aspects of their head nouns.

Examples in (19) and (20) are provided to contrast the grammaticalization of the notion of 'source' in Sanskrit and Apabhraṃśa:

(19) *hr̥dayād yadi niḥsarasi*
heart+ABL if out-go+2/SG (case)
'if you go out of [my] heart'

hiaya-ṭṭhiu jai nīsarahi [Hc 8.4.439]
heart=ABL if out-go+2/SG (postposition)
'if you go out of [my] heart'

(20) *kukavitvāt*
bad-poetry+ABL (case)
'because of being poetaster'

kukavitvena hetunā
bad-poetry+INSTR cause+INSTR (case and postposition)
'because of being poetaster'

kukavitta-resi [SR 21a]
bad-poetry=REF (postposition)
'because of being poetaster'

In (19) the ablative suffix in its concrete spatial sense was replaced by the postposition *ṭhiu*, whose source is the past participle *sthita* 'stood'; in (20) the causal relation 'due to/because of/on account of' is grammaticalized in several ways: in Sanskrit by the ablative suffix or by the postposition *hetunā*, which actually is the instrumental form of *hetu* 'cause' (also its head-noun is in the instrumental); in Apabhraṃśa there is one of the referential postpositions, such as *resi*.

On the whole, most of the Prākrit postpositions go back to their OIA namesakes, but some of the Apabhraṃśa postpositions are innovative and herald the NIA state of affairs. Table 4, constructed in a parallel fashion with Table 2, presents the MIA postpositional system.

1. *pāsi* 'at'	*kerau/ī* (Ap) 'of'
2. *kahũ* (Ap) 'to'	*honta(u)*, *ṭhiu* (Ap) 'from'
3. *ahĩ* (Ap) '(up)on'	(*ava-* 'off' as a preverb)
4. (*ud-* 'up' as a preverb)	(*ni-* 'down' as a preverb)
5. *majjhe* 'in(to)'	*bāhi/ar* 'out(side)'
6. *kehĩ*, *tehĩ*, *resĩ*, *taṇeṇa* (Ap) 'for'	(N+INSTR) 'by'
7. *agga* 'before'	*paccha* 'behind'
aggẽ (Ap)	*paccha(l)i/e* (Ap)
8. *samau*, *sa(h)u*, *saĩ/i* (Ap) 'with'	*viṇu*, *rahiyu*, *bāhire* 'without'
9. *sammuhu*, *paḍīva* (Ap) 'towards'	*majjhẽ* 'through'
10. *ãtar(i)* (Ap) 'between	? 'across'
11. *ãtar(i)* (Ap) 'among'	? 'about'
12. (*aha-*, *uva-* 'under' as a preverb)	*uvarĩ*, *(u)vari* (Ap) 'over'

Table 4: *Middle Indo-Aryan (Prākrit and Apabhraṃśa) postpositions*

The use of morphological cases (Gen, Abl, Loc, Instr) in 1, 2, 3 and 6 harks back to the OIA state of affairs. The old synthetic morphology had to be remodelled when, as a consequence of phonological changes, it became non-distinctive. This happened in Early MIA when the old ablative *devāt* lost the final *-t* and thus became homophonous with the plural nominative. Pāli helped the situation by adopting the pronominal suffix *-asmā* ~ *-amhā*, or the adverbial suffix *-to* (< *-tas*). The latter suffix is continued in Middle Prākrits in the form *-āo*. In Mahārāṣṭrī, in addition to the ablative suffixes *-ā* and *-āo*, there was a peculiar suffix *-ahi*, well documented in Hāla's *Sattasaī*:

(21) *tīa*	*muhāhi*	*tuha*	*muhã*	[Satta 179]
she+OBL	mouth+ABL	you+GEN	mouth	

'from her mouth (in)to your mouth'

It was shown by Insler (1993) that this suffix derives from the postposition *ádhi*, which as far back as Vedic could be attached to the ablative form of the noun in the meaning 'down from, out of' (competing with the postposition *áva*).

As far as the expressions for location are concerned, in OIA it was enough to say *gṛh+e* 'in the house' with the locative suffix *-e*; in MIA it became necessary to use the adverb *majjhe/i* 'inside' as an adposition with the noun in the genitive: *majjhe gharaho* ~ *gharaho majjhe*. In terms of dependency syntax the adverbial phrase 'inside the house' could be either left- or right-headed, as shown in (22):

(22) **Adverbial phrase 'inside the house' in Apabhraṃśa**

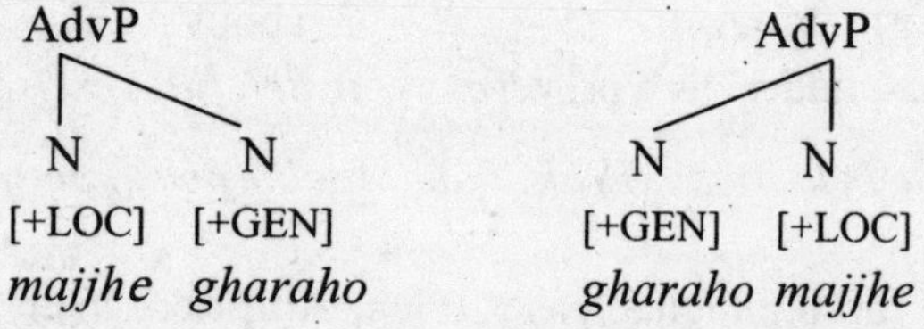

The projective notion of superiority 'over' in OIA was expressed by the adverb/adposition *upari* (with the noun in the Acc, Loc, Abl or Gen). In Apabhraṃśa literature, all sorts of examples are available ranging from (a) *uvari* detached from its (pro)nominal modifier to (b) immediately following one (as in *Kailāsaho upari* 'on the Kailasa') to (c) compound (as in *iyar'uvari* 'on another one').

The notion of proximity is realized by one of the adessive postpositions, most commonly *pās-i* 'in the proximity/nearness of'. Its concrete meaning used to be 'side, region of the ribs' (in OIA *pārśva*; cf. its derivatives *pārśva-ka* 'rib' and *pārśvaka-cara* 'attendant'). As shown in (23) in Apabhraṃśa literature, there are several morphosyntactic types realizing this notion: the left-headed *pāsu mahu* 'to/at me' or the right-headed *guru-pāsi* 'to/at the teacher' or *Vasudevaho pāsu* 'to/at Vasudeva':

(23) *āṇaho* *pāsu* *mahu* [Pc 27.3.9]
bring+IMP side I+GEN
'Bring to me!'

gayau *guru-pāsi* [Kp 101.1]
go+PP teacher-side+LOC
'He went to the teacher'

Vasudevaho *pāsu* *gau* [Riṭṭha 4.7.8]
Vasudeva+GEN side go+PP
'He went to Vasudeva'

Pāsu mahu, unlike *majjhe gharaho*, features the head-noun in the nominative. The left-branching *guru-pāsi* continues the locative form of the OIA compound noun **guru-pārśve* lit. at the teacher-side. *Vasudevaho pāsu* features the nominative form of the word *pāsu* while its dependent noun continues the OIA morphological genitive *Vasudevasya pārśve* lit. at Vasudeva's side. With its replacement by the phrasal possessive construction *=ke pās* we reach the NIA state of affairs of the postpositional phrase. This development from the compound noun and the adverbial phrase to postpositional phrase is sketched in (24).

(24) **Development from the compound noun and the adverbial phrase to the postpositional phrase in MIA**

OIA **guru-pārśve* 'at the teacher-side'

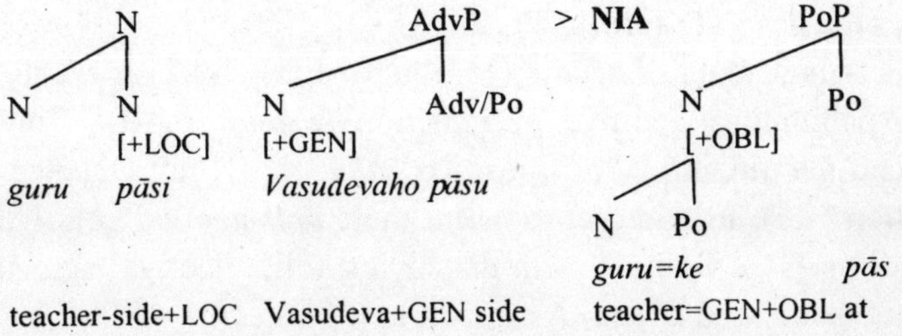

The notion of an opposing limit 'against, towards' was in OIA expressed by the postposition *prati* with the accusative (e.g. *devān prati* 'towards gods'). By the late MIA period, the meaning of *pai* (< *prati*) was reduced to that of a degree word 'only' and the emphatic particle (corresponding to Hindi *bhī*); in addition, the form *pai* was homophonous with *pai* 'husband' and *paĩ* 'you' (< *tvayā*). It is therefore no surprise that this postposition had to be recreated from OIA *pratīpam* 'towards' (lit. *prati-ap* 'against the water/stream') > Apabhraṃśa *paḍīva*.

In Vedic the notion of accompaniment was expressed by the preverb *sa(m)-*. The same *sa-* is found in the adposition *sahá* 'with', formed by the productive adverbial suffix *-dhā*; its simplified form is found in Pāli *i-há* 'here'. This adposition was recreated several times, yielding formations such as *sam-ám* (Acc) 'together with' and *sam-áyā* (Instr) 'altogether'; these two are case forms of the adjectival derivative *sam-á* 'similar, like, equal'; other formations include *sa-rátham* 'on the same car with' > 'together with' (by the process of grammaticalization); *sākám* 'together' is probably from **sa-añc* 'going together'; *sārdhám* is the accusative form of the compounded adjective *sa-ardha-* 'together with a half'; *samānam* 'jointly' is the accusative form of the adjectival derivative in *-na*, which itself is the derivative based on **sam*.

The privative adposition *viṇu* 'without' is used with the noun in the instrumental (in OIA it could also be used with the ablative and accusative). And finally there is also an antonym to *sahiya* 'accompanied by', namely *rahiya*, from OIA *rahita* 'devoid of', as in *dosahiṃ rahiu* 'without faults' (with the noun in the instrumental or the absolute form).

A new state of affairs (i.e. that of Early NIA) is heralded by the Apabhraṃśa genitive postposition *kerau/ī* 'of' (> Hindi *=kā/kī*) and the directional postposition *kahũ* 'to' (Hindi Dat/Acc postposition *=ko*). In addition to *kerau* there was another genitival postposition *taṇa*, both of them displaying full adjectival agreement with the possessed object. As shown in (25), in OIA and MIA agreement with the possessed could not be shown on the pronoun referring to the possessor:

(25) **Genitive postposition agrees with the possessed object**

	OIA	MIA	Apabhraṃśa	Hindi
'his brother'	*tasya bhrātā*	*tao bhāū*	*tao kerau bhāū*	*us=kā bhāī*
'his daughter'	*tasya duhitā*	*tao dhūya*	*tao kerī dhūya*	*us=kī beṭī*
'her brother'	*tasyā bhrātā*	*tahe bhāū*	*tahe kerau bhāū*	*us=kā bhāī*
'her daughter'	*tasyā duhitā*	*tahe dhūya*	*tahe kerī dhūya*	*us=kī beṭī*

We do not possess enough information regarding what happens when the head of the possessive construction is declined. In Hindi the genitival postposition takes on the form of the oblique case (observable only in the Masc Sg); e.g. 'with his/her brother' is *us=ke bhāī=ke sāth*. In Apabhraṃśa one would expect for the genitival postpositions *kerau* and *taṇa* to copy the case of their head nouns:

(26) **The head of the possessive construction is declined**

	tao	*ker(a)eṃ*	*bhāuṇa*	*saha*	(?)
	tao	*taṇeṇa*	*bhāuṇa*	*saha*	(?)
	he+GEN	GEN+INSTR	brother+INSTR	with	
cf.	*us=*	*ke*	*bhāī=ke*	*sāth*	(Hindi)

In my perusal of the Apabhraṃśa corpus (Bubenik 1998), I have not come across similar constructions. In their stead, sanskritic constructions *tao bhāuṇa saha* 'with his brother' and *tāe bhāuṇa saha* 'with her brother' are found:

(27) *tao bhāuṇa saha* (cf. Skt *tasya bhrātrā saha*)
'with his brother'
tāe bhāuṇa saha (cf. Skt *tasyā bhrātrā saha*)
'with her brother'

The notion of reference (*tādarthya* lit. being meant for that) was expressed by the dative in Sanskrit; in Apabhraṃśa the notion of reference came to be expressed by one of the postpositions attached to the genitive form or the stem of the noun: *kehĩ, tehĩ, resĩ, taṇeṇa*. None of them survived into Modern Indo-Aryan; in Hindi they were replaced by *=ke lie*. Their etymologies are more controversial. *Resĩ* can go back to the genitive form *keresĩ* of problematic form *kera* (*kera* is usually explained as the gerundive form *kārya* 'to be done'); *kehĩ* might go back to OIA *kṛte* (but its expected descendant should be *kie/kae*); and *taṇeṇa* is the instrumental form of the genitive postposition *taṇa*.

5. CONCLUSIONS

At the end of the MIA period we find the results of evolution from OIA, whose salient points are the following:

(i) The maintenance of four cases: the syncretic Nom/Acc (the future Direct of NIA), the syncretic Gen/Dat/Abl (the future Oblique), the Instrumental performing also the function of the Ergative case, and Locative.

(ii) It should be observed that several Late MIA postpositions were treated as locatives of place adverbs; in Table 4 those postpositions carry the nasalized locative suffix *-ĩ*; witness *ahĩ* '(up)on', relational *kehĩ* and *resĩ* 'for', *saĩ* 'with' and *uvarĩ* 'over'; see also the plural locative suffix in *-ahĩ*, which can be traced back to the pronominal locative form *-asmin* (as in *t-asmin*). *Aggẽ* 'before' and *majjhẽ* 'through' are formally instrumentals.

(iii) In spite of the fact that there is no phrasal noun (i.e. there are no required determiners and no fixed configuration), there is nevertheless a relatively fully developed postpositional phrase with a score of proper postpositions which still may appear preposed. In this respect MIA represents an intermediate state of affairs between non-configurational paradigmatic morphology of OIA and configurational phrasal syntax (both nominal and verbal) of NIA.

(iv) Postpositions attached to the instrumental form are limited to the relational pair 'with' versus 'without'. This remarkable perseverance of the instrumental (remarkable from the point of view of other IE languages such as Hellenic or Germanic) is explainable by the fact that this case also functioned as the agentive case in the ergative construction.

(v) This shift from the OIA syntax based on morphological agreement to an MIA syntax based on configurational phrases is an important shift in the history of the Indo-Aryan family of languages. We presented clear evidence that this shift began with the development of the postpositional phrase, in which what were originally adverbial particles became postpositions in the new syntax of the adpositional phrase.

REFERENCES

BEEKES, Robert S. P. 1995. *Comparative Indo-European Linguistics*. Amsterdam: John Benjamins.

BUBENIK, Vit 1996. *The Structure and Development of Middle Indo-Aryan Dialects*. Delhi: Motilal Banarsidass.

------ 1998. *Historical Syntax of Late Middle Indo-Aryan (Apabhraṃśa)*. Amsterdam: John Benjamins.

BUBENIK, Vit & John HEWSON (forthcoming). *From Adverbs to Adpositions in Indo-European Languages*. Amsterdam: John Benjmains.

INSLER, S. 1993. The Prakrit Ablative in *-ahi*. *Annals of the Bandarkar Oriental Research Institute* 72 & 73: 15-21.

MAYRHOFER, Manfred 1953/1956/1963/1976. *Kurzgefasstes etymologisches Wörterbuch des Altindischen*. Heidelberg: Winter.

TAGARE, Ganesh V. 1948. *Historical Grammar of Apabhraṃśa*. Poona. (Dissertation, 5) 1987 ed., Delhi: Motilal Banarsidass.

VAIDYA, P. L. 1980. *Prakrit Grammar of Hemacandra*. Poona: Bhandarkar Oriental Research Institute.

WHITNEY, William D. 1969 [1889]. *Sanskrit Grammar*. 2nd Indian ed. Delhi: Motilal Banarsidass.

TEXTS

Hc [= Hemacandra] *Prakrit Grammar of Hemacandra*. Ed. by P. L. Vaidya. Poona: Bhandarkar Oriental Research Institute, 1958/1980.

Kp [= Kumārapālapratibodha] *Der Kumārapālapratibodha*. Ed. by Ludwig Alsdorf. Hamburg: Friedrichsen, 1928.

Pc [= Paumacariu] *Svayaṃbhūdeva's Paūmacariu*. Ed. by Harivallabh C. Bhayani. Bombay: Jñānapīṭha-Mūrtidevī-Jaina-Granthamālā, 1953-60.

Riṭṭha [= Riṭṭhanemicariu] *Kavirāja Svayaṃbhūdeva's Riṭṭhanemi-cariu (Arishtanemi-charita)*. Ed. by Devendra Kumār Jain 1985.

RV [= Rig-Veda]

Satta [= Sattasaī] *Hāla's Sattasai. Stemma and Edition of Gāthās 1- 50, with Translation and Notes*. Dissertation by H. J. T. Tieken. Utrecht, 1983.

SR [= Saṃdeśarāsaka] *The Saṃdeśa Rāsaka of Abdul Rahman*. Translated by C. M. Mayrhofer. Delhi: Motilal Banarsidass, 1998.

Abbreviations

Abl = ablative
Acc = accusative
A(dj) = adjective
AdPo = adpositional phrase
Adv = adverb
AdvP = adverbial phrase
AMg = Ardha-Māgadhī
AOR = aorist
Ap = Apabhraṃśa
CL = clitic
Dat = dative
DU = dual
Gen = genitive
IE = Indo-European
IMP = imperative
IMPF = imperfect
INJ = injunctive
Instr = instrumental
Loc = locative
Masc = masculine
MED = middle (medium)
MIA = Middle Indo-Aryan
N = noun
NIA = New Indo-Aryan
Nom = nominative
NP = noun phrase
OBL = oblique
OIA = Old Indo-Aryan
PERF = perfect
PIE = Proto-Indo-European
PL = plural
Po = postposition
PoP = postpositional phrase
PP = past participle
Prev = preverb
PRT = particle
REF = reference
SG = singular
SOV = subject-object-verb (order)
V = verb

Notes on the instrumental case of the subject/agent vs. other cases in Buddhist Sanskrit

BORIS OGUIBÉNINE

Key words: S(ubject); A(gent); S and A are encoded either lexically or inflexionally; Instr-patterning vs. Nom-Acc patterning[1]; alternation of patterns.

The abbreviations showing the key words are used to present the basic encoding of syntactic patterns.

(**vs**) specifies that the quotation is from the verses.

The abbreviation *vs.* is used to point out the contrast between the quoted items.

Other abbreviations, in particular referring to grammatical terms, should be clear.

PPP past passive participle.

// separates the main and the subordinate or subordinate-like clauses.

The titles of Buddhist texts, if not explained below, are abbreviated as in BHSD.

1. The concern of this article is twofold. First, I attempt a systematization of the cases of subject (S), which some linguists term agent (A),[2] within the set of contrasting syntactic patterns: S/A_{Instr} O_{Acc} $V_{non\text{-}finite(Ger,\ PPP)}$ vs. $S/A_{Nom\ or\ Gen}$ O_{Acc} $V_{finite\ or\ infinitive}$

---

[1] Buddhist Sanskrit, as Classical Sanskrit, is a language with both patterning: Nom-Acc and Instr-Acc-patterning. Dixon 1995: 6-7 points out that in such languages S (intransitive subject alternatively labeled 'subject of intransitive verb') and A (transitive subject alternatively labeled 'subject/agent of transitive verb') naturally group together (S/A). The third 'primitive relation' or 'core argument' is O (transitive object is also labeled 'object of transitive verb'). The alternative denominations are given by Jamison 2000: 67.

[2] For example, Dixon 1995: 111 writes: "The 'subject' of a sentence is that NP whose referent *could* be the 'agent' that initiates and controls an activity; the subject NP is normally obligatory in a sentence, receives an unmarked case, may be cross-referenced in the verb, and is the pivot for operations of coordination and subordination".

in Buddhist Sanskrit of the Mahāsāṃghika-Lokottaravādins, which is fairly different from Classical Sanskrit and which is now commonly enough considered as Buddhist (Hybrid) Sanskrit.

Second, it is assumed that in our language these concomitant syntactic structures express more or less synonymous meanings. The synonymousness is especially pregnant in the case of the accusative gerundial clauses which are used besides the ergative gerundial clauses [as expressed by Tikkanen 1991: 133: "Sanskrit displays both accusative and ergative clause structures. The latter may be based on the passive gerundive and *ta-* participle[3] and are distinguished from passive structures in that they allow the Actor to be encoded as the instrumental or genitive agent[1] ([1]especially if animate and definite or given) and the Undergoer as the subject (...)"].

As is known, Instr is a predecessor of the ergative case in the Indo-Aryan languages (Dixon 1995: 190; Montaut 1997; see also a survey by Régamey 1954, although outdated). But, as will be seen, Instr is frequently matched by other cases of S/A. The investigation of conditions under which the Instr-patterning emerges, and proliferates in the discourse, is so more urgent.

I shall thus attempt to show that the use of different syntactic structures either beside one another or concomitantly is not free from any constraint, although these constraints are more tendentious than definitely operating (more in Oguibénine, forthcoming). Similar problems in relation with ergativity have recently been discussed by Jamison (she mentions particularly the "apparently mixed systems" of agent marking in the Niya documents and proceeds to "sort out what types of sentences receive which treatment" in order to support her claim that the distribution of different cases of the agents are not random, but favoured in "certain syntactic and functional areas", see Jamison 2000: 70ff.).

Special attention will be given to encoding the events by two main different argument patternings of the clauses: on the one hand,

---

[3] Of course, the *-na* participle is to be added.

Instr-patterning [S_{Instr}+$O_{Nom\ or\ Acc}$ +$PartPres_{Instr}$ (or $_{Ger}$)][4] and, on the other hand, Nom-Acc-patterning [A_{Nom}+O_{Acc} +V_{Finite}][5].

2.1. Sample text

A. Mv. 1.283.7-12 [1]*buddhena bhagavatā vaiśālīye sīmāṃ ākramantena sarve amanuṣyakā palānāḥ* [...] [2]*janakāyo* [...] *bhagavantaṃ pṛcchati kathaṃ* [1]*bhagavatā vaiśālīye sīmām ākramantenaiva sarve amanuṣyakāḥ palānāḥ* [3]*bhagavān āha kim* [...] *āścaryaṃ yan* [1a]*tathāgatena paramasaṃbodhiprāptena devātidevena sīmām ākramantenaiva sarve amanuṣyakā palānāḥ* [4]*anyadāpi mayā ṛṣibhūtena kampille nagare sīmām ākramantenaiva sarve amanuṣyakā palānāḥ* [...]

B. Mv. 1.283.14-15, 19-20; 284.1-2, 3-9; 11-13; 286.14-15; 17-19[5][...] *rājā brahmadatto nāma rājyaṃ kāresi* [...] [6]*so kāmeṣu ādīnavaṃ dṛṣṭvā anuhimavantaṃ gatvā ṛṣipravrajyāṃ pravrajito* [7]*tena* [...] *āśramaṃ māpetvā* [...] *jāgarikāyogam anuyuktena* [...] *catvāri dhyānāni utpāditāni* [...] [8]*so* [...] *kumāro brahmacārī* [...] *candramaṇḍalaṃ ca sūryamaṇḍalaṃ ca pāṇinā parāmṛṣati* [9][...] *amanuṣyavyādhi dāruṇo utpanno* [...] [10]*tena amanuṣyavyādhinā spṛṣṭā bahūni prāṇisahasrāṇi anayavyasanam āpadyante* [11]*rājñā brahmadattena taṃ kampille mahāntam ādīnavaṃ dṛṣṭvā* [...] *rakṣitasya dūto preṣitaḥ* [...] [12]*ṛṣir dūtavacanaṃ śrutvā anuhimavantāto kampillam āgato* [13]*tena ṛṣiṇā kampillasya sīmām ākramantena sarve te amanuṣyakā palānāḥ* [14]*ṛṣiṇā tahiṃ kampille svastyayanaṃ kṛtaṃ* [...] [15]*ahaṃ so* [...] *rakṣito nāma ṛṣi abhūṣi* [...,] [16]*eṣo rājā śreṇiko bimbisāro tadā kampille nagare brahmadatto nāma rājā abhūṣi* [17]*tadāpi maye ṛṣibhūtena kampille sīmām ākramantenaiva sarve amanuṣyakā palānāḥ* [18]*etarahiṃ pi maye vaiśālīye sīmām ākramantenaiva sarve amanuṣyakā palānāḥ*.

---

[4] As in Mv. 1.283.20-284.1 *tena dāni* [...] *āśramaṃ māpetvā* 'By him a hermitage being-caused-to construct' (see below). I translate the examples as literally as possible in order to make clear their semantics and syntactic structure.

[5] As in Mv. 1.283.8 *janakāyo* [...] *bhagavantaṃ pṛcchati* 'The crowd interrogates the Blessed One' (see more below).

A. [1]Once by the Blessed One-entering the confines of Vaiśālī all the demons ran away. [2]The crowd asked the Blessed One: "How do all the demons run away [while takes place] by the Blessed One-entering the confines of Vaiśālī?" [3]The Blessed One told "Is it a wonder that [1a]by the Tathāgata, by him-who-experienced-the supreme-enlightenment, by-him-who-is-superior-to-all-gods having-entered the confines [of Vaiśālī], all the demons ran away?" [4]On another occasion on which by-me-having-entered the confines of Kampilla all the demons ran away.

B. [5]There reigned a king Brahmadatta. [6]He [the priest's son Rakṣita] having-seen the peril in the pleasure of sensuous desire, went to the slopes of the Himālayas and embraced the religious life of a seer. [7]By him-having-caused-to-construct a hermitage, by him-practising the wakefulness the four meditations have been mastered. [8]The young holy man was [able] to touch the orb of the moon and that of the sun. [9]A terrible plague broke out. [10]Many thousands of beings infected by the demonic plague succumb to this calamity. [11]By the king this great calamity having-been-seen a messenger has been sent to Rakṣita. [12]The seer having-heard the messenger's words went from the Himālayas to Kampilla. [13]By the seer the confines of Kampilla having-been approached all the demons ran away. [14]By the seer well-being was established in Kampilla. [15]Such as I am, I was the seer Rakṣita. [16]At that time king Śreṇika Bimbisāra was the king Brahmadatta in Kampilla. [17]At that time by-me-having-entered the confines of Kampilla all the demons ran away. [18]Even now on my-entering the confines of Vaiśālī all the demons are running away.

2.2. To disclose the constraints determining the grammatical patterns, I have summarized below the argument structure and the grammatical features of the sentences numbered above.

A. (1) reports that the Blessed One enters the confines of Vaiśālī and prompts the demons to run away. The implementation of the Instr-patterning is peculiar here in that the sentence-initial Instr may be regarded either as the absolute Instr or as the agentive Instr of the opening clause (subordinate-like clause). The resulting complex sentence may be paraphrased as 'Once by the Blessed One the act-of-entering the confines of Vaiśālī' [has been performed], all the demons ran away'; the S_{Instr} of the opening clause is non-coreferential with A_{Nom} of the concluding clause. The argument structure and grammatical features of (1) are thus

(1) $S^{1}_{Instr}+O_{Acc}+V_{InstrPartPresIntrans}//S^{2}_{Nom}+V_{NomPresMiddlePartIntrans}$[6]

(2) refers to the next (new) event (the crowd is asking the Buddha about the preceding event): a new agent is introduced by an active-transitive Nom-Acc patterned clause ('the crowd asked') used to introduce a *kathaṃ*-clause (the how-clause) while the preceding clause is quoted in full (which does not change anything in the syntactic patterning):

(2) $A_{Nom}+V_{3SgPresTrans}+(1)$

(3) The Blessed One utters a question: why should the event reported under (1) be reckoned as a wonder (*bhagavān āha kim atra* [...] *āścaryaṃ*) ? The subordinated relative-interrogative *yaṃ*-clause (1a) is an extension of the argument S_{Instr} of (1) by multiplication: *yan tathāgatena paramasaṃbodhiprāptena devātidevena sīmām ākramantenaiva sarva amanuṣyakā palānāḥ*. The argument struc-

[6] Cf. the contrasting syntactic patterning referring to similar events Mv. 1.370.11-12 *bhagavāṃ* [...] *vaiśālīye ca sīmām ākrānto bhagavatā te amanuṣyakā palānā* 'The Blessed One came to the frontiers of Vaiśālī, [and] by the Blessed One the demons were [caused] to run away'. Here two simple sentences are conjoined. S_{Nom} of the first (*bhagavāṃ*) is coreferential with the quasi-agentive Instr (*bhagavatā*) of the second. The two conjoined sentences seem to result from an attempt to construe a complex sentence with S_{Instr} in one clause and S_{Nom} (*amanuṣyakā*) in the other, but the order of the two subjects is inverted and the whole utterance presents a defective syntactic structure, since the causativity is not expressed in *palānā*$_{NomPresMiddlePartIntrans}$. It can be inferred that the Instr in the second sentence is a clear witness of the pressure of the Instr-patterning, if even the opening sentence is Nom-patterned.

ture of (2) and (3) is the same, but an aggregate of lexical items in the subordinate clause replaces the single lexical item:

(3) $S/A^1{}_{Nom}+V_{3SgPfTrans}//Pron_{Interr}+Questioned\ Word//Relative\ Conjunction/S^1{}_{Instr}+S^2{}_{Instr}+O_{Acc}+S^3{}_{PartPresInstr}//S/A^2{}_{Nom}+V_{NomPresMiddlePartIntrans}$

(4) $S_{Instr}+O_{Acc}+S_{PartPresTransInstr}//A_{Nom}+V_{NomPresMiddlePartIntrans}$

In the section A, the recurrence of the argument structure accompanying the stylistic diversity [7] shows a relative rarity of the Nom-Acc-patterning[8], while the Instr-patterning prevails.

The section B begins with two clauses displaying the Nom-Acc pattern: (5) [...] *rājā brahmadatto nāma rājyaṃ kāresi* '[Once upon a time] reigned a king Brahmadatta':

(5) $A_{Nom}+ O_{Acc}+V_{3SgAor}$

(6) $A_{PronNom}+ O^1{}_{Acc}+V^1{}_{GerTrans}{}^1+O^2{}_{Acc}+V^2{}_{GerTrans}{}^2//O_{Acc}+V_{PPPCoref\ with\ A}$[9]

The alternation of the patterning takes place at this point. The clauses 7, 11-14 show the Instr-pattern, while the clauses 8-9 and 12, 15 show the Nom-Acc-pattern:

---

[7] By "stylistic diversity" I mean the use of two concomitant syntactic patternings which may also conflict.

[8] Only the clauses introducing a new agent asking the questions (the crowd and the Buddha) display the active Nom-Acc patterning.

[9] Two subordinate-like clauses (*so kāmeṣu ādīnavaṃ dṛṣṭvā* and *anuhimavantaṃ gatvā*) are identical, but the lexical items are different (O^1, Vb^1; O^2, Vb^2). $S_{PronNom}$ of the main clause is incorporated in the verb form (PPP), i.e. marked affixally in the verb form. Moreover, as according to Hendriksen 1948: 81 and 87, in Pāli, the PPP is only used about the present-past while the pure past is expressed by the finite preterite and that in the Ardhamāgadhī the tendency is to use the PPP to denote pure past in an active sense, it is instructive to compare [5]*kāresi* 3SgAor '[the king] made [the reign]' and [6]*pravrajito* PPP 'he went into the religious life'. The use of these two forms acknowledges once more the mixed nature of Buddhist Sanskrit.

(7) $S^1_{Instr}+O^1_{Acc}+V_{CausGer}+O^2_{Acc}+S_{PartPresInstr}//S^2+V_{PPP}$

(8) $A_{Nom}+O^1_{Acc}+O^2_{Acc}+V_{3SgPres}$

(9) $S_{Nom}+V_{PPP}$[10]

(10) $A_{Nom}+V_{3PlPres}$

(11) $S^1_{Instr}+O_{Acc}+V_{Ger}//S^2_{Nom}+V_{PPP}$

(12) $A_{Nom}+O_{Acc}+V_{Ger}//O_{Acc}+V_{PPPCoref\ with\ A}$[11]

(13) $S^1_{Instr}+O_{Acc}+V_{PartPresInstr}//S^2_{Nom}+V_{NomPresMiddlePart}$

(14) $S_{Instr}+O_{Acc}+V_{PPP}$

(15) $A^1_{Nom}+A^2_{Nom}+V_{3SgAor}$

(16) $A^1_{Nom}//A^2_{Nom}+V_{3SgAor}$

(17) $S^1_{Instr}+O_{Acc}+V_{PartPresInstr}//S^2_{Nom}+V_{NomPresMiddlePart}$

(18) $S^1_{Instr}+O_{Acc}+V_{PartPresInstr}//S^2_{Nom}+V_{NomPresMiddlePart}$

3. The above presentation of syntactic patterns shows the following:

a. *In the main clauses of the complex sentences*, the Nom-(Acc)-patterning prevails (**11** instances).

---

[10] In [9]*amanuṣyavyādhi dāruṇo utpanno* the intransitive subject (which may be called a reflexive subject) in the Nom is combined with PPP from the intransitive verb *utpadyati* 'to arise; to occur' and expresses the pure past in an active sense. Cf. Hendriksen 1948: 88 and 90 quoting, as example Uttarādhyayanasūtra 19.7 (ed. J. Charpentier, 1921-1922) *jāisaraṇaṃ samupannaṃ* 'the remembrance of his former births arose (in him)'. In our language the comparison of the latter construction with the passive construction [11]*rājñā* [...] *dūto preṣitaḥ* 'by the king a messenger has been sent', a converse to the active construction Mv. 1.128.15-16 *so* [...] *dūtam apreṣaye* 'he sent a messenger', shows that PPP *utpanno* is used in the same sense as PPP *preṣitaḥ*, made from the transitive verb *preṣayati* 'to send forth'. This is not new, but it is worth to show the extent to which Buddhist Sanskrit owes its syntax to Middle Indo-Aryan.

[11] As in (6), $S_{PronNom}$ of the main clause is incorporated in the verb form (PPP).

b. *In the subordinate or subordinate-like clauses of the complex sentences*, the Instr-patterning is more frequent (**8** instances); in all these instances (1, 1a, 4, 7, 11, 13, 17 and 18), S^1 and S^2 are non-coreferential. Indeed, *the subordinate or subordinate-like clauses* display the Nom-Acc-patterning in **2** instances only (in 6 and 12). In these two latter, S^1 and S^2 are coreferential.

c. *In the simple clauses* the Nom-Acc-patterning is found in 6 instances in 2(+1 conjoined)-3(+1a conjoined)-5(V_{3SgAor})-8-($V_{3SgPres}$)-15-16. This figure is actually to be added to that of main clauses since any simple clause can adjoin a subordinate or subordinate-like clause. Thus 11 + 6= 17.

d. The Instr-patterning occurs only in *one simple clause* (14).[12]

e. The Nom-patterning *in the simple clauses* with finite verb occurs in 5 instances: 2 (3SgPres)-5 (3SgAor)-10 (3PlPres)-15 (1SgAor)-16 (3SgAor).[13]

The simple sentences show a well-known contrast matching the opposition of the Instr-patterning vs. the Nom-patterning: in the former the predicate is a non-finite PPP, in the latter the predicate is a finite verb. The finite forms are, however, well known in the Instr-patterned simple clauses, but their salient feature is that they

[12] This single occurrence of S_{Instr} in the simple sentence contrasts with S_{Gen}, e.g. Mv. 1.35.1-2 *ciraṃ me śuddhāvāsaṃ devanikāyaṃ upasaṃkrāntasya* 'It is a long time since by me the Śuddhāvāsa devas have-been-approached'. S_{Gen} is also found in the subordinate-like clauses: Mv. 1.235.9-10 (vs) *atyunnatā ca namati natāpi atyunnatā bhavati bhūmiḥ praviśantasya bhagavato* 'The heaved earth subsides and subsided [earth] heaves [when] the Blessed One enters' (= by the Blessed One-entering); Mv. 1.263.14-15 *tehi bhagavato tarantasya paṃca cchatraśatāni pragṛhītāni* 'By them, [while] the Blessed One was-crossing [the Ganges], the five hundred sunshades were held' (in the latter case, if even the GenSg of the syntactic group *bhagavato tarantasya* may be understood as the case of the beneficiary within a simple sentence ('by them were held the sunshades for the Blessed One who crossed'), it should be stressed that the frequent and recurrent patterning suggests that we have here a complex sentence.

[13] The two latter (15 and 16) are equative clauses with the predicate 3SgAor of the intransitive verb *bhū-* 'to be, become', which anyway does not admit the Instr-patterning.

are PresPass forms, agreeing in number and gender with the transitive objects as shown by Mv. 2.70.5 *mama gomayena* [...] *devakāryāṇi ca kriyanti* 'By means [of my ordure] the gods' deeds are carried out' and Mv. 2.273.10-12 *rājñā dāni* [...] *ekam ekasya bhikṣusya* [...] *āsanaprajñaptī kriyati* 'By the king for each monk a seat is being made'. It should not be overlooked that, like in 14 (a simple sentence whose predicate is PPP *kṛtaṃ*), these finite forms denoting an achieved perfective aspect event are from the verb *kṛ-* 'to do; make', a high transitive verb[14]. Definite results are thus aimed at and the use of Instr partly involves the "naturalness condition 2" as suggested in Schlesinger 1989: 191 ("attention is drawn to the instrument by which an action is performed").[15]

f. The Nom-Acc patterning may occur when the action is referred to by V_{Ger} in the subordinate-like clause as in [12]*ṛṣir dūtavacanaṃ śrutvā anuhimavantāto kampillam āgato* 'The seer having-heard the messenger's words went from the Himālayas to Kampilla'. But it is only too clear that in the complex sentences with V_{Ger} *in the*

[14] For the definition of high and low transitivity, see Hopper and Thompson 1980. Transitivity is understood as "a global property [...], such that an activity is "carried-over" or "transferred" from an agent to a patient", high vs. low transitivity depends on "the effectiveness or intensity with which the action is transferred from one participant to another" (251-252). See also Tsunoda 1985: 387: the prototypical transitive verbs are defined as "those verbs which describe an action that not only impinges on the patient but necessarily creates a change in it", e.g. *kill, destroy, break, bend.* Moreover, the same author (Tsunoda 1985: 388) distinguishes, within the transitivity scale, the degrees of the affectedness of the patient in a two-place predicative structure, implying such meanings as direct effect on patient (resultative or non-resultative verbs meaning, on the one hand, 'kill, break', on the other hand 'hit, shoot, kick', cf. 'X kills Y' and 'X hits Y'), perception of the action by the patient (the patient can be more or less attained and the verbs will mean, on the one hand, 'see, hear, find', on the other hand 'listen, look', cf. 'X sees, hears, ... Y' and 'X listens to Y'); pursuit ('search, wait, await'); knowledge ('know, understand, remember, forget'); feeling ('love, like, want, need, proud, boast'); relationship ('possess, have, lack, correspond, consist, ...'); ability ('be capable, proficient, good'). Moving from the beginning of this range of meanings entails lowering of transitivity.

[15] Schlesinger's "natural condition 2" is more wide and applies to the expression of an inanimate instrument as the sentence subject in such English sentences as *The pencil draws very thin lines* or *This spray kills cockroaches instantly*. I do not fully follow his theory, but feel that his findings about naturalness are useful.

subordinate-like clause, and with the coreferential as well as the non-coreferential S^1 and S^2, both Nom- and Instr-patterning are possible (the former being imported from the simple sentences). Thus the examples discussed in more details below show the Instr-patterning (see 4.2.1.1.3).

This patterning contrasts with the use of the Nom-patterning:

[1] Mv. 1.32.8-12 *sthaviro tāṃ devānāṃ* [...] *tādr̥śīṃ samr̥ddhiṃ dr̥ṣṭvā* [...] *yatra devā* [...] *sanniṣaṇṇā* [...] *vāhyato devasabhāyāṃ dr̥śyanti* 'The elder [Mahāmaudgalyāyana] having-seen all this prosperity of the gods, while the gods staying together are being seen from outside in their assembly hall' (the syntax of this sentence is very awkward).

[2] Bhu-P 4.24 *yo puna bhikṣu bhikṣusya cīvaraṃ datvā* [...] *ācchindeya vā ācchindāpayeya* [...] *nissargikapācattikaṃ* 'Should a monk, after having given a robe to [another] monk, take it away or have it taken away, there is offence (called) *nissargikapācattikaṃ*' (more examples are given in 4.).[16]

It can be concluded that the Instr patterning has been rather favoured within the complex sentences. Although the non-coreferentiality of S^1 and S^2 seems to be preferred, this constraint is hardly compulsory. The other constraint that complies with the first constraint, although it is more loosely applied, is the adjoining of a subordinate or subordinate-like clause with the

[16] Here, besides the fact of the complex sentence, attention should be given to another fact: a low transitive (imperfective or non-terminative) verb *dā-* underlies the gerund *datvā* as far as no forcible movement is presupposed in the act to receive a gift [which does not exclude that, according to the distinctions defined by Deshpande, the verb *dā-* may have a built in perfective meaning as opposed to the verb *yam-* 'to extend, to offer': the offering does not necessarily entail acceptance, "while one cannot say "I have given *x*", unless someone has accepted the given item" (Deshpande 1992: 42-43)].

Instr-patterning to the Acc- patterned clauses. The chief data pointing to this constraint is the noticeable rarity of the Instr-patterned simple sentences.

4. Below I add some observations on the gerundial constructions with the Instr-patterning and with no Instr-patterning. In collecting the types of these two constructions, I intend to show the differing conditions of their occurrences. Both are most frequent in our language.

On the one hand, there are sentences with gerundial clauses whose syntactic features do not differ from those occurring in Classical Sanskrit (nominal or pronominal agent of the gerund in the Nom or in the Instr coreferential with the agent of the main verb).[17] On the other hand, there are sentences with gerundial clauses whose syntactic features are only possible in Classical Sanskrit, but which are more favoured in Buddhist Sanskrit.

Tikkanen (1987), when discussing the case of the agent (topical agent or subject of the gerundial clause), reminds us that, according to Pāṇ. 3.4.21, *samānakartṛkayoḥ pūrvakāle* '(the affix *ktvā* is applied to a root expressing that of two actions which) is situated earlier in time when (two successive actions) have the same agent' (as translated by Tikkanen 1987: 38, who adds p. 148, fn. 6: "the Pāṇinean rule 3.4.21 prescribing the identity of *Agents* (*kartṛ*) for the gerund and the superordinate clause cannot account for those cases where the controller is an oblique experiencer, affected possessor or foregrounded topicalized Undergoer").

4.1. As now expressed, "the Sanskrit (past) gerund in *-tvā́(ya)/-tvī́* and –′(*t*)*ya*/-′(*t*)*yā* is an invariable non-finite verb category that is chiefly used as the verb of a coreferentially constrained reduced clause, dependent on another clause (or verb phrase) and expressing

[17] Meenakshi 1983: 190 formulates a simple rule for Epic Sanskrit: the subject of the gerund is that of the main action; it usually refers to a nominative if the main verb is active, or to an instrumental if it is a passive.

a preceding action or resultative state (with possible causal and instrumental implicatures)" (Tikkanen 1991: 197).

Among the parameters of differential value for the syntax of the gerundial constructions, and consequently for the language of a given text or group of texts are: [1] the transitivity or intransitivity of the verb underlying the gerund, which may be either a high or a low transitive; [2] the coreferentiality or non-coreferentiality of the agent of the gerundial clause (the agent of the gerundial clause and that of the main clause verb are either the same or not); [3] the case of the agent of the gerund, which is either a noun or a pronoun or may be, if unexpressed, recovered from the context[18]; [4] the coordinate-like or subordinate-like function of the gerundial clause.

It is assumed that the coordinate-like gerundial clause, also called additive-sequential, is modally and operationally dependent on the main clause and shares its mood and tense as well as the topical agent, which is thus coreferential; and that the subordinate-like gerundial clause, also called restrictive or supplementive, is modally and operationally independent of the main clause and shares neither its mood nor the topical agent, which is thus non-coreferential.[19]

4.2. I single out the following syntactic constructions.

4.2.1. A low transitive verb underlies the gerund. The agent in the Nom controls the gerund.

---

[18] Tikkanen 1987: 147 states that in "standard non-periphrastic constructions, the gerundial clause is structurally incomplete in that it lacks an independent/non-coreferential subject (and/or agent, if passive), for the recovery of which it is thus dependent on some argument (mostly an actant/central participant) of the superordinate clause". As will be seen and as partly shown above, the recovery of the agent does not necessarily rely on the main clause but also on the immediate or even distant context.

[19] Tikkanen 1991: 197. His proposal is that the gerundial clause gets either an "additive-sequential" or "coordinate-like" reading (= 'S1 and [then] S2') or a temporally/circumstantially "restrictive/supplementive" or "subordinate-like" reading (= 'after having V-ed, upon/by V-ing'.

4.2.1.1. The nominal agent of the gerund is coreferential; the gerundial clause is subordinate-like; the verb of the main clause is in the present indicative or in the optative:

[3] Mv. 1.33.16-17 *sthavirasya śrutvā anekāni prāṇasahasrāṇi devamanuṣyāṇām amṛtaṃ prāpayanti* 'After having-heard the elder, many thousands of beings, devas and men, win immortality' (cf. J I, p. 29). Cf. with a pronominal agent:

[4] Mv. 1.57.2-3 *yaṃ nūnāhaṃ yena bhagavāṃs tenopagamitvā bhagavantam etam arthaṃ paripṛccheyaṃ* 'What now if I having-come to where the Blessed One is, I ask him about the matter?' Cf. with the verb of the main clause in the Aor(ist):

[4a] BhīVin §174 *satyaṃ tvaṃ nande śayyāsanasya arthāya yācitvā anyaṃ cetāpesi* 'Is it true, Nandā, [that] you, after having begged in order to obtain bed and seat, you barter something else?'

4.2.1.1.2. The nominal agent of the gerund is non-coreferential; the gerundial clause is coordinate-like. The verb of the main clause is an Imp(erative):

[5] Mv. 1.64.6-7 (vs) *gauravaṃ janiya sarvadarśiṣu śrūyatāṃ jinavarasya śāsanaṃ* '[Ye wise] while feeling reverence for the omniscient ones, may the noble Conqueror's teaching be heard!'

4.2.1.1.3. S/A[1] of the subordinate-like gerundial clause may be either non-coreferential (Mv. 1.38.9-10) or coreferential with S/A[2] of the main clause [Abhis-Dh(Mā-L) 85.15-86.1 (T 95.15)]. The gerunds are made either from the low transitive verbs (*okirati* 'to scatter, bestrew'; *āgacchati* 'to come to') or from a high transitive verb (*uppāḍeti* 'to tear off, uproot'):

[6] Mv. 1.38.9-10 *tena śatasahasrakeśareṇa bhagavantaṃ sarvābhibhūṃ* [...] *okiritvā* [...] *evaṃ cittaṃ utpādesi* '[Abhiya] after having scattered the hundred thousand pieces' worth of fragrant powder *keśara* on the Blessed Sarvābhibhū, the [following] thought occurred [to him].'[20]

[6a] Abhis-Dh(Mā-L) 85.15-86.1 (T 95.15) *apareṇa bhikṣuṇā āgacchiya uppāḍiya dantakāṣṭhaṃ khāyitaṃ* 'By the monk-having-come [to it], having uprooted [it, i.e. the mango-tree], [a part of] has-been-chewed as a tooth-stick.'

4.2.2. The pronominal agent of the gerund from a low transitive verb is coreferential; the verb of the main clause is in the present tense. The gerundial clause is subordinate-like:

---

[20] This sentence is embedded in the larger passage Mv. 1.38.4-10. It is instructive to see how the Acc-patterns and the Instr-pattern alternate within it.

Mv. 1.38.4-10. [1]*icchāmi* [...] *imasya śatasahasrasya keśaraṃ* [2]*parihariyāhaṃ bhagavato sarvābhibhūsya* [...] *adhikāraṃ karomi* [3]*pariharensuḥ* [...] *te duve gandhikamahattarakā śatasahasrakeśaraṃ* [4]*atha khalu* [...] *abhiyo bhikṣuḥ bhagavantaṃ sarvābhibhūṃ* [...] *khādanīyabhojanīyāsvādanīyena santarpayitvā bhuktāviṃ* [...] *viditvā tena śatasahasrakeśareṇa bhagavantaṃ sarvābhibhūṃ* [...] *okiresi* [...] [5]*okiritvā adhyokiritvā abhiprakiritvā evaṃ cittaṃ utpādesi* '[1]I want these one hundred thousand pieces' worth of *keśara* essence. [2]After having-taken care of it, I [shall] offer it to the Blessed Sarvābhibhū. [3]The two perfume dealers gave [him] a hundred thousand pieces' worth of *keśara* essence. Then the monk Abhiya after having-fed the Blessed Sarvābhibhū with plentiful and palatable food, both hard and soft, after having-seen [Sarvābhibhū] having-eaten, he bestrewed the hundred thousand pieces' worth of fragrant powder *keśara* on the Blessed Sarvābhibhū, after having-bestrewed [the powder] over and about [him], the [following] thought occurred [to him]'.

The passage begins with three Acc-patterned sentences; all three are present verb-initial clauses, which warrants their Acc-patterning (the VSO order is thus a syntactic feature of utmost importance for it precludes S_{Instr}). The complex sentence (4) with S_{Nom} *abhiyo* controls the gerunds of two low transitive verbs within two subordinate-like gerundial clauses (*santarpayitvā*, a low transitive verb and *viditvā*, a high transitive verb). In (5) the main clause-initial *tena śatasahasrakeśareṇa*$_{Instr}$ occurs along with the finite form *okiresi* 3 SgAor 'he bestrewed' (where the inflectionally marked pronoun is coreferential with the S_{Nom} *abhiyo*): that may be attributed to foregrounding of the instrument of action. It is to be noted that *tena* in the syntagm *tena śatasahasrakeśareṇa* [...] *okiritvā* cannot be the temporal-locative adverb 'then', but functions across the sentence boundary as the coreferential pronoun in syntagm with the gerunds of the next sentence (*okiritvā adhyokiritvā abhiprakiritvā*): 'by this one (= by him) having-bestrewed'.

[7] BhīVin §291 *sā dāni praticchādayitvā niṣkramati* 'After she covered [the bowl], she went out.'

4.3. A more complicated case is the combination of two gerundial clauses within one sentence:

[8] Mv. 1.3.13-15 *dr̥ṣṭvāna ca yācanakaṃ bhūyo 'sya mano prasāditvā cakṣūṇi ca mānsāni ca putradāraṃ dhanaṃ ca dhānyañ ca ātmā ca jīvitaṃ ca bhūyobhūyo parityaktā* 'On seeing a beggar time and again, after having-gladdened his [the bodhisattva's] heart, [the bodhisattva's] eyes, flesh, son and wife, wealth and grain, self and whole life were successively given up [to the beggar].'

In the first gerundial clause, the agent of the gerund *dr̥ṣṭvāna* of the high transitive verb *dr̥ś-* 'to see' is unexpressed. The unexpressed agent is coreferential with the possessive pronoun of the second gerundial clause where the gerund is made from a low transitive verb (*asya mano prasāditvā*; the bodhisattva sees a beggar and feels that this is an opportunity for charity, as stated J I, p. 4, fn. 6). This agent is non-coreferential with the subjects of the passive predicate (PPP *parityaktā*) of the main clause, which has the preterital meaning.

5. As in [8], transitive verbs of different intensity underlie the gerund. The agent controlling the gerund may be expressed or not expressed (it is impersonal in the second case, cf. Tikkanen 1987: 148). There is no coreference nor not-coreference with the non-agent of the gerundial clause and the agent of the main clause verb (but this is not a general case).

5.1. The predicate of the main clause is an obligational adjective. The gerundial clause is subordinate-like:

[9] BhīVin §293 *āraṇyakaṃ jentākaṃ varca kaṭhinaṃ uddharitvā avaśeṣā tathā eva kāryāḥ* [.] *abhisamācārikā dharmmāḥ* 'After having removed [the rules concerning] the dwelling in the forest, the hot bathroom, the feces and the wooden-frame for stitching the robes, then [only] the remaining *abhisamācārikā dharmā* have to be performed.'

5.2. The predicate of the main clause is a verbal phrase made including *kṣamati* 3SgPres followed by the infinitive:

[10] BhīVin §291 *gṛhṇītvā na kṣamati praticchādayitvā niṣkāsayituṃ* 'Once [the object] is taken hold of, it is not allowed [to the nuns] to bring [it] out after having-[it]-covered.'

[10a] BhīVin §240 *tāya pi dāni āliṃpiya na kṣamati abhyāgame pradeśe sthātuṃ* 'After smearing [her] with that [fragrance], she [the nun Bhadrā Kāpileyī] is not allowed to stay in a much visited place.'

In both examples the agent of the main clause *na kṣamati* + infinitive is impersonal; the verbs underlying the gerund and the main clause verb are equally intensive as to the degree of affectedness of the objects (patients[21]) involved, i.e. high transitive verbs.

5.3. In [11] the distantly expressed pronominal S/A_{Nom} is non-coreferential with the S_{Nom} of the main clause verb in the aorist. The first gerundial clause has a gerund of a low transitive verb (*upāgamiya*), while the second gerundial clause has a gerund of a high transitive verb (*dṛṣṭvā*). Both gerundial clauses are subordinate-like. The same applies to [11a] containing two gerunds of two low transitive verbs:

[21] See Hopper and Thompson 1980: 252 fn. 1: "The term 'patient' refers to an O[bject] which is in fact a 'receiver' of the action in a cardinal transitive relationship".

[11] Mv. 1.3.2-4 [*so*] *dīpaṃkaram upāgamiya* [...] *dr̥ṣṭvā tasya spr̥hācittam utpadye* 'After having-come to Dīpaṃkara and after having-seen him, the thought of emulating [Dīpaṃkara] arose to/in him.'

[11a] Mv. 1.60.1-2 *satkr̥tvā gurukr̥tvā tāṃ ca samitim anugr̥hṇanto taṃ ca śrāvakasaṃghaṃ anugr̥hṇanto cāyuḥpramāṇam anugr̥hṇanto evaṃ cittam utpādesi* 'After having-honoured [and] having-venerated the assembly [which he was] upholding [as he was] upholding the community of disciples and granting their due span of life [to all of their members], such a thought arose [in him].'

5.4. In [12] the common S/A designated by the proper name can be recovered from the preceding sentences while the coreferential pronominal S/A_{Nom} is retrievable from the verb of the main clause. The verb underlying the gerund is a low transitive verb and the gerundial clause is subordinate-like:

[12] Mv. 1.3.6-7 *jñātvā samudāgamaṃ saṃbodhau* [...] *svayaṃbhūsamatāye vyākārṣīt* 'After having-learnt about [his desire of] attainment of enlightenment, he [Dīpaṃkara] proclaimed [that he would win] an equality with the Self-becoming One.'[22]

6. A high transitive verb underlies the gerund. The agent in the Instr controls the gerund.

6.1. S/A_{Instr} of a gerund of a high transitive (telic, i.e. provided with an endpoint)[23] verb is coreferential with S/A of the main clause

---

[22] Senart (Mv I: 369) suggests that *samudāgam-* refers first of all to the striving after the enlightenment.

[23] Hopper and Thompson 1980: 252.

predicate (the PPP with the passive and preterital meaning). The gerundial clause is subordinate-like:

[13] Mv. 3.38.8-9 *śreṣṭhiputreṇa taṃ śatasāhasrikaṃ karaṇḍakaṃ utkṣipitvā etasya ādarśamaṇḍalasya abhimukhaṃ sthāpitaṃ* 'After the merchant's son has lifted the box containing the hundred thousand pieces, he set it in front of the mirror.'

6.2. S/A$_{Nom}$ (nominal or pronominal) of the gerund of a low transitive is coreferential with A of the main clause predicate (the PPP with the passive and preterital meaning from a high transitive verb):

[14] Mv. 1.63.2-3 *tāni mayā tasya bhagavato niryātetvā bodhāya anupraṇihitaṃ* 'After having-presented these [buildings] to the Blessed One, [by me] a vow to win the enlightenment has-been-made.'

6.3. S/A$_{Nom}$ of a high transitive (telic) verb is unexpressed and is non-coreferential with A of the main clause predicate which is, as above, the PPP with the passive and preterital meaning from a low transitive verb:

[15] Mv. 2.212.17 *ujjhitvā balavāhanā na kaścana taṃ pradeśam anuprāpto* 'After having-outstripped his [enemy's?] army, no one else has reached that spot.'

7. Now I will consider some examples where S of the gerundial clause is in the instrumental case.

In [16] the pronominal S/A$_{Instr}$ of the gerund of a high (telic) transitive verb is non-coreferential with S/A of the low transitive verb of the main clause in the imperative; the gerundial clause is subordinate-like:

[16] BhīVin §179 *etasyā mayā cīvaraṃ gr̥hītvā imām upasthāpehi* 'After by me from her the robe having-been-taken, do wait upon her' (but Nolot 1991: 178 translates as "prends le vêtement que je tiens de cette [probationnaire], et prends-la en charge").

Here the contextual constraints are decisive enough to allow the interpretation of the gerund in *mayā cīvaraṃ gr̥hītvā* as a passive gerund ('after her robe has been taken by me'): the whole context is rather unambiguous: the preceding sentences in BhīVin §179 make it clear that the nun Sthūlanandā stipulates the conditions under which the ordination of a śikṣamānā (female novice) can take place: Sthūlanandā must obtain from her a robe and this condition is mentioned repeatedly.

8. To account for the use of the gerundial constructions, two points are of peculiar interest. On the one hand, the phrase with a subordinate-like gerundial clause in which the pronominal agent standing in an oblique case (supposedly Instr) is common to both the gerundial clause and the main clause (it is thus coreferential) and the verb underlying the gerund is again the high transitive *gr̥h-*:

[17] BhīVin §179 *tāye cīvaraṃ gr̥hya na upasaṃpādayen niḥsarggikapācattikaṃ* '[If], after a robe has been taken by her[24], she does not ordain [the novice], there is offence [called) *niḥsarggikapācattikaṃ.*'

On the other hand, in the phrase meant as a gloss to [17] the S/A of the gerund of the same verb is in the Nom (since the gloss mentions only the act of taking the robe, it need not to be finished so that the main clause is simply missing):

---

[24] *tāye* and *tāya* are two alternative forms of the InstrSgf of the deictic pronoun *tad*, see Mv. 1.312.8 (Schneider 1950: 131) and Mv. 2.450.2.

[17a] BhīVin §179 *sā taṃ cīvaraṃ gr̥hṇitvā ti yathā sthūlanandā bhikṣuṇī* '"she having taken the robe" means "just as the nun Sthūlanandā" (the nun who has declined to ordain the novice).'

The statement of the offence called *niḥsarggikapācattikaṃ* in [17] is comparable to the statement in the Prātimokṣasūtra of Ma-Lo Bhu-P 17.16-18:

[18] Bhu-P 17.16-18 *yo puna bhikṣu bhikṣusya cīvaraṃ datvā yathā duṣṭo doṣāt kupito anāttamano ācchindeya vā ācchindāpayeya āharā bhikṣu cīvaraṃ na te* [*a*]*haṃ demīti vā vadeya nissargikapācattikaṃ* 'Should a monk, after having given a robe to [another] monk, if he is malignant [or] ill-willed, angry [and] displeased, take it away or have it taken away and say "Bring, o monk, the robe, I do not give it to you", there is offence [called] *nissargikapācattikaṃ.*'

In [16-17], the verb underlying the gerunds *gr̥hītvā* and *gr̥hya* is a high transitive verb since it implies the completion of the act to take in order to possess ('seize, take off, to get hold of'). Both S/A in [16-17] stand in the Instr and are non-coreferential. The action of the gerund *gr̥hītvā* is telic and volitional, since its effect on the patient (the robe) is quite apparent, while the pronominal S/A in [17a] stands in Nom although the gerund *gr̥hṇitvā* of the same verb is used (but an oblique case would be hardly conceivable in a gloss).

In [18] a low transitive (imperfective or non-terminative) verb *dā-* underlies the gerund *datvā* (about which see above, fn. 16).

9. A high transitive verb underlies the gerund. The S/A in the Instr controls the gerund.

9.1. The pronominal S/A stands in the Instr, the gerund of the high transitive verb is non-coreferential and the verb of the main clause is a verbal adjective with the preterital meaning; the gerundial clause is coordinate-like:

[19] BhīVin §152 *pūrvam ahaṃ kumārabhūtaḥ śākiyānāṃ saṃsthāgāraṃ praviṣṭaḥ tehi* [...] *saṃsthāgāraṃ* [...] *khānāpayitvā* [...] 'Previously, when I was a prince, I entered the assembly hall of the Śākiya, [while I] having-been-caused by them to dig [the ground] of the assembly hall.'

It is of course possible not to bind the gerund *khānāpayitvā* to the participle *praviṣṭaḥ* 'I entered' and to assume that *tehi* opens a new syntactic period and that the gerund stands for the finite verb (as it is done in Nolot 1991: 116). However, it is clear that the sentence includes a coordinate-like gerundial clause with a morphological gerund. Cf. the gerund standing for the finite verb also assumed by Sen (1927: 62):

[19a] Mv. 2.159.9-10 *kācit parasparasya udgr̥hya kācid vāmadakṣināto vikṣiptagātrā kāsāṃcit mukhāto lālā śravati* 'One [woman] embracing another, one [woman] with her limbs sprawling left and right, from the mouth of some [other women] the saliva trickled.'

The gerund *udgr̥hya* of a high transitive verb is controlled by the indefinite pronoun *kācit*$_{\text{Nom}}$ and, assuming that the sentence is not a concatenation of coordinate independent clauses, the agent of the last clause *lālā* 'the saliva' is non-coreferential with the agent of the gerundial clause opening the whole sentence.

However, it must be stated that the assumption of the finite verb replaced by the gerund is unnecessary in either case since the gerunds may be controlled by a non-coreferential agent either in the Nom or in the Instr within a subordinate-like gerundial clause.

9.2. [20] BhīVin §289 *labhyaṃ bhikṣuṇīye bhikṣūṇāṃ pratigrāhāpayituṃ sthāpayitvā jātarūpaṃ* 'The nun is allowed to be caused to take hold of [what is given by] the monks, with the exception of the gold (= the gold putting aside).'

The S/A of the causative gerund of a high transitive-causative verb *sthāpayati*[25] 'to let to put aside' is formally unexpressed; the agent of the main clause is in the Instr while its predicatc is the infinitive with an obligational meaning. There is no coreference between two agents (it is not the nun who puts aside the gold: the gerund *sthāpayitvā* is used in the sense 'excepting'). The gerundial clause is coordinate-like.

9.3. A more complicated case is:

> [21] Mv. 3.393.18-19 *tena dāni brāhmaṇena sā parivrājikā tridaṇḍaṃ ārūpayitvā chattropānāhāṃ ca gr̥hṇapetvā tato pariṣām adhyāto śiṣyadharmeṇa niṣkāsitā* 'The brahman made her raise his staff and hold his sunshade and shoes. She thus revealed herself in the eyes of the crowd to be in the state of pupillage.'[26]

The subordinate-like gerundial clause has two gerunds of two different high transitive causative verbs (*ārūpayitvā* 'having caused to rise' and *gr̥hṇapetvā* 'having caused to hold') which are controlled by a single non-coreferential agent in the Instr while the direct object of both gerunds is in the Nom (the pronoun *sā*); this direct object is coreferential with the agent of the verb of the main

---

[25] On causative morphemes as a mark of high (intensive) transitivity and causatives used in highly transitive constructions, see Hopper and Thompson 1980: 264.

[26] The quoted translation is by Jones 1956: 393. I have translated this sentence in Oguibénine 1996: 75 as 'Le brahmane fit lever son triple bâton à la femme-ascète et lui fit prendre parasol et sandales. Elle dut quitter l'assemblée (investie de dharma de) disciple' (*niṣkāsitā* is in fact from *niṣkāsayati* 'to drive, turn out, expel' while Jones translates it as if it were from **niṣkāśayati* which is unknown).

clause which is the verbal adjective *niṣkāsitā* with preterital meaning.

10. A low transitive verb underlies the gerund. The agent in an Oblique Case controls the gerund.

10.1. [22] Mv. 1.62.14-15 *jñātvānānityabalaṃ sudāruṇaṃ satkṛtasya anantaraṃ vīryārambho yojito anityabalasya vighātāya* 'The dreadful power of the impermanence having been apprehended by he who had worshipped [a Buddha], there has been performed the putting forth of energy to destroy the power of impermanence.'

The S/A (*satkṛtasya* 'one who has worshipped') of the gerund of a low transitive verb (*jñātvā*) stands in (the) Gen(itive); the gerundial clause is subordinate-like; the agent is non-coreferential and the predicate of the main clause is a verbal adjective with passive meaning.

10.2. A difficult case is [23]:

> [23] BhīVin §59 *upasaṃpādetu taṃ saṃgho itthannāmāṃ mayā itthannāmāya upādhyāyinīya anukampām upādāya* 'May the assembly let ordain [the woman] called so-and-so, with me called so-and-so as [her] preceptress, [while] taking pity of [her].'

Nolot (1991: 30) translates taking the noun phrase *taṃ saṃgho* as the agent of the gerundial clause: 'Que la communauté, par compassion, fasse conférer l'ordination à Une-telle, avec moi-même pour préceptrice'.

The gerundial clause is here coordinate-like and the verb of the main clause is in the imperative. But what is the S/A of the gerund of the low transitive verb *upādāya*? In Pāli the corresponding phrase *anukampam upādāya* is an idiomatic expression meaning 'out of pity or mercy' and the gerund *upādāya* functions as postposition with a preceding accusative (Rhys & Stede 1975: 149). However, in

Pāli *upādāya* is only originally the gerund of *upādiyati* 'to take hold of, to grasp, to cling to, to show attachment', whereas in Buddhist Sanskrit the meaning of the expression *anukampām upādāya* owes more to the gerund in its own function: it means 'employing (manifesting, showing) compassion or taking pity' (BHSD:145, cf. BHSG 126 and MadhK 27.30 *kampām upādāya* 'compassionately' as pointed out by Lindtner 1994: 271).

It seems likely that the gerundial clause *anukampām upādāya* 'taking pity' is controlled not by the nominative *taṃ saṃgho* from which it is too distant, but rather by the pronoun in the Instr *mayā* 'by me' which is the non-coreferential S/A of the gerund *upādāya*. Thus the translation of [23] by Nolot, which disregards a certain ambiguity (both the saṃgha and the preceptress take pity of the future novice?), would need more justification.[27]

In BhīVin the compassion will be shown both by the saṃgha and by the individuals, so that the grammatical argumentation in favour of the saṃgha or the preceptress showing compassion in [23] BhīVin §59 could be felt as insufficient. Indeed, [26] BhīVin §§40, 77 say *anukampatu me āryasaṃgho anukampako anukampām upādāya*, but [27] BhīVin §48 *bhagavatā* [...] *anukampakena anu-*

---

[27] The parallel text of the Bh(ikṣuṇ)ī-Ka(rma)vā(canā), which belongs to the school of the Mūlasarvāstivādins (Schmidt 1993: 254 and Schmidt 1994) proves, however, that not the preceptress, but the saṃgha is supposed to show the compassion.

The relevant text reads [24] BhīKaVā 17b2 *dadātv āryikāsaṃgho mamaivaṃ nāmikāyā brahmacaryopasthānasaṃvṛtiṃ anukampako 'nukampām upādāya* 'May the assembly of venerable nuns which is able to show the compassion, showing compassion give me [who is] so-and-so by name the permission to enter the religious life'. The gerundial clause is coordinate-like and both agents are identical (coreferential).

In the language of the Mūlasarvāstivādins, the use of the subordinate-like gerundial clauses with the high transitive-causative verb and the non-coreferential agent in the Instr is also known. BhīKaVā 17a5-17b1 reads [25] *tataḥ karmma kārikayā bhikṣuṇyā purastān niṣādāyitvā brahmacaryopasthānasa*[*mvṛ*]*tiṃ yācitavyā* 'Then after having-been set down by the presiding nun in front [of the assembly], [the nun to be ordained] should ask for the permission to enter the religious life'. It would be rewarding to find out whether the gerundial clause *anukampām upādāya* could be used in BhīKaVā in the same loose and ambiguous way as in BhīVin §59.

kampām upādāya [...] *trayo niśrayā abhijñāya deśitāḥ* 'The three basis have been taught by the Blessed One who compassionates while showing compassion, after having-acquired-supernatural-knowledge' (two gerundial clauses with the S_{Instr} which, however, differ in that the first is rather coordinate-like while the second rather subordinate-like).

The next example is noticeable in that it displays the gerundial clause *anukampām upādāya* with the coreferential S/A_{Nom}. This clause is coordinate-like:

[28] BhīVin §109 *ovadatu me āryo* [..] *anukampām upādāya* 'May the Ārya showing compassion instruct me!'

The gerundial clause *anukampām upādāya* has thus been used with both coreferential and non-coreferential agents, as a coordinate-like and as well as a subordinate-like clause. It is not excluded that the possibility to choose both types of agents and of gerundial clauses with *upādāya* is explained by the polyfunctionality of the latter being both postposition and gerund (which was losing its properly verbal nature).

11. A high transitive verb underlies the gerund. A non-coreferential agent of the main clause is retrieved from the agent in the vocative Case of the gerundial clause.

[29] Mv. 1.175.1-2 *aśīti koṭīyo bhūyo* [...] *vibhū* [...] *dametvā durgatīhi vimokṣitāḥ* 'After having-tamed eighty koṭis more of devas, O Lord, they have-been-delivered [by the Lord] from the ways of ill.'

12. A low transitive verb underlies the gerund. An unexpressed and impersonal non-coreferential agent controls the gerund of the subordinate-like clause:

[30] Mv. 1.175.17-18 (vs) *adbhutānāṃ ca dharmāṇāṃ viśuddhir upalabhyate / tvāṃ prāpya* is translated by Jones (1956: 139) as 'O Man of Light, thanks to thee, [...], the pure radiance of wondrous states is won', but it can be translated more appropriately, if also more literally, as 'One, after having-come to thee, the pure radiance of wondrous states is being won, etc.'

13. An intransitive verb underlies the gerund controlled by a non-coreferential agent which is a demonstrative pronoun in the Instr. The verb of the main clause is an obligational participle. The gerundial clause is rather coordinate-like:

[31] BhīVin §38 *tāya dāni āgacchitvā* [...] *sarvvāsāṃ pādā śirasā vanditavyāḥ* 'Coming close to the nuns, she should salute respectfully all of them by prosternating to their feet' (translated following partly the suggestions by Roth 1970: 35).

14. It is sometimes difficult to decide whether the gerundial clause is a coordinate-like or a subordinate-like. Among such cases the following is particularly intricate:

[32] BhīVin §139 *kāle ca vikāle ca marmāṃ praviśantāṃ niṣkrāmantāṃ dṛṣṭvā bhaviṣyati cittasya upakleśo*

Nolot (1991: 89 fn.10) suggests to read the opening as **teṣāṃ yuṣmākaṃ mārggaṃ* according to BhīVin §140 *teṣāṃ yuṣmākaṃ kāle ca vikāle ca niṣkrā*[*ma*]*ntāṃ* (*praviśantāṃ*). She emends (Nolot 1991: 474) the sentence and suggests the reading **praviśān dṛṣṭvā āryamiśrikāṇāṃ brahmacāriṇīnāṃ bhaviṣyati cittasya upakleśo*. As de Jong (1994: 376-377) asks whether **nagnāṃ* should be read instead of *marmāṃ* since the ascetics are nude (§140 *tīrthikanagnāḥ* according to Nolot 1991: 90 n. 14), the whole sentence thus emended might mean 'Their [of the nuns] thoughts while (or: after) seeing the nude [ascetics] enter and go out at different times will be stained'. The agent of the gerund of the low transitive verb meaning 'to see' is non-coreferential and stands in Nom. The verb of the main clause is in the future tense.

15. To conclude, the language of the Mahāsāṃghika-Lokottoravādins shows different concomitant syntactic structures meant to express more or less synonymous meanings which do not conflict despite their diversity. The synonymousness is especially pregnant in the case of the accusative gerundial clauses which are used besides the ergative gerundial clauses (cf. again Tikkanen 1991: 133 about Sanskrit displaying both accusative and ergative clause structures). Using both syntactic structures beside one another is not free from any constraint, although these constraints are more tendentious than definitely operating. Thus one notices that several parameters tend to co-occur (whether they are predictable remains to be investigated).

In the data I have surveyed, *low transitivity* of the verb underlying the gerund tends to be correlated with a *coreferential agent* standing in the *Nom*, the gerundial clause being *subordinate-like* (see [6], [7], [8], [12] and [18]). In [22] the agent is in Gen and in [30] the agent is unexpressed and non-coreferential. In [8], [15] and [20] the agent is *unexpressed* and in [8], [10a] and [30] it is *impersonal*.

On the contrary, *high transitivity* tends to be bound with *a non-coreferential agent in the Instr*, or in *non-Nom*, the gerundial clause being mostly *subordinate-like* (see [6a], [17], [17a], [19]; in [29] the agent is in Voc).

15.1. Once more one can observe the variability (but not the instability) of the linguistic norm (or, to say better, of the concomitant norms, see Oguibénine 1996: 24-25) implemented in Buddhist Sanskrit.

The syntactic constructions presented above belong most probably to different chronological layers of Sanskrit which the language of Ma-Lo uses synchronically, no doubt adapting them to speakers of various dialects (see more Oguibénine 2004).

15.2. It cannot be stated that the ergative construction is definitely among the syntactic features of our language. But, as various authors expressed it (a recent review of the different conceptions of the ergative in Indo-Aryan is Peterson 1998), the necessary conditions were provided for its emergence in Sanskrit and, we can add on the basis of the present survey, in Buddhist Sanskrit. By 'necessary conditions' I mean the sum of constraints that I tried to single out above.

REFERENCES

BHSD = EDGERTON, F. 1972. *Buddhist Hybrid Sanskrit Dictionary*. New Delhi: Motilal Banarsidass.

BHSG = EDGERTON, F. 1972. *Buddhist Hybrid Sanskrit Grammar*. New Delhi: Motilal Banarsidass.

DESHPANDE, M. M. 1992. Justification for verb-root suppletion in Sanskrit. *Historische Sprachforschung* 105: 18-49.

DIXON, R. M. W. 1995. *Ergativity*. Cambridge: Cambridge University Press.

JONG, J. W. de 1994. Review of Nolot 1991. *Indo-Iranian Journal* 37: 375-378.

HENDRIKSEN, H. A. 1948. A syntactic rule in Pali and Ardhamāgadhī. *Acta Orientalia* 20: 81-106.

HOPPER, P. J. & S. A. THOMPSON 1980. Transitivity in grammar and discourse. *Language* 56: 251-299.

JAMISON, S. W. 2000. Lurching towards ergativity: expessions of agency in the Niya Documents. *Bulletin of the School of Oriental and African Studies* 63: 64-80.

JONES, J. J. 1952 = J (see below: texts and translations)

LINDTNER, C. 1994. Review of H. Bechert (ed.), *Sanskrit-Wörterbuch der buddhistischen Texte aus den Turfan-Funden*. 6., 7., und 8. Lieferung. Göttingen 1990, 1992 und 1993. *The Adyar Library Bulletin* 58: 270-272.

MEENAKSHI, K. 1983. *Epic Syntax*. New Delhi: Meharchand Lachhmandas.

MONTAUT, A. 1997. L'ergativité en Indo-aryen. *Faits de Langues* 10: 57-64.

NOLOT, E. 1991. *Règles de discipline des nonnes bouddhistes*. (Publications de l'Institut de civilisation indienne, Fasc. 60.) Paris: Boccard.

OGUIBÉNINE, B. 1996. *Initiation pratique à l'étude du sanskrit bouddhique*. Paris: Picard.

------ 2004. Buddhist Sanskrit, ancient Indian grammarians and descriptive tasks. In: H.W. Bodewitz & M. Hara (eds.), *Gedenkschrift J.W. de Jong*: 99-116. (Studia Philologica Buddhica, Monograph Series XVII.) Tokyo: The International Institute for Buddhist Studies.

------ forthcoming. *A Descriptive Grammar of Buddhist Sanskrit.* Part 1.1. *The language of the textual tradition of the Mahāsāṃghika-Lokottaravādins.*

PETERSON, J. M. 1998. *Grammatical Relations in Pāli and the Emergence of Ergativity in Indo-Aryan*. München: Lincom Europa.

RÉGAMEY, C. 1954. À propos de la"construction ergative" en indo-aryen moderne. In: *Sprachgeschichte und Wortbedeutung. Festschrift Albert Debrunner gewidmet von Schülern, Freunden und Kollegen*: 363-381. Bern: Francke.

RHYS, T. W. & W. STEDE (eds.) 1975. *Pali-English Dictionary*. First Indian edition. Originally published in 1921-1925 by Pali Text Society, London. New Delhi: Oriental Books Reprint Corporation / Munshiram Manoharlal Publishers.

ROTH, G. 1970 = BhīVin (see below: texts and translations)

SCHLESINGER, I. M. 1989. Instruments as agents: on the nature of semantic relations. *Journal of Linguistics* 25: 189-210.

SCHMIDT, M. 1993 = BhīKaVā (see below: texts and translations)

------ 1994. Zur Schulzugehörigkeit einer nepalesischen Handschrift der Bhikṣuṇī-Karmavācanā. In: F. Bandurski, Bhikkhu Pāsādika, M. Schmidt & B. Wang, *Untersuchungen zur buddhistischen Literatur*: 156-164. (Sanskrit-Wörterbuch der buddhistischen Texte aus den Turfan-Funden: Beiheft 5.) Göttingen: Vandenhoeck & Ruprecht.

SCHNEIDER, U. 1950. *Die Deklination im Mahāvastu*. Inaugural-Dissertation, Universität Leipzig.

SEN, S. 1927. An outline syntax of Buddhistic Sanskrit. *Journal of the Department of Letters, University of Calcutta*, 17.

TIKKANEN, B. 1987. *The Sanskrit Gerund: A Synchronic, Diachronic and Typological Analysis*. (Studia Orientalia, 62.) Helsinki: Finnish Oriental Society.

------ 1991. On the syntax of Sanskrit Gerund constructions: a functional approach. In: H. H. Hock (ed.), *Studies in Sanskrit Syntax. A Volume in Honor of the Centennial of Speijer's Sanskrit Syntax (1886-1986)*: 197-217. Delhi: Motilal Banarsidass.

TSUNODA, T. 1985. Remarks on Transitivity. *Journal of Linguistics* 21: 385-396.

TEXTS AND TRANSLATIONS

Abhis-Dh (Mā-L) = B. Jinānanda (ed.), *Abhisamācārikā (Bhikṣuprakīrṇaka)*. Patna: K. P. Jayaswal Research Institute, 1969.

BhīKaVā = M. Schmidt (ed.), *Bhikṣuṇī-Karmavācanā*. Die Handschrift Sansk. c.25(R) der Bodleian Library Oxford. In: R. Grünendahl et al., *Studien zur Indologie und Buddhismuskunde. Festgabe des Seminars für Indologie und Buddhismuskunde für Professor Dr. Heinz Bechert*. Bonn: Indica et Tibetica Verlag, 1993.

BhīVin = G. Roth (ed.), *Bhikṣuṇī-Vinaya. Manual of Discipline for Buddhist Nuns*. Edited and Annotated for the First Time. Patna: K.P. Jayaswal Research Institute, 1970.

Bhu-P = N. Tatia (ed.), *Prātimokṣasūtram*. Patna: K.P. Jayaswal Research Institute, 1975. (Tibetan Sanskrit Works Series, 16.) Quotations by pages and lines.

J = J. J. Jones, *The Mahāvastu*. Translated from the Buddhist Sanskrit. Vol. I: London: Pali Text Society, 1952. Vol. II: London: Luzac & Co., 1956. Vol. III: London: Luzac & Co., 1973.

Mv = É. Senart (ed.), *Le Mahāvastu. Texte sanskrit publié pour la première fois et accompagné d'introductions et d'un commentaire,* I-III. Tokyo: Meicho- Fukyū-Kai, 1977.

T = Transcription of the Abhisamācārikā-Dharma in *A Guide to the Facsimile Edition of the Abhisamācārikā-Dharma of the Mahāsāṃghika-Lokottaravādin*. Abhisamācārikā-Dharma Study Group. The Institute for Comprehensive Study of Buddhism. Taisho University, 1998, pp. 43-129 (chapters I-IV).

INDEX OF QUOTATIONS

Abhis-Dh(Mā-L)
85.15-86.1 (T 95.15) 4.2.1.1.3

BhīVin
38 13
40 10.2
48 10.2
59 10.2
77 10.2
109 10.2
139 14
140 14
152 9.1
174 4.2.1.1
179 7
240 5.2
289 9.2
291 5.2

BhīKaVā
fn. 27

Bhu-P
4.24 3
17.16-18 8

Mv
1.3.2-4 5.3
1.3.6-7 5.4
1.3.13-15 4.3
1.32.8-12 3
1.35.1-2 fn.12
1.33.16-17 4.2.1.1
1.38.9-10 4.2.1.1.3
1.38.4-10 fn. 20
1.57.2-3 4.2.1.1
1.60.1-2 5.3
1.62.14-15 10.1
1.63.2-3 6.2
1.64.6-7 4.2.1.1.2
1.175.17-18 12
1.235.9-10 fn.12
1.263.14-15 fn.12
1.270.11-12 fn.6
1.283.7-12 2.1
1.283.6 fn.5
1.283.8 fn.5
1.283.14-15, 19-20 2. 1
1.283.20-284.1 fn.4
1.284.1-2, 3-9; 11-13 2.1
1.286.14-15; 17-19 2.1
1.312.8 fn.24
2.70.5 3
2.159.9-10 9.1
2.212.17 6.3
2.450.2 fn.24
2.273.10-12 3
3.38.8-9 6.1
3.393.18-19 9.3

Prākrit-like developments in Old Indo-Aryan: testing the 'Kölver-principle'

ERIK SELDESLACHTS

Owing to the working of the accent, nominal and verbal prefixes in Indo-Aryan tend to lose their initial or end vowel. This is particularly noticeable in the younger stages of Indo-Aryan, where this occurrence is part of a broader tendency towards the elision of short vowels.[1] So, e.g., *upaskara-* led via Prākrit **pakkhara-* to Nepali *bākhar*[2], and *anukrama-* to Singhalese *nukama*[3]. The chronology of this evolution is, however, not so clear-cut. Forms like Prākrit *bhittara-*, Hindi and Gujarati *bhītar* indicate Old Indo-Aryan **bhiyantara-*, alternating with the regular *abhyantara-*.[4]

Early reduced forms of this type are by no means limited to the domain of linguistic reconstruction. Since the early days of Indo-Aryan studies, the occurrence has been noticed of Sanskrit and Vedic forms with *ti* for *áti-*, *dhi-* for *ádhi-*, *pa-* for *ápa-* or *úpa-*, *pi-* for *ápi-*, *bhi-* for *abhí-*, *va-* for *áva-*, and *par-* for *pári*.-[5] Scholars pointed out the following doublets with identical or related meanings.[6]

[1] Cf. Pischel 1900: 109-113 §141-148.

[2] CDIAL 2265 *upaskara*[2] 'condiment, spice' (*'scattering').

[3] CDIAL 310.

[4] CDIAL 9504.

[5] E.g., Schmidt 1883: 23-24; Whitney 1896: 399 §1087a; Wackernagel 1905: 71-73 §29 γ-ζ; MW *passim*; and, closer to our time, Nand 1961: 455.

[6] Unless otherwise indicated, lexical meanings are taken from MW. In order to provide some time-depth, the oldest attestations are indicated, relying on MW.

Túgra-, name of Bhujyus's father and of an enemy of Indra R̥V, beside *Tyúgra-* TĀr.[7]

dhiṣṭhita- 'settled, regulated, appointed; superintending' Mbh.+, beside *adhiṣṭhita-* 'idem'.

parāga- 'pollen' Kāv.; 'dust' Ragh.; 'independence' Lex.+, next to *aparāga-* 'aversion, antipathy' Mn.

pidhā- in later Sanskrit beside Vedic *apidhā-* 'to place upon or into; to close, cover, conceal, etc.', with past participle *pihita-* Mbh.+, beside *apihita-* R̥V+; and *pidhāna-* 'cover, sheath, lid' Mbh.+, beside *apidhā́na-* 'covering' KātyŚr.; 'a cover, a cloth for covering' R̥V+.

pinaddha- 'tied or put on, fastened, covered, dressed' Mbh.+, beside *apinaddha-* 'closed, covered, etc.' R̥V+, past participle of, respectively, the later Sanskrit root *pinah-* and the Vedic *apinah-*.

pinasa- and, with unusual lenghtening of *i*, *pīnasa-*, 'cold (affecting the nose); catarrh' Suśr. < **apinasa-* and *apīnasa-*, the latter attested in the meaning of 'dryness of the nose, cold' Suśr.[8]

pinay- (*pinī-*) 'to put into, introduce' ĀpGr̥h., beside *apinay-* (*apinī-*) 'to lead towards or to, to bring to a state or condition' TS+.

vagāha- 'bathing, ablution' Vop.[9], next to *avagāha-* 'plunging, bathing; a bucket' Lex.

vataṃsa- 'a garland, ring-shaped ornament, ear-ornament, earring, crest' Kāv., beside *avataṃsa-* 'idem' Rām.

vatokā- 'a woman (or a cow) miscarrying from accident' Lex., beside *ávatokā-* 'idem' AV+.

---

[7] Mayrhofer 2003: 39 §2.1.199 *Túgra* ("wahrscheinlich zu *toj* 'antreiben'") omits any reference to *Tyúgra*.

[8] CDIAL 8237.

[9] Cf. also *vagāhya-* 'having bathed or dipped into or entered' MW *s.v.*

valamba- 'a perpendicular' W., beside *avalamba-* 'hanging down from or to; hanging on or from' Megh.; 'depending, resting upon; a perpendicular' Lex.; 'dependance, support, a prop, a stay' Ragh.

parṣad- 'assembly, audience, company, society' GṛS+, beside *pariṣád-* 'an assembly, meeting, circle, audience, council' ŚBr.+[10]

aparhāṇa- beside *aparihāṇa-*, both 'the state of not being deprived of anything' KauṣBr.

Taking a lead from such doublets, some scholars have assumed a limited number of shortened forms in cases where no full variant is attested:[11]

pavásta- 'a cover or garment (?)'; du. 'heaven and earth' ṚV < **apavasta-*; cf. *vas-* 'to cover'.

pidṛbh- 'to adhere firmly to; to hope in' ŚāṅkhBr. < **apidṛbh-*; cf. *dṛbh-* 'to fear , be afraid'.

piplu- 'a freckle, mark, mole' Nal. < *(a)piplu-*; cf. (?) *plu-* 'to float, swim; to hop, skip; to wash away, purify, etc.'.

pinākа- 'a staff, bow, or trident, esp. of Śiva' AV+, from the root **pinam-* = *apinam-* 'to bend, bow; to turn towards; to aim at; cf. *nāka-* 'vault of heaven'.

pīḍ- 'to press, squeeze' AV+; 'to hurt, harm, oppress, vex, etc.' Mn.+ < **pisd-* < **(a)pisad-*.

pyúkṣṇa- 'a covering for a bow'(?) ŚBr.+; comm.: 'on the bull', hence < **apyukṣṇa-* 'covered with sinews derived from the bull'.[12]

---

[10] ṚV also 'surrounding, besetting'.

[11] Except for those with a separate reference, the instances are gathered from MW, EWA and KEWA.

[12] Emeneau 1953: 86-87; considered "erwägenswert" by Mayrhofer, EWA II: 173 *s.v. pyúkṣṇa-*. I would rather derive from **(a)pivakṣaṇa-*, with Vedic *vakṣaṇa-* 'strengthening, invigorating; invigoration; the sides, flank'; even then,

bhiṣáj- 'to heal, cure' R̥V; and as a noun 'curing, healing; a healer, physician; a medicine' R̥V+ < **abhiṣaj* 'to attach, plaster'.

valāsaka- 'the koïl or Indian cuckoo' W.; 'a frog' Lex. < **avalāsaka-*; cf. *lāsaka-* 'moving hither and tither, playing; a dancer, actor'; *lāsa-* 'jumping, sporting, dancing'; *las-* 'to play, sport, frolic', but also 'to shine, flash, glitter'.

védi- (*vedá-?*) 'platform' R̥V+; etc. < **(a)vas(a)di-* 'seat'.[13]

Several of these etymologies gained some currency during the 19th and early 20th centuries, but not all of them have been readily accepted. The derivation of *bhiṣaj-* from **abhiṣaj-*, for instance, has been rightfully rejected on the basis of Avestan *-biš* in compounds like *vīspō.biš-* and the R̥gvedic impf. *abhiṣṇak*[14], which point to an Indo-Iranian root **bhiš-*[15]. Even those etymologies that withstood criticism are hardly noticed today, or are seen as very exceptional and isolated as far as Old Indo-Aryan is concerned. In this way, the relevance of the phenomenon of worn prefixes has been generally overlooked. There is one main exception, however.

More than a quarter of a century ago, the late Bernhard Kölver systematically explained a whole series of etymologically untransparent Sanskrit and Vedic words through this phenomenon. In many cases, Kölver noticed that stems are further affected by contractions and reductions. The contractions not only involve ordinary *saṃprasāraṇa* of *ya* to *i* and *va* to *u* (or *o*), but also more uncommon changes like *yā* to *ī* and *vā* to *ū*. The reductions involve the combination of initial stop with semivowel *y* before a vowel, in which *y* is dropped (rather than assimilated). However, *ty-* and *dhy-*

---

the etymology confirms Emeneau's claim that this word indicates the composite bow.

[13] Originally from K. F. Johansson, accepted a.o. by Thieme 1971: 691; not rejected by Mayrhofer, EWA II: 581 *s.v. védi-*.

[14] R̥V 10.131.5.

[15] Mayrhofer – on the basis of the arguments of a.o. Kuiper –, in KEWA II: 502-503 *s.v. bhiṣák* (*-áj-*) and EWA II: 264 *s.v. bhiṣaj-*, I: 91-92 *s.v. abhi-*.

not seldom change into the palatal stops *c-* and *jh-* respectively. A selection of the more than thirty etymologies proposed by Kölver may illustrate the working of the principle:[16]

ati- > *ti-* (*ty*V > *c*V- or *t*V-)

cañca- 'a basket', *cañcā-* 'anything made of cane or reeds, basket-work' Buddh., Lex. < **(a)tyañcā̆-* 'das Übergebogene';[17] cf. *añc-* 'to bend, curve'.

custa- 1. 'chaff, shell of fruit' Lex. < **(a)tivasta-*; from *vas-* 'to cover';
2. 'the burnt exterior of roast meat' Lex. < **(a)tyuṣṭa-* 'burnt (too) much'; from *oṣ-* (*uṣ-*) 'to burn'.

toraṇa- 'an arch, arched doorway, portal; decorations over doorways' Mbh.+ < **tyolana-*, **(a)tivalana-* 'overarching'; cf. *val-* 'to cover, enclose'.[18]

adhi- > *dhi-* (*dhy*V- > *jh*V- or *dh*V-)

jhaṣá- 'a large fish (of the Manu myth)' ŚBr.; 'a fish' MBh.+[19] < **(a)dhyr̥ṣá-*; cf. *arṣ-* (*r̥ṣ-*) 'to flow (quickly), glide, move with a quick motion' R̥V+.

dhūpa- 'incense, perfume' Kāṭh.+ < **(a)dhivāpa-*, interpreted by Kölver as 'Darübergestreutes, gelegtes; Hingestreutes'; cf. *vap-* 'to strew, scatter, throw, cast'.

api- > *pi-*

piśuna- 'slanderous, treacherous, malignant, base; a backbiter, informer, betrayer' R̥V+ < **apiśuna-* 'close to a dog, dog-like'; cf. *śuna-* 'dog'.

---

[16] All examples cited are from Kölver 1976: 12-41, except *jhaṣá-*, which is from Kölver 1975: 54-56.

[17] Gratuitously considered as "nicht weiterführend" by Mayrhofer, EWA III: 176 *s.v. cañca-*.

[18] Personally, I would prefer a derivation from **ativaraṇa-*; root *var-* (*vr̥-*) 'to cover'.

[19] 'Schnabeldelphin' according to Kölver.

apūpa- 'a sort of fine cake or bread', attested from the R̥V onwards, appears in the Mbh. as *pūpá-* < **(a)pyūpa-* < **pivāpa-*, corresponding to *apivāpá-* 'idem' TBr., in fact 'Ausgebreitetes' (*vap-*).

abhi- > *bhi-*

bhūṣaṇa- 'decorating, adorning; ornament, decoration' Mbh.+, sanskritisation of Prākrit *bhūsana-* < **bhivāsana-* 'covering', identical with *abhivāsana-* 'covering' comm. on TS and on Nyāyam.; cf. *abhivas-* 'to wrap one's self up in; dress up(?)'.

vi-V > *vy*V- > *v-*, *b-*

busá- 'vapour, mist, fog' R̥V; 'chaff, husks of grain, refuse or rubbish' Kauś.+ < **vyusa-* < **vivasa-* 'nach allen Seiten Umhüllendes, Umhüllung' or 'das, dessen Umhüllung auseinander [geht]'.

ni-

nīví-, *nīvī-* 'a loin-cloth, skirt or petticoat' VS+; 'a cord for tying together Kuśa-grass; a hostage' Lex.; 'capital' Daś., 'cash, content of the exchequer' Arth. < **ni-yu-i*; cf. *niyu-* 'to bind on, fasten; to procure' R̥V+[20].

Although Kölver offers a solid and very systematic explanatory model, his etymologies have drawn little or no support and have been generally neglected. Manfred Mayrhofer, who regularly refers to Kölver's etymologies in his latest etymological dictionary, mainly mentions them neutrally.[21] A few cases in which he rejects Kölver without explicit motivation may be justified. It is, for instance, possible that *dhūpa-* is not to be separated from *dhūmá-*[22], which has a generally accepted pedigree in Proto-Indo-European

[20] Derived from *ni-vye* by MW *s.v. ni-yu*.

[21] Though he is prudently appreciative in EWA III: 199 *s.v. coṣa-*.

[22] EWA I: 794-795 *s.v. DHŪP*; cf. Pokorny 1959-1969: I: 261-264 *s.v. dheu̯-*, *dheu̯ə-* (*dhu̯ē-*?).

**d^h^uHmós* 'smoke'. Nevertheless, such instances should not immediately lead to the rejection of the 'Kölver-principle' as a whole. To test the consistency of the principle, I tried to apply it to a wider range of Old Indo-Aryan forms. One should be aware that two principles are at work, in fact, for sometimes full prefixes accompany reduced roots and reduced prefixes sometimes go with full roots. However, as both phenomena often appear together, just like in Middle Indic[23], it is useful to consider them together. This investigation has yielded numerous new etymologies established according to clear patterns, of which I will present a few:

To begin with, there are more formal and (near-)semantical doublets:

> *balákṣa-*, *valakṣa-* 'white' TS+ resorts with *avalakṣa-* 'idem' Lex., which may be understood as 'with all distinguishing characteristics removed'; cf. *lakṣá-* 'a mark, sign, token' R̥V+. This suggests a similar origin for *palakṣa-* 'white' VS in **apalakṣa-*, literally also 'without characteristics'. An Indo-European explanation from **bel-* by Mayrhofer[24] stumbles on the *b-/v-* : *p-* alternation ("*pal°* wohl nach *palitá-*") and other formal and semantical shortcomings (e.g., what is *-(a)kṣa-?*).

The above example shows how words that have related meanings and are similarly built, except for the initial sound, may hide different prefixes combined with one and the same root or stem, as also in:

> *caṇḍa-* 'angry, fierce, violent, cruel, hot, ardent, passionate' Mbh.+[25] < **(a)tyaṇḍa-* 'having too much testicle (*aṇḍa-*)'[26], and, on the same nominal basis, but with other prefixes:

---

[23] Cf., e.g., the Middle Indic evolution *vyava-* > *vo-* (Schwarzschild 1965).

[24] EWA II: 215 *s.v. balákṣa-*.

[25] Also 'heat; passion, wrath' and 'circumcised' Lex. Usually connected with *candrá-* 'glittering, shining'.

vaṇḍá-, *baṇḍá-* 'maimed, defective, crippled' AV (*scholia* 'impotent, emasculated') < **vyaṇḍa-* 'without testicles'; and

paṇḍa(ka)- 'a eunuch, weakling' Nār.+, either, with Middle-Indic shortening of *-ā-* < **(a)pāṇḍa(ka)-* 'without testicles', or < **(a)pyaṇḍa(ka)-*, perhaps to be understood ironically as 'who surely has balls', unless *(a)pi-* also has a privative meaning as indicated by *piḍr̥bh-* : *dr̥bh-*, *supra*.

Conversely, there are pairs of words having the same prefix and root, but a different ending or suffix:

pallava- 'a sprout, shoot, twig, spray, bud, blossom; a strip of cloth, scarf, lappet; spreading, expansion; unsteadiness' Mbh.+[27] < **(a)padlava-*, **apadrava-*[28] 'offshoot; spreading out'; cf. *apadrav-* ŚBr.+ = *apadrā-* 'to run away' R̥V+.

pallavana- 'prolixity, useless speech' Naish. < **apadlavana-* 'running off *or* out'; cf. *dravaṇa-* 'running' TBr.+; etc. Formal identity with *pralapana-* 'prattling, talking' Pañcat., Sāh.; 'lamentation' Uttarar., is put forward by Mayrhofer[29]. In order to account for geminate *-ll-*, he assumes attraction by *pallava-*, which, however, is itself "[n]icht klar" to him[30]. If both words are explained together in Kölver's way, there is no need for any such gratuitous presumption.

The semantical parallelism between certain words is sometimes striking even when a formal similarity is not immediately visible:

---

[26] Or 'too much testosterone' as one would say nowadays.

[27] Hardly worth mentioning are the derivation by Wackernagel 1896: 223 §195 from **pad-lava-* 'Wurzelstückchen', and similar ones listed in KEWA II: 235 *s.v.* *pallavaḥ* and EWA III: 310 *s.v.* *pallavana-*.

[28] Cf. *bhadra-* : *bhalla-*; *Madra-* : *Malla-*, etc.

[29] EWA III: 310 *s.v.* *pallavana-*; KEWA III: 88-89 *s.v.* *lápati*.

[30] EWA III: 310 *s.v.* *pallava-*^{1}.

cavala(ka)- 'chick pea' < **(a)tyavala(ka)-*, with **avala-* as alternate form of *avara-* 'low, mean, unimportant, of small value'. The whole may have a kind of privative meaning 'beyond the mean; not unimportant', rather than 'very mean', in view of:

caṇa(ka)- 'chick-pea', but – at the end of a compound – 'renowned or famous for'. Contrary to Mayrhofer's opinion, both meanings are inseparable if derived from **(a)tyaṇa(ka)-*, to be understood as 'beyond the small or insignificant; not small or insignificant', hence 'significant'; cf. *aṇaka-* 'insignificant, small'. Likewise:

cañcu- 'renowned or famous for' (at the end of a compound) Mbh.+ < **(a)tyañcu-*; cf. *añc* (*áñcati*, *áñcate*) 'to reverence, honour', but also 'to bend, curve, curl', whence other meanings of *cañcu-*, like 'a beak, bill; a deer' Lex.

Kölver's principle is also relevant for toponymy, and onomastics in general:

Tū́rghna-, name of the northern part of Kurukshetra TĀr. < **(a)tyūrghna-* < **(a)tivārghna-* 'heavily striking the water'[31], with *vārghna-* containing *vār-* 'water' and *-ghna-* 'striking with; killing; destroying; removing'; cf. the synonymous *Tū́rṇāśa-* R̥V., with *-nāśa-* 'destroying, annihilating'; and also *Sṛughna-*, name of a town in the aforementioned region VaṛBṛS.+ 'hitting the current', from **sru-* 'flow, current', related to the verbal root *srav-* (*srávati*) 'to flow, stream, gush forth', and *-ghna-*. The town of Srughna is present-day Sugh in Ambala district, possessing a natural stronghold at the place where the Yamunā hits the plains.

---

[31] MW *s.v.* *Tū́rghna* interprets *tū́r-* as a variant of *tur-* 'running a race, conquering'; hence he awkwardly understands 'racer's death' as the literal meaning of the name.

Pulkasa- 'name of a primitive tribe' Gaut.+ < **pyulkasa-* < **(a)pivalkaśa-* 'covered with bark; bark-clothed'; cf. *valka-* 'bark of a tree' and *valkala-* 'bark, a garment made of bark' Yājñ.+[32], themselves < **vyalka-*, **vyalkala-*; cf. *vyálkaśa-* 'having various branches' according to Sāyaṇa, but to Mayrhofer 'nach allen seiten Wurzelfasern [*alka-*] habend'[33]. How precisely **vyalka-* is to be analysed is not clear, but *vyálkaśa-* probably means 'provided with bark'. *Pulkasa-* in final instance rests on **(a)pivyalkaśa-*, and thus contains two hidden prefixes.

Two successive prefixes are also encountered in the following words:

tomara- 'a lance, javelin' MBh.+ < **(a)tyavamara-* 'slaughtering excessively'; *ati-ava-* + *mara-* 'killing'.

pudgala- 'beautiful, handsome; the body, material object; person, Ego or individual'[34] < **(a)pyudgala-*; 'what inevitably perishes', or 'what trickles out *or* away'; cf. *ud-gal-* 'to trickle out, ooze out, issue in drops'; cf. *gal-* 'to vanish, perish, pass away'; *gala-* 'oozing'.

picu- 'cotton' Car.; *picavya-* 'the cotton shrub' Lex. < **(a)pityu-*, *(a)pityavya-*, and in second instance < **apyatyu-*, **apyatyavya-* 'surely to be liked very much'; based on *av-* 'to promote, to like'; cf. *cavya-* '*Piper chaba*; the cotton plant' < **(a)tyavya-*.

The last mentioned derivation is confirmed by other forms based on *av-*:

---

[32] Usually connected with *val-* 'to cover or enclose or to be covered', hence 'covering' (MW *s.v.* *2.valka*).

[33] EWA II: 592 *s.v.* *vyálkaśa-*; cf. also *valkā-* 'a kind of plant' ṚV.

[34] Mayrhofer gratuitously distinguishes two forms *pudgala-* (EWA III: 329 *s.v.* *pudgala-*^{1} and ^{2}).

cavana-, which not only designates the plant *Piper chaba*, but also carries the meaning 'giving particular joy', and is therefore derivable from **(a)tyavana-*; cf. *avana-* 'favour, preservation, protection; joy, pleasure'. *Piper chaba* or Javanese long pepper is precisely the most popular of all varieties of long pepper. Similarly also:

cūta- 'the mango tree' < **(a)tyūta-* 'liked very much'; cf. *ūta-* 'favoured, loved, promoted, helped, protected', again from √*av-*; or alternatively < **(a)tivāta-*; cf. *vāta-* = *vanita-* 'solicited, wished for, desired', past participle of *van-*. The development *(a)ty*V- > *c*V- here contrasts with *(a)ty*V- > *t*V- in:

tūta- 'the mulberry-tree', *tūda-* 'idem; cotton tree' < **(a)tyūta-* or **(a)tivāta-*.

In line with Kölver's observations, most of the words under scrutiny belong to specific spheres like nature, animal husbandry and agriculture, the household, the military, material culture, healing, shamanism, and ascetism. Their common denominator seems to be non-Brahmanical culture in general, from Kṣatriya chivalry to the very fringes of society. This indicates that they have been adopted from the speech of different non-Brahmanical strata of the population, a speech that clearly was Indo-Aryan, however. Apart from the examples already given, the following selection of etymologies may illustrate this:[35]

kūpa- 'a hole, hollow, cave' R̥V+; a pit, well' Śāṅkh.Gr̥S < **kvāpa-*[36] 'holding a good quantity of water'; cf. *āpa-* (from *ap-* 'water', cf. Pāṇ. 4.2.38) 'a quantity of water' Mallinātha on Śiś., also present in *anūpa-*; and the prefix *ku-*, from the interrogative pronoun 'how'. Note that *ku-*, which often implies 'depreciation, deficiency', apparently has a positive connotation here, as also in:

---

[35] Most of them not satisfactorily explained in Mayrhofer's opinion (EWA).

[36] Cf. **ku-áp-*, MW *s.v. kūpa.*

kūrma- 'a tortoise, turtle' < **kuvārma-*, **kuvarma-* or **kuvr̥ma-* 'well armoured'; cf. *varman-* 'defensive armour, shelter, defence, protection' R̥V+; root *var-* [*vr̥-*], 'to envelop'.

jhara- (*jharā-*, *jharī-*) 'a water-fall' Prab.+ < **(a)dhyara-* (°*ā-*, °*ī-*) 'falling from above'; cf. *ara-* 'swift, speedy Lex.; at the end of a compound 'going'; cf. *ar-* (*r̥-*) 'to move' in its specific meaning of 'to fall upon *or* into' R̥V+. However, it remains to be seen if this new etymology can hold out against the traditional classing of *jhara-* with *kṣar-* 'to flow, stream, trickle', cf. Pkt. *jharaï* 'tropft', younger Avestan *γžar-* 'to flow'.[37]

timi- 'a kind of whale or fabulous fish of an enormous size' Mbh.+; the ocean'; *tima-* 'a kind of whale' Lex. < **(a)timi-*, **(a)tima-* 'out of proportion, oversized'; cf. *mā-* 'to measure, mark off' R̥V+; *mi-* 'to mete out, measure' Var.Br̥S.; *ma-* 'a measure' L.

vīja-, bī́ja- 'seed, semen, seed-corn, grain' R̥V+; 'a runner (of the Indian fig-tree)' Vcar. < **vi-īja-* 'what is driven out *or* is thrown about' (making clear at once for *bī́ja-* the meaning 'the position of the arms of a child at birth' BhP.); cf. *īj-* 'to go'; *apej-* (*apa-īj-*) 'to drive away'; *samīj-* 'to drive together, collect' R̥V. Cf. also *vyaj-* 'to drive away; to go through or across, furrow' R̥V; 'to fan, ventilate' Suśr. (*vyaja-* 'a fan') = *vīj-* 'to fan, cool by blowing or fanning' Hariv.; to sprinkle with water Mbh.'. A few – rather marginal – attestations of the word exist in Iranian, viz. Buddhist Sogdian *byz'k* 'Saat, Same', Parāčī *bīz* 'Korn, Saatkorn', and perhaps Old Iranian **bīza-* in names[38]. Together with the Indian material, these indicate primacy of *b-* over *v-*, and thus speak against an Indo-Iranian form with

---

[37] EWA I: 428 *s.v. jhara-*; Bartholomae 1904: 530 *s.v. γžar-*.

[38] EWA II: 227 *s.v. bī́ja-*; Balōčī and Persian *bīj* are loans from Indo-Aryan.

**vi-*[39]. Might one suggest, as an alternative, Indo-Iranian **dvīǵa-* 'what is thrown about twice (i.e., first yielded by the plant and then sown by man)'?

cukra- 'vinegar' Hariv.+ < **(a)tyukra-* < **(a)tivakra-* 'very wry'; cf. *vakra-* 'crooked, curved, bent, twisted, wry'.

úgaṇa-, an adjective of uncertain meaning, VS+. The meaning adopted by different scholars seems dependent on the etymology they envisage. When, on the one hand, Monier-Williams gives this word the meaning '(an army) consisting of extended troops', he explicitly presumes an – improbable – corruption of **udgaṇa-* or **urugaṇa-*[40], containing *gaṇa-* 'a troop' R̥V+. On the other hand, 'machtvoll' adopted by Mayrhofer starts from **úgr̥-ṇa-*, containing an Indo-Iranian base **au̯gar-*[41]. Personally, I suggest that *úgaṇa-* is a reduction of **vigaṇa-*, which could have a meaning close to that given by MW, for the prefix *vi-*, among other things, expresses division, arrangement, order, but also variety or manifoldness.[42] R̥gvedic *ogaṇá-*, although attested earlier, may be a secondary *vr̥ddhi*-derivation of the reduced form *úgaṇa-*, at least if it really means 'assembled, united' as suggested by Sāyaṇa[43], and not again 'machtfoll'[44].

cāpa- 'a bow' Mn.+ < **(a)tyāpa-* 'obtaining much' or 'reaching beyond, hitting far'; cf. *āp-* 'to reach; to hit'; *āpa-* 'obtaining'.

tihan- 'a bow; sickness' Uṇ.Vr. < **atihan-* 'slaying (too) much' (the relation between the two meanings 'a bow' and 'sick-

---

[39] Bailey 1956: 41 unconvincingly suggests a connection with Avestan *mīz-* and ultimately with IE **meiǵ-* 'to sow seed' through a dubious variation *m* : *b*.

[40] MW *s.v. úgaṇa.*

[41] EWA I: 211 *s.v. úgaṇa-*, after K. Hoffmann.

[42] MW *s.v. 3.vi.* Note that *vi-* is reduced to *u-* when followed by a consonant other than a sonorant.

[43] MW *s.v. ogaṇá-.*

[44] As **ogr̥-ṇá-* (EWA I: 276-277 *s.v. ogaṇá-*, where reference is made to a still different interpretaion of *ogaṇá-* as a Prākritic development of**avagaṇa-* 'von der Schar sich entfernend').

ness' is the ability to kill); cf. *-han-* 'killing, a killer, slayer'; *atigha-* 'very destructive; a weapon, bludgeon; wrath' and *tomara-*, *supra*.

vraṇa- 'a wound, scar'; but also 'boil, ulcer, tumour' Mn.+[45] < **viraṇa-* 'absence of pleasure'; cf. *raṇa-* 'pleasure, gladness, joy' R̥V+; the verbal root *vraṇ-* 'to wound' Suśr+ is denominal from *vraṇa-* rather than directly from *raṇ-* or *ran-* 'to rejoice, take pleasure in; to gladden, delight'[46].

tyaj- 'to leave, abandon; to give up, resign, renounce' and *tyāgá-* (*tyā́ga-*) 'leaving, abandoning, forsaking' Mn.+; 'giving up, resigning; gift' KātyŚr.+; 'sacrificing one's life' R̥V are usually seen as resorting under an Indo-European root * *ti̯egᵘ̯-* also present in Greek *sébomai* 'feel awe *or* fear *or* shame; to worship, revere; etc.'[47] Tempted to reject this poorly demonstrated reconstruction, as an alternative I initially tried **(a)tiyaj-* 'to exceedingly offer, to completely sacrify' and **(a)tiyāga-* 'exceptional offer'; cf. *yaj-* 'to worship (esp. with sacrifice or oblations); to offer'; *yāga-* 'an offering, oblation, offer; grant, bestowal'. However, besides a lack of semantical persuasiveness, this etymology poses the problem of the additional syncope of *-i-*, so that one may rather consider with Migron, fully in Kölver's tradition, **(a)tyaj-*, i.e. **(a)ti-* + *aj-* 'to drive, propel; throw, cast'[48].

cor- (*cur-*) 'to steal, to rob; to cause to disappear' < **(a)tivar-* 'to excessively conceal'; *corá-* 'a thief' < **(a)tivara-*; cf. *var-* (*vr̥-*) 'to cover, conceal, hide'[49].

---

[45] The meaning 'a flaw, blemish' Mbh+ seems secondary.

[46] The question is, whether accepting this etymology necessarily implies that the not unattractive connection should be abandoned between *vraṇa-* and Alb. *varrë* 'wound', Russian *rána* 'idem'[46]? This kind of question is touched on below.

[47] Pokorny 1959-1969: I: 1086 *s.v.* *ti̯egᵘ̯-* ; EWA I: 673-674 *s.v.* *TYAJ*.

[48] Migron 1988: 82, relying on Stuart E. Mann, *An Indo-European Etymological Dictionary,* Vol. I, Hamburg: Buske, 1984: 11 (*non vidi*).

[49] *Caura-* 'thievish; a thief' is a secundary *vr̥ddhi*-derivation.

Finally, we have to confront the question whether the Old Indo-Aryan forms under scrutiny are late loans from Middle-Indic, or Prākrit-like developments in Old Indo-Aryan itself. It is possible that words attested only in late sources are late borrowings, like e.g., *pavana-* 'forest' in Sanskrit Buddhist literature, which corresponds to *upavana-* 'a small forest or wood, grove, garden' MBh.+ and which may be borrowed from Pāli.[50] One cannot fail to notice, however, that many of the forms dealt with up to now are already early Vedic. Some further words of R̥gvedic stock explicable along the same lines are:

carṣaṇí- 'active, agile, swift'[51] R̥V+; pl. 'men, people, race' R̥V; often explained as a palatalised variant of *karṣ* (*kr̥ṣ*)[52], but rather < **(a)tyarṣaṇí-* 'very active or mobile'; cf. *arṣaṇa-*, *arṣaṇin-* 'flowing, movable' *Nir.*; cf. *arṣ* (*r̥ṣ*) 'to flow, glide, move quickly'.

nákṣatra- 'star, heavenly body' R̥V+; 'lunar mansion' AV < **nyakṣatra-* 'protecting the universe'; cf. *nyakṣa-*[53] 'low, inferior; whole, entire; entireness' Lex. + *-tra-* 'protecting'.[54]

parjánya- 'a raincloud, cloud' R̥V+; 'rain' Bhag.; 'the god of rain (Indra)' R̥V+ < **parijanya-* 'produced all around'; cf. *janya-* (*jan-*) 'born, produced' *Bhāshāp.*+;[55] or < **para-janya-* 'produced far away'; *para-* 'far, distant, remote, opposite, ulterior, farther than, beyond, on the other or farther side of'.[56]

---

[50] EWA III: 311 *s.v. pavana-*².

[51] A meaning rejected for no clear reason by Mayrhofer, EWA I : 538.

[52] Hence "cultivating; cultivators" (MW *s.v. carṣaṇi*), or 'Grenze, (von Grenzen umschlossenes) Gebiet, (innerhalb dieser Grenzen lebendes) Volk' (EWA I: 538 *s.v. carṣaṇí-*).

[53] "Hardly fr. *ni* + *akṣa-*, but cf. Pā. 6.2.192 Sch." (MW *s.v. nyakṣa*).

[54] **nákt-kṣatra-* 'Herrschaft über die Nacht habend' (EWA II: 4 *s.v. nákṣatra-*) is only one of several attempts at clarifying this enigmatic word.

[55] Also 'a father' Lex. and 'a portent occurring at birth' Lex.; hence originally 'producer'?

[56] IE derivations discussed in EWA II: 96-97 *s.v. parjánya-* are all very uncertain.

Without entering that question now, it is also likely that the preclassical free accentuation of Old Indo-Aryan is partly responsible for the observed evolutions. Anyhow, the antiquity of the phenomenon should not surprise, as the presence of Middle Indic-like elements in Vedic is now widely accepted.[57] Whereas morpheme boundaries are usually fully preserved in Old Indo-Aryan, reflecting the Indo-European situation, the evolutions illustrated here are among the factors that have sporadically worn down these boundaries in even the oldest forms of Indo-Aryan.

Notwithstanding the antiquity of the phenomenon within Indo-Aryan, many of the words under investigation seem to have no direct Indo-European cognates and to be new formations within Indo-Aryan. Even a direct link with Indo-Iranian seems difficult to establish. The correspondence *bhiṣáj-* : Avestan *bišaz-* 'to heal', *baēšaza-* 'healing, medicine' cannot be invoked, as *bhiṣáj-* is not to be derived from **abhiṣáj-*, as explained above.[58] Possible genuine parallels in Iranian, like *pavásta-* : Old Persian *pavastā-* 'thin clay envelope to protect clay tablets'[59], are rather few and isolated. Yet, Middle-Iranian has a stock of shortened forms with, e.g., *bi-* < *abi-* in Saka *brre* < **birūji* < **abiroδa-*[60], but these seem mostly to have arisen independently from Indo-Aryan. One of the words treated by Kölver, *bhūṣaṇa-* (cf. *supra*), deserves to be reconsidered in this respect. That *bhūṣaṇa-* 'ornament' is based on **(a)bhivāsana-* 'covering' elucidates, in Kölver's view, the semantic field covered by the root *bhūṣ-*, which not only means 'to adorn', but also, already in the Ṛgveda, 'to strive after, use efforts for, be intent upon'.[61] This raises the question whether the direct cognate of *bhūṣ-*, Avestan *būš-*, *bauš-* can also be explained on Kölver's

[57] Cf., e.g., Elizarenkova 1986.

[58] Bartholomae 1904: 966-967 *s.v. bišaz-* 'heilen'; 914-915 *s.v. baēšaza-* 'heilend, heilkräftig, heiltätig; Heil-, Gesundheitsmittel, Arzenei; Heiltum'.

[59] Cf. EWA II: 105 *s.v. pavasta-*

[60] Bailey 1932: 73.

[61] Kölver 1976: 40-41.

terms. Generally, both *bhūṣ-* and *būš-*, *bauš-* are, with good reason, considered extentions of *bhav-/bav-* 'to become, be'.[62] The basic meaning 'to strengthen, make durable, perpetuate', that has been comparatively deduced for both, also seems acceptable.[63] Thus, either Kölver is wrong in equating *bhūṣ-* with **(a)bhivas-*, or there are, in fact, historically two roots *bhūṣ-* that have converged, the one meaning 'to adorn' < **(a)bhivas-/*(a)bhivās-* and the other 'to strengthen' < **bhū-s-*.

The more Indo-European languages are brought into the picture, the more complicated it becomes. In several language groups. instances are found that raise the question whether processes analogous to the ones assumed here for Indo-Aryan were already present in Proto-Indo-European. After all, for Indo-European, shortened prefixes have been reconstructed, notably *(h_1)pi-* for *$h_1$épi-*, *$h_1$ópi-*, **$h_2$pó-* for **$h_2$épo-*, *$(h_3)b^h$i-* for *h_3eb^hi-*, and **h_2u-* < **$h_2$eu-*.[64] Moreover, individual languages have other more isolated short forms, like Latin *de-* : Indo-Aryan *(a)dhi-*[65]. A reduced form may either have existed in Proto-Indo-European or have arisen independently in each Indo-European language. Even in the latter case, this could have important repercussions for our understanding of Indo-European.

The question is whether or not the many incompatabilities that are apparent between traditional Indo-European derivations and derivations according to the Kölver principle can be solved by extending that principle to Indo-European. Consider the following example. On the basis of Avestan and Greek cognates, for *udára-* 'the belly, stomach, bowels' ṚV+; 'the womb' MBh.+, PIE **udero-*[66] is reconstructed, but one could also recognise in it a reduced form of *vidara-* 'tearing asunder, rending' Lex. 'crevice,

---

[62] Wright 1962: 303-305; EWA II: 270-271 s.v. *bhūṣ-*.

[63] Wright 1962: 287, 303, reiterating Gonda.

[64] Schmidt 1883: 23-24; Kuhn 1895: 80; Wackernagel 1905: 71 §29γ. **$h_2$pó-* in OHGerm, Goth. *fan(a)* 'of, about, from'.

[65] Kuhn 1895: 80.

[66] Pokorny 1959-1969: I: 1104-05 *s.v. udero, u̯ēdero-*.

fissure' Naish.; cf. *vidar- (vidr̥̄-)* 'to tear asunder or to pieces'; *dar- (dr̥̄-)* 'to break asunder, split open; tear, rend, divide'. In order to let the proposed etymology fit in with the traditional one, **udero-* should be based on **u̯idero-*. However, besides the limited evidence for **u̯i-* outside of Indo-Iranian, the reduction of *-i-* in **u̯idero-* is difficult to account for in Proto-Indo-European.[67] More acceptable is a zero grade **h₂udero-* of **h₂eu̯dero-*, approximately corresponding to Indo-Aryan **avadara-* < **h₂eu̯edero-*;[68] cf. *avadar-* 'to split or force open, to rend or tear asunder' R̥V+; *avadaraṇa-* 'breaking, bursting, separating'.

The Indo-European derivation in fact corrects our derivation in this case: not Indo-Aryan *vidara-*, but Indo-European **h₂udero-* underlies *udara-*. Yet, with its reduced prefix, the coming about of this form bears some general similarity to what happened later within Indo-Aryan itself, where **avadarā̆-*, **avadarī-* led to *bádara-*, *vadara-* 'the jujube tree; another tree; the kernel of the fruit of the cotton plant; dried ginger'; *badarā-* 'the cotton shrub; a species of Dioscorea; *Mimosa octandra*; *Clitoria ternatea*'; and *badarī-* 'the jujube tree; the cotton shrub; *Mucuna pruritus*; name of a source of the Ganges'[69].

Interesting cases are found particularly in Germanic, with, e.g., *(h₃)bʰi-* in the frequently used prefix *be-*, *bi-*, corresponding to Indo-Aryan *(a)bhí-*[70]. The Germanic/Indo-Aryan comparisons fall outside the scope of the present paper, but in a future article I will (re)consider the possible relationship or at least parallelism between, e.g.,:

---

[67] Still, there are indications, on which I will not enter now, that it may be defended in other cases such as those involving prefixes in *-i-* .

[68] Also other forms listed in Pokorny 1959-1969: I: 1104-05 *s.v. u̯dero-, u̯ēdero-* may be explained along the same line, e.g., **h₂u̯eh₁dero-* in Lit. *vėdaras* 'Eingeweide (der Fische); Wurstmagen' and **n̥h₂uh₁dero-* in Skt. *anūdara-* 'bauchlos'.

[69] Differently, Johansson 1903: 329: related to *bindu-*; EWA II: 207; KEWA II: 204.

[70] As Kuhn 1895:80 remarks, "die einzige zweisilbige präposition im sanskrit [...], die den ton auf der endsilbe hat".

pakṣá- 'wing, feather, pinion; fin; shoulder' and OHGerm. *fahs*, Angl.Sax. *feax* 'hair (of the head)'[71]; and

púccha- 'tail', derived from *(a)pivakṣas-* by Kölver[72], and OHGerm. *fohs*, Anglo-Saxon, English *fox*[73].

The final conclusion seems warranted that, although individual etymologies are debatable and may eventually be rejected, in general the Kölver principle is an important but neglected instrument in the analysis of the Indo-Aryan lexicon. It reveals developments within Old Indo-Aryan, building further on tendencies that may reach back to Indo-European times, but which only culminate in the Prākrits. Owing to the preoccupation in the past with either a rigid Indo-European heritage or a supposed massive absorption of foreign, non-Indo-Aryan elements, the creativity of Old Indo-Aryan as a living language has been underestimated.

REFERENCES

Abbreviations

BSO(A)S	=	Bulletin of the School of Oriental (and African) Studies
KZ	=	Zeitschrift für vergleichende Sprachforschung auf dem Gebiete der indogermanischen Sprachen
MSS	=	Münchener Studien zur Sprachwissenschaft

BAILEY, H. W. 1930. To the Žamāsp-Nāmak I. *BSOS* 6 (1930-32/1): 55-85, 73.

------ 1955. Indo-Iranian Studies-II. *Transactions of the Philological Society* 1954: 129-156.

------ 1956. Iranian miṣṣa, Indian bīja. *BSOS* 18: 32-42.

BARTHOLOMAE, Christian 1904. *Altiranisches Wörterbuch*. 2. unveränderte Auflage, Berlin: De Gruyter & Co., 1961.

CDIAL = TURNER, Ralph 1966. *A Comparative Dictionary of the Indo-Aryan Languages*. London / New York / Toronto: Oxford University Press.

---

[71] Cf. Goldschmidt 1883: 327, who associated *fahs* with Sanskrit *pakṣman-*.

[72] Kölver 1977: 366-367.

[73] Wackernagel 1896: 155 §132 rejects this comparison.

ELIZARENKOVA, T. Y. 1986. About traces of a Prakrit dialectical basis in the language of the Ṛgveda. In: Colette Caillat (ed.), *Dialectes dans les littératures indo-aryennes. Actes du Colloque International organisé par l'UA, 1058* (Publications de l'Institut de Civilisation Indienne, Série in-8°, Fasc. 55): 1-17. Paris: Collège de France.

EMENEAU, Murray B. 1953. The composite bow in ancient India. *Proceedings of the American Philosophical Society* 97: 77-87.

EWA = MAYRHOFER, Manfred 1986-1999. *Etymologisches Wörterbuch des Altindoarischen.* Heidelberg: Carl Winter Universitätsverlag.

GOLDSCHMIDT, Siegfried 1883. Prâkṛtische miscellen. *KZ* 26 (NF 6): 327-328.

JOHANSSON, K. F. 1903. Arische Beiträge. 1. Zur Vertretung der indogermanischen Dentalgeminaten im Arischen. *Indogermansiche Forschungen* 14: 265-339.

KEWA = MAYRHOFER, Manfred 1956-1980. *Kurzgefaßtes etymologisches Wörterbuch des Altindischen / A Concise Etymological Sanskrit Dictionary.* 4 Bde. (Indogermanische Bibliothek, II: Wörterbücher.) Heidelberg: Carl Winter Universitätsverlag.

KÖLVER, Bernhard 1972. Zwei unerkannte Ableitungen der Wurzel *vap-*. *MSS* 30: 111-127.

------ 1975. Eine mittelindische Redewendung. *Studien zur Indologie und Iranistik* 1: 49-62.

------ 1977: Ai. *vakṣas-* und Verwandtes. *Zeitschrift der Deutschen Morgenländischen Gesellschaft* 127: 344-368.

------ 1976. *Verschliffene Präfixe im Altindischen.* (Abhandlungen für die Kunde des Morgenlandes, 42, 3.) Wiesbaden: Franz Steiner.

KUHN, A. 1895. Goth. *bi*, ahd. *bî*, nhd. *bei*. *KZ* 8: 80.

------ 2003. *Die Personnennamen in der Ṛgveda-Samhitā. Sicheres und Zweifelhaftes.* (Bayerische Akademie der Wissenschaften. Philosophisch-historische Klasse. Sitzungsberichte 2002, 3.) München: Beck.

MIGRON, Saul 1988. Living on in the son : Ṛgveda X.10.1cd. *MSS* 49: 79-84.

MW = MONIER-WILLIAMS, Sir Monier 1951. *A Sanskrit-English Dictionary.* New edition. Oxford: University Press. Repr. 1992 [^{1}1899].

NAND, Bidya 1961. Middle Indicism. *Journal of the Bihar Research Society* 47/1-4: 454-459.

PISCHEL, R. 1900. *Grammatik der Prakrit-Sprachen.* (Grundriss der Indo-Arischen Philologie und Altertumskunde I.8.) Strassburg: Karl J. Trübner.

POKORNY, Julius 1959-1969. *Indogermanisches etymologisches Wörterbuch.* Zwei Bände. Bern / München: Francke Verlag.

SCHMIDT, Johannes 1883. Die germanischen Präpositionen und das Auslautgesetz. *KZ* 26 (NF 6): 20-42.

SCHWARZSCHILD, L. A. 1965. The Middle Indo-Aryan prefix *vo-* 'off' and some phonological problems associated with it. *Journal of the American Society* 85: 350-354.

THIEME, Paul 1971. *Review of*: J. Wackernagel, Altindische Grammatik, II: 2 = A. Debrunner, Die Nominalsuffixe, Göttingen, 1954. In: *Paul Thieme, Kleine Schriften*, II: 661-695. Wiesbaden: Franz Steiner Verlag.

WACKERNAGEL, Jacob 1896. *Altindische Grammatik*, I. *Lautlehre*. Göttingen: Vandenhoeck & Ruprecht.

------ 1905. *Altindische Grammatik*, II: 1. *Einleitung zur Wortlehre. Nominalkomposition*. Göttingen: Vandenhoeck & Ruprecht.

WHITNEY, William Dwight 1896. *A Sanskrit Grammar. Including both the classical language and the older dialects, of Veda and Brahmana*. Fourth edition, Anastatic reprint, Leipzig: Breitkopf and Härtel, Boston: Ginn & Co., 1913.

WRIGHT, J. C. 1962. Vedic *bhūṣ-*, Iranian *būš-*, *baūš-*. *BSOAS* 25: 287-305.

Iranian elements in Sanskrit

HASSAN REZAI BAGHBIDI

1. INTRODUCTION

Iranian and Indian languages have been in close contact from the very beginning of their separation and the early stages of their development. Some lexical items and proper names in R̥gvedic hymns suggest the presence of Iranian speakers in northwestern India in the middle of the second millennium B.C. (Parpola 2002: 69). The establishment of the Achaemenian Empire in Iran in 550 B.C. and its subsequent domination over large parts of northwest India made the general conditions for linguistic borrowing between Iranian and Indian languages exceptionally favourable.

As a matter of fact, contact between Iranian and Indian languages increased when the troops of Cyrus the Great, the founder of the Achaemenian Empire, passed through Bactria and the Hindukush mountains and penetrated into northwest India through the Kabul Valley. From the very beginning of the establishment of the Achaemenian Empire, *Ga^{n}dāra* (Skt. *Gandhāra*) and *Θataguš* (Gk. Σατταγυδία), as they were called in Old Persian inscriptions, formed the easternmost conquests of the Achaemenians, and, from the time of Darius the Great (ruled 521-486 B.C.), they were organized as independent satrapies. Darius the Great extended the eastern frontiers of the Achaemenian Empire. Western India was subdued and formed into a new satrapy called *Hi^{n}duš* (cf. Av. *hindu-*, Skt. *sindhu-*). Maritime trade was opened up, and as a result a number of Iranian words found their way into Sanskrit. In some cases, however, loan translation occurred. The words borrowed from Iranian at this time often display Old Persian features and mainly have to do with military affairs and equipment, which is in accordance with the military superiority of the Achaemenians, e.g.

> **kurpāsa-**, **kūrpāsa-** 'bodice, cuirass, jacket', from OP. **kr̥p.pāça-* 'body-protection', Gk. LW *κυρβασία* (Herodotus V: 49, VII: 64). Cf. Av. *kəhrp-*, *kərəf-* 'body, form, shape', Zor.MP./MP.T. *kirb*, Pāz. *karf*, Arm. LW *kerp*; Av. **pāθra-* 'protection', in *pāθravant-* 'providing protection', Pth.T./MP.T. *pāhr* 'watch-post', Zor.MP./MP.T. *pās* 'guard, watch', NP. *pahra*, *pās*, Arm. LW *pah(ak)*, *pa(r)h* 'guard'. Cf. also Sog. B.M. *p'š'k*, C.M. *p'šy* 'guardian, protector' < **paθraka-*. (See also Hinz 1975: 154; Malandra 1973: 272; Mayrhofer 1956: I: 255; Thieme 1937: 90-91.)

> **phala-**, **phalaka-**, **phara-**, **pharaka-**, **pharatka-**, **pharaya-**, **sphara-**, **spharaka-** 'shield', Hin. *phar*, *pharak*, *pharī*, *phal*, *phalak*, (NP. >) *sipar*, from Med. **spara-*, Gk. gl. *σπαραβάραι* (Hesych). Zor.MP./MP.T./Pāz. *spar*, NP. *espar*, *separ*, Par. *separ*, Arm. LW *aspar*. (See also Hinz 1975: 226; Mayrhofer 1963: II: 392; Monier-Williams 1992: 1269; Turner 1989: 509.)

This state of affairs continued even after the collapse of the Achaemenian Empire in 330 B.C. During the Middle Iranian period which followed, especially during most of the first six centuries of the Christian era, the northwestern part of India was the scene of a series of invasions by other Iranian tribes, namely the *Pahlavas*, *Śakas* (second century A.D.), *Kuṣāṇas* and finally the Iranian-speaking tribes among the *Hūṇas* (fifth and sixth centuries A.D.). This also resulted in the adoption of a number of Middle Iranian words and names, first into Prakrit (principally northwestern Prakrit, i.e. Gāndhārī (see Bailey 1943), and eventually into Sanskrit.

A large number of Middle Iranian words and names, especially from Eastern Middle Iranian languages (e.g. Bactrian, Khotanese, Khwarezmian and Sogdian), are attested in Gāndhārī documents, including the two famous rock edicts of Aśoka (ruled c. 269-232 B.C.) in *Kharoṣṭhī* script at Śāhbāzgaṛhī and Mānsehrā (see Baghbidi 2002: 67-68; Emmerick 1983: 950; Fussman 1986: 780; Sims-Williams 1989: 166). Such elements are also abundant in the inscriptions in the *Brāhmī* and *Kharoṣṭhī* scripts of the *Śaka* and *Kuṣāṇa* periods (see Bailey 1958: 135-136; Salomon 2002: 119-134; Schmitt 1989: 103). Most of the Iranian words borrowed during this period belong to the spheres of administration, equitation, government and, of course, military equipment, e.g.

pavasta-, **pusta-**, **pustaka-**, **pustā-**, **pustikā-**, B.Skt. **postika-**, **pustaka-** 'book, manuscript', Kror. *-pothi*, Pal. *potthaka-*, Prak. *potthiā*, Hin. *pothā*, *pothī*, *pust(ak)*, *pustakī*, from Sog.B.S. *pwst'k*, *pwstk*, *pwst'y*, B.C.S. *pwsty* 'book, document, parchment, writing' (cf. Khot. *pūstya-*, Pth.T. *pōstag*), derived from Sog.S. *pwst(h)* 'skin, hide, leather'. Cf. Av. *pąsta-* 'skin', OP. *pavastā-* 'clay envelope of a tablet', Zor.MP./MP.T./Pāz. *pōst* 'skin, hide', Khwar. *pwst*, NP. *pust(a)*, *pusa*, Hin. LW *post*. (See also Bailey 1979: 247; Burrow 2001: 389; Mayrhofer 1963: II: 319; Turner 1989: 471, 478, 450.) It should be noted that the art of writing and the Aramaic script must have passed through Iran to the Indians, who developed their own *Brāhmī* and *Kharoṣṭhī* scripts from it.

vārabāṇa- (also **bāṇavāra-**) 'armour, mail', from MIr. **warbān* < OP. **vara^{h}.pāna-* 'protecting the breast, breastplate', Arm. LW *varapanak* 'cuirass'. Cf. Av. *varah-* 'breast, chest', Zor.MP./MP.T. *war*, Pāz. *var*, Khot. *vara* 'to, towards', NP. *bar*, *var* 'breast'; Av. *-pāna* 'protection', Zor.MP./MP.T. *-bān*, NP. *-bān*, *-pān*, Arm. LW *-pan*. (See also Burrow 2001: 56, 389; Mayrhofer 1976: III: 192.)

The spread of Islam in the Indian subcontinent by Persian-speaking missionaries and mystics, and the use of Persian as the official language of the court during Muslim rule in the different parts of India, paved the way for the penetration of New Iranian words into late Sanskrit texts. Such Iranian elements are abundant in the Sanskrit books written in Kašmīr, as one of the important centres for Sanskrit, especially during the time of Sultān Zayn al-Ābidīn (1420-1470 A.D.) of the Muslim family of Šāhmīr (see Naqavi 1974: 106-107), e.g.

añjīra- 'Ficus oppositifolia, fig-tree', Hin. *anjīr*, from NP. *anǰīr*, *anǰīl* < MP. *anǰīr* < OIr. **ana-čiθra-* 'not blooming, not blossoming, without flower' (according to the erroneous belief that the fig did not flower). Cf. Zor.MP. *anǰīr*, Sog.M. *'ncyr*, Ōrm. of Kaniguram *injīr*, Paš. *īnjar*, Uigh. LW (< Sog.) *ančīr*. (See also Laufer 1967: 411; Mayrhofer 1956: I: 24-25; Turner 1989: 9.)

seva-, sevi-, sevita- 'apple, jujube, fruit of Zizyphus jujuba' (possibly associated in popular etymology with *sevita-* 'cultivated'), Hin. *ṣeb*, *se'o*, *sew* 'apple', from NP. *sib*, *siv* < MP. *sēb*. Cf. Zor.MP. *sēb*, Par. *sēb*, Wax. *sēb*, Waṇ. *sēb*. (See also Mayrhofer 1976: III: 503; Turner 1989: 784.)

tarambuja- 'water-melon', Hin. *tarbuj*, *tarbūj*, *tarbuz(a)*, *tarbūz(a)*, from a NIr. language. Cf. NP. *tarboz(a)*, *torboza*, Paš. *tarbuja*, Sang. *tarbəz*, Šuγ. *tarbūz*, Wax. *tarbïz*, Bulg. LW *karpūz*, Gk. LW *καρπούσια*, Mong. LW *tarbus*, Russ. LW *arbūz*, Turk. LW *tarbuz*, *qarpuz*. (See also Baghbidi 2002: 73; Laufer 1967: 444; Mayrhofer 1956: I: 481.)

During Muslim rule in India some Arabic and Turkish elements, too, entered Sanskrit through Persian, e.g. **bahrāmakhāna-** 'PN' (< NP. *bahrāmxān*, from *bahrām* < Zor.MP. *wahrām* 'god of war and victory', cf. Av. *vərəθraγna-*; *xān* 'khan' < Turk. *xān* < Mong. *qā'ān*), **ka(ṁ)vūla-** 'name of the eighth Yoga in astronomy' (< Ar.

qabūl), **khāna-** 'Khan, Mogul emperor' (< Turk. *xān* < Mong. *qā'ān*), **mahalla-** 'a eunuch in a king's palace or in a harem' (< Ar. *maḥall*), **mahammada-** 'Muhammad' (< Ar. *muḥammad*), **majamudāra-** 'document-holder, record-keeper' (< NP. *majmu'ḍār*, from *majmu'* 'collected; collection' < Ar. *majmū'*; and *-dār* 'holder'), **malika-** 'king' (< Ar. *malik*), **maṇa-** 'a particular measure of grain' (< Ar. *man*), **mausula-** 'a Muslim' (< Ar. *muslim*), **murasidābāda-** 'name of a city' (< NP. *moršedābād*, from *moršed* 'PN' < Ar. *muršid* 'guide, leader'; and *ābād* 'populous, thriving, prosperous' < Zor.MP. *ābād*), **murāda-** 'Murād' (< Ar. *murād*), **mūsariḥpha-, mūsarīpha-** 'name of the fourth Yoga in astronomy' (< Ar. *muṣrif*), **muśallaha-** 'reconciliation (a term in astronomy)' (< Ar. *muṣāliḥa*), **muthaśila-** 'name of the third Yoga in astronomy' (< Ar. *muttaṣil*), **taravī-** 'quadrature (a term in astronomy)' (< Ar. *tarbī'*).[1]

2. CLASSIFICATION OF IRANIAN ELEMENTS IN SANSKRIT

Iranian loanwords in Sanskrit are almost entirely cultural words in the spheres of administration, agriculture, armament, equitation, government, military affairs, etc. It is clear that these words did not all enter Sanskrit at the same time and from the same Iranian language. Therefore, different chronological and dialectal layers of loanwords must be separated out.

Morgenstierne (1974: 273) distinguished for the first time between ordinary Iranian loanwords and Iranian words phonetically Sanskritized, i.e. Sanskrit words composed on the model of their Iranian equivalents. However, it seems more logical to study the Iranian elements in Sanskrit under the following headings: 1. loanwords, 2. loan translations, and 3. Sanskrit words semantically influenced by their Iranian equivalents. What follows is a list of such elements. It should be noted that some of the words discussed

[1] Such elements will not be dealt with in the present paper.

in the following pages are attested only in writers from Kašmīr, and some are found only in Sanskrit lexica.

2.1. LOANWORDS

akṣaṭa-, **akṣoḍa-**, **akṣoḍaka-**, **akṣoṭa-**, **ākṣoḍa-**, **ākṣoḍaka-**, **ākṣoṭa-**, **ākhoṭa-** 'Aleurites triloba, Croton moluccanum, walnut', Prak. *akkhoḍa-*, *akkhula-*, Hin. *a<u>kh</u>roṭ*, *akhroṭ*, *akroṭ*, *ākhoṭ*, from OIr. **axšar-ta-*[2]. Cf. Khot. *ṣara* 'nut, seed', Oss.D. *äxsärä*, Í. *äxsär* 'nut' (< **axšara-*); Khot. *tharka* 'walnut', Tib. LW *star-ka*, *star-ga*, *star-kha*, *dar-sga*, and probably Ōrm. *waṭk*[3] < **axšar-ka-*; Roš. *-xvōg* (in *xvit-xvō(y)g* 'walnut without outer skin') < **xšōḍ*. The base is Ir. *xšar-* (or possibly *fšar-*). Cf. also Oss.D.I. *äxsäräg* 'squirrel' (with **-aka*), Wax. *ṭōr* 'walnut'.

añjīra- 'Ficus oppositifolia, fig-tree', Hin. *anjīr*, from NP. *anǰīr*, *anǰīl* < MP. *anǰīr* < OIr. **ana-čiθra-* 'not blooming, not blossoming, without flower' (according to the erroneous belief that the fig did not flower). Cf. Zor.MP. *anǰīr*, Sog.M. *'ncyr*, Ōrm. of Kaniguram *injīr*, Paš. *īnjar*, Uigh. LW (< Sog.) *ančīr*.

bakanapati- 'shrine attendant', cf. Sog.B.S. *βγnpt(w)* 'priest, sorcerer'.

bandī, **vandī-** 'courtesan, female captive, female prisoner, female servant, robbed woman, slave-girl', formed with the feminine suffix *-ī*, from **banda-**, **bandin-**, **vandin-** 'captive, prisoner, slave', Hin. *baṅda* 'slave', *bandī*, *vandī* 'imprisonment, captivity; captive, prisoner; female slave', cf. OP. *ba^{n}daka-* 'servant, subject', Pth.T./Zor.MP. *bandag*, MP.T. *bannag*, Pāz. *banda*, Bac. *βανδγο* PN *βανδο*, Sog.B.M.S. *βnt'k*, C. *bnty*, M. *βndy(h)*, S. *βnty*, NP. *banda* 'servant, slave', *bandi* 'captive,

---

[2] According to Mayrhofer (1956: I: 16, 70), perhaps the OIr. word is from a non-Aryan source.

[3] Morgenstierne (1973: I: 412) considers Ōrm. *waṭk* a loanword from OInd. **akhoṭa-*.

prisoner', Yid. *bandɛ*, Arm. LW *band* 'prison'. Cf. **bandhakī-** 'whore', Hin. *bandhakī* 'unchaste woman' (< '*female servant').

bādāma-, **vadāma-**, **vādāma-**, **vātāma-** 'almond-tree', Hin. *badām*, *bādām*, from NP. *bādām* 'almond' < MP. *wādām*. Cf. Zor.MP. *wādām*, Ōrm. of Kaniguram *bādām*, Par. *bādām*, Sang. *bāδām̦*, Šuγ. *bādām*, Yid. *bādām*, Tib. LW *ba-dam*, Uigh. LW *badam*.

bāliśa- 'pillow' (cf. Skt. *barhis-* 'strew'), Hin. *bālish*, from MP. *bāliš* 'pillow' < OP. **bardiš-*, originally 'bed of grass, bundle of twigs' < OIr. **bardz* - 'to cover'. Cf. Av. *barəziš-*, Zor.MP. *bāliš(n)*, NP. *bāleš(t)*, Ōrm. of Kaniguram *bālišt*, Roš. *vāwz*, Sang. *vōzd*, Šuγ. *vīγ̌dz*, *vīγ̌dzēǰ*, Wax. *vōrz*, Yaz. *vawz*, Yid. *virzanë* (< **br̥zanaka-*), *vrazidinë*.

cobacīnī-, **copacīnī-** 'the root of Smilax pseudochina', Hin. *cob-cīnī*, cf. NP. *čub-e čini* 'China root'. Zor.MP. *čōb* 'wood', NP. *čub*; Zor.MP. *čīn* 'China', Sog.S. *cyn* 'China', *cyny* 'Chinese', NP. *čin* 'China', *čini* 'Chinese', Arm. LW *čen-k'* 'Chinese', *Čenastan* 'China'.

damana-, **damanaka-** 'Artemisia indica, wormwood', Hin. *daman(ak)*, cf. Zor.MP. *dramanag* (< **dramanaka-*), NP. *dar-mana*, *deramna*, *dermana*, Šuγ. *čūδm*, Yaγ. *dirawna*.

divira- 'clerk, scribe, secretary', Hin. *dabīr* (< NP.), cf. Pth.T./MP.T./Zor.MP. *dibīr* < OP. **dipīra-* < Elam.A. *tup-pi-ra*, A.N. *v.ti-pi-ra*, M.N. *ti-pi-ir*, O. *de-bi-ir*, *dè-pi-ir*, *di-bi-ra*, *te-ib-bi-ir*, *te-ip-pi-ir*, *te-pír*, O.M.N. *te-ip-pír* [dəpira].[4] Cf. Pāz. *divēr*, Bac. *λαβιρο*, Sog. LW C. *dpyr*, M.S. *δpyr*, NP. *dabir*, *davir*, Ar. LW *dabīr*, *dafīr*, *dawīr*, Arm. LW *dpir*. See also **divirapati-**, **lipi-**.

---

[4] The traditional explanation of this word by tracing it to OIr. **dipī.vara-* 'he who preserves the documents' (Nyberg 1974: 63), or to OP. **dipī.bara-* 'carrying documents/tablets' (Bailey 1979: 499) is unacceptable.

divirapati- 'chief scribe' (in an inscription from Kroraina from the year 496/7 A.D.), cf. Ins.Pth. *dpyrwpt* (Gk. transliteration: *διβιροπτ*), Zor.MP. *dibīrbed* < OP. **dipīra.pati-*. Cf. Sog.LW S. *δp'yrpt*, NP. *dabirbad*, Arm. LW *dprapet*. See also **divira-**, **lipi-**.

dumbaka- 'fat-tailed sheep, thick-tailed sheep', Hin. *dumba* 'fat-tailed sheep', *dum(b)* 'tail' (< NP.), cf. Av. *duma-* 'tail', Zor. MP. *dum(b)*, *dumbag*, Khot. *dumaa-*, Khwar. *δwm*, *δwmyk*, Sog. B. *δwnp'k*, B.S. *δwmph*, M. *δwm*, S. *δwnpy*, NP. *dom*, *domb(a)*, *donb(a)*, Ōrm. *dumb*, Oss.D. *dumäg*, I. *dymäg*, as second component D. *-dun*, I. *-dym*, Par. *dumb*, Paš. *ləm*, Sang. *dəmb*, Šuγ. *δum*, Wax. *dumb*, Yid. *lʊm*, Arm. LW *dmak* 'tail (of an army)'. See also **lūma-**, **lūman-**, **lūna-**.

gañja- 'treasury, grainstore', Hin. *ganj*, cf. Med. **ganza-*, OP. **ganδa-* (Hinz & Koch 1987: I: 430; cf. **ganǰa-* in: Bailey 1986: 461), Pth.T. *gazn*, MP.T. *ganz*, Zor.MP. *ganǰ*, Pāz. *ganž*, Sog.B.C.M. *γzn-*, NP. *ganǰ*, Oss. *γäzdug*, *γäznug*, Ar. LW *kanz*, Aram. LW *ginzā*, Arm. LW *ganj*, Elam. LW A. *gán-za-um*, *hh.qa-an-za*, *qa-in-za-um*, Gk. LW *γάζα*, Lat. LW *gaza*, Syr. LW *gazā*. See also **gañjavara-**.

gañjavara- 'treasurer', Gān. *gaṃñavara*, Hin. *ganjūr* (< NP.), cf. Med. **ganza.bara-*, OP. **ganδa.bara-* (Hinz & Koch 1987: I: 430), MP.T. *ganzwar*, Zor.MP. *ganǰwar*, Sog.B. *γznβr*, NP. *ganǰur*, *ganǰvar*, Arm. LW *ganjavor*, Elam. LW A. *gán-za-ba-ra*, *gán-za-bar-ra*, *hh.gán-da-bar-ra*, *h.qa-in-za-ba-ra*, *qa-an-za-ba-ra*, *qa-za-bar-ra*, Lyc. LW *gasabala*. See also **gañja-**.

gola- 'ball', Hin. *gol(a)*, cf. Khot. *gūla-* 'ball' < **gaula-*, **gauda-* < **gaud-* 'to be round', NP. *gul(l)a*, Oss.D. *γolä*, I. *qul*, Paš. *star-γalai* 'eye-ball', Yid. *γūlak* 'pellet-bow'. Cf. NP. *guy* < Zor.MP. *gōy* < OP. **gauda-*.

horaka- 'donator', from Kuš.Sak. *horaka*, cf. Khot. *haur-*, *hur-*, *hūr-* 'to give' < **fra-bar-*, Tum. *ror-*. Cf. OP. *fra-bar-* 'to grant, to proffer'.

hūṇa- 'Hun, name of a people incurring into the Punjab and western India during the fifth and early sixth centuries A.D.', Hin. *hūṇ(a)*, cf. Av. *hyaona-*, Zor.MP. *xiyōn* 'Turkish peoples in Central Asia and East Iran', Pāz. *hayūn*, Sog.S. *γwn*, *xwn*, NP. *hiyun*, *hun*, *xiyun*, Chin. LW *hiung-nu* 'Huns'. Cf. NP. *hayun* 'a dromedary used by express messengers'.

jagara-, **jāgara-** 'armour', cf. Ōrm. of Kaniguram *zγirɔ*, Paš. *zγara*.

kantha-, **kanthā-**, according to Pāṇini a dialectal word for 'town', also in place names, e.g. **āhvara.kantha-**, **dākṣi.kanthā-**, from OIr. **kanθa-*, **kanθā-*, perhaps originally 'built enclosure, covered place' < **kan-* 'to cover'. Cf. Zor.MP. *samarkand*, Khot. *kanthā-*, *kaṃtha*, *katha*, Sog.B.S. *knδ(h)*, *qnθ*, C. *knθ*, *qnt*, *kθ*, *qθ*, S. *sm'rknδc*, *smrknδc* 'Samarkand', NP. *kand*, *kant* 'name of a number of villages in Transoxiana', *samarkand*, *samar-qand*, *tāš-kand*, Oss.I. *känt* 'building', Paš. *kandai* 'ward', Ar. LW *Samar-qand*, Gk. LW *Μαρα-κανδα*.

karṣa- 'a certain weight, a weight of gold or silver', from OP. *karša-* '(unit by) weight = 83.33 gr.', which, in turn, may be from a western (perhaps Aramaic) resource. Cf. Elam. LW A. *kur-šá-am*, *kur-šá-um*. The OP. *karša-* was one-sixth of the Bab. *mana* 'mina'.

kākhorda- 'a kind of evil spirit; sorcerer', **kharkhoda-**, **khārkhoṭa-** 'a kind of magic', N.Prak. *khakhorna-*, *khakhorda-*, cf. Av. *kax^varəδa-* 'magician, sorcerer, wizard', Arm. LW *kaxard*.

kurpāsa-, **kūrpāsa-** 'bodice, cuirass, jacket', from OP. **kr̥p.pāça-* 'body-protection', Gk. LW *κυρβασία* (Herodotus V: 49, VII: 64). Cf. Av. *kəhrp-*, *kərəf-* 'body, form, shape', Zor.MP./ MP.T. *kirb*, Pāz. *karf*, Arm. LW *kerp*; Av. **pāθra-* 'protection', in *pāθravant-* 'providing protection', Pth.T./ MP.T. *pāhr* 'watch-post', Zor.MP./MP.T. *pās* 'guard, watch', NP. *pahra*, *pās*, Arm. LW *pah(ak)*, *pa(r)h* 'guard'. Cf. also Sog.B.M. *p'š'k*, C.M. *p'šy* 'guardian, protector' < **paθraka-*.

kuṣāṇa- 'Kušān', Prak. *kuṣaṇa-, khuṣaṇa-, kuṣūna-*, cf. Ins.Pth. *kwšn*, MP.T. *kušān* 'the Kušāns', Bac. κοÞανο (also miswritten as κορσολου, κορσνλ, κορονλ, χορανου), Sog.M. *kwš'n*, NP. *košān, kušān*, Arm. LW *K'oušan*, Chin. LW *kuei-shuang*.

kharbūja- 'melon, water-melon', Hin. *k͟harbuza, k͟harbūza, k͟harpuza, kharbujā*, from NP. *xarboz(a), xarbuza* < Zor.MP. *xarbūzag*. Cf. Par. *khȫrəbuǰ*, Sang. *xarbæ(a)*, Šuɣ. *xarbūz*, Yid. *xarbæ(a)*.

khola-, kholaka- 'a kind of hat, helmet', from a late new EIr. word with /l/ < OIr. */d/. Cf. Hin. *k͟hod* (< NP.), Av. *xaoδa-*, OP. *xaudā-*, Pth.T. *xōd*, MP.T. *xōy*, NP. *xud, xuy*, Oss.D. *xodä*, I. *xūd*, Paš. *xōl*. Most likely in origin 'a leather hat or helmet' < OIr. **xaud-* 'to cover'. Cf. Khot. *khauca, khoca* 'face', Wax. *skīd* 'cap' < **skauda-*, Arm. LW *xoyr* 'diadem, hat, headgear', Georg. *xoiri* 'headgear' (< Arm.).

limpi-, lipi-, lipī-, livi-, livī- 'alphabet, writing', also in **lipikara-, lipika-** 'scribe, writer', Pal. *lipi-* 'alphabet', Aśok. *dipi-, lipi-, lipī-* 'decree, edict, record, writing', *dipikara-* 'scribe, writer', Hin. *lip(i)* 'document, manuscript, writing', *lipikar, lipikār* 'copyist, scribe, writer', from OP. *dipi-, dipī-* 'inscription, script, tablet, writing' < Elam.A. *h.tup-pi*, A.N. *tup-pi*, M. *ti-ip-pi*, O. *te-bi* [dipi] < Bab. *ṭuppu* < Sum. *dup, dub*. **lipi-, lipī-** probably through association with *lip-* 'to smear', or contaminated by *likháti*, or perhaps an EIr. LW with /l/ < OP. */d/, cf. Bac. LW λιβο 'copy, document'. This word was borrowed during the period when the art of writing and the Aramaic script were transmitted beyond Iran to India. See also **divira-, divirapati-**.

lūma-, lūman-, lūna- 'tail', Hin. *lūm(a)*, from an EIr. word with /l/ < OIr. */d/. Cf. Av. *auma-*, Zor.MP. *dum(b), dumbag*, Khot. *dumaa-*, Khwar. δwm, δwmyk, Sog. B. δwnp'k, B.S. δwmph, M. δwm, S. δwnpy, NP. *dom, domb(a), donb(a)*, Ōrm. *dumb*, Oss.D. *dumäg*, I. *dymäg*, as second component D. *-dun*, I.

-dym, Par. *dumb*, Paṣ. *ləm*, Sang. *dəmb*, Šuγ. *δum*, Wax. *dumb*, Yid. *lʊm*, Arm. LW *dmak* 'tail (of an army)'. See also **dumbaka-**.

māḍhī- 'armour, mail', cf. Zor.MP. *mādīg* 'Median armour', Ar. LW *māδīya*. Cf. OP. *māda-* 'Media; Median', Ins.Pth./Zor.MP. *mād* 'Media', Arm. LW *mar-k'*, Bab. LW *ma-da-a-a*, Elam. LW A. *h.ma-da*, *v.ma-da*, *v.ma-da-be* (pl.), Gk. LW *Μηδοι*.

mihira- 'sun', Hin. *mih(a)r*, *mihir*, from Zor.MP. *mihr* 'Mithra; sun' < OP. **miça-* (LW *miθra-*, *mitra-*) 'friend; Mithras'. Cf. Av. *miθra-* 'contract; Mithra (Avestan god of the contract)', Ins.Pth./Pth.T./Ins.MP./Zor.MP./MP.T. *mihr* 'Mithra; sun', Pāz. *mihir*, Bac. *μιιρο*, *μιυρο*, *μιορο*, *μειρό*, *μιρο*, *μιρι*, *μιρρο* wrongly also: *μορο*, *μυρο*, *μευρο*, *μιιορο*, Khwar. *myθ* 'day', Sog.B. *'myδr-*, M. *myš-*, S. *myδr'* 'Mithra', C. *myθ* 'day', M. *myr* 'sun', NP. *mehr*, Ōrm. *mēṣ̌*, Ōrm. of Kaniguram *mēṣ̌*, Waṇ. *mīr*, Yid. *mīra*, Arm. LW *meh-*, *merh-*, *mihr*, *mirh* 'Mithra', Bab. LW *mi-it-ri*, Elam. LW A. *hh.mi-iš-šá* (PN), *hhh.mi-iš-šá*. See also **mitra-**.

moca-, **mocaka-** 'shoe', **maucika-**, **mocika-** 'cobbler, shoemaker, tanner', Hin. *mocī* 'shoe; shoemaker', *mocrī* 'shoe', *moza* 'boot', cf. Zor.MP. *mōg*, *mōz*, *mōzag* 'shoe', Pāz. *mōk*, NP. *muq*, *muza*, Par. *mōza*, Sang. *mus* 'clothes', Ar. LW *mauzaj*, *mūq*, Arm. LW *moyk*, *moučak* 'shoe', *mučak* 'shoemaker', Syr. LW *mōqā*.

mudrā- 'seal, signet-ring, stamp, token', also in **mudraṇa-** 'act of sealing up', **mudrayati** 'seals', **mudrākara-** 'maker of seals', Hin. *mohar*, *mŏhr*, *muh(a)r*, *muhur* (< NP.), from OP. **mudrā-*. Cf. Pth.T./MP.T. *muhr*, Zor.MP. *muhr(ag)*, Khot. *mūrā* 'jewel, name of a coin', *mūraka-* 'seal', Sog. M. *mwhrdyb* 'seal of letter', S. *myδr(y)* 'seal', NP. *mohr* 'seal', *mohra(g)* 'any round object', Arm. LW *mourhak* 'sealed document'.

nagnahu- 'leaven, yeast', cf. Early NP. *naγan*, *naγanxalān*, *naγnaxʷād*, *naγnaxʷāyin*, *naγnaxʷālān* 'aniseed' (literally 'sweetness of bread'). Cf. Pth.T. *naγn* 'bread', Sog.C.M. *nγn-*.

nūda-, **tūda-**, **tūla-**, **tūta-** 'the mulberry-tree', Hin. *tūt* (< NP.), *nūd*. Cf. Zor.MP. *tūt* 'mulberry', NP. *tud*, *tut*, Ōrm. *tūt*, Par. *tī*, Sang. *tūt*, Šuγ. *tūδ*, Wax. *tūt*, Waṇ. *tūwa*, Yid. *tūi*, *tūt*, Ar. LW *tūθ*, Aram. LW *twt'*, Arm. LW *t'ut'*. The Iranian word might also result in the Indo-Aryan dialectal forms **tul* and **tur*.

pahlava- 'Parthians; Persians (pl.)', Hin. *pahlav(a)*, cf. Zor.MP. *pahlawīg* 'Parthian', MP.T. *pahlawānīg*, NP. *pahla(v)* 'Parthia', *pahlavi* 'Parthian; later also Persian' < MP. **pahlaw* 'Parthia' < OP. *parθava-* 'Parthia; Parthian'. Cf. Sog. *pγr'w'n'k*, *pγl'w'n'k* 'Parthian (language)', C. *prθw'yq* 'Parthian', S. *pxl'w'n'k*, Ar. LW *fahla(w)* 'Parthia; later a northwestern district of Iran', *fahlawī* 'Parthian; later also any other northwestern Iranian dialect', Bab. LW *pa-ar-tu-ú*, Elam. LW A. *h.bar-tu-maš*, *v.bar-tu-ma*, *v.bar-tu-ma-ip* (pl.), *v.bar-tu-[ma-ra]* (sg.), *v.bar-tu-maš-be* (pl.), Gk. LW *Παρθία*. See also **parśu-**, **pārasa-**, ***pārasī-**, **pāraśava-**.

palyayana-, **palyāṇa-**, **paryayaṇa-**, **paryāṇa-** 'saddle', also in **palyāṇayati** 'saddles', **paryāṇayati**, Prak. *pallāṇa-*, *paḍā-yaṇa-*, Hin. *palān*, *palānā*, *pālān* (< NP.). Iranian in origin, but possibly assimilated in form to Skt. *paryāṇa-* 'circuit'. Cf. Sog.M.S. *pyrδn* 'saddle', NP. *pālān* 'pack-saddle', Par. *pālān*, Sang. *pāliŋg*, Šuγ. *bəδāṇ*, Wax. *pöδṇ*, Yid. *palan* < OIr. **pari-dāna-*.

parśu- 'name of a man, name of a woman', **parśavaḥ** (m. pl.) 'a northwestern warrior tribe', whose leader was called **Pārśava-**, Hin. *pār(a)s*, *pāris* 'Persia' (< NP.), *pārsī(k)*, *pārsik* 'Persian' (< NP.). Most probably connected with the OP. (actually Med.) word *pārsa-* 'Persia; Persian'. The name of the *Paštuns* and their language *Paṣ̌to* is also probably derived from **parsa-* or **parsu-* and connected with the *Πάρσιοι* placed in

Afghanistan by Ptolemy and with the **parśu-** of the Ṛgveda. Cf. Pth.T. *pārs* 'Persia', Zor.MP./MP.T. *pārsīg* 'Persian', Bac. *παρσο* 'Pars (?)', Sog.C. *p'rs* 'Persia', *p'rsyq* 'Persian', M.S. *p'rsyk*, NP. *pārs* 'Persia', *pārsi* 'Persian', Ar. LW *Fārs* 'Persia', *fārsī* 'Persian', Bab. LW *pa-ar-su*, Elam. LW A. *hh.bar-sìb-be* (pl.), *v.bar-sìp* (pl.), *v.bar-sir* (sg.), A.N. *v.bar-sir-ra* (sg.), N. *hw.bar-sìp* (pl.), *hw.bar-sir-ra* (sg.), Gk. LW *Πέρσης, Περσία.* See also **pahlava-**, **pārasa-**, ***pārasī-**, **pāraśava-**.

pavasta-, **pusta-**, **pustaka-**, **pustā-**, **pustikā-**, B.Skt. **postika-**, **pustaka-** 'book, manuscript', Kror. *-pothi*, Pal. *potthaka-*, Prak. *potthiā*, Hin. *pothā*, *pothī*, *pust(ak)*, *pustakī*, from Sog.B.S. *pwst'k*, *pwstk*, *pwst'y*, B.C.S. *pwsty* 'book, document, parchment, writing' (cf. Khot. *pūstya-*, Pth.T. *pōstag*), derived from Sog.S. *pwst(h)* 'skin, hide, leather'. Cf. Av. *pąsta-* 'skin', OP. *pavastā-* 'clay envelope of a tablet', Zor.MP./MP.T./Pāz. *pōst* 'skin, hide', Khwar. *pwst*, NP. *pust(a)*, *pusa*, Hin. LW *post*.

pārasa-, **pārasika-**, **pārasīka-** 'Persian', **pārasī-** 'Persian language', **pārasīka-** 'a Persian horse', also in **pārasīka-taila-** 'naphta', **pārasīka-yamānī-** 'an imported Persian medicine', **pārasīya-yavānī-** 'a remedy imported from Persia', Hin. *pār(a)s*, *pāris* 'Persia' (< NP.), *pārsī(k)*, *pārsik* 'Persian' (< NP.), cf. OP. (actually Med.) word *pārsa-* 'Persia; Persian'. The name of the *Paštuns* and their language *Pašto* is also probably derived from **parsa-* or **parsu-* and connected with the *Πάρσιοι* placed in Afghanistan by Ptolemy and with the **parśu-** of the Ṛgveda, Pth.T. *pārs* 'Persia', Zor.MP./MP.T. *pārsīg* 'Persian', Bac. *παρσο* 'Pars (?)', Sog.C. *p'rs* 'Persia', *p'rsyq* 'Persian', M.S. *p'rsyk*, NP. *pārs* 'Persia', *pārsi* 'Persian', Ar. LW *Fārs* 'Persia', *fārsī* 'Persian', Bab. LW *pa-ar-su*, Elam. LW A. *hh.bar-sìb-be* (pl.), *v.bar-sìp* (pl.), *v.bar-sir* (sg.), A.N. *v.bar-sir-ra* (sg.), N. *hw.bar-sìp* (pl.), *hw.bar-*

sir-ra (sg.), Gk. LW *Πέρσης*, *Περσία*. See also **pahlava-**, **parśu-**, ***pārasī-**, **pāraśava-**.

***pārasī-** 'walnut' (A Chinese-Sanskrit word transcribed as *po-lo-ši* in the Buddhist dictionary *Fan yi miṅ yi tsi*), the feminine form of the adjective **pārasa-** 'Persian'. Cf. Gk. *καρύα περσική*. See also **pahlava-**, **parśu-**, **pārasa-**, **pāraśava-**.

pāraśava- 'iron; made of iron', Hin. *pārśav* 'iron; an iron weapon', possibly from ***par(a)śava-** < OP. *parθava-* 'Parthia; Parthian', thus literally 'imported from Parthia'. Cf. Zor.MP. *pahlawīg* 'Parthian', MP.T. *pahlawānīg*, Sog. *pγr'w'n'k*, *pγl'w'n'k* 'Parthian (language)', C. *prθw'yq* 'Parthian', S. *pxl'w'n'k*, NP. *pahlavi* 'Parthian; later also Persian' (< MP. **pahlaw* 'Parthia' < OP. *parθava-*), Bab. LW *pa-ar-tu-ú*, Elam. LW A. *h.bar-tu-maš*, *v.bar-tu-ma*, *v.bar-tu-ma-ip* (pl.), *v.bar-tu-[ma-ra]* (sg.), *v.bar-tu-maš-be* (pl.), Gk. LW *Παρθία*. See also **pahlava-**, **parśu-**, **pārasa-**, ***pārasī-**.

pāyika- 'footman, foot-soldier', Hin. *pāyak*, *pāyik*, (NP. >) *paik*, Sanskritized form of Prak. *pāikka-*[5], cf. Pth.T. *padag*, Zor.MP./MP.T. *payg* 'foot soldier', in Zor.MP. also '(chess) pawn', Sog.B. *pδ'k* 'foot soldier; on foot', B.M. *pδ'y*, *pδδy*, *pδyy* 'on foot', M. *δδ'y* 'on foot', NP. *payg*, *payk* 'envoy', Ar. LW *fayj*, Arm. LW *payik* 'foot soldier', Syr. LW *paigā*.[6]

pīlu- 'elephant', Hin. *fīl* (< NP.), *pīl*, cf. OP. *piru-* 'ivory', Sog.B. *pyδ (h)*, Khwar. *pyz*, Pth.T. *pīl*, Zor.MP./MP.T. *pīl* 'elephant', in Zor.MP. also '(chess) bishop', NP. *fil*, *pil*, Ar. LW *fīl*, Aram. LW *pīl*, Arm. LW *p'iłapet* 'elephant-keeper'. Cf. Akk. *pīlu*, *pīru*.

phala-, **phalaka-**, **phara-**, **pharaka-**, **pharatka-**, **pharaya-**, **sphara-**, **spharaka-** 'shield', Hin. *phar*, *pharak*, *pharī*, *phal*, *phalak*, (NP. >) *sipar*, from Med. **spara-*, Gk. gl. *σπαρα-*

[5] It is not a corrupted form of *pādātika-* (as in Monier-Williams 1992: 619).
[6] Skt. *padāti(ka)-* (Nyberg 1974: 147) is not related.

βάραι (Hesych). Zor.MP./MP.T./Pāz. *spar*, NP. *espar*, *separ*, Par. *separ*, Arm. LW *aspar*.

rathyā- (feminine form of the adjective **rathya-**) 'carriage-road, high-road', also in **uparathyā-**, **virathyā-** 'by-road', Hin. *rathyā*, (NP. >) *rah*, *rāh*, from OP. **raθyā-* (< **raθa-* 'car, chariot') to denote, first of all, the Achaemenian roads. As we know the Achaemenian administration took great interest in the development of roads. Cf. Av. *raθa-*, *ra^{i}θī-*, *ra^{i}θyā-* 'road' (< *raθa-* 'car, chariot'), Pth.T./Zor.MP./MP.T./Pāz. *rāh* 'road' (< OIr. **rāθa-*), Sog.B.M.S. *r'δ(δh)*, C. *r'θ*, NP. *rah*, *rāh*, *rās*, Ōrm. *rāī* (< **raθī-*), Paš. *lyār*, *lār* (< **raθyā-*, **raθī-*), Yaγ. *rōt*, *rōs*, Sang. *rā*, Arm. LW *ŕah*, Ašk. LW *weriču*, *biriči* < **upa-rathyā-* or **vi-rathyā-*. Cf. also Pth.T. *reh* 'car, chariot', Zor.MP. *rah*, MP.T. *rah(y)*, Sog.B. *rδδ-* 'chair in chariot'.

seṭa- 'a particular measure or weight', Gān. *satera*, *sadera*, Hin. *ser* (< NP.), Sanskritization of a NInd. form. Cf. Zor.MP. *stēr*, Sog.B.M.S. *st'yr*, NP. *astir*, *estār*, *estir*, *setir*, *sir* < Gk. *στατήρ*.

seva-, **sevi-**, **sevita-** 'apple, jujube, fruit of Zizyphus jujuba' (possibly associated in popular etymology with *sevita-* 'cultivated'), Hin. *seb*, *se'o*, *sew* 'apple', from NP. *sib*, *siv* < MP. *sēb*. Cf. Zor.MP. *sēb*, Par. *sēb*, Wax. *sēb*, Waṇ. *sēb*.

sigatā-, **sikatā-** 'grain of sand; sand, gravel (usually pl.)', originally a collective formation from **sika-** (in **śveta-sika-druka-** 'scattering white sand'), Kror. *siǵata bhūma* 'sandy land', Hin. *siktā*, cf. OP. *θikā-* 'gravel, rubble', Zor.MP./MP.T. *sygd*, Khot. *siyatā-*, Sog.B. *šykth*, *škth*, Bal. *six* 'barren land; sand', Ōrm. *saga*, *sigo*, Oss.D. *sigit*, I. *sydžyt* 'earth, soil', Par. *seγa*, Paš. *šəga*, Waṇ. *səga*, Yaγ. *šōw*, Yid. *sëγio*, *siγiya*, Khow. LW *šuγur*, Kal. LW *šigal*, Phal. LW *šiga*.

sīsa-, **sīsaka-** 'lead', Prak. *sīsai*, Hin. *sīs(a)*, *sīsā* 'lead, blacklead', *siyāh* 'black', probably from OIr. **sai-*, **sy-au-* 'dark, dark-coloured', cf. Av. *sāma-*, *syāma-*, *syāva-* 'black', Pth.T.

syāw(ag), Zor.MP. *syā*, Pāz. *syāh*, Khot. *śāva-* 'copper; copper-coloured, red', Sog.B.M.S. *š'w*, C. *šw*, NP. *siyah*, *siyāh* 'black', Oss.D.I. *sau*, Sang. *ṣ̌ūi*, Wax. *ṣ̌ū*, *ṣ̌ū*, *šū*, *xui*, Arm. LW *seau*, Khow. LW *ṣ̌ā*. Skt. /ś/ often corresponds to Ir. /s/ (e.g. Skt. *śyāva-* ~ Av. *syāva-* 'black'); therefore, *s*-forms of Sanskrit are often loans from, or at least influenced by, Iranian. As for the suffix *-sa*, cf. Khot. *daujsä* 'lead' < **dāva-čū-* < **dav-* 'to burn' (cf. Skt. *dunoti*).

sorāka- 'nitre, potassium nitrate, saltpetre', Hin. *shora* (< NP.), cf. Zor.MP. *sōrag* 'salt (land)', NP. *šura* 'nitre, saltpetre', Ar. LW *šauraj*.

sthora- 'horse', Gān. *stora*, Hin. *sator*, *sutūr* 'beast of burden, quadruped' (< NP.), cf. Av. *staora-* 'bovine animal, draught animal', Pth.T. *istōr* 'cattle, horse', Zor.MP. *stōr*, Sog.B.S. *'st'wrh*, C.S. *stwr*, S. *'stwr* 'cattle, sheep', NP. *sotur*.

śaka- '*Saka*', also in **śaka.sthāna-**, Hin. *śak(a)*, cf. OP. *saka-* 'Scythia; Scythian', *sakā-* 'Scythia', Zor.MP./MP.T. *sag*, also in *sagān-šāh* 'king of the *Sakas*', *sakestān* 'Sakastan', Sog.C. *sγst'n* 'Sakastan' < OIr. **sak-* 'to wander about' (Szemerényi 1980: 46), not from Med. *σπάκα* (Herodotus I: 110), OP. **saka-* 'dog' in good sense, i.e. 'guardian of the flocks' (e.g. in: Kent 1953: 209). Cf. Elam. LW A. *hh.šá-ak-qa* (PN), *v.šá-ak-qa*, *v.šá-ak-qa-be* (pl.), Gk. LW *Σκύθης*, *Σκυθία*. The *Sakas*, known to the old Persians and Greeks from as early as 600 B.C., became overlords of northwest India in the second century A.D.

śav- 'to go', quoted by ancient Indian grammarians from the *Kambojas* in the extreme northwest. It must have belonged to a dialect containing Iranian features. Hin. *shudan* 'to become, to go' (< NP.), cf. Av.G. *š́yav-*, Y. *šav-*, OP. *šiyav-*, Pth.T./ Zor.MP./MP.T. *šaw-*, Khwar. **šw-* 'to come out (?)', Sog. *šw-*, Ōrm. *caw-*, Par. *čh-*, Sang. *š-*, Šuγ. *sāw-*, Wax. *c̣āw-*.

śāha- 'name of a country belonging to Kašmīr', also in **bhūmi.śāha-**, **nema.śāha-**, **phatiha.śāha-**, Hin. *shāh*, from NP. *šah*, *šāh* 'king' < MP. *šāh* < OP. *xšāyaθiya-*. Cf. Pth.T./Zor.MP./MP.T. *šāh*, Bac. *þαυι*, *þαυιο*, *þιυο* (< MP.), Khwar. *š'h* 'king (in chess)', Arm. LW *šah*.

tarambuja- 'water-melon', Hin. *tarbuj*, *tarbūj*, *tarbuz(a)*, *tarbūz(a)*, from a NIr. language. Cf. NP. *tarboz(a)*, *torboza*, Paš. *tarbuja*, Sang. *tarbəz*, Šuγ. *tarbūz*, Wax. *tarbïz*, Bulg. LW *karpūz*, Gk. LW *καρπούσια*, Mong. LW *tarbus*, Russ. LW *arbūz*, Turk. LW *tarbuz*, *qarpuz*.

tīra-, **tīrikā-**, **tīrī-** 'a kind of arrow', Hin. *tīr*, a late LW from Iranian. Cf. Av. *tiγri-* 'arrow', Zor.MP./MP.T. *tigr*, Pāz. *tīr*, NP. *tir*, Ōrm. *tīr*, Wax. *tīr-i-dast*.

ṭagara-, **ṭaṅga-**, **ṭaṅgaṇa-**, **ṭaṅka-**, **ṭaṅkana-**, **ṭaṅkaṇa-** 'borax', Hin. *tangār*, *tankār*, from NP. *tangār*, *tankār* 'crude borax found in lake-deposits of Iran, tincal, tincar'.

vārabāṇa- (also **bāṇavāra-**) 'armour, mail', from MIr. **warbān* < OP. **vara^h.pāna-* 'protecting the breast, breast-plate', Arm. LW *varapanak* 'cuirass'. Cf. Av. *varah-* 'breast, chest', Zor.MP./MP.T. *war*, Pāz. *var*, Khot. *vara* 'to, towards', NP. *bar*, *var* 'breast'; Av. *-pāna* 'protection', Zor.MP./MP.T. *-bān*, NP. *-bān*, *-pān*, Arm. LW *-pan*.

yavana- 'Greek, Ionian, in later times any foreigner', from **yauna-** 'name of a people', **yavanī-** 'yavana-woman', Hin. *jaun*, *jawan*, *yavan*, probably Sanskritization of the Prak. form *yona-* < OP. *yauna-* 'Ionia; Ionian' < Gk. *'Ιάονες*, *'Ιωνες*, *'Ιωνία*, though separate borrowing as **yavana-** cannot be excluded. Cf. Pth.T. *yōnāw* 'Greek (language)', Sog.C. *ywn'yq* 'Greek', NP. *eyuni*, *eyuniya*, *eyuniyā* 'Ionia', *yunān* 'Greece', *yunāni* 'Greek', Bab. LW *ya-ma-nu*, Elam. LW A. *hh.ya-u-na-ip* (pl.), *v.i-ya-u-na-ip* (pl.), *v.ya-u-na*, *v.ya-u-na-ap* (pl.), Hin. LW *yūnān* 'Greece', *yūnānī* 'Greek'. The same element is also seen in a number of cultural words: **yavana-** 'carrot,

Olibanum', **yavana.priya-** 'pepper', **yavanāla-**, **yonala-** 'Andropogon bicolor', **yavaneṣṭa-** 'Azadirachta indica, onion', **javanikā-**, **yavanikā-**, **yavanī-** 'curtain (in theatre)', **yamānikā-**, **yamānī-**, **yavānikā-**, **yavānī-** 'Carum copticum Benth.', Hin. *ajwān*, *ajwā'in*, *jawānī*, *jwā'in*.

2.2. LOAN TRANSLATIONS

aśvavāra- 'groom, horseman', Kror. *aśpavara-*, Prak. *āsavāra-*, Hin. *aśwavāra*, (NP. >) *aswār*, *sawār*, *suwār*, either directly from OP. *asa.bāra-* 'borne by a horse, horseman' (cf. Med. **aspa.bāra-*), or indirectly from Zor.MP. *aswār* (< OP. *asa.bāra-*). Cf. Bac. *ασβαρο-* in *ασβαροβιδο* 'leader of the horsemen', Khot. *aśśabārai*, NP. *asvār*, *savār*, Ōrm. *s(u)wâr*, Par. *sōwâr*, Paş. *swor*, Sang. *suvār*, Šuγ. *sawâr*, Wax. *s(u)wâr*, Yid. *s(u)wâr*. Av. *aspa-*, Med. **aspa-*, OP. *asa-*, Zor.MP./MP.T. *asp*, Khot. *aśśa-*, Sog. *'sp*, NP. *asb*, *asp*, Oss.D. *äfsä*, I. *jāfsā* 'mare', Paş. *ās*, Wax. *yaš*, Arm. LW *asp*. Riding was introduced into India from Iran.

kaṇṭhatrāṇa- 'neck-protector', Hin. *girebān*, *girībān* (< NP.), maybe a translation of Zor.MP. *grīwbān* 'gorget, neck-guard' < OIr. **grīvā.pāna-* 'neck-protector', Arm. LW *grīvpan* 'helmet'. Cf. Av. *grīvā-* 'neck', Zor.MP. *grīw*, NP. *gari* 'neck', *garibān* 'collar'. Cf. also Zor.MP. *grīkaft* '*neck-enclosure, *the head-protector of a horse in full armour, *τὸ προμετωπίδιον*'.

śirastrāṇa- 'head-protector, helmet', Hin. *sar*, *sār* (< NP.), maybe a translation of Zor.MP. *sārwār* < OIr. **sāra.vāra-* 'covering for the head'. Cf. Av. *sāra.vāra-* 'helmet', MP.T. *sārwār*, Arm. LW *sałauart* (< OIr. **sāra.varti-*). Cf. Av. *sarah-*, *sāra-* 'head', Pth.T./Zor.MP./MP.T./Pāz. *sar*, Sog.B. *s'r*, NP. *sar*, *-sār*, Ōrm. *sar*, Par. *sar*, *sōr*, Paş. *sar*, Sang. *sōr*, Wax. *sar*, Yid. *pusur*.

2.3. SANSKRIT WORDS SEMANTICALLY INFLUENCED BY THEIR IRANIAN EQUIVALENTS

āyatana- 'a place for the sacrificial fire, sacred place', perhaps influenced by OP. *āyadana-* 'sanctuary' < *ā-yad-* 'to worship', but phonetically doubtful.[7]

bodha(na)- 'burning incense, calling forth a perfume, exciting (of a perfume)', Hin. *bodhan(ī), bodhnī*, **bodhaya-** 'to revive the scent of a perfume', **prabodha(na)-** 'exciting (of a perfume), reviving (of an evaporated scent)', **udbodha-** 'fumigation'. The root **budh-** in the sense of 'to smell' is semantically influenced by Iranian. At a later date an EIr. form **βōla* 'gum-myrrh' (< OIr. **bauda-*) was borrowed into Skt. as **vola-** (or rather ***bola-**), Hin. *bol, vol, waul*. Hin. *bo, bū, bostān, būstān* (< NP.), cf. Av. *baod-* 'to perceive; to smell', *baoδah-* 'perception', *baoiδi-* 'fragrance, scent', Pth.T./Zor.MP./MP.T. *bōy* 'perception, scent, sense, smell', Pāz. *bōi*, Khot. *bū* 'incense, perfume', Sog.B. *βwδδh*, B.M. *βwδ*, B.M.S. *βwδh*, C. *bwd*, M. *βwδδ, βwwδ* 'incense, perfume, scent', NP. *bu(y)* 'smell', Ōrm. LW *būi* 'smell', Oss.D. *bodä*, I. *bud* 'incense', Par. LW *būi* 'smell', Sang. LW *būi*, Šuγ. LW *būi*, Wax. *vūl* (< **vūδ*), Yaγ. *vud, wud, wod*, Yid. LW *būi*, Arm. LW *boyr* 'perfume'; Pth.T. *bōδestān* 'garden', Zor.MP./MP.T. *bōyestān*, Pāz. *bōstą*, Sog.B.M.S. *βwδst'n, βwδstn*, C. *bwstn*, NP. *bostān, bustān*, Arm. LW *burastan*; Zor.MP. *bōy-* 'to smell', Khot. *buv-, bv-* 'to awake, to be aware, to know, to smell', Khwar. *'βwzy-* (< OIr. **ā-baudaya-*) 'to smell, perceive an odour', Sog.B. *βwδ-* 'to smell, to perfume'; Bal. *izbōxi* 'aniseed, migustum ajuwan' (< OIr. **uz-bauda(ka)-*); Oss.D. *bodän* 'garlic'.

kṣaharāta- 'a (dynastic ?) name on coins', from a later Ir. form *xšahr*. See also **kṣatra-, kṣatrapa-**.

---

[7] According to Bailey (1979: 109), *āyatana-* originally meant 'place' < *yat-* 'to place in its proper place'.

kṣatra- 'realm, territory', also in **ahi.kṣatra-** 'name of a town'. Skt. *kṣatra-* has only the abstract meaning 'dominion, might, power, sovereignty, supremacy', the concrete meaning (i.e. 'realm, territory') is influenced by Iranian. Hin. *shahr* (< NP.), cf. Av. *xšaθra-* 'dominion, kingdom', OP. *xšaça-*, Ins.Pth. *xšahr*, Pth.T./Zor.MP./MP.T. *šahr* 'city, country, kingdom, land, realm', Pāz. *šahar*, Bac. *þαυρο*, NP. *šahr*, Arm. LW *ašxarh* 'country, land, world' (< **axšahr* with a prothetic *a-*). See also **kṣaharāta-**, **kṣatrapa-**.

kṣatrapa-, rarely **chatrapa-**, **chatrava-** 'governor, (provincial) ruler, satrap' (recorded only at the beginning of the Christian era on coins and inscriptions, sometimes together with the name **kṣaharāta-**), probably from Pth. *xšahrap*. Cf. OP. *xšaça.pāvan-*, Ins.Pth. *xšahrap*, Ins.MP. *štrp*, Zor.MP. *šasab*, Bac. *þα(υ)ραβο* (< Pth.), NP. *šahrābān*, *šahrāvān*, *šahrbān*, *šahrvān*, Arm. LW *šahap*, *šahapet*, Gr. LW *σατράπης* < Med. **xšaθra.pāvan-*. Cf. also Aram. LW *'ḥšdrpn-*, wrongly vocalized (in pl.) *'ªḥašdarpᵉnayyā* (e.g. in Daniel 3: 2) for **axšadrapān-* < OP. **xšaça.pāna-*. See also **kṣatra-**, **kṣaharāta-**.

mitra- 'sun', Hin. *mitr(a)*, semantically influenced by Zor.MP. *mihr* 'Mithra; sun' < OP. **miça-* (LW *miθra-*, *mitra-*) 'friend; Mithras'. Cf. Av. *miθra-* 'contract; Mithra (Avestan god of the contract)', Ins.Pth./Pth.T./Ins.MP./Zor.MP./MP.T. *mihr* 'Mithra; sun', Pāz. *mihir*, Bac. *μιιρο*, *μιυρο*, *μιορο*, *μειρο*, *μιρο*, *μιρι*, *μιρρο*, wrongly also: *μορο*, *μυρο*, *μευρο*, *μιιορο*, Khwar. *myθ* 'day', Sog.B. *'myδr-*, M. *myš-*, S. *myδr'* 'Mithra', C. *myθ* 'day', M. *myr* 'sun', NP. *mehr*, Ōrm. *mēṣ̌*, Ōrm. of Kaniguram *mēṣ̌ʳ*, Waṇ. *mīr*, Yid. *mīra*, Arm. LW *meh-*, *merh-*, *mihr*, *mirh* 'Mithra', Bab. LW *mi-it-ri*, Elam. LW A. *hh.mi-iš-šá* (PN), *hhh.mi-iš-šá*. See also **mihira-**.

śaka.sthāna- 'Sakastān', a Sanskritization of Ir. *saka.stāna-*. Skt. *sthāna-* is used in a more abstract sense and not with reference to a country. Hin. *-stān*, *hindū-stān* (< NP.), cf. Zor.MP./MP.T. *sakestān*, Sog.C. *sγst'n*, NP. *sagestān*, *sakestān*, *sistān*,

Ar. LW *sijistān*, Arm. LW *-astan*, in e.g. *Hay-astan* 'Armenia'. See also **śaka-**.

vola- (or rather ***bola-**) 'gum-myrrh'. See **bodha(na)-**.

REFERENCES

BAGHBIDI, H. R. 2002. Ravābet-e Motaqābel-e Zabānhā-ye Irāni va Hendi-ye Bāstān va Miyāne [Reciprocal Relations between Old and Middle Iranian and Indian Languages]. *Nāme-ye Farhangestān 20*: 65-75.

BAILEY, H. W. 1943. Gāndhārī. *Bulletin of the School of Oriental and African Studies* 9: 764-797.

------ 1958. Languages of the Saka. In: *Handbuch der Orientalistik*. Erste Abteilung. Band IV. *Iranistik*. Abschnitt 1. *Linguistik*: 131-154. Leiden / Köln: E. J. Brill.

------ 1986. Iranian loanwords in Armenian. In: *Encyclopaedia Iranica*, II: 459-465. London / Boston / Henley: Routledge & Kegan Paul.

BURROW, T. 2001 [1955[1], 1973[3]]. *The Sanskrit Language*. Delhi: Motilal Banarsidass.

EMMERICK, R. E. 1983. Buddhism among Iranian Peoples. In: E. Yarshater (ed.), *The Cambridge History of Iran*, 3 (2): 949-964. Cambridge: Cambridge University Press.

FRYE, R. N. 1984. *The History of Ancient Iran*. München: C. H. Beck'sche Verlagsbuchhandlung.

FUSSMAN, G. 1986. Aśoka and Iran. In: *Encyclopaedia Iranica*, II: 780-781. London, Boston & Henley: Routledge & Kegan Paul.

HINÜBER O. von 1986. Zu einigen iranischen Namen und Titeln aus Brāhmī-Inschriften am oberen Indus. In: R. Schmitt & P. O. Skjaervø (eds.), *Studia grammatica Iranica: Festschrift für Helmut Humbach*: 147-162. (Münchener Studien zur Sprachwissenschaft, Beiheft 13.) München: J. Kitzinger.

HINZ, W. 1975. *Altiranisches Sprachgut der Nebenüberlieferungen*. Wiesbaden: Otto Harrassowitz.

LAUFER, B. 1967. *Sino-Iranica*. Taipei: Ch'eng-wen Publishing Company.

MALANDRA, W. W. 1973. A glossary of terms for weapons and armor in Old Iranian. *Indo-Iranian Journal* 15: 264-289.

MAYRHOFER, M. 1956, 1963, 1976. *Kurzgefaßtes etymologisches Wörterbuch des Altindischen*. Heidelberg: Carl Winter.

MODI, J. J. 1925. *King Akbar and the Persian Translations of Sanskrit Books*. Poona: Aryabhushan Press.

MONIER-WILLIAMS, M. 1992 [1899]. *A Sanskrit-English Dictionary*. Repr. Oxford: Oxford University Press.

MORGENSTIERNE, G. 1973. *Indo-Iranian Frontier Languages*. 3 Vols. 2nd ed. Oslo: Universitetsforlaget.

------ Early Iranic influence upon Indo-Aryan. In: *Acta Iranica* 1: 271-279. Téhéran-Liège: Bibliothèque Pahlavi.

NAQAVI, Š. 1353 A.H.S. = 1974. Ertebāt-e Fārsi va Sānskerit [The Relationship between Farsi and Sanskrit]. *Majalle-ye Dāneškade-ye Adabiyyāt va Olum-e Ensāni-ye Dānešgāh-e Tehrān* 85: 103-114.

PARPOLA, A. 2002. From the dialects of Old Indo-Aryan to Proto-Indo-Aryan and Proto-Iranian. In: Sims-Williams (ed.): 43-102.

SALOMON, R. 2002. Gāndhārī and the other Indo-Aryan languages in the light of newly-discovered Kharoṣṭhī manuscripts. In: Sims-Williams (ed.): 119-134.

SARKĀRĀTI, B. 1378 A.H.S.=1999. Širin Soxan: Pišine-ye Hend-o Orupa'i-ye Yek Estelāh-e Šā'erāne. In: *Sāyehā-ye Šekār Šode*: 349-361. Tehrān: Našr-e Qatre.

SCHMITT, R. 1989. Die Mitteliranischen Sprachen im Überblick. In: Schmitt (ed.): 95-105.

------ (ed.) 1989. *Compendium Linguarum Iranicarum*. Wiesbaden: Dr. Ludwig Reichert Verlag.

SIMS-WILLIAMS, N. 1989. Eastern Middle Iranian. In: Schmitt (ed.): 165-172.

------ 2002. Ancient Afghanistan and its invaders: Linguistic evidence from the Bactrian documents and inscriptions. In: Sims-Williams (ed.): 225-242.

------ (ed.) 2002. *Indo-Iranian Languages and Peoples*. Oxford: Oxford University Press.

SZEMERÉNYI, O. 1980. *Four Old Iranian Ethnic Names: Scythian-Skudra-Sogdian-Saka*. Wien: Österreichische Akademie der Wissenschaften.

THIEME, P. 1937. Über einige persische Wörter im Sanskrit. *Zeitschrift der Deutschen Morgenländischen Gesellschaft* 91: 88-146.

TURNER, R. L. 1989 [1966]. *A Comparative Dictionary of the Indo-Aryan Languages*. Repr. London: Oxford University Press.

Dictionaries consulted

BAILEY, H. W. 1979. *Dictionary of Khotan Saka*. Cambridge: Cambridge University Press.

BARTHOLOMAE, Ch. 1961 [1904]. *Altiranisches Wörterbuch*. 2nd ed. Berlin: Walter de Gruyter & Co.

BENZING, J. 1983. *Chwaresmischer Wortindex*. Wiesbaden: Otto Harrassowitz.

BOYCE, M. 1977. *A Word-List of Manichaean Middle Persian and Parthian.* (= Acta Iranica 9a.) Téhéran-Liège: Bibliothèque Pahlavi.

DAVARY, G. D. 1982. *Baktrisch, ein Wörterbuch auf Grund der Inschriften, Handschriften, Münzen und Siegelsteine.* Heidelberg: Julius Groos Verlag.

GHARIB, B. 1995. *Sogdian Dictionary (Sogdian-Persian-English).* Tehran: Farhangan Publications.

HENNING, W. B. 1971. *A Fragment of a Khwarezmian Dictionary.* Ed. by D. N. MacKenzie. London: Lund Humphries.

HINZ, W. & H. KOCH 1987. *Elamisches Wörterbuch*, I-II. Berlin: Dietrich Reimer Verlag.

KENT, R. G. 1953. *Old Persian Grammar, Texts, Lexicon.* New Haven, Connecticut: American Oriental Society.

MACKENZIE, D. N. 1971. *A Concise Pahlavi Dictionary.* 2nd ed. 1986. London: Oxford University Press.

NYBERG, H. S. 1974. *A Manual of Pahlavi*, II. Wiesbaden: Otto Harrassowitz.

PLATTS, J. T. 1911. *A Dictionary of Urdū, Classical Hindī, and English.* London: Crosby Lockwood and Son.

Abbreviations

A.	= Achaemenid (Elamite)	EIr.	= East Iranian
Akk.	= Akkadian	Elam.	= Elamite
Ar.	= Arabic	G.	= Gāθā (Avestan)
Aram.	= Aramaic	Gān.	= Gāndhārī
Arm.	= Armenian	Georg.	= Georgian
Ašk.	= Aškun	Gk.	= Greek
Aśok.	= Aśokan	gl.	= gloss
Av.	= Avestan	gr.	= gram
B.	= Buddhist (Sogdian)	Hin.	= Hindi
B.C.	= Before Christ	I.	= Iron (Ossetic)
B.Skt.	= Buddhist Sanskrit	i.e.	= *id est* (that is)
Bab.	= Babylonian	Ins.MP.	= Inscriptional Middle Persian
Bac.	= Bactrian	Ins.Pth.	= Inscriptional Parthian
Bal.	= Baluchi	Ir.	= Iranian
Bulg.	= Bulgarian	Kal.	= Kalāšā
c.	= *circa* (about)	Khot.	= Khotanese
C.	= Christian (Sogdian)	Khow.	= Khowar
cf.	= *confer* (compare)	Khwar.	= Khwarezmian
Chin.	= Chinese	Kror.	= Kroraina
D.	= Didor (Ossetic)	Kuš.Sak.	= Kušān Saka
e.g.	= *exempli gratia* (for example)	Lat.	= Latin

LW	=	loanword	pl.	=	plural
Lyc.	=	Lycian	PN	=	proper name
m.	=	masculine	Prak.	=	Prakrit
M.	=	Manichaean (Sogdian); Middle (Elamite)	Pth.T.	=	Parthian of Turfan
			Roš.	=	Rošanī
Med.	=	Median	Russ.	=	Russian
MIr.	=	Middle Iranian	S.	=	Sogdian (i.e. in Sogdian script)
Mong.	=	Mongolian	Sang.	=	Sanglīčī
MP.	=	Middle Persian	sg.	=	singular
MP.T.	=	Middle Persian of Turfan	Skt.	=	Sanskrit
N.	=	New (Elamite)	Sog.	=	Sogdian
N.Prak.	=	Niya Prakrit	Sum.	=	Sumerian
NInd.	=	New Indian	Šuγ.	=	Šuγnī
NIr.	=	New Iranian	Syr.	=	Syriac
NP.	=	New Persian	Tib.	=	Tibetan
O.	=	Old (Elamite)	Tum.	=	Tumshuqese
OInd.	=	Old Indian	Turk.	=	Turkish
OIr.	=	Old Iranian	Uigh.	=	Uighur
OP.	=	Old Persian	Waṇ.	=	Waṇecī
Ōrm.	=	Ōrmuṛī	Wax.	=	Waxī
Oss.	=	Ossetic	Y.	=	Younger (Avestan)
Pal.	=	Pali	Yaz.	=	Yazγulāmī
Par.	=	Parāčī	Yaγ.	=	Yaγnōbī
Paš.	=	Pašto	Yid.	=	Yidγa
Pāz.	=	Pāzand	Zor.MP.	=	Zoroastrian Middle Persian
Phal.	=	Phalura			

Further links between the Indo-Iranian substratum and the BMAC language

GEORGES-JEAN PINAULT

1. PRELIMINARY REMARKS

1.1. The present paper is a contribution to the prehistory of the Indo-Aryan languages, combined with the problem of language contacts in Central Asia. I take over the definition of the Indo-Iranian substratum proposed by Lubotsky (2001: 301-304): this part of the lexicon, while being safely reconstructed for the Indo-Iranian stage, constitutes a set of Indo-Iranian isolates that lack other Indo-European cognates; these words present characteristics of phonetic shape and word formation which preclude any Indo-European etymology.

This view had been anticipated by the numerous studies of Kuiper concerning the non-Indo-European sources of the Vedic vocabulary, which culminated in a reference book (1991). The claim has been made by Lubotsky (2001: 308), and about the same time by Witzel (1999: 342; 2000: 288), that a number of these words had been borrowed by the Indo-Iranians during their migrations from the north through Central Asia, and precisely before the entrance of the Indo-Aryans into the Indus basin. On their journey towards their future homelands, the Indo-Iranians, and perhaps the Indo-Aryans as the vanguard, wandering from the steppes, came into contact with a sedentary culture around the Oxus, also named BMAC, and were subject to multifarious influences from it.

1.2. BMAC stands for Bactria-Margiana Archaeological Complex, or the "Oxus culture" of the Bronze Age, ca. 2500-1500 BCE, flourishing in the period 2200-1700; it extended over a vast territory covering parts of northern Afghanistan, Turkmenistan, southern Uzbekistan, Tadjikistan, eastern Iran and Baluchistan. The restitution of this important urban culture of the Late Bronze Age is based on spectacular archaeological finds which have been the source of several conflicting hypotheses concerning the prehistory of the Indo-Aryans and Indo-Iranians.

I shall not discuss here the archaeological data, which lie beyond my competence (cf. Francfort 2001, with bibliography). I should like to add a further partner to the reconstruction of the words that have been adduced as borrowings from the time of the contacts of the Indo-Iranians (or Indo-Aryans) with the Oxus culture. This partner is Common Tocharian (henceforth CToch.), that is the ancestor of the two Tocharian languages, Tocharian A and Tocharian B, which are known from manuscripts found in the Tarim basin, in present-day Xinjiang (Western China), and ranging approximately from the sixth to eighth centuries CE. An anterior stage between 2500 and 1000 BCE of CToch. was the language of the Proto-Tocharians, the location of which was probably not confined to some oases in the Tarim basin.

In the debate on the diffusion of the lexicon of the language(s) spoken in the Oxus region around 2000 BCE, CToch. may offer interesting testimony, on two different grounds:

(i) In the Indo-European context, the respective prehistory of Tocharian and Indo-Iranian followed totally independent paths during the long period from their separation as dialects of Proto-Indo-European: they do not share common innovations in phonology, morphology or lexicon (cf. Adams 1984). Although the dialectal position of Tocharian vis-à-vis the other Indo-European languages is still a matter of debate among the few specialists, the fact of its independence from the Indo-Iranian branch is generally agreed upon..

(ii) There exists independent archaeological evidence for contacts between Xinjiang and BMAC and for the latter as a source of the material and non-material culture of the Proto-Tocharians: the use of mud bricks in domestic architecture, irrigation and agricultural techniques, various artefacts, the widespread use of Ephedra, especially in burials (cf. Mallory & Mair 2000: 269, 304-305, 311-313).

One may suspect that the Proto-Tocharians of the Late Bronze Age did borrow some lexical items together with the related technique: this fact is already documented by the word referring to the 'clay' used in building, that stays at the top of my list (see section 2.1). The source of this word is very probably identical with the corresponding item of the Indo-Iranian substratum: the CToch. word and the Indo-Iranian word are independent borrowings from a common source, located in the BMAC culture. Therefore one is justified to employ CToch. as a kind of "control language" for the assumption of connections between the Indo-Iranian and BMAC language(s) around 2000 BCE. The presence of the same items in CToch. would corroborate the evidence obtained from the Indo-Iranian substratum.

1.3. In the vocabulary of both Tocharian languages one can define a set of words that are isolates from CToch., on the basis of two arguments:

(i) They are without Indo-European etymology, or their morphological shape precludes any Indo-European etymology.

(ii) They cannot have been borrowed from Middle Iranian or Middle Indo-Aryan since they do not preserve the vowels with /a/ colour.

It is well known that the Tocharian languages have many loanwords from the Indian and Iranian languages, but those words belong to more recent stages in the development of these languages, when the speakers of Tocharian were in immediate contact with speakers of the Middle Iranian and Middle Indo-Aryan languages. After several decades of collecting the Tocharian loanwords, two dramatic phases seem to have been important, not excluding borrowings at other stages (Pinault 2002a: 243-246):

(i) the time when the speakers of Tocharian were in close contact with, and probably dominated by the Kushan empire (originally Yuezhi), whose official idiom was Bactrian, a Middle Iranian language which has passed on many words to CToch.;

(ii) the time of expansion of Buddhism in the Tarim basin, through missions from Gandhāra, which were responsible for the important impact of Indian and Buddhist culture along the roads to China.

With the progress of Sanskrit as the reference language, the later borrowings from Indo-Aryan were increasingly close to the Sanskrit norm. Nevertheless, there exists in the CToch. lexicon a definite layer of borrowings due to earlier contacts, which have been underestimated. Phonetic developments in these ancient borrowings are identical to developments from Old Iranian or even Indo-European sources: **a* > CToch. **æ* > Toch. B *e*, A *a*, cf. Toch. B *perne*, A *parāṃ* 'status, rank, glory' < CToch. **pærnæ* < Old Iranian (Scythian) **farnah* (cf. Lubotsky 2002: 191-195). Indo-European and Old Iranian **ā* > CToch. **å* > Toch. B *o*, A *a*, cf. B *procer*, A *pracar* 'brother' < CToch. **pråcær* < IE **bhrātēr*, etc. The examples analysed below will follow these basic principles.

2. RECONSTRUCTION OF SEVERAL WORDS, AS BORROWED INDEPENDENTLY BY COMMON TOCHARIAN AND INDO-IRANIAN IN THE LATE BRONZE AGE

All the following items are found in the lists of Witzel (1995, 1999 and passim) and Lubotsky (2001: 310-313), except Vedic *āṇí-* (2.3) and *paṇí-* (2.5), which, however, belong in the list of non-Aryan

RVic words established by Kuiper (1991: 90-93). It is likely that these lists are open to revision and correction, according to advances in research concerning possible contacts in the same geographical area. The scope may be modified by the perspective that can be gained with the aid of Tocharian, as well as from other non-Indo-European languages of Central Asia, if they can be identified with any precision.

2.1. **išt(i)*- 'clay, mud brick'

išt(i)*- 'clay, mud brick' has already been adduced by Witzel (1995: 103) as a borrowing from the BMAC language, cf. on the Indo-Iranian side, OPers. *išti*-, MPers. *xišt* 'brick', LateAv. *ištiia*- 'brick', *zəmōištuua*- 'brick of clay', Ved. *íṣṭakā*- fem. 'brick', *iṣṭikā*-, etc. (EWA I: 201; CDIAL: 72, No. 1600). Now, the corresponding Tocharian forms can be analysed more exactly: Toch. B *iścem* 'clay' (Adams, 1999: 67), *iścake (noted *iṣcake* in a St. Petersburg bilingual manuscript, the interpretation of which had long remained a puzzle) 'a kind of clay', from a paradigm Toch. B **iśce*, acc. sg. **iśc*, Toch. A **iśäc* (or **iśc*) borrowed into Old Turkic (Uighur) *išič*, *äšič* '(earthenware) cooking pot', through an easy way of metonymy (for the details, see Pinault 2002b: 326-331). The stem **išt(i)*- was integrated into the inflection of *i*-stems in Common Tocharian, according to a living morphological pattern: nom. sg. **iśce* < **istēy*, with regular phonetic developments. Accordingly, it remains uncertain whether the word was **išti*- at the time of its borrowing, and whether its interpretation as an *i*-stem furthered this new inflection: the Vedic and Iranian data are ambiguous on this point, since they are to some extent compatible with a stem originally ending in a consonant.

2.2. **athr̥* 'superior, overcoming force'

2.2.1. I reconstruct this lexeme as the missing link between the CToch. word meaning 'hero' and the well-known Indo-Iranian term reflected by Vedic *átharvan*- and Av. *āθrauuan*-/*aθaurun*-

(see Pinault 2003b for a more detailed discussion). This form would have become directly CToch. **æträ,* which ought to be remade as **ætræ* after the numerous stems in **-ræ* (< **-ro-*, cf. Toch. A *wir* 'vigorous, youthful' < **wiræ* < IE **wiHró-*, cf. Ved. *vīrá-*, Av. *vīra-*, Lith. *výras*, etc.) and because of the reference to a human being, hence Toch. B *etre* A *atär* 'hero' (compare Adams 1999: 81, without any convincing etymology). This noun is applied to Rāma, the famous figure of the Indian epos. The word in the Indo-Iranian substratum has been reconstructed as *$^*at^h$aru̯an-* 'priest' by Lubotsky (2001: 310), assuming an irrational variation *-ar-/-ra-* in order to account for the Iranian facts (2001: 303).

My own reconstruction differs on both the semantic and formal sides. There is now general agreement on the fact that the transposed Indo-Iranian lexeme **atharwan-* did not originally refer to a "fire-priest", but its etymological analysis remains an enigma (cf. EWA I: 60 and 805). On the Iranian side, Avestan *āθrauuan-/aθaurun-* (later Pehlevi *āsrōn*) means 'priest' (in general), and its formal shape can be explained by the secondary connection of the basic alternating paradigm **atharwan-/*atharun-* > **aθa(u)rwan-/*aθaurun-* (cf. Hoffmann & Narten 1989: 90 n. 14; Hoffmann & Forssman 1996: 56 and 145; somewhat differently, de Vaan 2003: 65), with the noun referring to 'fire', reflected by Avestan *ātar-* masc. (sg. nom. *ātarš*, acc. *ātrəm*, gen. *āθrō*, etc.).

This word *ātar-*, which is devoid of any matching Indo-Aryan form, has now received an independent etymology, from an IE root $*H_2eH_{1/3}$- meaning 'to be hot, burn', cf. Palaic *ḫā-*, Lat. *ātrium*, etc. (Melchert 1994: 78; Adams 1995: 209). In Indo-Aryan, Vedic *átharvan-* was not initially restricted to the realm of private sorcery. In the RV, *átharvan-*, being used mostly in the singular, refers to a mythical priest, one of the primaeval institutors of the sacrifice (Macdonell 1897: 139, 141). Later, in the lexicon of the AV, the plural *átharvāṇaḥ* gained the specialized meaning 'magicians, sorcerers', and was also used, by way of metonymy, as referring to auspicious magical charms (Bloomfield 1899: 1, 8-10). In Old

Indo-Aryan, the alternation of the final syllable of the stem was remade, hence the strong stem *átharvān-*, on the model of regular *-an*-stems.

The analysis of the Indo-Iranian word as **athar-wan-/-un-* remains morphologically possible, and is even more likely, since Indo-Iranian has other ancient religious terms with the same alternating suffix, cf. Ved. *maghávan-*, Av. *magauuan-* 'possessing or distributing gifts, liberal' (derived from *maghá-*, which may itself be of foreign origin, cf. Lubotsky 2001: 311), Ved. *r̥tā́van-*: Av. *aṣ̌auuan-/aṣ̌āun-* 'righteous, truthful' (derived from Ved. *r̥tá-*, Av. *aṣ̌a-*, whose IE pedigree is generally accepted). It is also recommended by the fact that ancient Vedic preserves some traces, albeit in rare and somewhat unclear words, of a stem **athar-*.

2.2.2. How can we combine the senses of the CToch. word meaning 'hero' and of the Indo-Iranian priestly title? Although 'hero' can be expressed by various lexemes in the IE languages, one may agree that a 'hero' is the incarnation of a victorious force, an all-powerful force. This concept of 'superior, overcoming force' can also be applied to the power of the "magician" or of the "priest" in general, who is in control of holy and supernatural forces. "Magic" has often been conceived as effective 'action', see Skt. *kr̥tyā-*, OEngl. *wicce-craeft*, Engl. *witchcraft*. On the Indo-Iranian side, an alternative scenario would presuppose that the original meaning of **athar-wan-* was 'a person endowed with a superior force' > 'powerful man', a designation that would fit the sense 'lord, king', effectively both king and priest (on the king-priest in Vedic, see Schmidt 1968: 238). The lexeme would have been later restricted, in both Avestan and Vedic, to the meaning 'priest', and alternatively 'magician' in the popular parallel tradition down to the AV.

A partly parallel development can be exemplified by another possible archaic designation of the original king-priest, cf. Vedic *kaví-* 'seer, sage, poet' (restricted to the religious sphere) vs. Av.

kauui- 'lord, prince'. One can find in the literature previous semantic interpretations of the lexical basis Vedic **athar-* as expressing 'magical power'. Actually, several passages of the RV preserve relics of this noun **athar-* in non-religious contexts: adj. *atharyú-*, *atharvī́-*, subst. *atharī́-*, all hapax legomena. The decisive locus is RV IV.6.8cd *uṣarbúdham athar(í)yo ná dántaṃ, śukrā́ṃ s(u)vā́sam paraśúṃ ná tigmám* '(this god, Agni) who awakes at dawn, who is bright like the tooth of the *atharī́-*, whose mouth is beautiful, who is sharp like an axe'. It has been correctly seen that the mysterious word, sometimes left untranslated, refers to a fierce animal (*mṛgá-*), which may be either an elephant or a boar, remarkable for its visible tusks or teeth. The second solution is supported by the existence in Indo-Iranian, and still in Vedic, of the mythological figure of the furious boar. The archaic theme of the sharp teeth is expressed in the above passage by *paraśúṃ ná tigmám* (in comparison with the flames) and elsewhere by the compound *áyo-daṃṣṭra-* 'having teeth (as sharp) as metal' (epithet of the boar, *varā́hu-*, in RV I.88.5d, concerning the Maruts), both expressions going back to Indo-Iranian phraseology, cf. Av. *tiži.dąstra-* 'with sharp fangs' in the description of Vərəθraγna in the shape of an aggressive boar, in Yašt X, 70. In other texts, this male hero is incarnated as a boar, *varāza-* (e.g. Yašt XIV, 15). In India as well as in Iran, the 'boar' was seen as the archetypal adversary and the animal double of the hero (Watkins 1995: 316, 325), cf. also 'boar' in many proper names in both onomastic traditions, cf. LateAv. *Varāza-*, MPers. *Barāz*, Skt. *Varāha-*, etc. Therefore, RV *atharī́-* can be interpreted as meaning 'endowed with superior, heroic force', hence 'formidable', used in RV IV.6.8c as a poetical substitute for the usual name of the animal: RVic *varāhá-*, *varā́ha-*, *varā́hu-*, corresponding to Av. *varāza-*, while these various forms reflect a lexeme which was also very probably found in the Indo-Iranian substratum (Lubotsky 2001: 311). The same replacement, maybe by force of taboo, can be assumed for *athar-yú-* (RV VII.1.1c, Agni as housemaster), *athar-vī́-* (RV I.112.10a, concerning the victorious female Viśpalā) 'chasing the formidable beast' (= the boar, as an incarnation of the superior force), cf. *takva-vī́-* 'chasing swift beasts', *varāha-yú-* 'hunting the boar', etc.

One may reconstruct the story as follows: when the foreign noun **athar-*, referring to a supernatural force, was borrowed into Vedic, it was not initially restricted to the priestly sphere: in a given part of the poetic tradition, it soon semantically shifted into a poetic term for the typical heroic animal, but did not remain in use, since no connection was any longer understood between this specialized usage and the new derivative Vedic *átharvan-* < **athar-wan-*, that became a living designation of the priest, having evolved from its early reference to the king-priest. On the phonetic level, the common compatible form for Common Tocharian and Indo-Iranian would be **athr̥* > **athar*, regularly in Avestan and partly (dialectally) in Old Indo-Aryan, cf. *ū́dhar* 'udder' < **ū́dhr̥* < IE **(H)uHdh-r̥*, related to Gk. *oûthar*, MHG *ūter*, etc. (Hoffmann & Forssman 1996: 91; Pinault 1989: 38-47).

2.3. **āni-* (**āṇi-*) 'hip'

2.3.1. The CToch. basis for this reconstruction is Toch. B *oñiye*, loc.sg. *oñi-ne*, translating Skt. *śroṇi-* (PK AS 2A [= Y1 Filliozat] a6), a word which has resulted from a new study of this bilingual medical manuscript (cf. Carling 2003: 40, 48, 64). The form Toch. B *oñiye*, which belongs to a well-known type of inflection in Tocharian, can be traced back to IE **āni-ēn*, borrowed from a non-IE source with a productive Tocharian nasal suffix. Since Tocharian does not possess retroflex consonants, the type of middle nasal in the source word cannot be determined.

I have proposed (see Pinault 2003a for a more detailed discussion) connecting the source **āni-* (or *āṇi-*) of this word with the noun Skt. *āṇi-*, which is known from early times. However, there is no Iranian match and until now its original meaning has remained in the dark, and consequently its etymology, too (EWA I: 161-162). In Indo-Aryan, *āṇí-* (MW: 134a) refers to two different things: (1)

'axle-pin' in the RV, that is a bolt or wedge used to secure the wheel of the chariot (*rátha-*) in its place (Sparreboom 1985: 30), later 'linch-pin, peg, bolt', also known in more recent Indo-Aryan, cf. Pāli *āṇi-*, etc. (CDIAL: 50, No. 1110); (2) 'the part of the leg just above the knee' (Suśruta). This word was for long interpreted as a borrowing from Dravidian, which in several languages displays a similar word of identical meaning, 'linch-pin' (cf. DED: 26, No. 295). It is now conceived rather as borrowed from Sanskrit into Dravidian (DED-R, App. 10: 509; see also Kuiper 1991: 89).

But the old question remains: how can we reconcile the two different meanings of the Sanskrit word? I assume that the primitive meaning was 'hip, haunch': the reference to a part of the leg in the medical terminology is due to an anatomical transfer by contiguity, according to a well-documented process, compare Fr. *cuisse* 'thigh' from Lat. *coxa* (cognate with Ved. *kákṣa-*, etc.) 'haunch'. Because of the importance of the chariot in RVic poetry, the most ancient meaning recorded refers to a part of this vehicle. The two linch-pins at both extremities of the axle of the chariot should have been named according to a well-known metaphorical transfer from parts of the body to corresponding parts of the chariot: they are (or they represent the essential constituent of) the 'hips' of the chariot, other parts of which have been named after various body parts, cf. *ratha-mukhá-* (AV) 'face of the chariot', *ratha-śīrṣá-* (ŚB) 'head of the chariot', referring to the forepart, see also *nā́bhi-* 'nave' of the wheel and 'navel', etc. (Sparreboom 1985: 122-133), and similar facts in other IE languages (Huld 2000: 103-111). Later, the transferred meaning 'linch-pin' of Indo-Aryan *āṇí-* was generalized and applied to other technologies.

2.3.2. The crucial evidence for the primitive meaning of Vedic *āṇí-* as the designation of a body part, and specifically 'hip, haunch', is concealed in a very famous adjective, Vedic *kalyā́ṇa-* 'beautiful'. This word has acquired later a wide range of positive meanings: 'agreeable, virtuous, good, salutary, prosperous, lucky, well, right'

(MW: 263b); it is known down to modern Indo-Aryan (cf. CDIAL: 150, No. 2952), but the reference to physical beauty is still pregnant in many Vedic examples. The adjective is mostly used as feminine, *kalyāṇī́-*, in the RV (3x, against 1x masculine in a relatively late hymn of Book I) as well as in the AV (13x, always feminine), hence it is reasonable to assume that the masculine was probably secondarily derived from the feminine form, cf. *sapátna-* masc. 'rival' after *sapátnī-*, originally feminine.

The word cannot be properly analysed as a derivative using a registered suffix: the retroflex nasal in the last syllable has remained a puzzle. The etymology from an IE compound **kali-ōlno-* (with Fortunatov's Law: **-ln-* > Indo-Aryan *-ṇ-*, parallel to IE **-lt-* > *-ṭ-*, etc.) 'having beautiful elbows' (according to Wackernagel, 1934), cf. Gk. *kalli-* and *ōllón*, *ōlên*, *ōlénê*, Lat. *ulna*, OHG *elina*, etc. (IE **(H)ol-en-* with various Ablaut grades), is very brilliant, but was never fully accepted (see EWA I: 325-326). Semantically, it is not especially appealing, since it applies to the ancient Vedic world an idealized and prudish view of feminine beauty, which was designed after the supposed canons of Homeric poetry.

We may now offer a much simpler interpretation, by reformulating the interpretation as a bahuvrīhi compound: **kaly-āṇi-H-*, recharacterized as feminine (of the *vr̥kī́*-type < **-i-H_2-*) in Old Indo-Aryan from **kaly-āṇi-* 'having beautiful hips', then simply 'beautiful' (of a woman). The reinterpretation as the regular feminine of a stem *kalyā́ṇa-* after a productive pattern was made easy by the obsolescence of the adjective **kali-* 'beautiful, good' in the standard Vedic language. Since in the same idiom *āṇí-* had became specialized as the name of the axle-pin, the compound structure became totally obscured. But the same concept had received other expressions in the conventional language of RVic poetry. The reconstructed meaning of *kalyāṇī́-* is quite banal. Actually, Proto-Vedic **kaly-āṇi-* is perfectly synonymous with Vedic *su-śroṇi-* 'having beautiful hips', and very close to other compounds describing the Indian ideal of feminine beauty, cf. *pr̥thu-śroṇi-*

'having large hips', *pr̥thu-jāghanā-* 'having large buttocks', etc. Therefore, **kaly-āṇi-* originally belonged to a variety of ancient Vedic characterized by dialectal differences from the standard language, as testified by the presence of the liquid /l/: taken from this "poetic dialect", the forms *kalyāṇī́-* and *kalyā́ṇa-* were integrated into the standard Vedic poetic language.

The new hypothesis confirms the IE pedigree of the first member **kal-i-*, which shows an IE morphological structure, with cognates in other languages, as seen by Wackernagel. There are still indirect remnants in Old Indo-Aryan of IE **kal-i-* 'beautiful, well done', see the proper name *Kalí-* (RV, name of a man whose beauty and vigour were restored by the gods Aśvin), and perhaps also the substantive *káli-* masc., which should be conceived as a euphemistic term for the losing result (number one) in the *akṣa* game, then naming the worst condition, the worst age, etc. (for various other solutions, see EWA I: 322). There is no further trace of a first compound member **kali-*, the place of which is occupied in Indo-Aryan by the overall positive prefix *su-* 'good'. As an equivalent of the "normal" Vedic compound *su-śroṇi-*, **kali-āṇi-* should have been coined through substitution of the second member, possibly from the expected form **kali-śloṇi-* 'having beautiful hips' in a Vedic *l*-dialect. While showing phonetic differences from the predominant Vedic dialect, which had the sole liquid /r/, this marginal dialect, bound to become obsolete, was also very archaic, by the preservation of the first compound member **kali-*, the match of which can be found in numerous ancient Greek (Homeric) compounds. Otherwise, standard Vedic kept *śróṇi-* 'hips and loins' (mostly dual) = Av. *sraoni-*, the ancient term inherited from Indo-European (EWA II: 671).

The precise motivation for the replacement of **ślóṇi-* (= *śróṇi-*) by *āṇí-* in this compound eludes us, and one can only present some hypotheses: it may be due to the desire, in some ancient Vedic "school" of poets, to avoid the usual and common name of this body part in a poetic compound. Another factor could have been the usage of this word in the donor language for referring to representations of women with prominent hips, which are known from numerous artefacts from the Oxus culture (cf. Francfort 1994: 407, 410-411) as well as from other adjacent cultures, to wit Elam and Indus (Francfort 2001: 154-155). This component of feminine beauty later became a permanent feature of Indian art.

2.4. ***ćarwa- 'hunting, living in the forest'**

ćarwa- is admitted by Lubotsky (2001: 311) as the name of a god, that would account for Vedic *Śarvá-* (AV +), one of the names of Rudra, and LateAv. *Sauruua-*, name of a Daēva 'demon'. I should like to broaden the scope of this reconstruction, by assuming as secondary the usage of the noun as a theonym in Indo-Iranian: it originally meant 'hunting, living in (from) the forest'. This reconstructed form is reflected directly in CToch. **śærwæ* > B *śer(u)we* A *śaru* 'hunter'. In Toch. B, the noun shows the inflection of an *n*-stem, with individualizing value, and consequently as from a base **særu-*, according to an internal process (see also the adjectival derivative *śerwäññe* 'pertaining to a hunter'): precisely, the verb Toch. B inf. *śeritsi* 'to hunt' can easily be analysed as the denominative based on this shorter form (stem CToch. **śærw-yä-* with the result of the IE suffix **-ye/o-*). The existence of this verb is incompatible with the previous etymologies of the Toch. noun (on which, see Adams 1999: 634). I have been unable to make sense of the IE connections that have been proposed so far:

(i) Adams prefers the derivation from the IE noun for 'wild animal' (cf. Gk. *thêr*, Lith. *žvėr̃is*, OCS *zvěrĭ*, Lat. *ferus*, etc.), hence IE **ĝʰwēr-wo-*, which is semantically possible, but the function of the suffix would remain problematic, and the development of the initial cluster would be unexpected.

(ii) Another current etymology is from IE **k̂ērw-o-*, connected with the abundant word family of 'horn' (Nussbaum 1986: 8, taking over a suggestion of Jasanoff, cf. Lat. *cervus*, Welsh *carw* 'stag', Ved. *śarabhá-* '(a kind of) deer', for possible comparanda in the Nuristani languages, cf. CDIAL: 715, No. 12341), but the resulting gloss as 'he of the stag' (which bears some kind of Germanic flavour) is not particularly appealing, since hunting was never limited to stags or horned animals, especially in Central Asia.

Therefore, one should go back to the consequences to be drawn from the striking formal resemblance of the CToch. noun to Vedic *Śarvá-* and Av. *Sauruua-*. The connection between the CToch. nouns meaning 'hunter' and Indo-Iranian was already made by Bailey, but he interpreted the relevant forms as genuine Indo-Iranian, as derived from IE. Besides the above theonym, Iranian **sarw-* > **saur-* is also the basis of Ossetic Digor *sorun, surd*, Iron *sūryn, syrd* 'to chase, hunt' (Bailey 1970: 23), Digor *sird*, Iron *syrd* 'wild beast', Khotanese *hasūrä, husure* < **fra-saura-* 'quarry, hunted beast' (Bailey 1975: 11 n. 22; 1979: 474).

Alternatively, one may assume that there existed a prehistoric basis **ćarw-* 'to hunt' for the noun **ćarwa-* 'hunter'. Going back to Indo-Aryan, the Vedic god *Śarvá-* is frequently associated with the god called *Bhavá-* in the AV: both names are, among several others, assigned to Rudra, although these two gods seem to have been regarded in the AVic tradition as distinct from one another and from Rudra (cf. Macdonell 1897: 75). They are invoked in order to slay enemies with their destructive arrows. Accordingly, the name *Śarvá-* was secondarily connected with *śáru-* fem. 'missile, spear, arrow' (see the literature in EWA II: 621), but this does not go beyond the scope of popular etymology (still represented in MW: 1057a).

The god Śarva shares many features of Rudra, as master of the wild beasts, and as the protector of hunters. He is depicted as an 'archer' (*ástr̥-* in AVŚ VI.93.1, 2, *iṣvāsá-* in AVŚ XV.5.2), although other gods are called *iṣvāsá-* in the last-mentioned hymn (cf. AVŚ XV.5.1, 3-7). Therefore, one should consider the formal source **ćarwa-* as having a full semantic content which originally referred to hunting and living in the wilds. The semantic evolution in Indo-Iranian was relatively straightforward: 'hunting, hunter' = 'living in the wilds' > 'god of the wilds, killer of living beings'.

2.5. *_pani-_ (*_paṇi-_) 'wealthy' (or 'wealth, possession')

This lexeme is reconstructed as the source of Vedic *paṇí-*, masc., which is basically the proper name of foreign (non-Aryan) people, who were mythologized as a class of hostile demons, together with the Dāsas and the Dasyus, see for instance the famous RVic dialogue hymn X.108 concerning the recovery of the cows retained by the Paṇis in a rocky fortress. In the RV, the name is attested in both the singular (22 times) and the plural (28 times): the singular can be interpreted as referring to the chief of the Paṇis or to the "typical" man representative of these people, that is the rich lord who does not give the proper remuneration to the priest or the poet (cf. RV I.182.3, IV.25.7, VI.53.3, VIII.45.14, VIII.64.2, X.60.6), because the Paṇis in general do not observe the rules of Aryan religion and culture (cf. *áhaviṣ-* I.182.3, *ásunvant-* IV.25.7, *aśraddhā́-*, *ayajñá-* VII.6.3, *avratá-*, *ádevayu-* VIII.97.3). The traditional figure of the Paṇis hiding their treasures (*nidhí-*, *vásu-*, *maghá-*, etc.) and keeping watch over their wealth is maintained in the mythological narratives which depict them as primaeval enemies of the Aryan people (cf. RV I.32.11, II.24.6, IV.58.4, VI.39.2, IX.111.2, X.108.2, 7).

It is now generally accepted that the traditional interpretation with an appellative sense, as 'bargainer, miser, niggard' (see for instance MW: 580b, from the root *paṇ-*, whose verbal forms and derivatives are much more recent, see below) was mistaken: it inspired the most usual renderings of this noun in the current translations of the RV (Oldenberg, Geldner, Renou, etc.). It was first demonstrated by Hillebrandt (1916), and more recently confirmed with other arguments by Schmidt (1968: 209-214), that this name referred to non-Aryan adversaries, secondarily conceived as demons. This fact was clearly seen in accordance with the shape of the word, which does not have any well-founded IE etymology

(EWA II: 70). Since they were, according to the location of a battle (RV VI.61.1), residing in Arachosia (cf. Hillebrandt 1916: 519), they could be easily identified as an Iranian tribe, which is known from Greek sources as the *Párnoi*, living originally in the Oxus region, and more precisely in Margiana (cf. Parpola 1988: 222-224). Corresponding to an Iranian form **Parna-* (> Gk. *Párnos*), the Vedic form *paṇí-* could be interpreted as going back to **pr̥ṇi-* with "Prakritic" development (Wackernagel 1918: 411; Parpola 1988: 224). There are two objections to this scenario:

(i) The variation of suffix and Ablaut between **parna-* and **pr̥ṇi-*, which is very difficult to account for, if it really refers to the same foreign tribe, remains an *ad hoc* hypothesis.

(ii) From the alleged point of departure, one would rather expect Indo-Aryan **puṇí-*, because of the preceding bilabial consonant (von Hinüber 2001: 127), without any motivation for later reintroducing the /a/ vocalism.

Therefore, I see another possibility, by introducing into the debate a CToch. word that could be a loan from this noun, as known in the Oxus region: **pæniyā* > B *peñiyo* (adj. *peñiyatstse* 'splendid') A *pañi* 'splendour'. This Tocharian lexeme is deprived of any good IE etymology (cf. the tentative analysis mentioned in Adams 1999: 394). The CToch. form may be interpreted as an abstract of a productive type based on the foreign word **pani-* (or **paṇi-*, see above the same problem for Toch B *oñiye* from **āni-* or **āṇi-*) meaning 'wealthy, rich'.

Alternatively, the original meaning of **pani-* (**paṇi-*) could have been 'wealth, richness' and CToch. **pæniyā* was some kind of re-characterization based upon this word. Accordingly, the foreign class of men named by the Aryans *Paṇáyaḥ* were already conceived in their original language as 'the rich ones' or the personification of wealth: this name, secondarily affected to an imaginary hostile people, corresponded to a precise part of this foreign society, to which belonged the owners of wealth, either landlords or merchants. The original meaning of the noun was adequately reflected by the predominant characteristic of the Paṇis in the RV: they personified the possessors of archetypal 'wealth', but full of bad connotations, that is the wealth that is not given for pious actions, but kept for private use and exchanged in trade, contrary to the precepts of Aryan society. Hence, they were conceived as forming a group of hostile people, dwelling in remote and fortified places: does this latter image refer to original ware-houses? Once adapted in Indo-Iranian (or Indo-Aryan), the name did not preserve its appellative sense.

Consequently, the identification with the people known by Greek historians as *Párnoi*, living in Arachosia, may still stand: one may interpret this form as reflecting a local variant (extended from Indo-Aryan to Iranian) of the original name *Paṇí-*, plural *Paṇáyaḥ*, with "intrusive" *-r-*, that is original *-ṇ-* "naturalized" as *-rṇ-* (on this widespread phenomenon, see Kuiper 1991: 70-81). This process is indirectly proven by the proper name *Parṇáya-*, which in the late RV (I.53.8, X.48.8) designates an enemy of King Atithigva.

However, the story of *paṇi-* in Indo-Aryan does not end here: one is tempted to seek another possible reflex of this foreign word **pani-* (*paṇi-*) meaning 'wealth' or 'wealthy' in the nominal derivative *páṇya-* nt. 'an article of trade, a ware' (ŚB +), perhaps originally meaning 'provided with trading value'. Starting from this derivative, the verbal root which was formerly assumed as the basis of the name *paṇí-*, may have been secondarily extracted: *paṇ-*, present *páṇate* 'to negotiate, bargain, barter' (JB +).

This root has traditionally been interpreted as coming from a "Prakritic" form of a thematized nasal present: **paṇāti* < **pr̥ṇā-ti*, cf. Gk. *pérnêmi*, OIr. *renim* 'to sell' (EWA II: 69). It is contradicted by the development of Vedic (RV +) *pr̥ṇā́ti, pr̥ṇáti* 'to fill' and *pr̥ṇā́ti* 'to give' from two different IE roots. The detailed discussion of this last moot point, which goes beyond the reconstruction of the BMAC word **pani-* (*paṇi-*), should be reserved for a later occasion.

2.6. ***anću- ‘rusty red (brown)’**

2.6.1. ***anću-*** is admitted by Lubotsky (2001: 304, 310) as meaning ‘Soma plant’, being the substratum source of Ved. *aṃśú-* ‘Soma plant’ and LateAv. *ąsu-* ‘Haoma plant’; the original term should “probably” refer to Ephedra. This claim presupposes that the Soma/Haoma cult had been borrowed from the BMAC culture together with the name of the plant. I shall not further discuss the implications of this view, which are of dramatic importance for Indo-Iranian religion (cf. Parpola 1995). It is better to set aside the archaeological and botanical problems surrounding the alleged traces of Ephedra in vessels that have been found at BMAC sites (see most recently Bakels 2003).

While accepting that the Soma/Haoma plant was some kind of Ephedra, I shall not dwell further within the limited scope of this paper on this much debated issue. It may suffice to refer to the two papers published by Falk on this problem: the first (1989) reviews the whole previous literature and concludes with the identification of the prototype of the plant with Ephedra, and the second (2003) answers objections, discusses more recent literature and puts forward additional arguments in favour of this identification. The same conclusion is put forward by Kashikar (1990). A very useful discussion of the whole problem, with abundant bibliography, has been provided by Houben (2003), in his report of the conference held at Leiden University in July 1999. I shall simply recall that one of the strongest arguments for Ephedra is the following: various kinds of Ephedra that are still in use in the same area (the Indus valley and surroundings in Afghanistan) bear names that ultimately go back to the descendants of Indo-Iranian **sauma-* (Flattery & Schwartz 1989: 68-70; Falk 2003: 149): *hum/huma*, *hom*, *um/uma*, *som*, *sumani*, etc.

One should not place too much importance on the frequent use of the action noun *máda-* for describing the effects of Soma drinking: it means ‘excitement, inebriation’, which is not the same as hallucination or ecstasy, implying loss of contact with plain reality.

Judging from the description of poetic inspiration by the poets themselves, Soma drinking did help them, as a stimulant, to compose poetry, and this fact blatantly contradicts the concept of Soma as a hallucinogenic beverage: one would not compose such elaborate hymns under the negative effects of drugs. The so-called *laba-sūkta* (RV X.119), which is full of "ecstatic" imagery, is in itself not probative, since the poet places the text, as 'self-praise' (*ātma-stuti*), in the mouth of a god: it does not describe an actual experience of Soma drinking by humans (even under the gratuitous supposition that they were shamans of sorts), as a clinical or ethnological report would do. Starting from Lubotsky's reconstruction, I would nevertheless modify the semantic description of the Indo-Iranian lexeme. It is a well-known fact that Indo-Iranian **sáu-ma-* (> Ved. *sóma-*, Av. *haoma-*) was not originally the name of the plant but of the product derived from it by pressing: it meant 'what is pressed' (from the root Ved. *su-* 'to press'), and actually referred to the juice. This motivated and transparent name, that fits the level of sacred speech, obviously results from the early thinking of learned Indo-Iranian people.

One is, of course, too easily tempted to find the "true" name of the Soma/Haoma in another word, preferably one of obscure form. It is true that Ved. *aṃśú-* (45 occurrences in the RV, from which only five plural forms; besides, three occurrences of the adjective *aṃśumánt-*) is used in the hymns as one of the names of the Soma plant (see Macdonell 1897: 104-105; Brough 1971: 336-338), but one may doubt that it had solely this reference. The concrete meaning 'thread' is known later from Pāli *aṃsu-*, as well as 'fibre' (of plant or fruit) in the modern Indo-Aryan languages (CDIAL: 1, No. 4). The semantic evolution is expected if the Soma plant was seen as fibrous or characterized by dense twigs. The reference to the 'stalk' or 'stem', while being possible in several passages of the RV (and preferred by some translators, such as Geldner and Renou), is clearly implied by the usage of the noun in the ritual literature, especially by the reference to several (two, six, etc.)

'twigs', 'sprigs' or 'stalks' of the plant (cf. Caland & Henry 1906: XXIII, 63, 153-158). Various ritual actions are performed by handling several 'units', that is sprigs or stalks, of Soma (cf. for instance TS VI.4.5.3-5-7, ŚB 4.1.1.3-4, XI.5.9.6-8-12, XII.6.1.19). The contrast between Soma as a god and *aṃśú-* as a material unit is clear from the following mantra (TS I.2.11a, etc. quoted in ŚB III.4.3.19) *aṃśur-aṃśuṣ ṭe deva somāpyāyatām indrāyaikadhanavide* 'Let stalk after stalk of thine swell strong, O divine Soma, for Indra, the winner of one part of the booty!'. It is true that in Vedic literature, *aṃśú-* refers only to the twigs of the Soma plant, and not of any other plant, but it is only to be expected, given the prestige of the hymns, where the word was used in hieratic language for the whole Soma plant: in this poetic usage, it can be explained by a commonplace metonymy, and by the pressure to give many names to Soma. Therefore, I shall assume that **anću-* originally referred to the 'twig' or 'stalk', as a special term given to the "body" of the holy plant, which was the most important part for ritual purposes.

2.6.2. There exists in Tocharian no word of similar form referring to a plant or part of a plant. From the Tocharian vocabularies, we have Toch. A **añcu* 'iron', the basis of the derived adjective *añcwāṣi* 'made of iron', to which corresponds Toch. B *eñcuwo*, with the parallel derived adjective *eñcuwaññe* 'made of iron'. These words are well attested, and the meaning is ensured by their occurrence as translating Skt. *ayas-* 'iron'. The two forms go back to CToch. **æñcuwæn-*, nom. sg. **æñcuwō*, the final part of which is a regular product of IE **-ōn*. Nasal enlargement (< IE **-on-*) of nominal stems is very common in Tocharian. This noun is deprived of any convincing IE etymology (cf. Adams 1999: 80), which is not surprising, since IE did not have a common word for 'iron'. The connection with an Iranian form **aśwanya-* according to Bailey (1957: 55-56), which does not fit in with the first cluster, was later abandoned (Bailey 1979: 32, 487). The CToch. form may reflect a term proper to the Central Asiatic region, cf. Chorasmian *hnčw* 'iron' ('iron tip', see Benzing 1983: 319) < Iranian **anśuwan-* (Schwartz, 1974: 409): the formal shape is extremely close to the CToch. transposition, so that the Iranian and Tocharian words may have been borrowed from a common substratum language.

The problem now becomes: if the original meaning of **anću* had been 'sacred plant', or the like, it would become impossible to explain the meaning of the CToch. loan-word. A simple solution to this dilemma is near at hand. Metals are not named from designations of plants, but they are often named after the colour, see for instance Ved. *híraṇya-* and *suvárṇa-* 'gold', *rajatá-* 'silver', *lóhita-* or *lohá-* 'copper', etc. (Rau 1974: 18-24). A secondary differentiation (from AV onwards) was also provided by colour adjectives, cf. *lóhitam ấyaḥ* 'reddish metal' (for 'copper') vs. *śyāmám áyaḥ* 'dark metal' (for 'iron'). The primitive system opposed Ved. *áyas-* (Av. *aiiah-*) 'metal of utility' to *híraṇya-* 'noble metal': the former term originally referred to « copper », later to « iron ». I recall that the prominent colour of iron ore is rusty red, reddish-brown. Besides Toch. B *eñcuwo* (A **añcu*), we know several names of metals in Tocharian: B *yasa* (A *wäs*) 'gold', B *ñkante* (A *nkiñc*) 'silver', B *pilke* 'copper', B *lant** (adj. *läntaṣṣe*) 'lead'. Interestingly enough, the name of copper is obviously derived from the root *pälk-* 'to shine': it originally meant 'shining like fire, gleaming', as corresponding to Skt. *loha-*, *lohita-*, which referred to copper for its red colour. It would be likely that the name of iron be derived from another colour, that is 'rusty (brown)'. Compare the designations of the colours in Tocharian: B *ratre* A *rtär* 'red', B *tute* 'yellow', AB *tseṃ* 'blue', B *motartstse* 'green', B *erkent-* A *arkant-* 'black', B *kwele* 'grey'.

2.6.3. Going back to Vedic, we may assume that the borrowed word **anću-* referred to the characteristic colour of the twig or stalk of the sacred plant. The Soma plant is qualified and also designated by various colour adjectives: *hári-*, *aruṣá-*, *aruṇá-*, *babhrú-*. The terms *hári-* (cf. Av. *zairi-*) 'yellow, fawn' to 'green', and *aruṣá-/aruṇá-* ‘tawny-orange’ are not specific of the juice or the dried plant, but probably refer to the Soma (personified) as a divine horse, as a celestial being, etc. (cf. Brough 1971: 349-352; Falk 1989: 85-86 and 2003: 147). They were used as poetic epithets, secondarily as names of the Soma: they cannot be used to determine the botanical nature of the plant. More specific is the term *babhrú-* ‘greyish-brown, reddish-brown, tawny’ (MW: 721c), which is used, contrary to the other colour terms, exclusively for the flow(s) of Soma (see RV IX.31.5, 33.2, 63.4.6, 98.7, 107.19.20), and secondarily for the plant (Kapadia 1959: 4-5). It probably referred to the colour of the essential part of the plant, the marrow inside the stalk, from which the juice was extracted after crushing. As a designation of the “heart” of the plant, it could easily be transposed as the name of its twig or stalk, and finally of the whole plant. Actually, it fits quite well with the hypothesis of Ephedra (Falk 1989: 86). It corresponds to the colour of the ‘chocolate powder’ contained in the central part of some sorts of Ephedra, as described by Qazilbash (1960: 499): “The central portion of dried mature twigs collected in autumn contains a powdery material of rusty red colour” (emphasis mine).

The same range of usage can be assumed for the term **anću-* ‘rusty red (brown)’ as the source of the Vedic noun *aṃśú-*. In addition, one finds in the RV the fixed phrase *aṃśúṃ duh-* (I.137.3b, III.36.6d, 7c, V.36.1d, V.43.4d, IX.72.6a, 95.4b, X.94. 9b): this implies that the juice of the Soma is compared to the milk obtained from a cow, as shown by other passages (RV II.13.1, III.48.2, VIII.9.19, IX.6.7, IX.107.12, X.94.8, etc.). Literally, this expression could have originally meant ‘to extract (by pressing) the brown product’ from the plant. The same word could be applied to the result of the operation, that is the juice itself. When illuminated by the sun, the juice shines like gold: RV I.46.10ab *ábhūd u bhā́ u aṃśáve, híraṇyam práti sū́ryaḥ* ‘Radiance has come into existence for the brown juice, the sun (has appeared) like gold’. Of course, at the stage of the RVic hymns, the term *aṃśú-* became simply a name of the Soma, which is fully integrated into the phraseology. It is all the more interesting to find an isolated reference to foreign (non-Aryan) people who also practise the Soma cult, while using *aṃśú-*: RV VIII.53.4c (Vālakhilya hymn) *śī́ṣṭeṣu cit te madirā́so aṃśávaḥ* 'Among the Ś. also the exciting [Soma] plants belong to you [Indra]'. The form *śī́ṣṭa-* with variants *śī́ṣṭra-*, *śī́rṣṭra-* testifies to a non-Aryan name with "intrusive *-r-*" (Kuiper 1991: 7, 70). It would be one of the last echoes of the widespread practice of the cult of the sacred plant in Central Asia.

To summarize my present contribution to the Soma/Haoma problem, I should like to point out the most important provisory results:

(i) The term Ved. *aṃśú-*, Av. *ąsu-* goes back to a noun borrowed from some donor language of Central Asia, as confirmed by CToch. **æñcuwæn-*.

(ii) Since the original meaning referred to the colour of the marrow, that is the internal part of the twigs of the plant, one may wonder whether the designation of the heart of the plant as 'the rusty red one' had already been coined by the ritualists of the donor language, or whether this denomination was conceived by the speakers of Indo-Iranian, in order to possess a supplementary secret term to designate this holy substance.

3. CONCLUDING REMARKS

3.1. The last interpretation is admittedly tentative, because it concerns one of the most discussed issues of Indo-Iranian studies, and it will certainly be refined and tested according to other parameters. I should point out that this example is not fundamentally different from others which have been discussed previously. Once it is admitted that Ved. *aṃśú-*, Av. *ąsu-* are of foreign origin, it is legitimate to look for the most similar form in other languages of Central Asia. Since one finds a corresponding noun of very close, almost identical, formal shape, but with a very different meaning, referring to 'iron', there are two possible strategies: either the similarity is due to a mere coincidence, or the difference of designation can be explained by sound arguments. I have, I hope, shown that the semantic gap is not insurmountable, provided that diverging ways of evolution from a common source are assumed.

A similar situation is exemplified by the religious designation Ved. *átharvan-*, Av. *āθrauuan-/aθaurun-* vis-à-vis CToch. **ætræ* meaning « hero »: in this case, a missing link can be found between the diverging designations by reconstructing in Indo-Iranian the figure of the king-priest. This reconstruction is based on independent evidence. Furthermore, an internal clue is provided in the most ancient layer of the Vedic language by the remnants of the lexeme **athar-*, which corroborates the possible heroic scope of the original meaning.

In the same vein, in the case of the epithet Ved. *kalyāṇī́-* meaning 'having beautiful hips', the new interpretation can be gained by arguments that explain within Indo-Aryan the semantic evolution of *āṇí-* from its original meaning 'hip': this interpretation can be dissociated from the loan-word hypothesis. The word Toch. B *oñiye* 'hip' provides only corroborative evidence, as it appears that the word *āṇí-* cannot be of IE origin.

I would thus insist on the fact that this research on substratum influence in Central Asia involves a definite amount of *reconstruction*, as does any research on the prehistory of dead languages. It would be superficial to transpose to the remote past the meaning of hitherto obscure Vedic or Avestan words as recorded in our dictionaries. One should take into account an interval of five to eight centuries between the probable period of borrowing by contacts with BMAC people and the time of our most ancient documents, that is the nucleus of the collection of RV hymns. During this time, it is reasonable to admit some range of semantic evolution, parallel to the formal adaptation of these foreign words to different morphological structures. But this evolution of meaning should not be conceived as arbitrary or random: it followed some patterns of the receptor language and culture. From the Vedic point of view, a striking fact is that several words are doublets or substitutes for words of the standard language of the RV, cf. *āṇí-* and *śróṇi-*, *aṃśú-* and *babhrú-*, *atharī́-* and *varāhá-*. This implies that these borrowed words originally belonged to a variety of the Vedic language that later became obsolete or marginal, by integration into the conventional language of the RV: the latter was some kind of standard "pan-Vedic" language.

Another consequence of the above reconstruction is the following, which is not new, but should be restated explicitly: there already existed some kind of poetic and religious Indo-Iranian language at the time of the borrowings, which could respond to the needs of sacred speech. This process can be deduced from the evolution of the noun, which happened to become a designation of the holy plant: in the donor language, **anću-* was probably not the special name of this plant, but referred to one of its characteristics (actually, the colour of its internal part); in the receptor languages, it served as a special (originally alternative) designation of the stalk and the plant itself.

3.2. Judging from this limited material, the semantic range of the loan-words does not seem limited to one particular lexical field. On this point, my conclusions are at variance with the claim of Lubotsky, who places great emphasis on words of the religious sphere (2001: 304). In fact, the religious usage of given words (cf. for instance 2.2.2 and 2.6.3) may be due to a secondary interpretation by Indo-Iranian (or, separately, Iranian or Indo-Aryan) speakers. Some words point to sociological and technological differences between Indo-Iranians, Proto-Tocharians and BMAC people. Words for fierce animals (2.2.2) and hunting (2.4) are notoriously unstable and subject to replacement. Without anticipating deeper investigations, the above results do not seem in contradiction with what is known from the BMAC material culture. The fortified dwellings of the Paṇis (2.5), where their goods were kept, may be compared with the circular or quadrangular citadels typical of BMAC archaeological remains.

Concerning the language of the BMAC, as in the title of this paper, a caveat should be expressed, since it would be rash to admit that all the words that have been listed so far belong to a single language. The Tocharian data are important, because they may add complementary evidence for determining the original form and meaning of the words of the common source.

Concerning the phonetic aspect of this substratum language (if all the above items belong to one and the same language), one may note the following features: voiceless aspirate stops, syllabic liquids (cf. also Ved. *gr̥dá-*, *mr̥gá-*, *vr̥kká-*), several palatal stops and palatal clusters. Vedic *āṇí-* (2.3.1) and *paṇí-* (2.5) would corroborate each other and confirm the existence of retroflexes in this language, because it would be less economical to admit two cases of spontaneous development of the dental nasal (cf. von Hinüber 2001: 169).

Having such characteristics around 2000 BCE, the BMAC language would not belong to the Indo-European family; it does not seem to be related to Dravidian either. The above examples constitute only a first sample, showing that new insights may be gained by including in the perspective other languages of Central Asia, such as Tocharian. New identifications and reconstructions will certainly help to define more precisely the contours of the BMAC vocabulary in Indo-Iranian, as well as in Tocharian.

REFERENCES

Abbreviations

BSOAS = Bulletin of the School of Oriental and African Studies
EJVS = Electronic Journal of Vedic Studies

ADAMS, Douglas Q. 1984. The position of Tocharian among the other Indo-European languages. *Journal of the American Oriental Society* 104: 395-402.

------ 1995. Tocharian *āṣtär*, B *astare* 'clean, pure' and PIE *$*h_2eh_x(s)$-* 'burn'. In: Wojciech Smoczyński (ed.), *Kuryłowicz Memorial Volume. Part One* (Analecta Indoeuropaea Cracoviensia, Vol. II): 207-211. Cracow: Universitas.

------ 1999: *A Dictionary of Tocharian B*. (Leiden Studies in Indo-European. 10.) Amsterdam - Atlanta: Rodopi.

BAILEY, Harold W. 1957. Adversaria indoiranica. *BSOAS* 19: 49-57.

------ 1970. A range of Iranica. In: Mary Boyce & Ilya Gershevitch (eds.), *W.B. Henning Memorial Volume*: 20-36. London: Lund Humphries.

------ 1975. The second stratum of the Indo-Iranian gods. In: John R. Hinnells (ed.), *Mithraic Studies*. Proceedings of the First International Congress of Mithraic Studies (Manchester University, 1971), I: 1-20. Manchester: Manchester University Press.

------ 1979. *Dictionary of Khotan Saka*. Cambridge: Cambridge University Press.

BAKELS, C. C. 2003. The contents of ceramic vessels in the Bactria-Margiana Archaeological Complex, Turkmenistan. *EJVS* 9, Part I, 1c.

BENZING, Johannes 1983. *Chwaresmischer Wortindex*. Wiesbaden: Harrassowitz.

BLOOMFIELD, Maurice 1899. *The Atharvaveda and the Gopatha-Brāhmaṇa*. Strassburg: Trübner.

BROUGH, John 1971. Soma and *Amanita muscaria*. *BSOAS* 34: 331-362.

CALAND, Willem & Victor HENRY 1906. *L'Agniṣṭoma*. Description complète de la forme normale du sacrifice de Soma dans le culte védique. Tome premier. Paris: Ernest Leroux.

CARLING, Gerd 2003. Fragments bilingues du Yogaśataka. Révision commentée de l'édition de Jean Filliozat. *Tocharian and Indo-European Studies* (Reykjavik) 10: 37-68.

CARPELAN Christian, Asko PARPOLA & Petteri KOSKIKALLIO (eds.) 2001. *Early Contacts between Uralic and Indo-European: Linguistic and Archaeological Considerations* (Papers presented at the international symposium, Tvärminne, 8-10 January, 1999) = Suomalais-Ugrilaisen Seuran Toimituksia, 242. Helsinki: Suomalais-Ugrilainen Seura.

CDIAL = TURNER, Ralph Lilley 1966. *A Comparative Dictionary of the Indo-Aryan Languages*. London / New York: Oxford University Press.

DED = BURROW, Thomas & Murray B. EMENEAU 1961. *A Dravidian Etymological Dictionary*. Oxford: Clarendon Press.

DED-R = BURROW, Thomas & Murray B. EMENEAU 1984. *A Dravidian Etymological Dictionary*. Revised 2nd ed.. Oxford: Clarendon Press.

ERDOSY George (ed.) 1999. *The Indo-Aryans of Ancient South Asia. Language, Material Culture and Ethnicity*. Berlin / New York: Walter de Gruyter.

EWA = MAYRHOFER, Manfred 1986-2001. *Etymologisches Wörterbuch des Altindoarischen*, 3 vols. Heidelberg: Winter.

FALK, Harry 1989. Soma I and II. *BSOAS* 52: 77-90.

------ 2003. Decent drugs for decent people: further thoughts on the nature of Soma. *Orientalia Suecana*. Vol. LI-LII (2002-2003): 141-155.

FLATTERY, David Stophlet & Martin SCHWARTZ 1989. *Haoma and Harmaline. The botanical identity of the Indo-Iranian sacred hallucinogen "Soma" and its legacy in religion, language, and Middle Eastern folklore.* (University of California Press. Near Eastern Studies, Vol. 21.) Berkeley / Los Angeles: University of California Press.

FRANCFORT, Henri-Paul 1994. The Central Asian dimension of the symbolic system in Bactria and Margiana. *Antiquity*, Vol. 68 (No. 259): 406-418.

------ 2001. The archaeology of protohistoric Central Asia and the problems of identifying Indo-European and Uralic-speaking populations. In: Carpelan et al. (eds.): 151-168.

HILLEBRANDT, Alfred 1916. Die Paṇi's im R̥gveda. *Zeitschrift der Deutschen Morgenländischen Gesellschaft* 70: 512-520.

HINÜBER, Oskar von 2001. *Das ältere Mittelindisch im Überblick*. 2., erweiterte Auflage. Wien: Österreichische Akademie der Wissenschaften.

HOFFMANN, Karl & Bernhard FORSSMAN 1996. *Avestische Laut- und Flexionslehre*. Innsbruck: Innsbrucker Beiträge zur Sprachwissenschaft.

HOFFMANN, Karl & Johanna NARTEN 1989. *Der Sasanidische Archetypus. Untersuchungen zu Schreibung und Lautgestalt des Avestischen.* Wiesbaden: Reichert.

HOUBEN, Jan 2003. The Soma-Haoma problem: Introductory overview and observations on the discussion. *EJVS* 9, Part I, 1a.

HULD, Martin E. 2000. Reinventing the Wheel: the technology of transport and Indo-European expressions. In: Karlene Jones-Bley et al. (eds.), *Proceedings of the 11th Annual UCLA Indo-European Conference* (Los Angeles, June 4-5 1999) = *Journal of Indo-European Studies. Monograph Series*, 35: 95-114. Washington D.C.: Institute for the Study of Man.

KAPADIA, B. H. 1959. *A critical interpretation and investigation of epithets of Soma*. Vallabh Vidyanagar: V. P. Mahavidyalaya.

KASHIKAR, C. G. 1990. *Identification of Soma.* (Tilak Maharashtra Vidyapeeth, Research Series, No. 7.) Pune: C. L. Kshirsagar.

KUIPER, F. B. J. 1991. *Aryans in the Rigveda*. (Leiden Studies in Indo-European, 1.) Amsterdam / Atlanta: Rodopi.

LUBOTSKY, Alexander 2001. The Indo-Iranian substratum. In: Carpelan et al. (eds.): 301-317.

------ 2002. Scythian elements in Old Iranian. In: Sims-Williams (ed.): 189-202.

MACDONELL, Arthur A. 1897. *Vedic Mythology*. Strassburg: Trübner.

MALLORY, James P. & Victor H. MAIR 2000. *The Tarim Mummies*. London: Thames & Hudson.

MELCHERT, H. Craig 1994. *Anatolian Historical Phonology*. (Leiden Studies in Indo-European, 3.) Amsterdam / Atlanta: Rodopi.

MW = MONIER-WILLIAMS, Monier 1899. *A Sanskrit-English Dictionary*. Oxford: Clarendon Press.

NUSSBAUM, Alan 1986. *Head and Horn in Indo-European*. Berlin / New York: Walter de Gruyter.

PARPOLA, Asko 1988. The coming of the Aryans to Iran and India and the cultural and ethnic identity of the Dāsas. *Studia Orientalia* 64: 195-302.

------ 1995. The problem of the Aryans and the Soma: Textual-linguistic and archaeological evidence. In: Erdosy (ed.): 353-381.

PINAULT, Georges-Jean 1989. Reflets dialectaux en védique ancien. In: Colette Caillat (ed.), *Dialectes dans les littératures indo-aryennes* (Actes du colloque international, Paris, Fondation Hugot du Collège de France, 16-18 septembre 1986): 35-96. Paris: Collège de France/de Boccard.

------ 2002a. Tocharian and Indo-Iranian: Relations between two linguistic areas. In: Sims-Williams (ed.): 243-284.

------ 2002b. Tokh. B *k$_u$caññe*, A *k$_u$ciṃ* et skr. *tokharika*. *Indo-Iranian Journal* 45: 311-345.

------ 2003a. Sanskrit *kalyāṇa-* interprété à la lumière des contacts en Asie Centrale. *Bulletin de la Société de Linguistique* 98: 123-161.

------ 2003b. Une nouvelle connexion entre le substrat indo-iranien et le tokharien commun. *Historische Sprachforschung* 116: 175-189.

QAZILBASH, N. A. 1960. Ephedra of the Rigveda. *The Pharmaceutical Journal*, No. 26 (November 1960): 497-501.

RAU, Wilhelm 1974. *Metalle und Metallgeräte im vedischen Indien*. Mainz. Akademie der Wissenschaften und der Literatur. Abhandlungen der Geistes- und Sozialwissenschaftlichen Klasse, Jg. 1973, Nr. 8. Wiesbaden: Steiner.

SCHMIDT, Hanns-Peter 1968. *Bṛhaspati und Indra*. Wiesbaden: Harrassowitz.

SCHWARTZ, Martin 1974. Irano-Tocharica. In: Philippe Gignoux & A. Tafazzoli (eds.), *Mémorial Jean de Menasce*: 399-411. Louvain: Imprimerie Orientaliste.

SIMS-WILLIAMS, Nicholas (ed.) 2002. *Indo-Iranian languages and peoples* (Proceedings of the British Academy, Vol. 116.) Oxford: Oxford University Press.

SPARREBOOM, Marcus 1985: *Chariots in the Veda* (Memoirs of the Kern Institute, No. 3.) Leiden: Brill.

de VAAN, Michiel 2003. *The Avestan Vowels*. (Leiden Studies in Indo-European, 12.) Amsterdam / New York: Rodopi.

WACKERNAGEL, Jacob 1918. Indoiranisches. *Sitzungsberichte der Berliner Akademie der Wissenschaften* 1918: 380-411 (= 1953: 229-330.)

------ 1934. Indoiranica.- 12. *kalyā́ṇa-*. *Zeitschrift für vergleichende Sprachforschung auf dem Gebiete der Indogermanischen Sprachen* 61: 191-197 (= 1953: 352-358.)

------ 1953. *Kleine Schriften*, I-II. Göttingen: Vandenhoeck & Ruprecht. (2nd ed., 1969.)

WATKINS, Calvert 1995. *How to Kill a Dragon. Aspects of Indo-European Poetics*. New York / Oxford: Oxford University Press.

WITZEL, Michael 1995. Early Indian history: linguistic and textual parameters. In: Erdosy (ed.): 85-125.

------ 1999. Aryan and non-Aryan names in Vedic India: data for the linguistic situation, c. 1900-500 B.C. In: J. Bronkhorst & M. Deshpande (eds.), *Aryan and Non-Aryan in South Asia: Evidence, Interpretation and Ideology*. (Harvard Oriental Series, Opera Minora, 3): 337-404. Cambridge [Mass.].

------ 2000. The Home of the Aryans. In: Almut Hintze & Eva Tichy (eds.), *Anusantatyai. Festschrift für Johanna Narten* (Münchener Studien zur Sprachwissenschaft. Beiheft 19): 283-338. Dettelbach: J. H. Röll.

Abbreviations of languages and texts

Av.	=	Avestan	MHG	=	Middle High German
AV	=	Saṃhitā of the Atharvaveda	MPers.	=	Middle Persian
			OCS	=	Old Church Slavonic
AVŚ	=	Saṃhitā of the Atharvaveda, Śaunaka	OEngl.	=	Old English
			OHG	=	Old High German
Gk.	=	Greek	OPers.	=	Old Persian
IE	=	Indo-European	RV	=	Saṃhitā of the Ṛgveda
JB	=	Jaiminīya-Brāhmaṇa	ŚB	=	Śatapatha-Brāhmaṇa
Lat.	=	Latin	Toch.	=	Tocharian
Lith.	=	Lithuanian	TS	=	Taittirīya-Saṃhitā

Indo-Aryan and Dravidian convergence: gerunds and noun composition

HARTMUT SCHARFE

1. NORTH-SOUTH-INDIAN RELATIONS

The idea that the northern Indian or Indo-Aryan languages have been influenced by the Dravidian languages to the South has circulated for almost two centuries. Pott suggested in 1833 that the retroflex consonants of Sanskrit might have developed under the influence of autochthonous speakers,[1] Gundert suggested Dravidian origin of several Sanskrit words,[2] and so did Caldwell.[3] The idea of India as a linguistic area or "Sprachbund" gained prominence with the publications of Emeneau[4] and Kuiper[5]. Their work balanced the obvious fact that the Indo-Aryan languages, beginning with Sanskrit, had an enormous influence on the Dravidian and Munda languages with evidence that some striking similarities between these language families could best be explained as originating in a Dravidian language. They point *inter alia* to the retroflex consonants (which are found only sporadically in Iranian and some Euro-

---

[1] "Ein Erzeugniss des indischen Bodens" (A product of the Indian soil) (Pott 1833: 78) and "mehrere Indische Sprachen wimmeln von diesen Lauten und haben wahrscheinlich das eingewanderte Sanskrit angesteckt" (several Indian languages teem with these sounds and have probably infected the immigrant Sanskrit) (Pott 1836: 19).

[2] Gundert 1869: 517-530.

[3] Caldwell 1961: 565-579. The first edition of 1856 was not at my disposal.

[4] E.g., Emeneau 1954: 282-292 and 1956: 3-16.

[5] Kuiper 1967: 81-102.

pean languages), the so-called absolutives or gerunds (which play only a minor role in Iranian and Greek,[6] never as a kind of subclause), and the quotation end-marker *iti* (which was not used in this way outside Indo-Aryan).[7]

Building on their work, Hock and Witzel proposed some thorough revisions of their theses. Hock[8] pointed to the paucity of likely loanwords from Dravidian in the Ṛgveda versus several likely loanwords from a Muṇḍa language, and Witzel[9] differentiated this argument, pointing out that he could not find clear Dravidian loanwords (or at least not many) in the oldest parts of the Ṛgveda (which he defined as books IV, V, VI, and maybe II),[10] though such words "suddenly appear" in the books he considered later (III and VII, and then I, VIII, and X). While Hock and Witzel proposed that the first contacts of the Aryan immigrants were with speakers of a Munda (or Para-Munda or Austro-Asiatic) language rather than a Dravidian language, retroflex consonants, gerunds, and the use of *iti* are found in all the books of the Ṛgveda – how can these features then be a calque of Dravidian constructions?[11] The difficulty increases when we consider that the gerunds are derived from stems that are obsolete in Vedic. According to the older explanation,[12] the *-tvā* forms were derived from a *-tu* stem – but *-tu* stems with zero grade of the root are not found in Vedic Sanskrit except for a few that may be of recent origin.[13] If we follow Hamp's explanation of the uncompounded gerunds as

[6] Hock 1975: 105; Hamp 1986: 103-108.

[7] But see Hock's articles quoted in fn. 59.

[8] Hock 1975: 76-125, especially 85-89.

[9] Witzel: 1999b: 12-16, 20. (This paper is almost identical with the one in *IJDL* 30 (2001): 1-94, which itself is a reproduction of the *Electronic Journal of Vedic Studies* 5 (1999) issue 1 [Sept.].)

[10] Witzel 1995b: 329-332, 343; 1999b: 7; 2000: 550-551, 564.

[11] van Driem 1999, on the contrary, held to the belief that the similarities go back, at least ultimately, to Dravidian, acknowledging at the same time early Munda influence on Ṛgvedic vocabulary and mythology. A larger influx of Dravidian language material is noted in late Vedic literature, i.e., after 500 B.C.

[12] Defended by Tikkanen 1987: 249-252.

[13] Wackernagel & Debrunner 1954: 652-656, 666.

instrumentals of nouns in *-tva* with zero grade of the root, attested in Slavic (*šitvo* 'sewing') and Gothic (*waúrstw* 'work'), the forms must have arisen when that suffix was still in use, i.e., long before the composition of the Vedic hymns. The compounded gerunds in *-(t)yā* or *-(t)ya* are derived from verbal abstracts with the suffix *-ya*[14] and find their correspondence in compounds like Latin *nau-frag-ium* and *in-i-t-ium*, i.e., in case forms like *initiō*, literally 'with the going in', then 'in the beginning, initially'.

Witzel (1999b: 8) rightly remarks: "By way of caution, it must be stressed that neither the commonly found Drav. nor Munda etymologies are up to the present standard of analysis, where both the root and all affixes are explained." Sometimes Indo-European etymologies proposed for words that might instead be of Dravidian or Munda origin appear belabored; but the critics overlook the fact that these derivations from Indo-European often attempt to explain every detail of a word's formation – while they themselves offer only vague alliterations which they declare to be striking. The word *mayūra* 'peacock' does not fit an Indo-European pattern, and the bird was unknown in the IE homeland (Thieme 1955: 440). The older Indo-European etymologies that linked *mayūra* to a root *MĀ* 'bellow, bleat', *māya* 'bellowing', *maya* 'horst', etc. are less than convincing; they are also only root etymologies that leave the word formation unexplained. But what the Dravidologists offer is no better: *mayūra* shares with the Dravidian word for this bird (*mayil*) the first three phonemes, but the rest differs; the link to Munda *ma-ra'* 'crier' is tenuous at best, and the word formation (or formations: *mayūra* / *mayil*) is not explained.[15] If Bailey (1957: 59) is right in regarding Saka *mur-āsa* 'peacock' as a very old loanword, the borrowing may predate the R̥gveda (Hock 1975: 86).

There are other aspects that urge caution. Accidental similarities cannot be ruled out, especially in proper names whose meaning-

---

[14] Wackernagel & Debrunner 1954: 778-779.

[15] Emeneau 1971: 46-47; Witzel 1999b: 16-17, 33. Witzel's assumption of a "northern" form *mayur* and a southern form *mayil/r* pushes the dilemma only further into the past; cf. also Witzel 1999a: 350.

content is usually unknown: Witzel (1999b: 43) issues a note of caution, referring to a River Kankai in Eastern Nepal whose name sounds strikingly like the Tamil form of the name of the great river Gaṅgā – yet it is extremely unlikely that there is any Tamil connection. The similarity of the names Aṅga, Vaṅga, Kaliṅga, Triliṅga, etc. has long been noted: Shafer (1954: 14, 122) saw here Tibetan suffixes *-nga*, Witzel (1999b: 38, 41-42) various Munda prefixes to a base *-anga*.

The old name of the modern River Gaṇḍak (a tributary of the Ganges coming from the Himalayas), Sadānīrā, may contain in its second part the word *nīra* 'water' which is said to derive from Dravidian *nīr* 'water': 'always-having-water'. But it is disconcerting that the word *nīr* is not attested in the neighboring North Dravidian languages;[16] one cannot therefore rule out an explanation that remains within Sanskrit: *Sadānīlā 'always dark (or blue)' as in the Rivers Asiknī 'black' and Kr̥ṣṇā 'black' (cf. *nadī nīlā* in Rāmāyaṇa IV 42 931*5); the Sadānīrā (or a neighboring river?) was also known as Gaṇḍakī or Kāla-gaṇḍikā 'Black Gaṇḍikā' (Witzel 1999b: 42). Note how the different colors of the Ganges (loamy yellow) and Yamunā (blue) at their juncture at Allahabad are often described (e.g., Raghuvaṃśa XIII 54-57)!

When the son repeats his father's chant *akhkhalīkr̥tyā* 'syllabizing' in RV VII 103, 3, the poet uses a colloquial form corresponding to correct Sanskrit **akṣarīkr̥tya* (Thieme 1954: 109) with clearly identifiable word-elements. It strains the reader's credulity when it is argued that the Nihali word *akkal* '(to cry) loudly in anguish' offers a better explanation of the Vedic word (Witzel 1999b: 43-44). Nihali is the language of a hill-tribe in Madhya Pradesh that has been described only in the last half century.

Bad etymologies based on careless scholarship are avoidable: Mundlay (1996: 6) compares the (Munda?) word "*Kol* or *kor*,

---

[16] Witzel 1999b: 42; Witzel 1999a: 379-381 considers the possibility that all parts of the name may be nothing but popular reinterpretations (sanskritizations) of an original Munda name.

meaning 'people'" to place names in India, e.g. *Kolapur*, *Kolam* in Kerala, and *Koromandala* (Coromandel). In fact, the real name of modern Quilon in Kerala is Kollam, and the old Tamil name of the Coromandel coast is *Cōḻa-maṇḍalam*, a reference to the ruling dynasty of that area, the Cōḻa-s; except in some modern mutilations of the name, the word never had a *k*-sound at the beginning.[17]

These remarks do not mean a refusal to discuss possible outside influences on Vedic or classical Sanskrit, but they indicate the tentativeness (and the sometimes even visionary character) of many of the theories offered so far. More uncertain yet are the attempts of the "long rangers" to connect the language families found in India and their suspected substratum languages to distant language families on the basis of typological similarities or the similarities of a few words. Trask (1995: 193) has some amazing Greek-Hawaiian "equations" (yet Odysseus never reached Hawaii), and Southworth (1982) ironically "proves" that Tamil is closely related to English.

In the following two studies I intend to trace two developments that show Dravidian influence on Indo-Aryan: one that took place within the Vedic tradition and became an integral feature of the syntax of the Indo-Aryan languages, and another that left its mark on classical Sanskrit and Prakrit literature but did not become integrated into the ordinary spoken language.

2. ABSOLUTIVES OR GERUNDS

Absolutives or gerunds are sometimes claimed to be a peculiarity of Sanskrit; but similar words (similar in function, not in their morphology) are found in Homeric Greek and maybe some Iranian dialects. Greek has σχεδόν 'near' from ἔχω and ἀγχίμολον 'moving close'; the latter in its composite structure reminds one of Indic *pādagṛ́hya* 'seizing by the foot', *śṛtaṃkṛ́tya* 'having cooked thoroughly', and *namaskṛ́tya* 'doing homage'; forms with *-kṛtya* are still popular in classical Sanskrit, e.g. *puraskṛtya* (Mahā-

[17] Caldwell 1961: 20-23 and Yule & Burnell 1968: 256-258.

bhārata), *nirdhanīkṛtya* (Daśakumāracarita chapter 2). The Greek forms are used like adverbs, never forming a sub-clause with an object or other complements. Tikkanen counted 173 gerunds in the Ṛveda from sixty-five different roots.[18] The distribution among the family books is as follows. The three books that I (Scharfe 1996: 351-377) have previously considered as belonging to the border area with Afghanistan have few examples: book IV has six, book V five, and book VI six gerunds. Of the books hailing from the Punjab, book II[19] has eighteen, book III sixteen, and book VII five gerunds. (It is surprising that the short book II has so many more than book VII.) Books VIII with eleven, IX with five do not deviate from this pattern. A major break occurs with the later part of book I (thirty-seven) and the whole of book X with sixty-five gerunds. But this is not the only development. Gerunds can stand alone in a sentence (as in Greek), they can have objects or complements that precede or follow, and they can have a combination of both. The incidence of "bare" gerunds may not have statistically significant variations; in Book IV two out of six stand alone, in Book X fifteen out of sixty-five; book VI has none.

While "bare" gerunds and compounded forms like *pādagṛ́hya* or *mithaspṛ́dhya* 'mutually emulous' are inherited types, the increasing occurrence of objects or other complements is statistically significant. Preceding objects and complements versus following objects and complements[20] occur in the following ratios: book IV 4 : 0, book V 3 : 2, book VI 2 : 4, book II 7 : 9, book III 4 : 7, book VII 1 : 3, book VIII 5 : 5, book IX 2 : 3 , book I 15 : 13, and book X 37 : 17. In a few instances objects or complements can both

---

[18] Tikkanen 1987: 351-360 lists sixty-five different forms, many of them occurring repeatedly. A few instances are doubtful, because the forms may not be gerunds at all or the reading is disputed. The figures given by Witzel 1999b: 15-16 undercount several books.

[19] Witzel 1995b: 331 fn. 61 has a different division that joins books II, IV, V and VI as the "Oldest Books", located in the western border area; but his localization of book II rests largely on doubtful identifications of rivers (Sarasvati as the Iranian Harahvaiti rather than the Indian Sarasvatī). It may well be, though, that these books are older.

[20] RV II 12, 3 *hatvâhim*, V 53, 14 *hitvâvadyam* and VI 50, 5 *śrutvā havaṃ*.

follow and precede (e.g., VIII 92, 6 and IX 23, 7 *asyá pītvā́ mádānām*).

The trend continued in the Atharvaveda. Of the 282 gerunds (from 68 different roots) listed by Tikkanen, approximately[21] 136 have a preceding object, fifty-five a preceding complement, and only twenty-three have a following object. The approximately twenty-four following complements are almost all supplements to a preceding object. Only circa twenty-six gerunds stand without direct dependencies. A check of the use of *kr̥tvā* in the Aitareya-brāhmaṇa showed eleven occurrences with a preceding object, and in books I to VI of the Śatapathabrāhmaṇa showed *kr̥tvā* forty-four times with a preceding object, and once *kr̥tvāya* in a quoted formula with a following object (I noticed also one *unmucya kr̥ṣṇâjinam*). Chapters 2 and 3 of the Daśakumāracarita yielded 197 gerunds, of which thirty were bare, 144 had a preceding object, thirteen a following object, a few had parts of the object and complement preceding and following (e.g., *vittair krītvā ... dāridryam*) and five times the object stood between gerund and verb, being the object of both (e.g., *bhartsayitvā māṃ samabhy-abhāṣata*). Initial position of the gerund is clearly a stylistic device, for dramatic effect, as at the beginning of chapter 1 *śrutvā tu bhuvana-vr̥ttāntam*)[22] or for variation at the end of a chain of gerunds (e.g., *sarvaṃ saṃdiśya, sarvaṃ kṣiptvā, kr̥tvā ca rājavāhanam*). Such chains were unknown in the more western (and perhaps earlier) parts of the R̥gveda (books IV, V, and VI) and occur first in some of the later books: II 37, 3; III 32, 1 and 48, 4; I 104, 1; X 15, 6, X 109, 7, and 162, 5[23]. They are common in

[21] The figures are approximate not only because of possible errors on my part, but mainly due to the ambiguous nature of some formulations. Stanzas taken from the R̥gveda have not been counted.

[22] Note also the chiastic word order in Mahābhāṣya I 13, 13-14 *na hy anupadiśya varṇān iṣṭā varṇāḥ śakyā vijñātum* 'for without teaching the sounds, the desired sounds cannot be discerned'.

[23] Overlooked by Hock 1975: 105. RV X 162, 5 has two parallel gerunds, whereas in the other instances the gerunds are sequential (X 109, 7 has three sequential gerunds).

the Brāhmaṇas and extremely popular in classical Sanskrit literature. At the end of this evolution the sentence structure involving gerunds is quite parallel to the Dravidian sentences with adverbial participles (*viṉaiyeccam* 'requiring a verb supplement'). These can be "bare" as in (modern Tamil) *pōyiṭṭu varām* 'having gone away, come back > good-bye = Auf Wiedersehen' or they can have an object as in *āṇai koṇṭu vantāṉ* 'having taken the elephant, he came = he brought the elephant', or adverbial and other complements as in *avaṉ vīṭṭukku ppōy* 'having gone to his house...' or *pūṉai tiṉantōṟum eṉṉiṭattiṟku vantu* 'the cat having come to me daily...' (Arden 1942: 200). Often long chains of parallel adverbial participles are employed before a finite verb that concludes the sentence.[24] Surprisingly, grammars almost never[25] refer to the word order which is apparently taken for granted: the adverbial participle precedes the finite verb and is itself preceded by its object or other complements if any.

When we compare the use of gerunds in the Veda with Dravidian usage, we find that the formation of the Vedic gerunds is of IE origin, the "bare" use and the use of short compounds is likewise inherited. New is the use of an object and other (adverbial) complements that may precede or follow. The Dravidian languages are not a likely source for this innovation, because in them object and complements regularly precede.[26] In the latest parts of the Ṛveda there are no following complements (though there are still following objects), and there we find chains of gerunds. In Vedic prose the construction with following objects became almost extinct, and in

[24] The Old Tamil poem Puṟanāṉūṟu 47, 1-7 has a string of eleven adverbial participles; see below p. 216-217.

[25] The one exception I found is remarkable, because it is a specifically motivated exception to the rule. In old Kannaḍa inscriptions the object may follow the adverbial participle – but only in metrical texts, apparently for the sake of the meter: Narasimhia 1941: 230-231.

[26] We may note as an exception a sentence in which the object of the sentence is at the same time the agent of the main verb: *pāmpu kaṭittup paiyaṉ cettup pōṉāṉ* 'The snake bit the boy and he died' (lit. 'the snake haven bitten [the boy], the boy died') given in Steever 1981: 65.

classical Sanskrit it is employed as a stylistic device, exploiting its status as an exception.

I conclude that the gerund is of Indo-European, not Dravidian, origin, but that its use in the sentence gradually conformed to a Dravidian pattern. Its use continued in the Middle Indo-Aryan and New Indo-Aryan languages, as in Pali *mātugāmasaddo nāma purise khobetvā tiṭṭhati* 'for the word *woman* stirs the men mightily' (Saddharmapuṇḍarīka (K) II, 228, 2), Mahārāṣṭrī (Sattasaï 226 *kāūṇa gehavâvāram* 'doing housework'; 506 *saddaṃ soūṇa* 'hearing the sound'), Hindī *bartan lekar kū'āṇ* [for *kuẽ* – editor's note] *par gayā* 'having taken (= with) a vessel he went to the well' (Spies & Bannerth 1945: 41). Chatterji (1926: 175) compared Bengali *låïyā āïså, niē ēsō* 'having taken, come (= bring)' and Hindi *lē-āo* > *lāo* with Tamil *koṇḍu vā* 'having taken, come (= bring)' and gives a sentence with a string of fifteen gerunds.[27] A string of three gerunds is found in Premcand's Hindi novel *Godān*: *vah kitābẽ naqal karke kapṛe sīkar laṛkõ ko paṛhākar apnā guzar kartā thā* 'He used to get by copying books, sewing clothes, teaching young boys'.[28]

3. NOMINAL COMPOSITION IN THE VEDAS

In Vedic language nominal compounds are generally limited to two members; three members are very rare and only one example of the type *jīvá-pīta-sarga* 'whose out-pourings are drunk by the living' RV I 149, 2) was found. This pattern conforms to the compound structure inherited from Indo-European and found in classical Greek, Old Germanic, etc. Renou (1956: 96-116, 97 fn. 1, 98), referred to rare late Avestan compounds with three members; even the readings of these compounds are uncertain.

---

[27] Chatterji 1926: 1011, 175 suggests Dravidian influence.

[28] Premcand, *Godān*, p. 80 line 6 from bottom (quoted from Tikkanen 1987: 261); the translation was kindly furnished by Dr. G. Mahajan. Jacobi 1897: 97-98 translated a Telugu sentence with several verbal participles into Sanskrit, showing the similarity of expression.

Classical Sanskrit literature, both in prose and in poetry (and Prakrit literature as well), contains nominal compounds of enormous length; Bloch (1934: 106) called them "monstrueuse". Some of them contain participles that serve almost as verbs of subordinate clauses, while others consist merely of long strings of nouns and adjectives. I will try to demonstrate that these constructions have their root in patterns of Dravidian language and poetry. Earlier treatments merely refer to their peculiar length with no attempt to explain them : "...sometimes they are entirely artificial (e.g., the growth of noun compounding in later Sanskrit)" (Masica 1991: 56). Such compounds were not unknown in Middle Indo-Aryan. Sen (1960: 188) wrote: "The literary prose of MIA (viz. Pali, Ardhamāgadhi, the dramatic Prakrits and Jaina Apabhraṃśa) following the model of Classical Sanskrit rejoiced in long and tedious compounds. This was against the spirit of MIA." Hauschild hinted at Dravidian influence without elaboration (Thumb & Hauschild 1958: 108, 124-125).

In the Veda we already find all the compound types known from Sanskrit. There is the nascent type of dvandva or copulative compounds, not inherited from IE and emerging, as it were, before our eyes:

náktā ... uṣā́sā 'Night and Dawn' (separated by intervening words, each of the two words in dual form and with its own accent)

dyā́vā pṛthivī́ 'heaven and earth' (standing together, but separate,[29] each word in dual form and with its own accent)

indrā-pūṣṇóḥ 'of Indra and Pūṣan' (together, each word in dual form, but only the last with accent and proper case ending)

[29] Insler 1998: 285-290.

indra-vāyū́ 'Indra and Vāyu' (together, the first word in its stem form, and only the second with case ending and accent). The latter one emerges as the standard type.

As the name implies, they were originally expressions for two paired objects; in the tenth book of the Ṛgveda we begin to see "plural dvandvas" (a contradictory term) as in *ajā́vayas* 'goats and sheep'. Then there are determinative or tatpuruṣa compounds like *havir-ád* 'eating the oblation', *viś-páti* 'lord of the clan', *vīrá-jāta* 'born of a hero', etc., and possessive or bahuvrīhi compounds like *índra-śatru* 'having Indra as a foe', *ugrá-bāhu* 'powerful-armed', and *iddhā́gni* 'whose fire is kindled'. The last subtype, with initial participle perfect passive (*iddhā́gni* and *práyata-dakṣiṇa* 'by whom honoraria are given'), is an Indian innovation (Renou 1956: 98). Only twelve compounds in the Ṛgveda contain three full words (if we leave aside words with the negation *a/an-*), all of them hapax legomena. In this small number there are only two compounds with a central participle: *jīvá-pīta-sarga* 'whose outpourings are drunk by the living', and *śukra-pūta-pā* 'drinking clear purified [Soma]' On the contrary, such a construction is generally avoided. It is even rare that a participle in attributive position has a dependent noun, though examples are not totally lacking:

yamena dattaṃ trita enam āyunak ... 'Trita harnessed him (i.e., the steed) given by Yama' (attribute with agent) (RV I 163, 2)

vayaṃ namo bharanta emasi 'We come bearing reverence' (attribute with object) (RV I 1, 7)

dhāsiṃ kṛṇvāna oṣadhīr bapsat agnir ... 'Making [the plants] his nourishment, [and] chewing the plants, Fire ...' (attribute with object) (RV VIII 43, 7)

âyam, janā, abhicakṣe jagāmêndraḥ, sakhāyaṃ sutasomam icchan 'This Indra, O people, has come to look, because he desires a friend who presses *soma*' (object with both verb and participle) (RV V 31, 12)

ahann ahiṃ parvate śiśriyāṇam 'He slew the snake lying on the mountain' (attribute with qualifying locative) (RV I 32, 2)

agniḥ pūrvebhir ṛṣibhir īḍiyo nūtanair uta 'Fire was to be regaled (honored) by the earlier poets and also by those of today' (predicate with agent) (RV I 1, 2)

vatsair viyutā yad āsan 'since they were separated from their calves' (predicate with supplement) (RV V 30, 10)

striyā aśasyam manaḥ '[that] the mind of a woman cannot be taught' (predicative with supplement) (RV VIII 33, 17)

vājaṃ viduṣā cid arghyam 'prize that can be won by one who knows' (predicate with agent) (RV V 44, 10)

bhagaṃ na nṛbhyo havyam 'like Bhaga to be called upon for the men' (predicate with supplement) (RV X 39, 10)

yo dabhrebhir havyo yaś ca bhūribhir 'who is to be called upon by the few and by the many' (predicate with agent) (RV X 38, 4)

sa nābhānediṣṭhaṃ brahmacaryaṃ vasantaṃ nirabhajat

'He deprived Nābhānediṣṭha, who was a student, of any portion' (attribute with object) (TS III 1, 9, 4)

cetavyo hy asya bhavati 'For he is to be built up by him' (predicate with agent) (ŚB VI 1, 2, 16)

In later Vedic literature we see a growth of compounds involving dvandvas, as in *prāṇâpāna-vyānôdāna-samānā*[*s*] in Taittirīya-āraṇyaka X 51, often as part of another compound, as in *aṅga-hīnâśrotriya-ṣaṇḍha-śūdra-varjam* 'with the exception of those crippled, not Vedic scholars, eunuchs, [and] śūdras' in Kātyāyana-śrautasūtra I 1, 5. Long dvandvas became common in the scholarly śāstras, from Pāṇini's grammar to the Arthaśāstra and the Nyāya- and Vaiśeṣikasūtras.

Expanded compounds other than dvandvas often involve numerals or suffix-like elements that were not seen as independent entities: *prāṇaîkaśata-vidha* 'like hundred and one breaths' in Śatapathabrāhmaṇa. The author of the late section Aitareyabrāhmaṇa VII 18, 10 dared *para-ṛk-śata-gātha* 'having more than a hundred stanzas and gātha-s'. The Baudhāyanadharmasūtra has many recent elements and shows familiarity (if not even closer links) with South India. While its date is difficult to ascertain and its composition may have extended over a good length of time, it belongs either at the end of what one might call "Vedic literature" or rather at the beginning of post-Vedic literature. It exceeds earlier texts in the use not only of long dvandvas (as BaudhDhS II 3, 31 *prabhū-taîdhôdaka-yavasa-samit-kuśa-mālyôpaniṣkramaṇam* 'where fuel, water, fodder, sacred fuel, kuśa grass, and garlands are plentiful'),[30] but also other long compounds such as *nānā-varṇa-strī-putra-samavāye* 'when there is a concurrence of sons of women of different social orders' (II 2, 10) (Renou 1956: 108). Pāṇini, who occasionally uses dvandvas of extraordinary length (e.g., I 1, 58; I 3, 32; II 1, 6), allows a few tatpuruṣa compounds of three members as in II 1, 51. Patañjali gives as an example *pañca-gava-priya* 'dear to one who has five cows'.[31] No text offers compounds that compare in complexity or length to those found in classical Sanskrit and Prakrit literature.

4. TAMIL COMPOUNDS

Traditional Tamil grammar classifies compounds (*tokai*), following more or less the Sanskrit pattern.[32] A compound behaves as one

---

[30] Cf. Renou 1956: 107. BaudhDhS I 10, 18 has a dvanda consisting of four tatpuruṣa-compounds: *brahmahatyā-gurutalpagamana-suvarṇasteya-surāpāneṣu* 'in case he has slain a Brahmin, has violated the bed of a guru, has stolen gold, or has drunk liquor'.

[31] Mahābhāṣya (ed. Kielhorn) I: 396, 4.

[32] Tolkāppiyam, Collātikāram 406-414 (in the SISSW edition with the commentary of Iḷampūraṇar; 412-420 in the editions with the commentaries of Ceṉāvaraiyar and Nacciṉārkkiṉiyar); later Tamil grammarians follow this pattern with minor differences: Sastri 1934: 205-215; Shanmugam 1967: 106-110.

word according to Tolkāppiyam, Collātikāram 414[33] – which may be said to correspond to Pāṇini's II 1, 1 *samarthaḥ pada-vidhiḥ*, best translated as 'Operation concerning finite words, having the same purpose (i.e., single meaning)' (Scharfe 1983: 55-56). Caldwell in his pioneering *Comparative Grammar* hardly discussed compounds at all. He stated that nouns, often with certain affixes or modification at the end, are used "as adjectives" attached to a following noun, taking, as it were, the place of Sanskrit compounds. He compared the common English way of considering the first word in phrases like *gold watch* as an adjective, while in the sentence *gold is more ductile than silver* it would be considered a noun. (Caldwell 1961: 308-311.)

The question of adjectives in Dravidian is tied up with the question of compounds: *poṉ muḍi* can equally be translated as 'gold crown' or 'golden crown', containing the word *poṉ* 'gold'. Bloch (1954: 107) denied that the Dravidian languages had a category of adjectives (Dravidian "adjectives" are really substantives, in his opinion), and he was followed by several other scholars. Andronow claimed that forms like *nalla* 'good' acquired status as adjectives only in modern Tamil.[34] A different stand was taken by Zvelebil (1990: 19 fn. 64; 27-28) who argues that even if the number of true Dravidian adjectives does not exceed a dozen, this does not justify denying them the status of a separate class. Zvelebil's position was also taken by several other scholars, e.g., Burrow (1947: 254-255), Lehmann (1994: 24-26) and Rajam (1992: 434-442).

---

[33] Tolkāppiyam, Collātikāram 414 *ellāt tokaiyum orucol naṭaiya* 'All compounds behave as one word.'

[34] Andronow 1972: 1-9; cf. also Andronov 1989: 131. It would not be proper to argue that the Tamil grammarians did not recognize a separate class of adjectives, because they copied the pattern of Sanskrit grammar, where nouns and adjectives are both called *nāman* 'name', even though the Sanskrit language has a clear distinction: nouns have a fixed gender, adjectives follow in their gender the noun of reference and can be called *guṇa-vacana* in that role. This distinction is not found in Tamil.

Zvelebil (Zvelebil & Vacek 1970: 66, 76) admitted the existence of compounds in early inscriptional Tamil (*ūṭupokku* '[tax on cultivation that] comes between' and *nāḍukāval* '[fee for] province watching'), as did Vacek in the same work (Zvelebil & Vacek 1970: 125-128) for modern Tamil; but nineteen years later, Vacek recognized no compounds: "As we can not see any grammatical reasons for the existence of compounds in OTa[mil], we feel that even words like *kōṭṭu mīṉ*[35], *mu-k kōl*[36] do not differ from other syntagmas morphologically and should be considered as syntagmas from the formal point of view. If semantically they refer to a single object, they may be interpreted as 'naming units', not compounds."[37]

Lehmann (1994: 17) differentiated between phrases and real compounds where the combined words have a new meaning, not merely the sum of its elements. Another criterion adduced by Lehmann is the inability to separate the two members by an inserted qualification. *malar uṇ-kaṇ* 'flower[like] eye' (Paripāṭal IX 59) is, he argued, not a compound, because we find expressions like *malar am kaṇ* 'flower[like], beautiful eye' (Kalittokai 44, 6), *malar maḻai kkaṇ* 'flower[like], moist eye' (Naṟṟinai 85, 1) and *malar neṭuṅ kaṇ* 'flower[like], large eye' (Aiṅkuṟunūṟu 315, 1). But the parts of *kaṭu-mīṉ* 'shark' (i.e., *kaṭu* 'wild' and *mīṉ* 'fish') cannot be separated and still denote a shark; similarly *āṇ* 'maleness' and *talai* 'head' in *āṇtalai* 'rooster'.

His argument followed essentially that in an earlier publication of Zvelebil (1967: 103-104), who stressed the difficulty in drawing a hard and fast line between phrases and compounds when the expressions are strings of mere stems. Bloch remarked: "It goes without saying that a group being treated as a simple noun, the group can be extended indefinitely in principle; and the learned poetry has abundantly used this liberty." (Bloch 1954: 109).

---

35 *kōṭu* 'crookedness' + *mīṉ* 'fish' > 'shark'.

36 *mūṉṟu* 'three' + *kōl* 'stick' > 'trident, staff of ascetic, *tri-daṇḍa*'.

37 Vacek in Vacek & Subrahmaniam 1989: I: xxxvii. Similarly Narasimhia 1941: 188-190 has declined to call most of these expressions compounds.

The longest undeclined nominal compound of this kind found in the anthologies has ten members:

mān	*taḷir*	*mēṉi*	*neṭu*	*meṉ*	*paṇai*	*ttōḍ*	*kuṟun*
mango	shoot	color	long	soft	bamboo	arms	small
toṭi	*makaḷir*[38]						
bangle	women						

'mango shoot[like] complexioned women with tender bamboo[like] long [and] soft arms [and] small bangles'

Vacek's rejection of compounds in Tamil may be too narrowly based on a concept of nominal compounds as it is found in Vedic Sanskrit or Greek, where the bare stem of the initial member and a single pitch accent for the whole compound constitute objective criteria. *rāja-putráḥ* 'king's son, prince' is a compound – marked by the absence of an inflectional suffix after *rāja* and a single pitch accent – whereas *rā́jñaḥ putráḥ* 'son of the king' and *rā́jā putráḥ* 'The son is a king' are not. By the standard applied by Vacek, English may have hardly any compounds, though both *gold watch* and *shoelace* are generally considered as such. Whether the words are written together or not is merely an arbitrary convention. Paul (1937: 328) refers to Middle High German manuscripts where compounds formed according to the traditional Indo-European pattern are often written as separate words. As Paul (1937: 328-330) recognized, the line between compound and phrase is fluid and based largely on the perception of the speakers; but the concept is useful for differentiating casual combinations and those that have become single entities with a special notion: compounds that express a single concept different from the meanings of the

[38] Paripāṭal VIII 38/39; cf. Rajam 1992: 468. Following Rajam 1992: 467, 470, 717, the words are here not hyphenated. Rajam, like many other scholars, is not always consistent; he occasionally writes short "compounds" as one word (*pakuttūṇ* 'shared food', *pāṇmakaḷ* 'female bard', *taṭakkai* < *taṭam* + *kai* 'big trunk') or separate (*kaṭu vaḷi* 'gusty wind', *puli ppal* 'tiger's teeth'), sometimes hyphenates a short compound (*i-p-paṇpu-il-tāy* 'this mother without qualities'), and sometimes not (*nī kātta nāṭu* 'the land which you protected').

separate components. A good example of such a development is Tamil *taṇṇīr* 'water', a compound of *taṇ* 'cool[ness]' and *nīr* 'water', originally 'cool water'. It can nowadays be qualified by *cūṭu* 'hot' as in *cūṭu taṇṇīr* 'hot water', indicating that *taṇṇīr* was no longer felt to be a compound but had acquired a new simple meaning 'water'.

Dunkel, in a recent publication (1999: 47-68),[39] differentiates between univerbations (e.g., Śúnaḥ-śépa with two accents, Νεάπολις with only one, but with the feminine form of the adjective)[40] and true compounds (like ἀκρόπολις), and suggests that true compounds (also called *stem compounds*) like *rājaputrá* developed secondarily from instances of univerbation where the first element regularly exhibited no case suffix (e.g., *vasu-víd*). He thus rejected the idea first put forward by Jacobi (1897) that the stem compounds hark back to an (assumed) stage of Proto-Indo-European before the accretion of case suffixes – there is, alas, no proof for such a stage of Indo-European.

I am unaware of any explanation for the genesis of the long compounds in Tamil; but could the explanation offered by Dunkel be applicable to them too? Note that Dravidian has no suffix to denote the nominative, and that a word for an inanimate being usually has no marker that indicates its being an object (accusative) – and even a word denoting humans under certain conditions.[41] It matters little in this context, whether we call the Tamil forms syntagmas, phrases or compounds, since the Tamil grammarians all

---

[39] Cf. also Schindler 1997: 537-540.

[40] *dāsyāhputra* 'son of a servant girl > bastard' postulated by Pāṇini VI 3, 22 was treated as one word as the loss of intervocalic /p/ in its Middle Indic form shows: *dāsīeutta*, a derogatory term common in the dramas.

[41] Meenakshisundaran 1965: 103: "Even in the case of humans, the case sign may be avoided if a cohesive unit is marked by the doubling of the initial plosive of the second word: *avar* 'they' + *piriyēn* 'I will not leave' > *avar-p-piriyēn* ('I will not leave them' instead of *avarai-piriyēn*)". [Meenakshisundaran reverses the standard transliteration of alveolars and dentals – editor's note.] The commentators of the Tolkāppiyam are divided on the issue as to whether *nilan-kaṭantān* 'he crossed the land' is a compound or not in the sense 'he has crossed the ground'; it is a compound when it means 'one who has crossed the ground': Sastri 1934: 214-215 and Meenakshisundaran 1965: 103.

treated them as corresponding to Sanskrit compounds (*samāsa*). It is solely the *Sprachgefühl* of the contemporary speaker of these languages that matters in this case of a possible influence across language borders.

The doubling of an initial stop in a juncture that is often taken to indicate a compound (Meenakshisundaran 1965: 97) is not always realized in the texts (Zvelebil 1967: 103; Vacek & Subrahmanian 1989: I: xxxvii). The rules in the old Tamil grammar Tolkāppiyam regarding this juncture are quite confusing and not clearly supported by other authorities (Vijayavenugopal 1968: 201-204). There is an alleged difference between *nāy kōṭpaṭṭāṉ* 'he was held by the dog' and *nāy-kkōṭpaṭṭāṉ* 'he suffered the holding of the dog'. In the first instance *nāy* represents an instrumental, in the second a genitive – in which case the following /k/ will be doubled. Nothing comparable is found in the other Dravidian languages, and this may be merely a dialectal feature.

In the following section I shall give some examples of Old Tamil compounds (or phrases) taken from Vacek & Subramanian (1989). First I list compounds that string noun stems[42] together:

Kuṟuntokai 40, 4	*cem pula*	*ppeya*[*l*]	*ṉīr*	*pōla*	
	red soil	rain	water	like	
	'like rain water on red land'				
Kuṟuntokai 122, 2	*kuṇṭu*	*ṉīr*	*āmpal-uṅ*		
	deep	water	lily	too (connector at the end)	
	'even the lilies of deep water'				
Aiṅkuṟunūṟu 1, 4f.	*naṉaiya*	*kāñci*	*cciṉaiya*	*ciṟu*	*mīṉ*
	budding	kāñci	spawning	small	fish
	yāṇar	*ūr=aṉ*			
	wealth	town=man			

[42] Some could be considered verb stems, or at least stems/roots from which only verbal derivatives are known.

'man of the wealthy town with budding kāñci-[flowers] and spawning small fish' (three parallel attributes with participles, personalizer at the end)

Aiṅkuṟunūṟu 163, 2	*iruṅ*	*kaḻi*	*ttuvalai-y*	*oliyiṉ*	
	black	backwater	drop	sound[OBL]	

'in the sound of the water-drops of the black backwaters'

Akanāṉūṟu 46, 2	*ūr*	*maṭi*	*kaṅkuliṉ*		
	city	sleep	night[OBL]		

'at night when the city is sleeping'

Akanāṉūṟu 46, 3	*kūr*	*muḷ*	*vēli*		
	sharp	thorn	fence		

'fence with sharp thorns'

Akanāṉūṟu 46, 13	*oḷiṟu*	*vāṭ*	*ṭāṉai*	*kkoṟṟa*	*cceḻiyaṉ*
	shiny	sword	army	victory	Ceḻiyaṉ

'victorious Ceḻiyaṉ with an army of glittering swords'

Akanāṉūṟu 170, 10	*kataṟ*	*ciṟu*	*kākkai*	*kāmar*	*peṭaiyoṭu*
	sea	small	crow	beauty	hen [OBL]

'with the beautiful hen of the small sea crow'

Next I shall list compounds that end in a verbal participle (*viṉaiyeccam*), comparable to the Sanskrit absolutive/gerund (the sentence concludes with a final verb):

Kuṟuntokai 3, 3	*karuṅ*	*kōṟ*	*kuṟiñci*	*ppū*	*kkoṇḍu*
	black	stem	kuriñci	flower	having=taken

'having taken from the flowers of black-stemmed kuriñci'

Kuṟuntokai 163, 1f. *pūḻiyar ciṟu talai veḷḷai ttōṭu*
Pūḻiyar small head sheep herd
parantu
having=dispersed
'The Pūḻiyar's herd of small-headed sheep having dispersed'

Puṟanāṉūṟu 190, 1 *viḷai pata cciṟ iṭa nōkki*
ripen time little place aiming
'aiming at a little place at the ripening time'

Naṟṟiṇai 172, 3 *ney pey tīm pāl peytu*
ghee pour sweet milk having=poured
'pouring sweet milk into which ghee was poured'

Puṟanāṉūṟu 163, 1 *niṉ ṉayant*[*u*] *uṟainarkku,*
you (acc.) liking dwellers
nī nayant[*u*] *uṟainarkk-um*
you (nom.) liking dwellers and
'To the dwellers liking you and to the dwellers whom you like'

This line shows how the gerunds can be object directed or agent directed, playing the role assumed in other languages by active and passive constructions (cf. the adjectival participle in Aiṅkuṟuṉūṟu 296, 1 below).

A chain of eleven adverbial participles with their complements is found in Puṟanāṉūṟu 47, 1-7:

vaḷḷiyōr ppaṭarntu puḷḷiṟ pōki neṭiya-v-eṉṉātu curampala kaṭantu /
vaṭiyā nāviṉ vallāṅku pāṭi pperṟatu makiḻntu cuṟṟam arutti /
ōmpāt[*u*] *uṇṭu kūmpātu vīci varicaikku varuntum ipparicil vāḻkkai* /
piṟarkku ttīṭaṟint aṉṟō viṉṟē...

'This reputation-destroying living on donations while hoping for (*paṭarntu*) rich patrons and moving (*pōki*) around like birds, traversing (*kaṭantu*) many deserts without [even] calling (*eṉṉātu*) them long, singing (*pāṭi*) to the best of one's ability with one's imperfect tongue, rejoicing (*makiḻntu*) at what one receives and feeding (*arutti)* one's kinsmen, eating (*uṇṭu*) without saving (*ōmpātu*) and giving away (*vīci*) without stinting (*kūmpātu*), does it bring harm to others? Certainly not!...'[43]

Note that the three negative adverbial participles (*eṉṉātu*, *ōmpātu*, and *kūmpātu*) are each subordinate to the adverbial participle following it.

Finally I list compounds, in several subgroups, that contain an adjectival participle (*peyareccam*). Dravidian participles lack case or gender suffixes and could thus look to the speaker of an Indo-Aryan language like bare stems, part of a *stem compound*.

a) the participle is preceded by the object or instrument of its action:

Aiṅkuṟunūṟu 261,1

meṉ ṟiṉai meynta taṟukaṭ paṉṟi
soft millet having=eaten valor boar
'a bold boar which has grazed on soft millet'

Naṟṟiṇai 172, 8f.

valam puri vāṉ kōṭu naralum
right turn beautiful conch sounding
ilaṅku[m] nīr tturai keḻu koṇka[ṉ]
shining water shore brilliant chief
'brilliant chief of a seashore with shining waters resounding with right-turning beautiful conches' (with two adjectival participles)

[43] Text from Puṟanāṉūṟu (ed. Cāminātaiyar); translation after Tikkanen 1987: 300.

b) the participle is preceded by the agent of its action:

Kuṟuntokai 396,4-7	*oruttal ...*	*maḻai*	*muḻaṅku*	*kaṭuṅ*
	male elephant	cloud	thunder	harsh
	kural	*ōrkkum ...*	*iṭai*	
	sound	listening	place	

'The place where ... the male elephant ... listens to the harsh sound of the thunder of the clouds'

Aiṅkuṟuṉūṟu 105, 2	*tirai*	*taru[m]*	*muttam*	*veṇ*	*maṇal*
	wave	giving	pearl	white	sand
	imaikkum	*taṇṇ*	*aṇ*	*tuṟai-v-aṉ*	
	shining	cool	beautiful	shore=man	

'The hero of the cool and beautiful shore where on white sand pearls are shining which the waves gave'
(with two adjectival participles)

Puṟanāṉūṟu 191, 7	*[cāṉṟōr palar]*	*yāṉ*	*vāḻum*	*ūr-ē*
		I	living	town

'[there are many wise men in] the town in which I live'

Puṟanāṉūṟu 163, 8	*paḻan*	*tūṅku[m]*	*mutirattu*	*kkiḻavaṉ*
	fruit	hanging	Mutiram	chief

'The chief of Mutiram where fruit is hanging'

Puṟanāṉūṟu 163, 9	*kumaṇaṉ*	*[n]alkiya*	*vaḷaṉ-ē*
	Kumaṇaṉ	granted	wealth

'wealth granted by Kumaṇaṉ'

c) agent-centered participles and object-centered adjectival participles are combined:

Aiṅkuṟuṉūṟu 296, 1 *koṭicci* *kākkum* *peruṅ* *kural*
mountain=woman watching big ear
ēṉal *aṭukkaṉ* *maññai*
millet mountain peacock
kavaru[*m*] *nāṭa*[*ṉ*]
stealing country=man
'The hero of the country where a mountain peacock steals millet with big ears which a mountain woman guards'

d) adverbial and adjectival participles can be combined:

Kuṟuntokai 124, 1 *umaṇar* *cērntu*
salt=vendors having=joined
kaḻinta *maruṅkiṉ*
passing track
'on the track where salt vendors pass jointly'

Meenakshisundaran claimed that the strings of bare stems or roots developed into a mix of adjectival and verbal participles. The string (or compound) *vari-ppunai-paṉṭu*[44] tie-adorn-ball 'the ball which was adorned by being tied tightly' developed into the phrase *varintu punaiṉṯa paṉṯu* (adverbial and adjectival participles + noun) 'having-tied, adorned ball'.[45] Indeed the long strings of bare stems or roots seem to be absent from the later language, while phrases with verbal and adjectival participles are common (Arden 1942: 93-96; Andronov 1989: 353-354). Modern Dravidian reformers are against long compounds which they regard as Sanskrit influenced (Sridhar 1981: 210).

---

[44] Tirumurukāṟṟuppaṭai 68; cf. Maturaikkāñci 723 *vari-ppunai-pāvai*.

[45] Meenakshisundaran 1965: 97 [cf. fn. 41 on transliteration - editor's note]; similar already Caldwell 1961: 312.

5. PRAKRIT COMPOUNDS

Neither the Prakrit nor the few Sanskrit inscriptions dating from before the second century A.D. have significant long compounds. Aśoka has *dvādasa-vāsâbhisitena* 'anointed for twelve years' and *mitā-saṃstuta-ñātīnam* 'friends, acquaintances, [and] relatives' (RE 3, Girnār) (Sircar 1993: 18-19). The Sohgaurā Bronze Plaque Inscription (circa 3rd century B.C.) in which Renou (1956: 112) believed to find a long compound, is read differently by Sircar (1993: 82).[46] Long compounds (aside from a few long dvandvas) are found in a Prakrit inscription from the Indian Northwest (possibly the Pakistan-Afghan border) dating from the first century A.D.:

line 4c *parama-vaśi-pratipata + ṇirdhada-malakasa*
'who has attained highest control and has been cleansed of impurities'

line 4d *aṇega-kapa-śata-sahasa-kuśala-mula-samudaṇidasa*
'who has collected the basis for bliss over several hundred thousand eons' (von Hinüber 2003: 22)

But there is no "hinged" compound. Long compounds of noun stems and "hinged" compounds where an attributive participle is at the same time the "governing" predicate of a subordinate clause are found in an early Prakrit inscription, the Nasik Cave inscription of Vāsiṣṭhīputra Puḷumāvi from his nineteenth regnal year (A.D. 149), e.g.:[47]

lines 1-2 *himavata-meru-mandara-pavata-sama-sārasa*
[long string of nouns]
(≈ Himavat-Meru-Mandara-parvata-sama-sārasya)

---

[46] The long Hāthigumphā inscription of Khāravela contains some long dvandvas; the readings of many passages are disputed due to the poor preservation of the inscription.

[47] Senart 1905/1906: 60-61; Sircar 1993: 203-204.

'who was equal in strength to Mount Himavant, Mount Meru, Mount Mandara'

line 3 *sava-raja-[loka-maṇ]ḍala*-patigahīta-*sāsanasa*
[long "hinged" compound]
(≈ sarva-rāja-loka-maṇḍala-pratigṛhīta-śāsanasya)
'whose commands were obeyed by the circle of all kings on earth'

divasakara-kara-vibodhita-*kamala-vimala-sadisa-vadanasa* [long "hinged" compound]
'whose face was beautiful and pure like the lotus opened by the rays of the sun'

line 4 *abhayôdaka-dāna*-kilina-*nibhaya-karasa*
[long "hinged" compound]
(≈ abhayôdaka-dāna-klinna-nirbhaya-karasya)
'whose fearless hand was wet by the water poured out to impart freedom from fear'

line 6 *sava-maṇḍal*âbhivādıta-*caraṇasa*
[long "hinged" compound]
'whose feet were saluted by all provinces'

The Mahāparinibbānasutta of the Dīghanikāya, though a canonical text, is not considered one of the older parts of the canon, though its exact date is unknown. It has some compounds of moderate length, such as e.g., *dhamma-vicaya-sambhojj-aṅga* (ch. 9) 'branch of knowledge [known as] acquisition of righteousness'.

The Sattasaï, an anthology of approx. 700 stanzas attributed to the Sātavāhana King Hāla (first or second century A.D.), is a collection of early Mahārāṣṭrī poetry dating from the first few centuries A.D. The language is not totally uniform but shows traces of dialectal variation. The ethnic affiliation of the Sātavāhana dynasty is unknown, but the Sātavāhanas proudly pointed to their support of the Brahmanic way and perhaps called themselves Brahmins (Scharfe 1989: 30). Their inscriptions were composed in Prakrit, which seems to have been their court language.[48] The Sattasaï has many long compounds, often with a participle which like a "hinge" links a subordinate action with a noun which is part of the main action. A simple compound of three nouns is *kuḍumva-vihaḍaṇa-bhaeṇa* 'out of fear of breaking up the family' (stanza 59); five members are found in *maaṇa-chuh-āüla-kaḍakkha* (≈ madana-kṣudhâkula-kaṭâkṣa) 'whose eye glances are fluttering with the thirst for love' (stanza 582) and *paḍhama-ras*[*a*]*-ubbhea-pāṇa-lohillo* 'eager to drink the first outpouring of sap' (stanza 615).

In a stanza inserted after stanza 100, a long compound ends with a participle:

kaï-vacchala-pamuha-sukaï-ṇimaie
(≈ kavi-vatsala-pramukha-sukavi-nirmite)
'composed by Sukavi who is foremost among the friends of poets'

In many instances the participles serve as "hinges":

ahi-rakkhia-*ṇihi-kalase* (≈ ahi-rakṣita-nidhi-kalaśe)
'treasure jug watched by a snake' (stanza 577)

rosâruṇa-paḍimā-samkaṃta-*gori-muhaaṃdaṃ* (< mukha-candra)
'on which Gauri's moon of a face is reflected with an image red with anger' (stanza 1)

ṇava-sūa-pīa*-peūsa-matta-pāḍī*
(≈ nava-sūta-pīta-pīyūṣa-matta-pāḍī)
'calf wild with beestings drunk by the new-born' (stanza 65)

---

[48] Rājaśekhara, Kāvyamīmāṃsā I 10.

ṇav-abbha–daṃsaṇa-kaṇṭh-āgaa-jīviam
(≈ navâbhra-darśana-kaṇṭâgata-jīvita)
'one whose life came into his throat because of the sight of new clouds' (stanza 336)

The compounds may contain two participles in parallel or hierarchical position:

bahu-puppha-bhar-oṇāmia-bhūmi-gaa-sāha
(≈ bahu-puṣpa-bharâvanamita-bhūmi-gata-śākha)
'with branches bent by the great load of flowers [and] gone to earth' (stanza 103)

raï-keli-hia-ṇiaṃsaṇa-kara-kisalaa-ruddha-ṇaaṇa-jualassa
(≈ ratikeli-hr̥ta-nivasana-kara-kisala-ruddha-nayana-yugalasya)
'whose pair of eyes were obstructed by the hand-buds by whom the dress was removed in love play' (stanza 455)

*jhaṃjhā-vā-*uttiṇa-*ghara-vivara-*paloṭṭanta-*salila-dhārāhiṃ*
'rain floods that stream though the gaps in the house which is turned into straw by the monsoon storm' (stanza 170)

Though participles of the perfect passive dominate, participles of the present are also common (as in the last quoted passage). Later learned poetry took composition to new extremes. Rājaśekhara (lived circa 900 A.D.) has an eight-member compound in Act I stanza 29 of his Karpūramañjarī:

*bhing-*āaḍḍhia-*kea-aggima-dala-ddoṇī-saricchа-cchavī*
'whose brilliance was like that of the cavities of the petals on the tips of the ketakas where the bee sucks'[49]

His use of long compounds in his Prakrit drama cannot be separated from that found in contemporary Sanskrit literature.

---

[49] Konow's edition, p. 28. Further examples in Davane 1956: 43-46.

6. SANSKRIT COMPOUNDS

Among the early inscriptions, the number of those in Sanskrit is insignificant compared to those in Prakrit, and they are short, containing no intricate compounds. The first Sanskrit inscription with long compounds is the Junāgaṛh Rock Inscription of Rudradāman I of circa A.D. 150 on the Kathiawar peninsula (Sircar 1993: 175-180):

lines 6f. *yuga-nidhana-sadr̥śa-parama-vora-vegena*
'[by a storm] of a most tremendous fury befitting the end of an eon'

line 19 *yathāvad-artha-dharma-vyavahāra-darśanair*
'through displays of proper material and moral activity'

with "hinge" participle and instrument or cause:

line 13 *pāraṇa-dhāraṇa-vijñāna-prayog*âvāpta-*vipula-kīrttinā*
'who had attained wide fame by studying and remembering, by the knowledge and practice [of grammar...]'

line 14 *kanaka-rajata-vajra-vaiḍūrya-ratnôpacaya-*viṣyandamāna-*kośena*
'with a treasury overflowing with an accumulation of gold, silver, diamonds, beryls and [other] precious things'

line 14 *...-śabda-samayôdār*âlaṃkr̥ta-*gadya-padya-...* (instr.)
'prose and verse noble and ornamented with clear, light, sweet, colorful and lovely words and conventions'

The Kānākheṛā Stone Inscription[50] of Śrīdharavarman (circa 279 A.D.) has a few long compounds but none with "hinge" participles:

sva-rājyâbhivr̥ddhi-kare
'effecting the growth of his kingdom'

kalyāṇâbhyudaya-vr̥ddhy-artham
'for the sake of increasing the prosperity of the kalyāṇa festival'

akṣaya-svarggâvāpti-hetor
'for the sake of obtaining heaven permanently'

The Allāhābād Stone Pillar Inscription of Samudragupta (latter half of the fourth century A.D.)[51] has many long compounds, some consisting of solely nouns and adjectives:

...-sphuṭa-bahu-kavitā-kīrtti-rājyam (line 6)
'sovereignty in consequence of fame for copious lucid poetry'

kavi-mati-vibhavôtsāraṇam (line 16)
'which outdistances the greatness of the genius of [other] poets'

'neka-go-śatasahasra-pradāyinaḥ (line 25)
'the giver of many hundred-thousands of cows'

loka-samaya-kriyânuvidhāna-mātra-mānuṣasya (line 28)
'a human being, only as far as he performs the rites and conventions of the world'

and others with "hinge' participles:

*..aneka-praharaṇa-*virūḍhâkula-*vraṇa-śatâṅka-śobhā-samudayô*pacita-*kāntatara -varṣmaṇaḥ* (line 18)

[50] Banerji 1921/1922: 232; Sircar 1993: 186-187.
[51] Chhabra & Gai (eds.) 1981: 211-220; Sircar 1993: 262-268.

'whose body was most charming, being covered over with the plenteous beauty of the marks of hundreds of promiscuous scars' (participles with subordinate instruments)

...-grahaṇa-mokṣânugraha-janita-*pratāpa-...* (line 20)
'valor [was] caused by [his first] capturing and [thereafter showing] the favor of releasing' (participle with instrument)

sarvva-kara-dānâjñā-karaṇa-praṇāmâgamana-paritoṣita-*pracaṇḍa-śāsanasya* (lines 22f.)
'whose formidable rule was propitiated with the payment of all tributes, execution of orders and visits [to his court]' (participle with cause)

sarvva-pr̥thivī-vijaya-janitô*daya*-vyāpta-*nikhilâvani-talām kīrttim* (line 29)
'fame having pervaded the entire surface of the world with [its] rise caused by the conquest of the whole earth' (participles with instrument and cause)

Turning now to Sanskrit literature, Aśvaghoṣa is probably the first poet of classical Sanskrit whose work we have.[52] He was reportedly a contemporary of King Kaniṣka, whose exact date is still under dispute. Aśvaghoṣa is generally believed to have flourished early in the second century A.D., and the Saundarānanda is supposed to be his earliest work.[53]

Here we find compounds with four or more members, e.g.:

I 6 *cāru-vīrut-taru-vanaḥ*
'It had groves of lovely shrubs and trees' (4 members)

---

[52] That Sanskrit poetry goes back further in time has been made clear by Bühler 1890.

[53] Johnston1928: v-vi; Lienhard 1984: 164-169.

I 31 *tad-āśrama-mahī-prāntam*
'along the boundary of the land of that hermitage'
(4 members)

IX 51 *sattvāśayânuśaya-bhāva-parīkṣakāya*
'in examining the dispositions, tendencies and feelings of beings' (5 members, including a dvandva)

X 12 *mayūra-picchôjjvala-gātra-lekhāḥ*
'with limbs striped with gleaming peacock's feathers'
(5 members)

VI 5 *sa-pādukâikārdha-vilamba-pādā*
'with her feet half hanging out of her slippers'
(6 members)

with a "hinge" participle and its agent:

VII 42 *cittôdbhava*-bhinna-*varmā*
'with his armor pierced by the mind-born [god]'

I 33 *nemi*-cihnita-*lakṣaṇe*
'which is defined by the track of your wheels'

with a "hinge" participle and an instrument or cause:

IV 9 *parasparâśleṣa*-hṛtâ*nga-rāgam*
'body paint rubbed off by their mutual embraces'

IV 17 *nakha-prabh*ôdbhāsitâ*ṅgulibhyām*
'the toes of which gleamed with the brilliance of their nails'

VI 4 *kheda*-saṃsvinna-*lalāṭakena*
'her forehead dripping with anxiety'

with "hinge" participle and location or object:

I 35 *hasta*-viṣṭhita-*kārmukāḥ*
'with bows in their hands'

II 65 *vana-gamana*-kṛta-*manāḥ*
'determined to go to the forest'

In some stanzas, construction with a "hinged" compound is artfully avoided:

IV 23 *kāraṇḍava*-kliṣṭam *ivâravindam*
'resembled a lotus pressed down by a karaṇḍava bird'

XVIII 48 cūrṇita-*naur ivôrmibhiḥ*
'like a man whose ship has been broken by the waves'

The Buddhacarita offers similar evidence, a compound with six or seven members, depending on whether *abalā* is regarded as part of the compound or not:

IV 30 *srastâṃsa-komalâlamba-mṛdu-bāhu-latâbalā*
'one young woman with tender arm-creepers, which hung down loosely from her drooping shoulders'

and compounds with "hinge" participles:

V 41 *cala-kuṇḍala*-cumbitâ*nanābhir*
'with faces kissed by ear-rings, swinging to and fro'

V 49 *ṛju-ṣaṭpada-paṅkti*-juṣṭa-*padmā*
'whose lotuses are enjoyed by straight rows of bees'

The date of the thirteen dramas ascribed to Bhāsa is still disputed; if they are preserved in their original shape, they would fall in the period between Aśvaghoṣa and Kālidāsa. In his Cārudattam we find long compounds and "hinged" compounds in both the Prakrit and the Sanskrit passages:

śarīra-pariṇāha-sukha-praveśam
'easy entrance [fitting] for the size of my body' (p. 227)

daddha-sarīra-rakkhaṇatthaṃ
'for the sake of protecting his burned body' (p. 219)

kattavvakara-tthī-kida-saṃkedo
'[like a Buddhist monk] who has made an assignment with a servant girl' (p. 228)

dīpa-prabhā-vyaktīkṛta-rūpam 'whose form was revealed by the lamp's light' (p. 230)

Śūdraka's Mṛcchakaṭika, which is assumed to be a remake (or completion) of the Cārudatta, has similar compounds:

loha-kaḍāha-pariattaṇa-kasaṇa-sārā
'quite black through the turning around of an iron pot' (act I after stanza 8)

sura-jaṇa-pīda-sesassa
'whose remainder is drunk by the gods' (act I after stanza 11)

nṛpati-puruṣa-śaṅkita-pracāra
'whose activity is viewed suspiciously by the king's officers' (act III stanza 10)

The Kauṭalīya Arthaśāstra (compiled in the first or second century A.D., but containing older material)[54] contains – like Pāṇini's grammar and the philosophical sūtras – dvandva

---

[54] Scharfe 1993: 293.

compounds of great length, and compounds whose length is caused by long embedded dvandvas:

sattva-prajñā-vākya-śakti-saṃpannānām (I 11, 19)
'endowed with spirit, intelligence and eloquence'

A modest example of the long dvandvas in the lists of book II is II 15, 1 listing revenue sources:

sītā-rāṣṭra-krayima-parivartaka-prāmityakâpamityaka-saṃhatikânyajāta-vyaya-pratyāyôpasthānāni

Some compounds contain "hinge" participles, mostly with a subordinate instrument or location, but apparently not with an agent:

yantra-baddha-*talâvapātam*
'floor fixed to a mechanism [and thus] capable of sinking down' (I 20, 2)

snāna-pragharṣa-śuddha-*śarīraḥ*
'with bodies cleansed by a bath and rubbing' (I 20, 20)

sva-bhūmy-avasthita-*prakṛti-saṃdhim*
'agreements with constituents remaining in his own territory' (VII 15, 23; with location)

sva-deśâbhiṣyanda-vamanena
'by shifting the overflow from his own country' (II 1, 1) is a simple compound with four nouns.

hīna-śakti-pratāpa-pūraṇârtham
'for the sake of recouping his diminished powers and might' (VII 7, 9) is a long indeclinable compound (avyayībhāva).

A "hinged" compound is avoided in:

dauvārikâbhigr̥hītās tīkṣṇāḥ
'the assassins, seized by the doorkeepers' (V 1, 25).

From the medical Carakasaṃhitā Sūtrasthāna, I wish to quote only two of many examples:

8, 4 *tad-arthâtma-sampad*-āyatta-*ceṣṭam*
'[mind] whose activity is based on the contact with its objects and the self'

28, 3 *antar-agni*-saṃdhukṣita-*balena* (prose) (instr.)
'[fire] whose strength is stimulated by the internal fire'

The redaction and reworking of the Mahābhārata continued for centuries, and it is difficult to be certain of the date of an individual passage; in Mahābhārata III 282, 5 *kuśa-kaṇṭhaka*-viddhâ*ṅgau* 'whose limbs are pierced by kuśa grass and thorns' we have a "hinged" compound. It is unnecessary to document the feature from the works of Kālidāsa and the other great classical poets. In the words of Whitney (1889: 480), "But the later the period, and, especially, the more elaborate the style, the more a cumbrous and difficult aggregate of elements, abnegating the advantages of an inflective language, takes the place of the due syntactical union of formed words into sentences."

Burrow (1955: 55) declared that "This practice is not only at variance with the earlier usage and with Indo-European usage in general, but it is also obviously incompatible with any form of popular speech which can have prevailed in India during the period. This linguistic development is a purely literary development, and it is a sign of the growing artificiality of the Sanskrit language as the difference between it and the vernacular Middle Indo-Aryan grew wider."

By contrast with this rather uncharitable view, we quote the warm appreciation by Lienhard: "The numerous compounds grouped round the heart of the sentence are carefully selected to give euphony and, as there are often several ways in which they can be resolved into their component parts, they may be interpreted by the reader in two, sometimes three different meanings ... attaining the greatest possible fullness and concentration of style." (Lienhard 1984: 231).

The poet and theorist Daṇḍin declared that "a wealth of compounds [not only] gives strength [to poetic expression; it also gives] life to the prose."[55] In the works of Daṇḍin, Bāṇa and Bhavabhūti, to name only a few, compounds have sometimes reached fantastic size. A stanza in Bhavabhūti's drama Mālatīmādhava (act V stanza 23) has four compounds with from 21 to 54 syllables; of the two com-pounds with 54 syllables one contains 24 and the other 23 words.

7. CONVERGENCE

We have seen in the preceding chapters the rise of gerunds and of ever longer compounds – with and without "hinge" participle – in Sanskrit and Prakrit literature (i.e., essentially North Indian, though quite a few authors were South Indians), making the language seemingly more similar in type to the Dravidian languages, a convergence typical of a "Sprachbund" or linguistic area.

It is well known that Sanskrit and Prakrit have had an enormous influence on all Dravidian languages (and the Munda languages as well), just as the culture and social structure behind them has influenced all inhabitants of the subcontinent in a process often called sanskritization or brahmanization. On the other hand, Sanskrit and its successor languages have adopted a good number of loanwords from these other languages. How has this convergence come about? It is frequently assumed that there was a long

---

[55] Daṇḍin's Kāvyâdarśa I 80 *ojaḥ samāsa-bhūyastvam etad gadayasya jīvitam.*

period of bilingualism, since the borrowing goes well beyond the casual adoption of single culture words, as would easily occur between adjacent language groups.

The Indo-Aryans are generally assumed to have entered India towards the beginning or the middle of the second millennium B.C., coming from the northwest and encountering a native population. It has often been taken for granted that these native inhabitants were the Dravidians, even though their status as natives is only relative; they most probably also entered India at some time from the northwest. If the Dravidians were the carriers of the Indus Valley civilization (also called Harappa, Mohenjo-Daro Civilization after the major excavation sites), their arrival would have preceded that of the Indo-Aryans by at least a millennium. Speakers of Dravidian languages are found nowadays mostly in South India, with smaller tribal groups in Central India and a group of about two hundred thousand, the Brahui, in Baluchistan (a small tribal group in the Nepalese Tarai is a recent transplant), and it is frequently assumed that they populated more or less the western half of India. As their land was conquered by the Aryan invaders, so the reasoning goes, they gradually gave up their language in favor of that of their new masters, but not without carrying some traces of their old language into the new idiom.

This view has been challenged by Hock and Witzel who following earlier work by Kuiper noted a paucity of Dravidian loanwords in the earlier books of the R̥gveda but several likely borrowings from a language related to the Munda languages.[56] At the same time, they questioned the standard items of supposed Dravidian influence on Vedic Sanskrit: the retroflex consonants,[57] the

[56] Parpola 2002: 94-95 questioned the evidence for Munda influence and points to a likely loanword from Dravidian (*ukha* 'hip' in RV IV 19,9) in an ancient hymn.

[57] Hock 1979: 47-62; 1984: 102-105 and Hamp 1996: 719-723 demonstrate that the retroflex sounds of Indo-Aryan can be derived effortlessly from Common Indo-European by internal forces.

gerunds,[58] the quotative use of the particle *iti*.[59] They assumed that the Vedic Aryans came into contact with Dravidian speakers only later, at the time that the younger parts of the Ṛgveda were composed, i.e., when the Vedic Aryans had entered the Punjab. They assumed that the Dravidians entered India at about the same time as the Aryans did, but taking a more southerly route along the coast of the Arabian Sea, whereas the Indo-Aryans entered through the mountain passes of the Northwest (Khyber, Bolān, Swat). Even if one concedes the absence (or near absence) of Dravidian influence on the oldest parts of the Ṛgveda hailing from the extreme northwest near the Afghan border, it does not necessarily follow that the Dravidians could not have settled in India earlier. They could have been a component of the Indus Valley Civilization and stayed closer to the coast. As the Indus Valley Civilization decayed, possibly for climatic reasons, their people spread through settlements in Gujarat, Rajasthan and Punjab.[60]

This area, consisting of the Indus Valley, Gujarat, Rajasthan and parts of Punjab, would have been the first area of bilingual contact between Dravidian and Aryan speakers. But this contact cannot explain the similarities that developed in the post-Vedic and early classical period described in the preceding chapters. Even if we were to accept Lewy's thesis (1913: 110-120) that substratum influences on the general mode of expression ("innere Sprachform") show up only long after the speakers have completely switched to their new language, the gap of many centuries is too great to bridge. We should look for a new area of bilingual speakers and cultural exchange.

---

[58] Hock and Hamp point out that gerunds/absolutives are also known from other IE languages, even if the morphemes do not always match (above fn. 6); see also above pp. 198 and 201.

[59] Hock 1982: 39-85; 1984: 98-102 points to very similar forms of quotation in the Avesta and parallels in several other old IE languages.

[60] If graffiti, discovered in Mysore and Tamilnadu (Lal 1960: 4-24; Mahadevan 2001: 379-385), are indications of settlements further south is uncertain; they are similar to the writing found in the Indus Valley, but the similarity could be accidental.

The most likely scenario of "the descent of the Dravidians" has been sketched by Zvelebil: as the Dravidians came from Iran into India, the Brahui branched off in Baluchistan, and on their further advance along the shores of the Arabian Sea towards South India, the Central Dravidian language groups stayed in the Dekkhan, and the South Dravidian group moved into the tip of the Indian subcontinent, splitting eventually into Tamil, Kannaḍa, Malayalam and several others (Zvelebil 1972: 57-63 [map on p. 61]). Zvelebil's model suggests that at some time the western coast of India was peopled by speakers of a Dravidian language, and certain peculiarities of the modern Indo-Aryan languages of this region were pointed out long ago.

Caldwell (1961: 414-415) compared the contrast of the inclusive and exclusive 'we' in Dravidian languages with the similar feature in some Western languages. Marathi (inclusive *āpaṇ*, exclusive *āmhi*), Gujarati[61] (inclusive *āpaṇ*, exclusive *ame*), and Mārwāṛī[62] (inclusive *āpā̃*, exclusive *mhẽ* compares with Tamil inclusive *nām* 'we' (which includes the person or persons addressed) versus *nāṅkaḷ* 'we' (which excludes them).[63] According to Bloch,[64] the peculiar development of the cluster /jñ/ > /dñ/ is similar to that in Telugu and a Muṇḍa dialect. Many place names in Sindh, Gujarat and Maharashtra contain the element *palli/v[a]li / oli*, which has been taken by some scholars to be the Dravidian word for village

---

[61] Grierson (ed.) 1908: 340-341; Cardona 1965: 92.

[62] Grierson (ed.) 1908: 23.

[63] There are potential difficulties: Kannaḍa, the language most likely to have been the substrate language, does not have this feature (nor do Gōṇḍī and Brāhūī), and the feature itself has been called by Konow 1906: 4, 293-294 and others (e.g., Meenakshisundaran 1965: 170-171) a secondary development under Munda influence. But their argument has been rejected by Burrow 1943-1946: 596-597 (repr. 1968: 116-118) and Krishnamurti 1968: 189-202: "The existence of two plurals, one exclusive and one inclusive, is certainly a Proto-Dravidian feature" (194). Andronov 1975: 14-16 identified traces of the inclusive/exclusive contrast in Old Kannaḍa. But it remains odd that Kannaḍa should have lost this feature, while the Indo-Aryan languages acquired it under Dravidian influence.

[64] Bloch 1970: 112 with reference to Konow 1906: 169, 479, 586.

(*paḷḷi*).[65]

Southworth (1974: 212) gives a statistical argument: dental consonants are 2.0 to 4.4 times more frequent than retroflex consonants in Western Indo-Aryan languages (i.e., Marathi, Gujarati, Western Panjabi), in Dravidian languages 2.0 to 3.3 times. But in Western Hindi/Urdu dentals are 8.0 to 11.7 times more frequent, and in Bengali "at least" 15.7 times. Languages in an intermediate belt show ratios of from 4.1 to 7.4 in favor of dentals. The statistical closeness of the relations in the Western Indo-Aryan and the Dravidian languages, he argues, supports the suggestion that these Western Indo-Aryan languages represent an expansion of Indo-Aryan into a region originally dominated by Dravidian languages.

But the most reliable evidence comes from written documents. The Kannaḍa literary critic Nṛpatuṅga (ninth century A.D.), in his Kavirājamārga stated that the Kannaḍa language extended from the Kāvēri River in the south to the Godāvari River in the north (Ritti 1997: 3). Kannaḍa inscriptions have been found in the districts of Osmanabad, Nanded, Solapur, and Kolhapur in the present Maharashtra State, beginning with an inscription from A.D. 1013 (Ritti 1997: 6). Inscriptions in Marathi appear only towards the end of the twelfth century (Ritti 1997: 14). The dramatist and theorist Rājaśekhara (circa 900 A.D.) listed in his Kāvyamīmāṃsā (p. 9, lines 11-12) Mahārāṣṭra with Kerala, Gaṅga, Kaliṅga, etc. as being in the southern region (*dakṣiṇā diś*), and two stanzas preserved in two different versions list the Gauḍa and the Drāviḍa. The stanzas are found in the Vallālacarita[66] of Ānandabhaṭṭa[67] in describing the classes of Brahmins:

[65] Sankalia 1949: 53-54; Southworth 1995: 271; Witzel 1999b: 23. Prabhoo 1987: 185-200 finds this suffix also in place names in Bastar District (Madhya Pradesh) where Goṇḍī is spoken. The attempt by Khaire 1978: 14-25; 1979: 78-83; 1980: 79-93 to derive a great number of names and ordinary Marathi words from Tamil is not credible; the same author's book *Dravida Maharastra*, Pune 1977, I have not seen.

[66] Haraprasād Shāstrī's edition, p. 2.

[67] 1432 Śaka era = 1510/11 A.D. acc. to the dedication XXVII 16.

sārasvatāḥ kānyakubjā gauḍā maithilakôtkalāḥ /
pañcagauḍāḥ samākhyātāḥ vindhyasyôttaravāsinaḥ /13/
kārṇāṭāś caîva tailaṅgāḥ gurjjarā rāṣṭravāsinaḥ /
andhrāś ca draviḍāḥ pañca vindhyadakṣiṇavāsinaḥ /14/
'The people living near the Sarasvati (i.e., in Punjab), in Gauḍa (Bengal), Mithilā, Utkala (Orissa) are called the five Gauḍa, living north of the Vindhya [mountain range]. The Kārṇāṭaka, Telingana, Gụrjara and those living in the 'kingdom' (Mahārāṣṭra), and the Āndhra are the five Draviḍa, living south of the Vindhya [mountain range].'

The problem with the second stanza is that the Tailangas and Āndhras (which are usually taken to refer to the same people) are mentioned separately, while the Tamils are omitted (even though Draviḍa supposedly is equivalent to Tamil and is used as the name of all members of that family).[68] The two stanzas are found in nearly identical form in the Skandapurāṇa (after the seventh paṭala of the śakti-saṃgama-tantra) according to the Śabdakalpadruma, except that we find here *Gujjarā* for *Gurjarā* and *Drāviḍa* for *Draviḍa*.[69]

Böhtlingk & Roth (1855-1875: III: 797) quote a different version of the second stanza from a manuscript of the Vajrāsanasādhana

āndhrāḥ karṇāṭakāś caîva gurjarā draviḍās tathā /
mahārāṣṭrā iti khyātāḥ pañcaîte draviḍāḥ smṛtāḥ //

in which the Tamils are included. The oddity that Draviḍa is used twice here – once for the Tamils and then as a comprehensive term for all five ethnic groups – is mitigated by the fact that the same happens with the term Gauḍa in the first stanza. The parallelism of the ending of the two stanzas ('living north/south of the Vindhyas')

[68] Cf. Sastri 1967: 10-11.

[69] The tradition of the Skandhapurāṇa is notoriously vague. The stanza is not found in the text studied by Hans Bakker (oral communication).

is lost – or was the desire to have parallel endings the cause for the rewriting that led to the omission of the Tamils from the list in the Vallālacarita? Which set of stanzas is the older?

The expression *panca-dravida* is found in the Tamil Lexicon (and in the earlier Tamil dictionaries of Winslow and the Tamil-French Dictionary), and Munshi (1967: 17-18) spoke (therefore?) of a Tamil tradition. But it is obvious that the term (for which no reference is given) is taken over in its Sanskrit form and does not constitute an authentic Tamil tradition. It is probable that the border of the Marathi and Kannaḍa languages shifted further southward in recent times.[70]

Though our knowledge of the Kannaḍa language essentially begins with inscriptions dating from the sixth century A.D. and literary works somewhat later, there may be evidence of earlier literary activity. A papyrus found in Egypt and dating from the second century A.D.[71] may contain sentences in Kannaḍa, according to Hultzsch[72] – or in Tulu (a related Dravidian language) according to Rai[73]; or it may contain nothing but gibberish[74]. The comedy skit that envisions a Greek sailor's voyage to "the coast of a barbarian country bordering on the Indian Ocean"[75] is assumed to be a creation of the late first or early second century A.D.[76] The text is written without word breaks, and the Greek alphabet is not always

---

[70] Southworth 1974: 220 suggests, with reference to Gumperz & Wilson 1971: 151-168 that the border of Marathi and Kannaḍa may have shifted southward in recent times. Spate 1957: 663 points to the destruction of Vijayanagar and the later Maratha dominance combined with the administrative and commercial influence of Bombay in explaining the southward spread of Marathi. Cf. also Alsdorf 1955: 266.

[71] Grenfell & Hunt 1903: 41-57; Page 1950: 336-349.

[72] Hultzsch 1904a: 307-311 and 1904b: 399-405. He was criticized by Aiyar 1975 (repr. 1987: 268-270) who saw in the non-Greek parts of the fragment mostly Sanskrit words.

[73] Rai 1985: 320-330.

[74] Barnett 1926: 13-15; Page 1950: 337.

[75] Page 1950: 337.

[76] Hunt in Grenfell & Hunt 1904: 44. Rai 1985: 321-322, based on his identification of the language as Tulu, surmises that the scene of the drama was near the modern port of Mangalore.

ideal for expressing Indian sounds; but some of the alleged Indian expressions have Greek translations that make the identifications less of a wild guess, and an inscription in Prakrit found in the same place and era confirms the presence of Indians in Roman Egypt.[77] Of course, literary sources and excavations in South India have made us aware of trade between India and Egypt in the distant past.

Tamil is attested much earlier, in short inscriptions found in caves and attributed to Jainas and in extensive anthologies of elegant poetry. While the earliest inscriptions have tentatively been dated to the second or first century B.C., the poems of the so-called Sangam anthologies are dated mostly to the first to third centuries A.D., some secondary works a couple of centuries later.

This dating has recently been challenged by Tieken (2001), who claims that they are no older than the end of the eighth or the beginning of the ninth century A.D.[78] Since such a late dating would obviously have a bearing on the thesis put forward in the preceding pages, Tieken's claims have to be taken into account. Tieken rejects the common notion that these works are true anthologies, gathered from a large body of literary creations and claims instead that "the poems were composed only at the moment of their compilation" (Tieken 2001: 92), as proved by the steady interlocking of vocabulary between adjacent poems.[79] But Tieken's method is flawed, since in his samples he lists only those occurrences of words that occur in clusters, omitting all others. Thus on pp. 237-242 he lists in his test sample of Kuṟuntokai 1-110, e.g., *kātalar* only from poems 48, 51 (*kātaleṉ*), 103, and 104, creating the impression of two clusters. But this impression would vanish if he had included all occurrences of the word: poems 4, 24, 41, 48, 51, 60, 75, 103, and 104. Naturally the occurrences would not be

[77] Salomon 1991: 731-736 and 1993: 593; also 1994: 7-16.

[78] Tieken's thesis met with strong scepticism and outright rejection by reviewers: Cox 2002: 407-410, Monius 2002: 1404-1406, and Hart (forthcoming in *JAOS*, preview on the Internet).

[79] Such linkage has been demonstrated for Kālidāsa's Meghadūta: Schubring 1955: 331-337.

evenly spread throughout the 110 poems, but the apparent bunching of words is as meaningless as that of numbers in a random drawing of numbers (as in a numbers lottery) or the apparent vertical white lines in a newspaper column. Hart points out that with a finite vocabulary some of the same words are bound to occur in poems that precede or follow closely, and in a counter test of ten non-contiguous poems from the Kuṟuntokai he found even greater overlapping of vocabulary. With that demonstration Tieken's main argument collapses. Furthermore, his claim is unpersuasive that a poet under the revived Pandya dynasty concocted dynastic histories, archaic social conditions and an archaic language in what could only be called an elaborate forgery, much grander in scale than James Macpherson's Ossian Hymns and his concocted "original" text in bad Gaelic.[80] And how would an author of the ninth century know of King Atiyamāṉ 'son of the Atiyars' (Puṟanāṉūṟu 101, 5) corresponding to Satiyaputo in Asokas Rock Edict 2?[81]

In many of his discussions Tieken has displayed his "tin ear" for poetry, when he sees everywhere indications that the authors wished to show the stupidity of the so-called heroines (who cannot believe that the monsoon has arrived, since the lover has not yet returned [p. 50], or blame the royal servant's chariot that does not know how to return home [p. 30 fn. 41]). Pretended animation of inanimate objects is a common feature of speech, especially of poetic language, as already Kātyāyana and Patañjali observed (Thieme 1960), a device used beautifully by Kālidāsa in his Meghadūta. Perverse stubbornness in his pursuit is also evident in Tieken's treatment of Kuṟuntokai 359, the idyllic picture of a father playing with his little son: since in some poems it is the love of his

[80] *Chambers's Encyclopædia*, new rev. ed., Oxford 1967, vol. 8, p. 783; *The New Encyclopædia Britannica*, 15th ed., Chicago 2003, Micropædia, Vol. 8, p. 1031.

[81] Aiyar 1937: 18 and Burrow 1947: 136-137 (repr. 1968: 158-159). Initial /s/ was lost in Southern Dravidian before our oldest texts (e.g., *iñci*[*vēṟu*] > Pali *siṅgivera*, Sanskrit *śr̥ṅgavera* 'ginger root').

little son that brings the unfaithful husband back to his suffering wife, even this sweet poem (and there are more!) must surely hide some awful secret (pp. 45-49)! And how could such joyless poetry serve to glorify a revived Pandya dynasty, as the author claims?

Of the seventy-three Tamil inscriptions found in natural caves, some are even older, dating from the first or second century B.C. (Mahadevan 1968: 57-73; 1971: 73-103). Some of the inscriptions which Mahadevan assigns to the "early" period (i.e., 2nd - 1st cent. B.C.) have lengthy compounds: no. 27 from Cittannavacal *erumi-nāṭu-kumuḷ-ūr-piṟanta* [*kavuṭi itenku*] '[to Kavuṭi Iten] born at Kumuḷ-ūr in Erumi-nāṭu, no. 28 *eḻaiy-ūr-aritiṉ-paḷi* 'monastery of Aritj of Eḻai-ūr', and no. 51 *erukāṭ-ur-īḻa-kuṭumpikaṉ-polālaiyaṉ* 'Polālaiyaṉ of Erukāṭṭ-ūr, a householder from Ceylon'.

If then the Sangam texts and some Tamil inscriptions are as old and even older than the oldest Prakrit and Sanskrit texts exhibiting long compounds, the immediate conclusion would be that this peculiar style originated in Dravidian poetry. But sceptics might argue that the synchronicity – even antecedence – of Tamil records does not absolutely rule out borrowing in the opposite direction. This argument can be answered on two levels. We have traced the development of composition from Vedic to Prakrit and Sanskrit and found no trend in favor of long compounds except for dvandvas (a new type of compound following its own trajectory). On the Dravidian side, long compounds mark even the oldest Tamil texts; the development leading up to this style is lost in prehistory, but can partially be recovered through comparative linguistics. Unfortunately, most of our available reference works on Dravidian linguistics are virtually silent on the topic of compounds. But there can be no doubt that Proto-Dravidian had nominal compounds or something close to them. There is the cluster of names of relationship treated by Emenau: *entai* 'my father', *nuntai* 'your father', *tantai* 'his/her father', etc., that combine a pronoun with a term of relationship and are attested in several Dravidian languages (Emeneau 1953: 339-353). *kaṇṇīr* 'tear', a compound of *kaṇ* 'eye' and *nīr* 'water', *eṇṇey* 'sesame oil', a compound of *eḷ* (or *eṇ*) 'sesame' and *ney* 'oil' are found in several Dravidian languages,[82] and so are the compound names of several fruits, e.g. *tēṅkāy* 'coconut'[83], and *māṅkāy* 'unripe mango fruit'[84]. Bloch (1954: 101, 108) gives an example of a compound with three members from Kui, a Central Dravidian language from Orissa: on *kēta* 'low land' and *nēḍa* 'high land' one can form with the appellative *gaṭanju* (implying agency)[85] a derivative *kēta-nēḍa-gaṭenju* 'peasant', and another from Kurukh in the Ḍekkhan: *mainā-kukk-pello* 'maina-headed girl, a girl with smoothly combed hair'. Compounds with uninflected words are thus established as a feature of Dravidian speech. Some case "suffixes" are still also used as independent words: *il* 'house' and *kaṇ* 'place' mark a locative, indications of the "agglutinative" character of Dravidian (Bloch 1954: 18-21; Meenakshisundaran 1965: 101-102).

The same can be demonstrated for compound-like constructions with participles that link as "hinges" subordinate actions to the main action of a sentence. These adjectival participles (*peyar-eccam*) are besides the adverbial participles (*viṉaiyeccam*) the only means of creating sentences with subordinate actions, since Dravidian has neither relative clauses (Caldwell 1961: 520-521) nor temporal, conditional or concessive dependent clauses.

The influence of South Indian literary style on Sanskrit and Prakrit literature should come as no surprise: southern poets were considered "masters of literary effect" by the poet Bhartṛhari.[86] Some Sanskrit poets, like Daṇḍin, were South Indians themselves.[87] We found evidence of long compounds in poetry and

---

[82] Burrow & Emeneau 1961: nr. 726.

[83] Burrow & Emeneau 1961: nr. 2806 (*teṉ* 'coco-nut tree' + *kāy* 'fruit').

[84] Burrow & Emeneau 1961: nr. 3919 (*mā* 'mango'+ *kāy* 'fruit').

[85] Winfield 1928: 90, 93, 134; 1929 (repr. 1985: 40).

[86] Śatakatraya III 58: [*agre gītaṃ*] *sarasa-kavayaḥ* [*pārśvato*] *dākṣiṇātyāḥ*. The almost identical stanza in Subhāṣitāvali 3467 has no reference to southern poets.

[87] Daṇḍin may even have been aware of the Tamil anthologies, if the commentators are right in taking *saṃghāta* in Kāvyâdarśa I 13 as *dramiḍasaṃghāta*

inscriptions from the Western Dekkhan. Eventually, though, long compounds became rather more the characteristic of North Indian (*gauḍa*)[88] poetry than that from the South (*vidarbha*)[89]. The poetician Bhāmaha (fourth or fifth century A.D.?) refers to a notion of *gauḍa* and *vaidarbha* style[90] and declares that avoidance of long compounds lends sweetness and clarity, and that some authors use compounds to exhibit "power"[91]. Dandin (late seventh century) says the *gauḍīya* style cultivates "strength" (*ojas*) through long compounds in both verse and prose (a practice he dislikes), whereas the *vaidarbha* style uses "strength" through the use of compounds sparingly, except in prose, where it is essential.[92]

Actually, none of the modern Indian languages, Indo-Aryan or Dravidian, use long compounds now – except that Dravidian languages continue to use constructions with verbal and adjectival participles (*viṉaiyeccam* and *peyareccam*) that can be very long. The use of long compounds of nouns without case endings – if it ever was part of spoken Tamil – has in historical times apparently always been a strictly literary style, not a form of spoken discourse.[93] It certainly did not gain a foothold in the Modern Indo-Aryan languages.[94] The same may be the case with some of the

---

'collections of Tamil' rather than as "ein in einem und demselben Metrum abgefasstes Gedicht" (Böhtlingk & Roth), "a poem composed in one and the same metre" (Monier-Williams).

[88] The name Gauḍa 'sugar country' refers to modern Gaur in Bengal and the neighboring territory.

[89] The name Vidarbha refers to modern Berar in Maharashtra.

[90] Kāvyâlankāra I 31-33.

[91] Kāvyâlankāra II 1-2.

[92] Kāvyâdarśa (*alias*) Kāvyalakṣaṇa I 80-84; Warder 1972: 94-95. Vāmana (Kāvyâlaṃkārasūtra II 19) declares that "pure" *vaidarbhī rīti* has no compounds and Rudraṭa flatly declares that the *vaidarbhī* is without compounds (Warder 1972: 96, 100). Similarly Rājaśekhara, Kāvyamīmāṃsā p. 8, lines 14-15 (*samāsavat... gauḍīyā rītiḥ*), and p. 9, lines 22-23 (*asamāsam ... vaidarbhī rītiḥ*).

[93] This was seen already by Burrow, but he wrongly attributed it to "the growing artificiality of the Sanskrit language" versus the vernacular Middle Indo-Aryan dialects (above p. 231).

[94] Long nominal compounds have arisen in literal and bureaucratic German (and Russian), e.g. *Vierwaldstätterseedampfschiffahrtsgesellschaft* (Henzen 1947: 243). In English, diplomats speak of a *United Nations Security Council Resolution (UNSCR).*

lexical borrowing. Bloch has suggested that individual literary men may have brought Dravidian terms into Sanskrit and that the use of these words remained provincial.[95]

Noun composition in Indo-European, especially the common form of stem-compounds, has intrigued scholars for a long time – especially the use of long compounds that we find in classical Sanskrit. An early, daring attempt at an explanation was Jacobi's booklet *Compositum und Nebensatz* (1897). Jacobi (1897: 92-93) pointed out that the long compounds surface first in Prakrit inscriptions,[96] the Jaina canon and the Purāṇas, i.e., not in learned works, and are not connected with the nominal style.[97] He was wrong in assuming that an ancient IE feature resurfaced here, one that had by-passed the Vedic literature. He and the many scholars who followed him had assumed that there was a stage in the early development of Indo-European when bare stem forms were not yet firmly connected with free-moving particles (that would eventually develop into case endings). Virtually the only proof of this stage in the development of Indo-European were these same stem compounds.

But, as Dunkel has shown, such a stage is extremely unlikely.[98] The stem compounds developed already in Common Indo-European before the break-up, analogically from certain forms of univerbation. While Jacobi saw correctly the similarity of long Sanskrit compounds with Dravidian compounds (he used Telugu as the Dravidian prototype rather than Tamil), he mistakenly believed that he had found a parallel,[99] a language structure similar to that of

[95] Bloch 1928-1930: 744; similarly Burrow 1968: 325-326 and Masica 1979: 138-139: several loanwords in Sanskrit from Dravidian did not survive into Middle Indo-Aryan, where the inherited words prevailed: *toya* 'water', *mīṉ* 'fish', and *heramba* 'buffalo'.

[96] Kielhorn 1905/1906: 39-40.

[97] Renou 1956: 96-116 tried to link the development of long compounds to the development of the sūtra-style.

[98] See above p. 213.

[99] Jacobi's remark 1897: 119 fn. 2 shows that he did not consider mutual influence likely.

his assumed early stage of Indo-European. If the use of long stem-compounds represented the surfacing of popular usage – why did it leave no trace in modern spoken dialects? Burrow (1955: 55), who called "This linguistic development .... a sign of the growing artificiality of the Sanskrit language as the difference between it and the vernacular Middle Indo-Aryan grew wider" (cf. above p. 231), overlooked the fact that the trend made its first vigorous appearance in Prakrit texts. But it is gratifying that we can ultimately agree with Jacobi on the rise of compounds in Prakrit and the similarity with Dravidian usage, with Renou on the spread of long dvandas in the sūtra literature, with Hauschild on the Dravidian influence, and with Bloch and Burrow on the literary aspects of this development.

REFERENCES

Abbreviations

BSO(A)S	=	Bulletin of the School of Oriental (and African) Studies
EI	=	Epigraphia Indica
IIJ	=	Indo-Iranian Journal
IJDL	=	International Journal of Dravidian Linguistics
JAOS	=	Journal of the American Oriental Society
JRAS	=	Journal of the Royal Asiatic Society of Great Britain and Ireland
JTS	=	Journal of Tamil Studies
MT	=	Mother Tongue
SLS	=	Studies in the Linguistic Sciences
ZDMG	=	Zeitschrift der Deutschen Morgenländischen Gesellschaft

AIYAR, K. G. Sesha 1937. *Cēra Kings of the Śangam Period*. London.

AIYAR, R. Swaminatha 1975. *Dravidian Theories*. Repr. Madras 1987.

ALSDORF, Ludwig 1955. *Vorderindien. Bharat – Pakistan – Ceylon.* Braunschweig.

ANDRONOV, M. S. 1972. Notes on the nature and origin of the adjective in Tamil. *IJDL* 1(2): 1-9.

------ 1975. Dravidian pronouns: a comparative study. *JTS* 7: 14-18.

------ 1989. *A Grammar of Modern and Classical Tamil.* 2nd ed. Madras.

ARDEN, A. H. 1942. *A Progressive Grammar of Common Tamil.* 5th ed. Madras.

BAILEY, H. W.1957. *Dvārā matīnām. BSOAS* 20: 41-59.

BANERJI, R. D. 1921/1922. The Sanchi Inscription of Svamin Jivadaman: the 13th Year. *EI* 16: 230-233.

BARNETT, L. 1926. The alleged Kanarese speeches in P. Oxy. 413. *Journal of Egyptian Archaeology* 12: 13-15.

BLOCH, Jules 1930. Some problems of Indo-Aryan philology. *BSOS* 5: 719-756.

------ 1934. *L'indo-aryen du Véda aux temps modernes*. Paris.

------ 1970. *The Formation of the Marāṭhī Language*. Translated by Dev Raj Chanana. Delhi. (French original 1914.)

------ 1954. *The Grammatical Structure of Dravidian Languages*. Trans. Ramkrishna Ganesh Harshé. Poona.

BÖHTLINGK, Otto & Rudolph ROTH 1855-1875. *Sanskrit-Wörterbuch*. St. Petersburg. Repr. Delhi 1990.

BÜHLER, Georg 1890. Die indischen Inschriften und das Alter der indischen Kunstpoesie. *Sitzungsberichte der Akademie der Wissenschaften, Wien*, Vol. 122: 11: 1-98.

BURROW, Thomas 1943-1946. Dravidian studies V: Initial *y* an *ñ* in Dravidian. *BSOAS* 11: 595-616. (= Burrow 1968: 113-149.)

------ 1947. Dravidian studies VI: The loss of initial *c/s* in South Dravidian. *BSOAS* 12: 132-147. (= Burrow 1968: 150-177.)

------ 1955. *The Sanskrit Language*. London.

------ 1958. Sanskrit and the Pre-Aryan tribes and languages. *Bulletin of the Ramakrishna Mission*. (= Burrow 1968: 319-340.)

------ 1968. *Collected Papers on Dravidian Linguistics*. Annamalainagar.

BURROW, Thomas & M. B. EMENEAU 1961. *A Dravidian Etymological Dictionary*. Oxford.

CALDWELL, Robert 1961 [1875]. *A Comparative Grammar of the Dravidian or South-Indian Family of Languages*. 3rd ed., repr. Madras.

CARDONA, George 1965. *A Gujarati Reference Grammar*. Philadelphia.

CHHABRA, B. & G. S. GAI (eds.) 1981. *Corpus Inscriptionum Indicarum*, III. *Inscriptions of the Early Gupta Kings*. Revised by D. R. Bhandarkar. New Delhi.

Chambers's Encyclopædia 1967. New rev. ed. Oxford.

CHATTERJI, Suniti Kumar 1926. *The Origin and Development of the Bengali Language*. Repr. London 1970.

COX, Whitney 2002. Review of H. Tieken, *Kāvya in South India*. *JRAS* 2002: 407-410.

DAVANE, Gulab V. 1956. *Nominal Composition in Middle Indo-Aryan*. Poona.

DRIEM, G. van 1999. On the Austroasiatic Indus theory. *MT*, Special Issue (October), Appendix: 75-83.

DUNKEL, George 1999. On the origins of nominal composition in Indo-European. In: H. Eicher & H. C. Luschützky (eds.), *Compositiones Indogermanicae in Memoriam Jochem Schindler*: 47-68. Praha.

EMENEAU, M. B. 1953. Dravidian kinship terms. *Language* 29: 339-353.

------ 1954, Linguistic prehistory of India. *Proceedings of the American Philosophical Society* 98: 282-292. Philadelphia.

------ 1956. India as a linguistic area. *Language* 32: 3-16.

------ 1971. Dravidian and Indo-Aryan. In: A. F. Sjoberg (ed.), *Symposium on Dravidian Civilization*: 33-68. Austin.

ERDOSY, G. (ed.) 1995. *The Indo-Aryans of Ancient South Asia: Language, Material Culture and Ethnicity*. Berlin.

GRENFELL, B. P. & A. S. HUNT (eds.) 1903. *Oxyrhynchus Papyri*. Part III. London.

GRIERSON, G. A. (ed.) 1908. *Linguistic Survey of India*. Vol. IX: 2. Calcutta. Repr. Delhi 1973.

GUNDERT, Hermann 1869. Die dravidischen Elemente im Sanskrit. *ZDMG* 23: 517-530.

GUMPERZ, J. J. & R. WILSON 1971. Convergence and creolization: a case for the Indo-Aryan/Dravidian border. In: D. Hymes (ed.), *Pidginization and Creolization of Languages*: 151-167. Cambridge.

HAMP, Eric P. 1986. On the morphology of Indic gerunds. *IIJ* 29: 103-108.

------ 1996. On the Indo-European origins of the retroflexes in Sanskrit. *JAOS* 116: 719-723.

HART, George 2003. Review of H. Tieken, *Kāvya in South India*. (On the Internet; forthcoming in *JAOS*.)

HENZEN, Walter 1947. *Deutsche Wortbildung*. Halle.

HINÜBER, Oskar von 2003. *Beiträge zur Erklärung der Senavarma-Inschrift*. (Abhandlungen der Geistes- und sozialwissenschaftlichen Klasse / Akademie der Wissenschaften und der Literatur, 1.) Mainz.

HOCK, Hans Henrich 1975. Substratum Influence on (Rig-Vedic) Sanskrit? *SLS* 5(2): 76-125.

------ 1979. Retroflexion rules in Sanskrit. *South Asian Languages Analysis* 1: 47-62

------ 1982. The Sanskrit quotative: a historical and comparative study. *SLS* 12(2): 39-85.

------ 1984. (Pre-)Rig-Vedic convergence of Indo-Aryan with Dravidian? Another look at the evidence. *SLS* 14: 89-108.

HULTZSCH, Eugen 1904a. Zum Papyros 413 aus Oxyrhynchos. *Hermes* 39: 307-311.

------ 1904b. Remarks on a Papyrus from Oxyrhynchus. *JRAS* 1904: 399-405.

INSLER, Stanley 1998. *mitrāváruṇā* or *mitrā́ váruṇā*? In: J. Jasanoff, H. C. Melchert & L. Oliver (eds.), *Mír Curad* (Festschrift Calvert Watkins) (= Innsbrucker Beiträge zur Sprachwissenschaft, 92): 285-290. Innsbruck.

JACOBI, Hermann 1897. *Compositum und Nebensatz*. Bonn.

JOHNSTON, E. H. 1928. *The Saundarananda of Aśvaghoṣa*. Edited and translated. Lahore. Repr. Delhi 1975.

KHAIRE, Vishvanath 1977. *Dravida Maharastra*. Pune. [not seen]

------ 1978. Tamil, the language of prehistoric Maharashtra. *JTS* 15: 14-25.

------ 1979. Tamil, the language of prehistoric Maharashtra. *JTS* 16: 78-83.

------ 1980. Tamil alveolars in Marathi vocabulary. *JTS* 17: 79-93.

KIELHORN, Franz 1905/1906. Junagadh Rock Inscription of Rudradaman: the Year 72. *EI* 8: 36-49.

KONOW, Sten 1906. *Muṇḍā and Dravidian Languages*. In: G. A. Grierson (ed.), *Linguistic Survey of India*. Vol. IV. Repr. Delhi 1967.

KRISHNAMURTI, Bhadriraju 1968. Dravidian personal pronouns. In: B. Krishnamurti (ed.), *Studies in Indian Linguistics (Festschrift M. B. Emeneau)*: 189-205. Poona.

KUIPER, F. B. J. 1967. The genesis of a linguistic area. *IIJ* 10: 81-102. Reprinted in *IJDL* 3:1 (1974): 135-153.

LAL, B. B. 1960. From the Megalithic to the Harappa: tracing back the graffiti on the pottery. *Ancient India* 16: 4-24.

LEHMANN,Thomas 1994. *Grammatik des Alttamil*. Stuttgart.

LEWY, Ernst 1913. Zur Frage der Sprachmischung. In: *Beiträge zur Sprach- und Völkerkunde. Festschrift für Alfred Hillebrandt*: 110-120. Halle. (= E. Lewy, *Kleine Schriften*: 1-9. Berlin 1961.)

LIENHARD, Siegfried 1984. *A History of Classical Poetry. Sanskrit – Pali – Prakrit*. Wiesbaden.

MAHADEVAN, Iravatham 1968. Corpus of the Tamil-Brahmi Inscriptions. In R. Nagaswamy (ed.): *Kalveṭṭu karuttaranku. Seminar on Inscriptions 1966*: 57-73. Madras.

------ 1971. Tamil-Brahmi inscriptions of the Sangam Age. In: R. E. Asher (ed.), *Proceedings of the Second International Conference-Seminar of Tamil Studies, Madras, India 1968*, Vol. I: 73-106. Madras.

------ 2001. The Indus-like symbols on Megalithic pottery: new evidence. In: K. Karttunen & P. Koskikallio (eds.), *Vidyārṇavavandanam. Essays in Honour of Asko Parpola*: 379-385. Helsinki.

------ 2003. *Early Tamil epigraphy*. (Harvard Oriental Series, 62.) Cambridge [Mass.].

MASICA, Colin 1979. Aryan and Non-Aryan elements in North Indian agriculture. In: M. Deshpande & P. E. Hook (eds.), *Aryan and Non-Aryan in India*: 55-151. Ann Arbor.

------ 1991. *The Indo-Aryan Languages*. Cambridge.

MEENAKSHISUNDARAN, T. P. 1965. *A History of Tamil Language*. Poona.

MONIER-WILLIAMS, Sir Monier 1899. *A Sanskrit-English Dictionary*. 2nd ed.. Oxford.

MONIUS, Anne E. 2002. Review of H. Tieken, *Kāvya in South India*. *Journal of Asian Studies* 61: 1404-1406.

MUNDLAY, Asha 1996. Who are the Nihals? What do they speak? *MT* 2: 5-9.

MUNSHI, Kanaiyalal M. 1967. *Gujarāt and its Literature*. Bombay.

NARASIMHIA, A. N. 1941. *A Grammar of the Oldest Kanarese Inscriptions*. Mysore.

The New Encyclopædia Britannica 2003. 15th ed. Chicago.

PAGE, Sir Denys L. 1950. *Select Papyri. Literary Papyri Poetry*, III. London.

PARPOLA, Asko 2002. From the dialects of Old Indo-Aryan to Proto-Indo-Aryan and Proto-Iranian. In: N. Sims-Williams (ed.), *Indo-Iranian Languages and Peoples* (Proceedings of the British Academy, 116): 43-102. Oxford.

PAUL, Hermann 1937. *Prinzipien der Sprachgeschichte*. 5th ed., repr. Halle.

POTT, August Friedrich 1833, 1866. *Etymologische Forschungen auf dem Gebiete der Indo-Germanischen Sprachen*, I-II. Lemgo.

PRABHOO, Lalitha R. 1987. Place nominalising bridge attributes and the Northern regional-areal limits of South India. In: P. Ramachandran (ed), *Perspectives in Place Name Studies*: 185-200. Trivandrum.

RAI, P. Shivaprasad 1985. *Sariti*. *IJDL* 14: 320-330.

RAJAM, V. S. 1992. *A Reference Grammar of Classical Tamil Poetry*. Philadelphia.

RENOU, Louis 1956. Sur l'évolution des composés nominaux en Sanskrit. *Bulletin de la Société de linguistique* 52: 96-116.

RITTI, Shrinivas 1997. Kannada inscriptions in the Maharashtra State. *Quarterly Journal of the Mythic Society* 88: 1-18.

SALOMON, Richard 1991. Epigraphic remains of Indian traders in Egypt. *JAOS* 111: 731-736.

------ 1993. Addenda to "Epigraphic remains of Indian traders in Egypt." *JAOS* 113: 593.

------ 1994. Epigraphic remains of Indian traders in Egypt. *IJDL* 23: 7-16.

SANKALIA, H. D. 1949. *Studies in the Historical and Cultural Geography and Ethnography of Gujarat*. Poona.

SASTRI, K. A. Nilakanta 1967. *Cultural Contacts between Aryans and Dravidians*. Bombay.

SASTRI, P. S. Subrahmanya 1934. *History of Grammatical Theories in Tamil*. Madras.

SCHARFE, Hartmut 1983. Secondary noun formation in Pāṇini's grammar - what was the great option? In: S. D. Joshi & S. D. Laddu (eds.), *Proceedings of the International Seminar on Studies in the* Aṣṭādhyāyī *of* Pāṇini: 53-57. Pune.

------ 1989. *The State in Indian Tradition*. Leiden.

------ 1993. *Investigations in Kauṭalya's Manual of Political Science*. 2nd ed. Wiesbaden.

------ 1996. BARTHOLOMAE'S Law revisited or how the Ṛgveda is dialectally divided. *Studien zur Indologie und Iranistik* 20: 351-377.

SCHINDLER, Jochem 1997. Zur internen Syntax der indogermanischen Nominalkomposita. In: E. C. & J. G. Ramón (ed.), *Berthold Delbrück y la sintaxis indoeuropea hoy*: 537-540. Madrid / Wiesbaden.

SCHUBRING, Walther 1955. Jinasena, Mallinātha, Kālidāsa. *ZDMG* 105: 331-337.

SEN, Sukumar 1960. *A Comparative Grammar of Middle Indo-Aryan*. Poona.

SENART, E. 1905/1906. The Inscriptions in the caves at Nasik. *EI* 8: 59-96.

SHAFER, Robert 1954. *Ethnography of Ancient India*. Wiesbaden.

SHANMUGAM, S. V 1967. *Naccinarkkiniyar's Conception of Phonology*. Annamalainagar.

SIRCAR, D. C. 1993. *Select Inscriptions Bearing on Indian History and Civilization*, I. Delhi

SOUTHWORTH, Franklin C. 1974. Linguistic stratigraphy of North India. *IJDL* 3: 201-223

------ 1982. Dravidian and Indo-European: the neglected hypothesis. *IJDL* 11: 1-21.

------ 1995. Reconstructing social context from language. Indo-Aryan and Dravidian prehistory. In: Erdosy (ed.) 1995: 258-277.

SPATE, O. H. K. 1957. *India and Pakistan. A General and Regional Geography*. 2nd ed. London.

SPIES, Otto & Ernst BANNERTH 1945. *Lehrbuch der Hindūstānī-Sprache*. Leipzig & Wien.

SRIDHAR, S. N. 1981. Linguistic convergence: Indo-Aryanization of Dravidian languages. *SLS* 8(1): 197-215.

STEEVER, S. B. 1981. *Selected Papers on Tamil and Dravidian Linguistics*. Madurai.

THIEME, Paul 1954. *akhkhalīkṛtya. Zeitschrift für vergleichende Sprachforschung (auf dem Gebiete der Indogermanischen Sprachen)* (begründet von A. Kuhn) 71: 109. (= Thieme 1971: I: 138.)

------ 1955. Review of T. Burrow, *The Sanskrit Language. Language* 31: 428-448. (= Thieme 1971: II: 696-716.)

------ 1960. Beseelung in Sprache, Dichtung und Religion. *Paideuma* 7: 313-324. (= Thieme 1971: I: 374-385.)

------ 1971. *Kleine Schriften*, I-II. Wiesbaden.

THUMB, A. & R. HAUSCHILD 1958. *Handbuch des Sanskrit*. I. Teil: *Grammatik*, 1. *Einleitung und Lautlehre*. Dritte, stark umgearbeitete Auflage von Richard Hauschild. Heidelberg.

TIEKEN, Herman 2001. *Kāvya in South India. Old Tamil Cankam Poetry*. Groningen.

TIKKANEN, Bertil 1987. *The Sanskrit Gerund: A Synchronic, Diachronic and Typological Analysis*. (Studia Orientalia, 62). Helsinki.

TRASK, R. L. 1995. Response to the Comments. *MT* 1: 172-198.

VACEK, J. 1970. The Tamil of a 19th century ballad. In: Zvelebil & Vacek (eds.) 1970: 103-222.

VACEK, J. & S. V. SUBRAMANIAN 1989. *A Tamil Reader*, I-II. *Introducing Sangam Literature*. Madras.

VIJAYAVENUGOPAL, G. 1968. *A Modern Evaluation of Nannul*. Annamalainagar.

WACKERNAGAL, J. & A. DEBRUNNER. 1954. *Altindische Grammatik*, II: 2. *Die Nominalsuffixe*. Göttingen.

WARDER, A. K. 1972. *Indian Kāvya Literature*, I. Delhi.

WHITNEY, W. D. 1889. *Sanskrit Grammar*. 2nd ed. Leipzig. Repr. Delhi 1962.

WINFIELD, W. W. 1928. *A Grammar of the Kui Language*. Calcutta.

------ 1929. *A Vocabulary of the Kui Language*. Calcutta. Repr. Delhi 1985.

WITZEL, Michael 1995a. Early Indian history: Linguistic and textual parametres. In: Erdosy (ed.) 1995: 85-125.

------ 1995b. Ṛigvedic history: poets, chieftains and polities. In: Erdosy (ed.) 1995: 307-352.

------ 1999a. Aryan and non-Aryan names in Vedic India: data for the linguistic situation, c. 1900-500 B.C. In: J. Bronkhorst & M. Deshpande (eds.), *Aryan and Non-Aryan in South Asia: Evidence, Interpretation and Ideology* (Harvard Oriental Series, Opera Minora, 3): 337-404. Cambridge [Mass.].

------ 1999b. Early sources for South Asian substrate languages. *MT*, Special Issue: 1-71.

------ 2000. Die sprachliche Situation Nordindiens in vedischer Zeit. In: B. Forssman & R. Plath (eds.), *Indoarisch, Iranisch und die Indogermanistik*: 543-579. Wiesbaden.

YULE, H. & A. C. BURNELL 1968. *Hobson-Jobson*. New ed. W. Crooke. Repr. Delhi.

ZVELEBIL, Kamil 1967. The language of Peruṅkuṉṟūṟ Kiḻār: Early Old Tamil, ca. 160 to 200 A. D. In: K. Zvelebil, Yu. Glasov & M. Andronov, *Introduction to the Historical Grammar of the Tamil Language*, I: *Preliminary textual analysis*: 9-101. Moscow.

------ 1970. The language of earliest Tamil inscriptions. In: Zvelebil & Vacek (eds.) 1970: 9-101.

------ 1972. The descent of the Dravidians. *IJDL* 1:2: 57-63.

------ 1990. *Dravidian Linguistics; an Introduction*. Pondicherry.

ZVELEBIL, Kamil & J. VACEK (eds.) 1970. *Introduction to the Historical Grammar of the Tamil Language*. (Dissertationes Orientales, 25.) Prague.

TEXTS

Aiṅkuṟuṉūṟu. Ed. by C. Turaicāmippiḷḷai. Annamalai University 1957/1958.

Akanāṉūṟu. Ed. by M. Kācivicuvanātan Ceṭṭiyar. Cennai 1946, repr. 1959.

Karpūramañjarī (of Rājaśekhara). Ed. by Sten Konow. Harvard Oriental Series, IV. Cambridge [Mass.] 1901. Repr. Delhi 1963.

Kāvyâdarśa *alias* Kāvyalakṣaṇa. Ed. by Dharmendra Kumar Gupta. Delhi 1973.

Kāvyālankāra. Ed. by V. Naganatha Sastry. 2nd ed. Delhi 1970.

Kāvyamīmāṃsā (of Rājaśekhara). Ed. by M. C. Dayal & R. A. Sastry. 3rd ed. Baroda 1934.

Kuṟuntokai. Ed. by U. Vē. Cāminātaiyar. 4th ed. Cennai 1962.

Mahābhāṣya. Ed. by F. Kielhorn. 3rd ed. by K. V. Abhyankar. Poona 1962-1972.

Maturaikkāñci. In: Pattuppāṭṭu. Ed. by U. Vē. Cāminātaiyar. 6th ed. Madras 1961.

Naṟṟiṇai. Ed. by South India Saiva Siddhanta Works Publishing Society. 3rd ed. Madras 1962.

Paripāṭal. Ed. and transl. by François Gros. Pondichéry 1968.

Premcand: *Godān*. Ilāhābād 1936, repr. 1976.

Puṟanāṉūṟu. Ed. by U. Vē. Cāminātaiyar. 5th ed. Madras 1956.

Śatakatrayam (of Bhartr̥hari). Ed. by Rāmakr̥ṣṇaśarman & Dāmodaraśarman. Ānandāśrama Sanskrit Series 127. 2nd ed. Pune 1977.

Sattasaï (of Hāla). Ed. by A. Weber. Leipzig 1881.

Saundarānandakāvya (of Aśvaghoṣa). See JOHNSTON 1928.

Subhāṣitāvali. Ed. by P. Peterson & Durgāprasāda. 2nd ed. by Raghunath Damodar Karmarkar. Poona 1961.

Tirumurukāṟṟuppaṭai. In: Pattuppāṭṭu. Ed. by U. Vē. Cāminātaiyar. 6th ed. Madras 1961.

Tolkāppiyam: Collātikāram. South India Saiva Siddhanta Works Publishing Society editions with the commentaries of Iḷampūraṇar. Madras 1963, of Ceṉāvaraiyar, Madṛas 1959, and of Nacciṉārkkiṉiyar, Madras 1962.

Vallālacaritam. Ed. by Haraprasād Shāstrī. (Bibliotheca Indica, New Series, 164.) Calcutta 1904.

Vāmana Kāvyâlaṃkārasūtra. Ed. by Hargovinda Shastri. Varanasi 1989.

The Sanskrit translation of the Avestan Haoma Liturgy in the light of recent research

JOHN S. SHELDON

1. INTRODUCTION

When Abraham Anquetil Duperron brought his hard-won manuscripts from India to Paris in 1764 they contained the whole of the existing Avesta[1]. Some texts were equipped with interlinear translations and exegetical notes (Zand) in Pahlavi[2]; in some cases there was in addition a Sanskrit translation. In 1771 Anquetil published his edition of the Avesta with a French translation based upon the explanation of the texts which he had received during his years of study with learned Parsis in Surat. He had no real understanding of Pahlavi[3] and it seems that he did not know Sanskrit[4]. He did not publish the Pahlavi or Sanskrit versions. William Jones, who was then still at Oxford, but was later to become the founder of

---

[1] Written in the Old Iranian language now called Avestan (earlier erroneously Zend or Zend-Avesta) in a clear alphabet based on middle Persian scripts derived from Aramaic and containing vowel letters.

[2] The Middle Iranian language of the Sassanian court written in a highly ambiguous alphabet derived from Aramaic with only twelve consonantal signs and many ideograms of Aramaic words equipped with Iranian terminations. Zand means the translations and commentaries on the Avesta in Pahlavi.

[3] Anquetil's edition of the Avesta contains a glossary of Pahlavi terms no doubt provided by his learned informants.

[4] See Sir William Jones, *Asiatic Researches*, II §3 quoted by Darmesteter 1880: xx. The fact that an easy key to translation lay to hand in the Sanskrit and that Anquetil did not use it is further proof.

European Sanskrit scholarship, led the charge against Anquetil impugning the authenticity of the documents. In the following decades little interest in the subject was displayed by the scholarly world owing to the perception that the works were forgeries in some form of debased or corrupted Sanskrit.

When Sylvestre de Sacy deciphered the early Sassanian Pahlavi inscriptions 1793, he made use of the glossary of Pahlavi terms provided in Anquetil's edition, a break-through which led later to the decipherment of the Persian cuneiform inscriptions; this discovery of the Old Persian language of the Achaemenian Empire[5] provided the final decisive proof of the authenticity of Avestan which was seen to be a closely related dialect. An important contribution to a proper understanding of Avestan as representing an independent branch of the Indo-European language family, related to Sanskrit but closer to Persian, was made by the Danish scholar Rasmus Rask in his treatise published in 1826.

The first man to use the Sanskrit translation contained in the manuscripts in order to gain better understanding of the meaning of the Avesta was, it seems, Eugène Burnouf[6], who between 1833 and 1835 published a commentary on the Yasna. In this he made judicious use of the methods of comparative philology recently developed by Franz Bopp to provide a valuable insight into the grammar and vocabulary of Avestan, especially in its relationship to Sanskrit.

Meanwhile little progress was made with Pahlavi, which was seen as a mixed language extraordinarily difficult to interpret owing to its highly ambiguous writing system. In 1839 Josef Müller, who had been working on the Pahlavi in the manuscripts, published a ground-breaking article on the subject in the Journal of the Royal Asiatic Society. Thus it was that Ferdinand Spiegel,

---

[5] Rawlinson published his transcription and translation of the Old Persian Behistun inscription in 1846.

[6] Burnouf worked on the Behistun inscription and went quite far in correct decipherment independently of Rawlinson and the German scholars.

when he published his edition of the Avesta in 1853 and 1858, was able to include the Pahlavi translation[7].

After this much work was done to elucidate the Pahlavi which was seen by some to provide an essential key to an understanding of the original language.[8] James Darmesteter provided an important new translation of the Avesta in 1892-1893[9] in which much reliance was placed on the Pahlavi, Persian and Sanskrit translations. When in 1904 Christian Bartholomae produced his monumental *Altiranisches Wörterbuch*, the cornerstone of all future Avestic studies, he provided most words with the equivalent Pahlavi and Sanskrit translation. Henceforth these Pahlavi and Sanskrit versions were usually considered in any translation or interpretation of Avestan passages.[10]

The Sanskrit version has always been regarded as of secondary importance to the Pahlavi, as it claims to be a translation of that language, not of the original Avestan. Its authorship is attributed to Neriosangh, son of Dhaval, a Parsi cleric who lived in the latter part of the 12th Century and the early part of the 13th Century in Gujarat. Neriosangh's native tongue would have been Old Gujarati;[11] it is possible that he may have known New Persian as well.[12] Old Gujarati has much in common with Sanskrit in vocabulary and word formation, though it would take a trained linguist to see more than certain obvious resemblances, just as an Italian can

---

[7] He calls it Huzvāresch.

[8] Hübschmann 1872a sounded a strong note of warning about too much reliance on Pahlavi particularly in the Gāthas.

[9] This was preceded by his English versions of considerable portions of the Avesta published in *The Sacred Books of the East* series from 1880.

[10] For some years Avestan scholars have been generally divided into two schools of thought: those who continue to place great emphasis on the value of the Pahlavi translation in elucidating the text and those who seek to find explanations by studying parallel passages within the surviving Avesta and in the Old Indian Vedic texts, especially the Rigveda. See Humbach 1991: I: 72-73. Humbach is a strong advocate of the latter approach.

[11] An Old Gujarati translation appears in some mss. but it is fragmentary and according to Barucha 1910 it is not the work of Neriosangh. Westergaard 1852-1854: 11, 12 attributes it to Framji Aspandiarji.

[12] See Spiegel 1861: 10.

recognize some Latin without knowing that language. As a Dastur, Neriosangh must have received much instruction in the understanding of texts according to traditional interpretation. His training in Sanskrit was no doubt part of the schooling in India at the time. He may well have spoken as well as read and written the language. The fact that his written Sanskrit diverges from Classical usage[13] and displays idiosyncratic features which have been attributed to Gujarati influence on 'Parsi Sanskrit' is not surprising. It was no doubt the vernacular Sanskrit of the schools. His knowledge of Avestan is a more complex question.[14] *Prima facie* one is tempted to assume that this liturgical language, although deciphered in the Iranian context through the Pahlavi Zand, revealed some of its form and meaning to a reader of Sanskrit through the obvious similarity of some of its words.[15]

The inflexions, syntactical and grammatical structures of these two languages of comparable antiquity at times reveal their similarity even to the linguistically untrained eye. To take one striking example – at Y, X, 14 (c) 'I give this body which to me', the Avestan reads daδąmi imąm tanūm yā mē and the Sanskrit translation uses exactly the same words **dadāmi imāṃ tanuṃ yā me**[16] **(Example 1)**. The Pahlavi, on the other hand, looks quite different *dahēm ēn ī man tan kē.* It would not be difficult for any reader to draw the conclusion that Avestan and Sanskrit had some common bond which separated them from Pahlavi. It might simply have been seen as a mark of antiquity; it might have been attributed to some form of borrowing; it is even possible that scholars thought of the possibility of a common source to explain some of these

[13] For example, see IX, 28 (a) Av vī... bara, Pah *be... barē,* Skt **vinā... kuru** 'remove' where N gives the meaning of separation by use of the preposition **vinā** but departs from normal Skt usage by treating it as a prefix separated from its verb.

[14] Geldner 1896: Prolegomena xxxiii comments 'his Avesta knowledge was not at any rate profound.'

[15] There is no reason to doubt N's ability to read the Avestan alphabet, since he reads the very similar Pazand and has translated many texts in that alphabet.

[16] N usually translates 'body' by **vapus** and he may be consciously imitating Av here.

remarkable similarities. We may safely assume that a fuller understanding of Avestan phonology, morphology and syntax as known to modern philologists would not have been possible for even the most learned Zoroastrian clerics. Nevertheless the degree of this understanding may have been underestimated by Avestan scholars of the modern era.

2. NERIOSANGH'S TRANSLATION

In her recent survey of the Pahlavi technique employed in translating *Hōm Yašt*, Judith Josephson[17] has identified the two chief aims of the translator as (1) 'to determine the value of the words of the original and establish what he considers the closest lexical equivalent' and (2) 'to maintain the words in the same sequence as that of the Avestan so that the translation would truly reflect the original text.'[18] She also notes that despite these two constraints he tries to write correct and comprehensible Pahlavi using established vocabulary and its predetermined sequence of words as much as possible. In attempting the task of rendering a highly inflected language into one which has lost many of its inflections and used prepositions, enclitic pronouns and fixed word order to create meaning, the translator has to confront a continual conflict in reconciling his two chief aims. It seems clear that Neriosangh had the same two chief aims, although in his case it was to give the meaning by establishing lexical equivalents in Sanskrit and maintaining the same sequence of words so that his version could be used as a key to an understanding of the Pahlavi. Like the Pahlavi translator he attempts to write correctly and comprehensi-

---

[17] The research of Judith Josephson into the Pahlavi translation of *Hōm Yašt* (1997) has been the starting point for this examination. Her clear presentation of the material has been an invaluable aid in the work of comparing the Sanskrit translation with the Pahlavi. The earliest treatment of the subject (Spiegel 1861) is still of great value. The other work to which I am chiefly indebted is Unvala 1924. The edition of the Sanskrit translation by Barucha 1906 remains an important tool for this work.

[18] A good example of this is N's use of participles corresponding to Av in places where Pah usage requires periphrasis.

bly, although his language diverges from the norms of classical usage at times. Occasionally it is ungrammatical.

Example 2[19]

Av - mā ciš pauruuō būiδiiaēta nō vīspe pauruua būiδiiōimaiδe
'may no one recognize us first! May we first recognize all!'

Pah - *ma kas pēš wēnād (pēš az) amā az harwispīn pāš wēnām*
'may no one recognize us first (before) us! May we recognize before all!'

Skt - **mā kaścit purā paśyatu puro 'smād vayaṃ sarvebhyaḥ puraḥ paśyāma** 'may no one see first before us! May we see before all!' [IX, 21 (b)]

The Av optative, subjunctive in Pah, becomes 3rd sing. imperative in Skt; otherwise the imitation of Pah produces .two awkward sentences. Av accusative nō 'us' is changed to the nominative producing grammatical anomalies in Pah and Skt.

From the time that Pahlavi came to be understood and used as a tool for interpreting Avestan by European philologists, it was recognized that its translations were of uneven quality, hence usefulness, for this purpose.[20] *Hōm Yašt* has been regarded as one of the more satisfactory of these versions, but since it is itself of inconsistent quality, it has been attributed to the work of several authors of varying competence. Study of the Sanskrit translation of *Hōm Yašt* reveals, I believe, a similar situation. At its best the translation is the work of a highly competent writer who is learned in religious lore and sensitive to the nuances in his texts. We may reasonably assign this to Neriosangh himself. In a few places the text is aberrant, sometimes wildly so, and although corruption may

---

[19] From here on the following abbreviations are used: N for Neriosangh; Av for Avesta or Avestan or the Avestan version; Pah for Pahlavi or the Pahlavi translator; Skt for Sanskrit or the Sanskrit version.

[20] Hübschmann 1872b: 639 drew attention to the fact that the translation of Vīdēvdāt and the Young Avestan parts of Yasna were of much better quality than the Gāthas.

be at work, it cannot be the sole cause of this; in such cases attribution must be made to less competent and probably later editorial work. Such editing is more evident in the later sections of each of the three individual *Yašts* and more evident in *Yašts* X and XI than in *Yašt* XI.

Sometimes the meaning of the original Avestan seems to have been altered by the Pahlavi translators to reflect shifts in emphasis in religious practice and these are usually followed in the Sanskrit version. Most notable among these are avoidance of reference to animal sacrifice and the use of Haoma to produce intoxication. The former has led to deep-seated alteration in various places which has reduced the comprehensibility of the text and led to further distortion, which Neriosangh seems to have attempted to correct at times.

Example 3

Av - yasə tē bāδa haoma zāire-gauua iristahe baxšaite 'whoever continually partakes of you, oh golden Haoma, mixed with cow['s milk / meat]'

Pah - *kē tō bāstān hōm ī zarren ō gōšt gumēzēd* (...) *baxšēd* (*pad bahr*) 'whoever continually mixes you, oh golden Haoma, with meat (...) (and) distributes you (in portions)'

Skt - **ye tvāṃ nityaṃ hūma suvarṇābha gosaṃśliṣṭaṃ vibhajanti** 'those who continually partake of you, oh golden Haoma, mixed with cow['s milk]' [X, 13 (d)]

Av gauua iristahe seems to mean 'mixed with cow['s milk / meat]' and this is faithfully followed by N in his translation **gosaṃśliṣṭaṃ.** Pah *o gōšt gumēzēd* 'mixed with meat' is immediately followed by an explanatory gloss (not in N) to explain that *šir* 'milk' is meant.[21]

---

[21] It is possible that N has simply followed the meaning given in the gloss and for this reason does not translate it, but this does not accord with his usual practice. For a discussion of the possible dilution of Haoma with milk or water following reforms of Zaraθuštra see Humbach 1991: 71.

Example 4

Av - gāuš zaotārəm zauuaiti 'the cow curses the priest (??)'

Pah - *gāw zōt rafēd* 'the cow curses the priest'

Skt - **gauḥ gr̥hītāram ākrośayati** 'the cow curses the one who seizes him' [XI, 1 (c)]

In the parallel sections[22] the horse curses his rider and Haoma curses his drinker. Here the cow must be cursing his eater, not, it would seem because meat-eating is evil, but because the zaotār does not distribute the cooked meat, keeping it selfishly for the consumption of himself and his family. If zaotār here has its usual meaning of 'priest', one cannot avoid the conclusion that the earliest form of this passage related to a time when sacrificial meat was distributed by priests.

With regard to the avoidance of the use of Haoma as an intoxicant, the Avestan text itself already shows that earlier favourable references to such use remain in isolated passages which have been overlaid by later writers replacing 'intoxication' with 'knowledge' or 'wisdom'.

Example 5

Av - nī tē zāire maδəm mruiiē 'I call down your intoxication/knowledge, oh golden one'

Pah - *be tō zarrēn māyišn gōw* 'you golden one, proclaim intoxication/knowledge!'

Skt - **nitāntaṃ tvaṃ suvarṇābha vidyām brūhi** 'speak emphatically knowledge, you golden one!' [IX 17 (a)][23]

---

[22] Bartholomae 1904: 1880 sees a tripartite division Priester-, Krieger-, Bauerstand represented here by the cow, the horse and Haoma. It seems unlikely.

[23] N seems not to understand that Av nī and Pah *be* are preverbs belonging to the verbs in (a) and (f). His **nitāntaṃ** must be an attempt to ape the first syllable of Av. Repeated emphatic preverbs recur throughout this text and N does not understand them as tmeses. See example 12. **nitāntam** is similarly used to translate Av preverb nī in IX 18 (a) and X, 12 (d).

Av maδəm clearly originally meant 'intoxication', but N translates the word unambiguously as 'knowledge'. This is the norm in the Pahlavi translation. Neriosangh is obviously part of the later tradition reflected to the present day in the homeopathic use of a small quantity of ephedrine in the Parsi Yasna ceremony.

I have had cause to suspect bowdlerizing in some places where the original may have seemed to be improper by reason of sexual references; in one such place Neriosangh may have been less coy,[24] but the state of the text is too poor for absolute certainty about this.

Example 6

Av - auuaŋhərəzāmi janiiaoš ūnąm mairiiaiiå əuuītō-xarδaiiå 'I renounce the ... of the ... evil woman'

Pah - *u-t be hilom pad zanišn (...) un (sū<rag>) ī marān* 'and for you I renounce (?) ... the ... (hole) of evil men'

Skt - **avakṣepaya apaghāte śroṇiṃ nr̥śaṃsānāṃ paribhraṣṭa-buddhīnām** 'I cast aside in defence the loins of the crazed wicked ones' [X, 15 (a)]

The Avestan hapax ūnąm may well be a word thought too crudely descriptive of the female anatomy by the Pah translator who seems engaged in bowdlerizing here. N, perhaps influenced by the less inhibited Sanskrit tradition, is likely to give a better clue to the original meaning with **śronim**.[25] It is therefore surprising that his translation has not been used in elucidating the passage.[26] The Pah translation of the first line is deeply flawed. The word *un* (apparently a creation to represent the isolated Av form) has been glossed with *swlg* 'hole'[27] which has in turn been partly overwritten by the

[24] X, 15 (a). See also IX, 28 (d) (example 12).

[25] Unvala 1924 translates the word metaphorically as 'band' i.e. 'gang' – a meaning not attested in Monier-Williams 1889 – to suit Pah *gilistag* in the gloss.

[26] Bartholomae 1904: 1407 makes no mention of it. See further Josephson 1997: 99 fn. 57 with references. In Tocharian B *oñiye* translates **śroṇim** and it is conceivable that the Tocharian form conceals a cognate of Av ūnąm.

[27] *sūrāg* is given in MacKenzie 1971.

gloss (*gilistag ī wattarān* 'abode of the evil ones') continuing the change from fem. sing. in Av to masc. plur. which is followed by N.[28] There is no translation of Av əuuītō-xareδaiią̊ for which various meanings have been suggested[29] and Bartholomae based his meaning on N's **paribhraṣṭabuddhīnām** 'those whose minds are astray'. The Pah phrase *pad zanišn* surely conceals an earlier version in which *zan* 'woman' was used in translating Av janiiaoš.

There are a few places where the Sanskrit translator shows independence, no doubt for the benefit of his readers in Gujarat, by introducing some local colour. A good example of this is his substitution of 'tigers etc' for 'wolves' at IX, 18 (c).

Example 7

Av - mairiianąmca bizaṇgranąm ašəmaoγanąmca bizaṇgranąm vəhrkanąmca caθβarə.zaṇgranąm 'of two-legged rascals and two-legged deceivers of the religion and four-legged wolves'

Pah - *mar-iz ī dō-zang ud ahlamōγ-iz ī dō-zang gurg-iz ī cahār-zang* 'of two-legged rascals and two-legged deceivers of the religion and four-legged wolves'

Skt - **nr̥śaṃsānāṃ ca dvicaraṇanānāṃ āsmogānāṃ ca dvicaraṇanānāṃ vyāghrādīnāṃ ca caturaṃghrīṇām** 'of two-legged rascals and two-legged deceivers of the religion and four-footed tigers etc' [IX, 18 (c)]

This is an unusually blatant case of deliberate alteration.[30] Can it possibly be that the similarity of the appearance of the words in Av and Skt has influenced the translator in making the change?

Parsi marriage custom has been seen to lie behind the use the causative form of the root **yāc** in IX, 23 (a) in reference to a suitor who engages another to press his suit. Similarly an otherwise unex-

---

[28] See discussion by Josephson 1997: 99 who refers to the article by Schmidt on this subject 1969: 124-132.

[29] Flattery & Schwartz 1989: 113 suggest 'filthy'.

[30] Unvala 1924 *ad loc.* describes it as 'typical', but gives no parallels.

plained change from feminine to masculine in the liturgical context of X, 15 (c) has been attributed to 'the Parsi custom, which does not allow a woman to offer a sacrifice'.[31]

Example 8

Av - yā taṯ yaṯ haomahe draonō nigå̊ŋhəṇti nīšhiδaiti nōiṯ tąm āθrauuō.puθrīm naēδa dasti hupuθrīṃ lit. '(the evil woman) who sits down to devour[32] Haoma's share she will not be given priest-sons, good sons'

Pah - *kē ēdōn ān ī hōm sūr ō jōyišn be nihēd* (...) *nē ōy ān ī āsrō pus* (...) *u-š nē dahīhēd hu-pusīh* (...) lit. '(she) who thus sets down Haoma's feast to devour (...) not for her (will there be) priestly sons (...) and she will not be given (a gift of) good sons'

Skt - **evaṃ yo hūmasya utsavaṃ khādanāya nivedayati (...) na tasmai ācaryaṃ putraṃ datteca suputratvam** lit. 'thus to him who announces the feast of Haoma for consuming he (Haoma) does not bestow a (religious) teacher son (and) a good provision of sons' [X, 15 (c)]

It may, of course, be nothing more than the ambiguity of Pah *kē* (masc. fem. sing or plur.) that has caused the alteration. Difficulty in interpreting Av has led to awkward translations, although the meaning is clear enough and is made clearer in the glosses. Those who approach the Haoma rite simply to consume the sacred beverage or eat a share of the meat without true devotion will not be accorded good sons worthy of priesthood.

Although Neriosangh claims in his introduction to be translating the Pahlavi and makes no mention of the Avestan,[33] it is highly

---

[31] Unvala 1924 *ad loc.* draws attention to the Parsi Gujarati form **ejayate** instead of Classical Skt *yājayati* in the gloss following **nivedayati.**

[32] Bartholomae 1904: 1754.

[33] **idam ijisnijaṃdapustakaṃ mayā niriosaṃghena dhavalasutena pahlavijaṃdāt saṃskṛtabhāṣāyām avatāritam** 'this book the Yasna has been translated from Pahlavi into Sanskrit by me Neriosangh, son of Dhaval'.

likely that he would have had the Avestan text in front of him as he wrote, since his assumed exemplar derives from the manuscript of Farnbag (ca. 1100 CE)[34] which combined Avestan and Pahlavi.[35] It is interesting therefore that he departs from the Pahlavi text quite frequently. There are a number of possible reasons for this. The first is that he may have been working from a Pahlavi text different to that which appears with our earliest copies of his translation.[36] This was the view of Spiegel (1861: 3). A second possibility is that there are times when he misunderstands the Pahlavi and translates erroneously. Finally he may decide that the text in front of him is incorrect and emends accordingly. In making the emendation, he may either base this on commonsense, informed guesswork or knowledge derived from some third source; but it is also possible that he is correcting the Pahlavi from his knowledge of the Avestan, such as it was. Some examples which illustrate these possibilities follow.

Example 9

(here N may have a different text or misunderstand Pah or emend independently)

Av - haomō təmcit̰ yim kərəsānīm apa.xšaθrəm nišāδaiiat̰ 'Haoma put down from his sovereignity him who is Keresani / the robber / the Christian (?)'

Pah - *hōm awēšān kē karsāgīg hēnd ā-šān be az xwadāyīh nišānēd* 'Haoma puts down those who are robbers / Christians (?) - those (he puts down) from their sovereignty'

Skt - **hūmas tāṃścit ye kalaśiyākāḥ aparājyān niṣādayati** 'Haoma puts down from their sovereignity those who are K......' [IX, 24 (a)]

---

[34] Geldner 1896: Prolegomena xxxiii, xxxiv *et passim.*

[35] Humbach 1991: I: 66.

[36] S1 and J3 (earliest surviving trilingual texts) are thought to derive from the lost Pahlavi-Sanskrit Yasna and are two to three centuries later than Neriosangh's original.

Following Bartholomae (1904: 470), who bases his translation on Pah, Av kərəsānīm is usually taken as a proper noun referring to an enemy of the true religion. Pah writes *karsāgīg* which is not given in MacKenzie's dictionary and must be interpreted from the context here. N translates **kalaśiyākāḥ**, an apparent transliteration, but the gloss which follows suggests the meaning 'Christians'[37]: **yeṣām prabodhaḥ tarśākadīniḥ** 'whose faith is the Trembling Religion'. The appellation **tarśaka** or **tarśāka** is, according to Unvala[38], one given to Christians and he compares 'Quakers'. MacKenzie gives *tarsāg* [*tls'k*] "Christian', quoting also Manichaean Middle Persian *trs'g* and New Persian *tarsā*. It is therefore not unreasonable to see this meaning in the Pah which may have originally had an initial 't' altered later to bring the form into line with Av. The isolated kərəsānīm can therefore be assigned the same meaning, if we make the reasonable assumption that additions to Av were made in later times.

Example 10

(here N seems to use knowledge of Av in correcting Pah)

Av - zaraθuštra nmānahe pourušaspahe vīdaēuuō ahura.tkaēšō 'in the house of Pourušaspa, oh Zarathustra opposed to demons, supporting the religion of Ahura'

Pah - *zardušt andar mān ī porušasp ī jud-dēw ī ohrmazd-dādestān* 'oh Zarathustra, in the house of Pouṛušaspa (who is) separated from demons and (adhering) to the law of Ahura Mazda'

---

[37] The meaning 'Christians' is adopted by Barucha and by West 1880 (repr. 1965: 200) who writes that Alexander was thought to be a Christian and a Roman: "To a Persian in Sasanian times Alexander was the representative of an invading army which had come from countries occupied by the eastern empire of the Christian Romans..."

[38] Unvala 1924 in his additional notes suggests reading Pah as *kilisyāk* which he equates with Mid. Pers. *kilisyākīh* from Greek ἐκκλησία.

Skt - **jarathūśtra mandire pauruśaspīye vibhinnadevo hormijdanyāyī** (same as Av with genitive pourušaspahe translated by adjectival **pauruśaspīye**) [IX, 13 (c)]

Pah by incorrect use of the izāfa transfers epithets belonging to Zarathustra to Pourušaspa. N follows Av thus correcting the Pah.

Example 11

(here N may have a different text or misunderstand Pah or emend independently)

Av - yō #as vərəθrająstemo abauuat̰ mańiiuuå dāmąn 'who became the most victorious of the creation of the two spirits'

Pah - *kē hast kū pērōzgartar dād ēstē az ān ī mēnōgān dām* 'it is you who have been created more victorious than those creations of the spirits.'[39]

Skt - **yo'si**[40] **vijayavattamaḥ jātaḥ paralokināṃ**[41]. **sṛṣṭibhyaḥ** '(you) who are born most victorious with/by/from (usually translated "among") the creations of the super(preter)natural ones' [IX, 15 (b)]

The mysterious and probably corrupt 'as'[42] in Av is understood to be from the verb 'to be' by Pah and this involves a change to the third person singular. N also opts for the verb 'to be', but assumes that it is second person singular (a reasonable inference from Av) and turns Av abauuat̰ (for which he could have used the exactly cognate form **abhavat**) into periphrastic **asi**... **jātaḥ**.[43] Where Pah for no obvious reason changes the next adjective to the compara-

---

[39] Not, as Josephson 1997, "the most victorious of the creations of the spirits".

[40] **asti** is suggested by Barucha 1906 in his app. crit.

[41] The same translation of *mēnōgān* as **paralokināṃ** occurs at X, 16 (g). N does not use the important dual of the Av to refer to the two creating spirits, good and evil.

[42] For this vexed question see Josephson 1997: 55 fn. 32.

[43] The only two examples in *Hōm Yašt* of Av imperfect with augment occur in this stanza: N translates Av ākərən<a>uuō by **akaroḥ.**

tive, N retains the Av superlative. Av dāmąn is an anomalous genitive singular. I suspect that it should be emended to genitive plural dāmanąm 'of the creatures' which may have been read by N to judge from his translation.

Example 12

(here N may have a different text or emend independently)

Av - pairi šē uši vərənūiδi 'twist his ears / turn aside his mind (?)'

Pah - *be ān ī ōy uš wardēn* 'twist off his ears'

Skt - **prakr̥ṣṭaṃ tasya caitanyaṃ parivartaya** 'forcefully turn aside his understanding' [IX, 28 (d)]

Pah uses *uš*[44] to translate 'ears' for Av uši. The word in Av, however, has a derived meaning 'understanding' (Bartholomae 1904: 414) and it may well be that N preserves the correct tradition when he translates **caitanyam** 'reason, understanding'. The governing imperative Av pairi...vərənūiδi would seem to have the meaning 'turn aside' (Bartholomae 1904: 1363) and is taken in this way by N as **parivartaya**. It seems therefore that Pah misunderstood Av in the brutal sense 'pull off his ears' and translated accordingly *be ān ī ōy uš wardēn*. This may reflect a different tradition known to N or it may conceivably be an instance of better understanding of Av on his part.

Example 13

(here N does not seem to follow either Av or Pah and may be working from a different version)

Av - imå hən̨ti cicašānå 'these are your sayings'

Pah - *u-t awēšān hēnd cēgām-iz-ē cāšišnīh* 'and these are your teachings of all kinds'

Skt - **kāścit āsvādanāḥ** 'these are some tastings' [X, 18 (b)]

---

[44] MacKenzie 1971 does not give the word, but it is attested in New Persian, see Bartholomae 1904: 414.

Av cicašānå has caused problems for the translators. Bartholomae (1904: 584) is no doubt correct to derive the word from root kaš- 'teach' and give the meaning 'teachings'. Pah has written *cēgām-iz-ē cāšišnīh* and Bartholomae saw *cēgām-iz-ē* as an attempt to translate the first two letters of Av as though they were from an indefinite pronoun. Interpretation of the Pah form is difficult. Progress, however, can now be made by considering two forms which are given by MacKenzie in his Pahlavi Dictionary (1971: 22): Manichaean Middle Persian *cyg'myc*, which he equates with Pah *cyk'm-c* = *'cēgām-iz-ē* 'a little, whatever', and New Persian *č(ag)āma* Pah *cegāmag* 'song'. If the latter, perhaps unfamiliar, word originally stood in the text, it is easy to see how it could have been replaced with the assumedly more familiar *cēgām-iz-ē* and *cāšišnīh*, an imitation of cicašānå, would then have been added to complete the meaning. In any case, N writes **kāścit āsvādanāḥ** which would seem to mean 'some tastings', a meaning which cannot be equated to Av or Pah. It formally resembles the latter and shows that he understood *cēgām-iz-ē* as indefinite. I think it possible that he looked at the Avestan (possibly Pah) and saw something resembling Skt **aśana** 'eating'.

3. CONCLUSION

The result of this study suggests that the Sanskrit translation of *Hōm Yašt*, while basically a key to the Pahlavi and not an attempt to translate the Avestan, shows sufficient independence from its Pahlavi exemplar and sufficient consideration of the original Avestan to warrant being consulted in cases where the text is in doubt as it may be found to point to a correct reading.

REFERENCES

BAILEY, H. W. 1979. *Dictionary of Khotan Saka*. Cambridge: Cambridge University Press.

BARTHOLOMAE, C. 1904. *Altiranisches Wörterbuch*. Strassburg: Trübner. Repr. Berlin 1961.

BARUCHA, S. D. 1906. *Collected Sacred Writings of the Parsis,* I. Bombay: Nirṇaya-Sāgara Press.

------ 1910. *Collected Sacred Writings of the Parsis,* II. Bombay: Nirṇaya-Sāgara Press.

DARMESTETER, J. 1880. *The Zend-Avesta,* I. *The Vendīdād.* (The Sacred Books of the East, IV.) Repr. Delhi: Motilal Banarsidass 1965.

DEGENER, A. 1991. Neryosanghs Sanskrit-Übersetzung von *Škand gumānīk vicār*. In: R. Emmerick and D. Weber (eds.), *Corolla Iranica. Papers in honour of Prof. Dr. David Neil MacKenzie on the occasion of his 65th birthday on April 8th, 1991*: 49-58. Frankfurt am Main.

FLATTERY, D. S. & M. SCHWARTZ 1989. *Haoma and Harmaline.* Berkeley: University of California Press.

GELDNER, K. F. 1896. *Avesta, the Sacred Books of the Parsis,* I. Stuttgart.

------ 1904. *Awestalitteratur.* In: W. Geiger & E. Kuhn (eds.), *Grundriss der Iranischen Philologie,* II: 1-53. Strassburg: Trübner.

HÜBSCHMANN, H. 1872a. Beiträge zur Erklärung des Avesta. *Zeitschrift der Deutschen Morgenländischen Gesellschaft* 26: 453-460.

------ 1872b. Zur Beurtheilung der traditionellen Übersetzung des Avesta. *Sitzungsberichte der philosophisch-philologischen und historischen Klasse der königlichen Bayerischen Akademie der Wissenschaften zu München,* Bd. II: 637-710.

HUMBACH, H. 1991. *The Gāthas of Zarathustra,* I-II. Heidelberg: Carl Winter Universitätsverlag.

JONES, William 1799. The sixth discourse: On the Persians (delivered 19 Febr. 1789). *Asiatic Researches* II: 43-66. London.

JOSEPHSON, J. 1997. *The Pahlavi Translation Technique as Illustrated by Hōm Yašt.* (Acta Universitatis Upsaliensis. Studia Iranica Upsaliensis, 2.) Uppsala.

MACKENZIE, D. N. 1971. *A Concise Pahlavi Dictionary.* London / New York / Toronto: Oxford University Press.

MONIER-WILLIAMS, M. 1889. *A Sanskrit-English Dictionary.* Oxford: Oxford University Press. Repr. Delhi 1993.

RASK, R. 1826. *Über das Alter und die Echtheit der Zend-Sprache und des Zend Avesta.* Berlin. (Original Danish title: *Om Zendsprogets og Zendavestas Ælde og Ægthed.* Det Skandinaviske Litteraturselskabs Skrifter XXI. København 1826.)

SCHMIDT, H. P. 1969. Avestan *unā* and *ūnā*. In: *K. R. Kama Oriental Institute Golden Jubilee Volume*: 124-132. Bombay.

SPIEGEL, F. 1861. *Neriosanghs Sanskrit-übersetzung des Yasna.* Leipzig.

UNVALA, J. M. 1924. *Neryosangh's Sanskrit Version of the Hōm Yašt.* Vienna.

WEST, E. W. 1880. *Pahlavi Texts,* I. *Bahman Yast, or Zand i Vohûman Yasno.* (Sacred Books of the East, V.) Repr. Delhi: Motilal Banarsidass 1965.

WESTERGAARD, N. L. 1852-1854. *Zendavesta or the Religious Books of the Zoroastrians.* København.

WILLIAMS, A. 1990. *The Pahlavi Rivāyat Accompanying the Dādestān ī Dēnīg,* I-II. (Historisk-filosofiske meddelelser 60; 1. Det Kongelige Danske videnskabernes selskab.) København.

A preliminary study of Gāndhārī lexicography

ANDREW GLASS

INTRODUCTION

Prior to 1994 the Khotan Dharmapada was practically the only known manuscript in Gāndhārī. Since then, the discovery of three major collections of Gandhāran manuscripts – not to mention continuing discoveries of other documents and inscriptions – has dramatically increased our knowledge of the Gāndhārī language and its literature. Work on the new manuscripts, at times, must draw on vocabulary from across the whole range of Gāndhārī materials.

It is now highly desirable to think of compiling a dictionary of Gāndhārī. Previous works on specific Gāndhārī texts or collections have included word indices, such as: Konow's *Kharoṣṭhī Inscriptions with the Exception of Those of Aśoka* (1929, more than 1000 entries); Boyer & Rapson & Senart's *Kharoṣṭhī Inscriptions Discovered by Aurel Stein in Chinese Turkestan* (1920-1929, approximately 6000 entries); and Brough's *Gāndhārī Dharmapada* (1962, about 2000 entries). Turner's *Comparative Dictionary of the Indo-Aryan Languages* (CDIAL) incorporated more than 1000 Gāndhārī words in its articles and indices.[1] However, no attempt

[1] The Gāndhārī terms listed in CDIAL are divided among separate indices: the Aśokan Inscriptions (mixed Gāndhārī + Prākrit, Turner 1969: 19-22); the Gāndhārī Dharmapada (22); Kharoṣṭhī Inscriptions from Niya (22-24); and the Corpus Inscriptionum Indicarum II (24-25). Indices consisting of or containing

has yet been made to produce a comprehensive dictionary of Gāndhārī. There is also no evidence of a lexical tradition found in the texts themselves, so it is probable that there has never been a dictionary of this language.[2]

It is a common feature of discussions on lexicography to bemoan the problems of dictionary work, and the present paper will be no exception.[3] A dictionary of Gāndhārī will suffer from many of the difficulties common to other dictionary projects, and even more so, as it will be the first attempt at a lexicon for this language. It will also be the victim of a host of problems of its own – those stemming from the peculiarities of the Gāndhārī language and the state of its corpus.

This paper discusses the various problems and issues involved in making a dictionary of the Gāndhārī language, with a view to preparing the ground for the work ahead. I have tried to anticipate some of the problems which may be encountered and suggested possible solutions in the form of recommendations and samples for both a dictionary in book format and an electronic database. But first there is the question: what is Gāndhārī?

Gāndhārī words can also be found in: Hultzsch 1925: 231-258 (mixed Gāndhārī + Prākrit); Burrow 1937: 71-134; Brough 1996: 503-504. Tsukamoto 1996 (mixed Gāndhārī, Prakrit, Epigraphical Hybrid Sanskrit, Sanskrit); Salomon 2000: 227-234; Allon 2001: 325-336; Hinüber 2001 (mixed Gāndhārī + Prākrit); Lenz 2002: 259-266.

[2] The earliest Sanskrit lexicons predate the Kharoṣṭhī period by several centuries. The earliest, the Nighaṇṭu, is thought to predate another important early lexicon, the Nirukta, by several centuries (Patkar 1981: 2). The latter work itself has been dated to around the 8th century B.C. (Patkar 1981: 4). The first dictionary of Pali, the Abhidhānappadīpikā, dates from around 12th century A.D. (Norman 1983: 166). The first Prakrit lexicon, the Pāialacchīnāmamālā, was composed in VS. 1329 (= 1271/2 A.D., Ghatage 1996: 2). So it appears that lexicography of the Middle Indo-Aryan languages was not productive until after the Kharoṣṭhī period.

[3] "The worst criminals should neither be executed nor sentenced to forced labour, but should be condemned to compile dictionaries, because all the tortures are included in this work." J. J. Scaliger paraphrased in Zgusta 1971: 15. "*Dull,* To make dictionaries is dull work" Johnson 1755: s.v. 'dull' (8th definition).

WHAT IS *GĀNDHĀRĪ*?

In 1943 Harold Bailey proposed the single term "*Gāndhārī*" to refer to the dialect that had hitherto been known as "northwestern Prakrit." Within this term he proposed to include:

> Those inscriptions of Aśoka which are recorded at Shahbazgaṛhi and Mansehra in the Kharoṣṭhī script, the vehicle for the remains of much of this dialect. To be included also are the following sources: the Buddhist literary text, the Dharmapada found in Khotan, written likewise in Kharoṣṭhī, . . . the Kharoṣṭhī documents on wood, leather, and silk from Caḋota (the Niya site) on the border of the ancient kingdom of Khotan, which represented the official language of the capital Krorayina, 摟蘭 K[arlgren 1923:] 572, 512 *lou-lan* < *lə̯u-lan* (*lou* in a series with alternation of *k* and *l*) of the Shan-shan kingdom, and of document, no. 661, dated in the reign of the *Khotana maharaya rayatiraya hinajha dheva vijida-siṃha*. With this more copious material must be grouped the scattered traces of the same Middle Indian dialect in Khotanese, Tibetan, Agnean, Kuchean, the earlier Chinese Buddhist transliterations, as, in particular, in the Dīrghāgama of the Dharmaguptaka sect and the remains in Sogdian, Uigur Turkish, and in Mongoḷ (in living use), and also in Manchu texts. The modern Dardic languages Ṣiṇā, Khowar, Phalūṛa and others represent the same type of Middle Indian. (Bailey 1943: 764-765.)

Bailey's suggestion won more or less immediate acceptance, and is now the standard term for the Middle Indic language/dialects of the northwest written in the Kharoṣṭhī script. However, since Bailey's pioneering article, much new material has come to light, particularly manuscripts, such that his definition needs to be reviewed in order to determine the extent of the Gāndhārī language, and thus its lexical inventory.

Anything written in the Kharoṣṭhī script is Gāndhārī

A the risk of blurring the distinction between language and writing system, I propose extending Bailey's observation that the Kharoṣṭhī script was "the vehicle for the remains of much of this dialect" (764) to serve as a complete definition for Gāndhārī. Such a definition eliminates the grey area involved in distinguishing exactly when a Prakrit becomes hybrid Sanskrit or 'pure' Sanskrit.

However, this definition will admittedly include many hybrid spellings and a few Sanskrit words, which may, by some standards, not be regarded as proper Gāndhārī. This definition will exclude the "traces of the same Middle Indian dialect" (765) which Bailey spoke of in Khotanese, Tibetan, etc.; as well as any document not written in the Kharoṣṭhī script that might otherwise be connected with Gāndhārī. It will also limit the chronological extent of the language to that of the Kharoṣṭhī script, so we need not be concerned with the transition to the late Middle Indo-Aryan forms of the language and their ultimate transition to the New Indo-Aryan languages of the region which may ultimately derive from Gāndhārī.

Gāndhārī Hybrid Sanskrit and Kharoṣṭhī

Salomon (2001: 241) coined the term "Gāndhārī Hybrid Sanskrit" to refer to the hybrid language of the now many Kharoṣṭhī materials dating from the second and third centuries A.D. which display Sanskritic features. Such documents typically show developments in orthography more than morphology. For example, in the MPS-G Salomon notes that the genitive singular regularly has the Sanskritized ending *-sya,* but the other nominal endings are typically Middle Indic (Salomon 2001: 245-246). Other documents show yet higher degrees of sanskritization and even hyper-sanskritization.

> Typical features of this late variety of Gāndhārī are manifested in spellings like *smi* (8A, a2 etc.), *-prapta* (8A, a3), *bhaviṣyami* (H24, a2), *anuyukta* (9A, b2), *amithya* (118, a1), and *veśaradhyaṇi* (8A, a2), where consonant clusters that would normally be reduced or assimilated in spoken Gāndhārī (*mi, prata, bhaviśami, anuyuta, amicha, veśarajaṇi*) are represented as in Sanskrit. In some cases such spellings are actually hypersanskritisms, as in *paṣyadi* (9A, b1) which is evidently wrongly Sanskritized from Gāndhārī *paśadi* on the basis of the rule that Sanskrit *ṣy* goes to *ś* in Gāndhārī. This development was probably influenced by analogy with the forms of future tense, which in standard Gāndhārī has the affix *-iśa-*, but which in the Sanskritized variety is restored to *-iṣya-*, as in *bhaviṣyami*. (Salomon forthcoming a.)

A dictionary of Gāndhārī should be a diachronic dictionary since the corpus itself spans almost 1000 years[4], and one of its primary functions will be to illustrate historical and etymological connections with other Indo-Aryan languages (primarily Sanskrit and Pali). Consequently, the hybrid forms attested in some of the later documents and inscriptions should be included in the lexicon as they establish a trajectory in the development of the written language towards Sanskrit, which ultimately replaced Gāndhārī as the literary language of the Northwest. It is likely that when all the data has been compiled, the process of sanskritization as witnessed in the Gāndhārī materials will shed light on the same process at work in the twin phenomena of Buddhist Hybrid and Epigraphical Hybrid Sanskrit.

Classical Sanskrit and Kharoṣṭhī

Besides the isolated Sanskrit formulas in otherwise Gāndhārī inscriptions noted by Fussman (1989: 486, see also Salomon 1998b: 135), there are at present just two known Kharoṣṭhī fragments written in more or less Classical Sanskrit, viz.: the four verses on the reverse of Niya document 523; and one of the fragments in the Pelliot Collection. The editors of the former text observed that "Quant à la langue, c'est un Sanskrit que déforment des prākritismes et des incorrections" (Boyer & Rapson & Senart 1918: 322). Salomon has said of the latter: "it appears to have been written in more or less standard Sanskrit, as opposed to Buddhist Hybrid Sanskrit, although there is at least one apparent case of a hybrid-type form (*yaṃ*) and one probable nonstandard orthographic practice (*-sajña*)" (Salomon 1998b: 134). The Pelliot fragment does not indicate long vowels, as is generally the case with Kharoṣṭhī,

---

[4] It is possible, and perhaps even desirable, to think of producing a synchronic dictionary based on a single collection of manuscripts, e.g. the British Library collection, and other contemporaneous materials. However, the greatest advantage to scholarship will certainly come from a complete lexicon to the language in all its attested stages.

whereas, the Niya document does indicate vowel length, though not always correctly for Sanskrit.

Since the intention of the authors/scribes of these documents was to write Sanskrit, and they did so more or less successfully in the opinions of the modern editors, we might consider revising the above definition of Gāndhārī to exclude these items. However, since the number of actual words is very small, it is perhaps worthwhile for the time being to include these items in the corpus and preserve the clarity of the definition as they complete the trajectory established by the hybrid documents. If many more Kharoṣṭhī documents in classical Sanskrit should come to light, it may be necessary to develop a separate classification.

Loan words from Gāndhārī

Bailey's outline of what constitutes Gāndhārī, quoted above, includes "traces of the same Middle Indian dialect" in a variety of other languages. However, this remark should not be taken as a prescription for including loanwords into other languages as headings in a Gāndhārī dictionary. Rather, reference to the form of the loan in the receiving language should be given under the source word in Gāndhārī. For example, under the heading *goni* = Skt. *goṇī* 'sack' the Khotanese cognate *gūña,* might be given with reference to Lüders (1936: 6) and Bailey (1943: 767).

Gāndhārī but not Kharoṣṭhī

Fussman has rightly observed that "rien n'interdit de supposer l'existence de textes gandh. en brāhmī: lorsque la khar. cessa d'être en usage au Gandhāra, la gandh. ne cessa pas d'y être parlée et d'y être écrite."(1989: 439). While this is certainly true, we do not yet possess any examples of Gāndhārī written in a script other than Kharoṣṭhī.

Damsteegt claims to have found evidence of northwestern influence in the Mathurā Brāhmī inscriptions by identifying terms and phrases found in Kharoṣṭhī inscriptions before they occur elsewhere.[5] The following table summarizes Damsteegt's evidence for NW influence in the Mathurā inscriptions (1978: 159-166).

	Kharoṣṭhī Inscriptions[6]	Mathurā Inscriptions
1	*sarvabudhana puyae* Bīmarān 1, Mathurā 84, Taxila 1, 3	*sarvabudhapujāye* M 29, 80, 123, 157
2	*hidasuha-* Pājā 1 *hidasuhartha[ṃ]* Shāh-jī-kī Ḍherī 1	*sarvasatvānaṃ hitasukhāye* or *-sukhārthaṃ* M 1, 2, 135
3	*arogadakṣiṇae* Taxila 3	*ar[o]g[a]dākṣiṇ[ā]y[e]* M 44 *arogyadakṣiṇ[ā]ye* M 46 *ārogyadakhiṇa* M 180
4	*catudiśa-* Mathurā 84, Taxila 5 *cadudiśa-* Bedadi 1, Takht-i-Bāhī 3	*că̄turdiśa-* M 31, 33, 35, 39 *c[a]tudiśa* M 35
5	*desama-paricaga-* Taxila 3 *de[yadharma-pa]rityaga-* Tor Ḍherai 1	*deyadharma-parityāga-*M 29, 46, 60–62, LL 16a
6	*dha[rma]kathi-* Sui Vihār 1	*dharmakathika-* LL 16a
7	*pratigraha-* Shāh-jī-kī Ḍherī 1, Tor Ḍherai 1	*pratigraha-* M 150, 157
8	*matapitaraṃ puyayaṃto* Taxila 1 *madu pidu puyae* Takht-i-Bāhī 1	*mātāpit(ṛ)ṇa pujārtha* LL 17a *mātāpit[r]ina pujāye* M 90
9	*[vi]hara(ṃ)svam[i]s(r)a* Peshāwar 2 *viharasvamiṇi(ṃ)* Sui Vihār 1 *viharasvamis(y)a* Tor Ḍherai 1	*vihārasvāmin-* M 136
10	*śakamuṇisa* Swāt 1, Tīrath 1, Taxila 1 *śakyamuṇe* Wardak 1 *śakyamunisa* Kurram 1	*śākyamuni-* M 29, 180
11	*sadayarisa* Loriyān Tangai 3 *sadaviyarisa* Loriyān Tangai 1	*sārdhaṃvihārin-* M 44, 45, LL 16a

While the evidence in the above table does show some similarities between the two sets of inscriptions, particularly in 1, 3, 4, 6, 7,

[5] Damsteegt's purpose was to identify loan words and influence from Gāndhārī rather than to identify inscriptions in Gāndhārī and Brāhmī script.

[6] Kharoṣṭhī inscriptions are referenced by the geographical designations found in Tsukamoto 1996. References to the Mathurā inscriptions are taken from Damsteegt 1978.

9, and 10, the suggestion that the language of any of the Mathurā inscriptions is Gāndhārī cannot be proven conclusively, as similarities in consonant clusters could be attributed to the process of sanskritization. If these terms originated in Gāndhārī and were borrowed into the local language, as Damsteegt argues, then the terms here represent loan words and would therefore be covered under the previous section.

THE GĀNDHĀRĪ CORPUS

Having established a working definition of Gāndhārī, the initial task of preparing the dictionary lies in assembling a catalogue of all Gāndhārī literature. An ongoing attempt at this is available online at: http://depts.washington.edu/ebmp/gdintro.php. This aims to provide a list of all known Kharoṣṭhī materials, published and unpublished. Obviously such a catalogue needs to be circulated among scholars in the field so that it can be checked and supplemented. In outline, the corpus consists of four groups of materials:

1. Inscriptions: We now know of more than 200 inscriptions spanning from the Aśokan inscriptions at Shāhbāzgaṛhī and Mānsehrā, ca. 250 B.C., to around the 3rd century A.D. (Salomon 1998a: 47).
2. Coin legends: Coins with Kharoṣṭhī legends have been found from throughout the greater Gandhāra region as well as a few specimens of biscript Kharoṣṭhī and Chinese coins from Central Asia. The coins date from the 2nd century B.C. to the 2nd century A.D.
3. Buddhist Manuscripts: There are now more than 200 fragments in nine collections, spanning from the 1st to the 3rd centuries A.D.
4. Secular documents: These materials now number almost 1000 items. Most are written on wood, some on leather and other materials. They come from various sites in Central

Asia and can be dated between the 2nd and 7th centuries A.D. (see Salomon 1998a: 47).

METHODOLOGY AND GUIDELINES

The following outline for the stages in the preparation of a Gāndhārī dictionary is based on Geiger's (de Lanerolle 1950: 19-20, quoted in Bechert 1998: 25) suggestions for the *Dictionary of the Sinhala Language* and the *Siṃhala Śabdakoṣaya,* adapted slightly to Gāndhārī and to the tools of the twenty-first century:

1. Creating electronic versions of all Gāndhārī documents in the catalogue so that all words and phrases from inscriptions, coins, manuscripts and documents can be compiled into a list.
2. Generating numerical sort codes or otherwise arranging the words in alphabetical order.
3. Systematizing basic materials:
   - 3.1 examining every individual entry under a single word or phrase, referring it back to its original source, and ascertaining the meaning it bears in that particular context;
   - 3.2 setting up hyper-links between individual entries and quotable passages in the electronic texts;
   - 3.3 adding cognates in Sanskrit and Pali;
   - 3.4 separating those entries that bear the same word into homonymic categories;
   - 3.5 studying the development of meaning under each homonym in historical order;
   - 3.6 noting down in each case the idiomatic uses and specialized meanings;
   - 3.7 tracing the historical development of forms by means of fresh researches.
4. Writing rough articles.

5. Revising rough articles with special attention to philological and comparative information.
6. Consulting experts and incorporating their advice.
7. Type-setting the articles on a computer and reading the first proofs.
8. Reading the second proofs and checking the references and cross-references.
9. Reading and passing page proofs.

The principal difference between Geiger's scheme and the modern one is in the automation of collecting words. If we can produce electronic versions of all Gāndhārī materials, it is a simple matter to produce a list of all occurring words and compounds with complete textual references. It is also a fairly simple matter to alphabetize this list, make a reverse index, or otherwise sort the data. The real work of the lexicographer, writing the articles, cannot be automated, but electronic searching, hyperlinks, and other modern tools should provide considerable assistance.

PART I – A DICTIONARY IN BOOK FORMAT

Since new mediums can take considerable time to develop the same sense of scholarly authority as traditional forms of publication, it may be desirable to produce a Gāndhārī dictionary in book format. Such a work will have to take into account a number of difficulties, for to publish a dictionary is to set a standard, and Gāndhāṛī is a language not used to standards. Furthermore, the fragmentary nature of many of the materials will mean that many words can not be read with certainty; others will only be read with partiaḷ reconstruction. A further complication arises in that new materials in the Kharoṣṭhī script come to light fairly regularly. Inevitably new materials will contain new orthographies and spellings for familiar words, and less often completely new words. This is akin to the problem of the lexicographer of any modern language – that the dictionary will be out of date as soon as it is published – but this is no reason not to begin.

A Gāndhārī dictionary in book format will also need to consider some basic, but troublesome questions. What will be the headword: Gāndhārī, Sanskrit, or some hypothetical stem/root? How will the lemma be sorted: like Sanskrit, like Sanskrit but not taking into account long vowels and other modifiers, or according to the native ordering system, the Arapacana? How will variant orthographies be treated? In the case of variant spellings, which one should be entered as the lemma, which shall be listed as the deviants? When there is a graphic and phonetic merger of two sounds (e.g., *t* and *d*), should the transcription reflect the etymological value or the nearest graphic value? The following is an attempt to address these and other issues by suggesting a standard format for the dictionary's articles. Sample articles are given in fig. 1 to illustrate the proposed format for the beginning of the alphabet. Similarities between the Kharoṣṭhī manuscripts and the Sanskrit manuscripts from Turfan make the format of the SWTF a natural starting point for developing a format for the Gāndhārī dictionary. The following outline for the entries is based on the scheme of the SWTF (Schmidt 1994: xlviii):

1. Entry word(s)
2. Deviant spellings
3. Sanskrit cognate
4. Pali cognate
5. Cognates in other languages
6. Grammatical category
7. Definition
8. References to other modern works
9. Grammatical form
10. Reference to sources
11. Citation
12. Fragmentary entries
13. Compounds

𐨀 A

𐨀 [1]*a*, the first letter of the varṇamālā alphabet as applied to Gāndhārī in modern works and the first letter of the traditional alphabet called Arapacana; the vowel inherent in consonants.

𐨀 [2]***a***, *ā*, ind. up to, towards (see Burrow 1937b §92). Shāh 13.9†; Mān 13.9, 10; Niya 419, 549.

𐨀 [3]***a***, *see ca.*

𐨀 [4]***a***, *see va.*

𐨀𐨀 ***aa***, *see aha.*

𐨀𐨀𐨎 ***aaṃ***, *see aha.*

𐨀𐨀𐨁 [1]***aï***, *see aya.*

𐨀𐨀𐨁 [2]***aï***, *see idha.*

a+√i, reach, attain. *aed(*i)* pres. ind. 3 sg. P, Dhp-G^{K} 95d.

𐨀𐨅𐨡𐨁 ***aedi***, see a+√i.

𐨀𐨎 ***aṃ***, *see ya.*

𐨀𐨐𐨐𐨭 ***a-kakaśa***, *akarkaśa*, *akakkasa*, mfn. not hard, tender. Acc. sg. Dhp-G^{K} 22a. ~ *viñamaṇi gira saca udiraï* Dhp-G^{K} 22ab.

𐨀𐨐𐨑𐨂 ***akakṣu***, *ākākṣā*, *ākaṅkhā*, mfn. desire, wish. Acc. sg. Dhp-G^{K} 249c. *śrudiviñati ~ ta bhayea tadhavidha* Dhp-G^{K} 249cd.

𐨀𐨐𐨡𐨒𐨡𐨁 ***a-kada-gadi***, *akathaṃkathika*, *akathaṃkathin*, mfn. not questioning. Acc. sg. Dhp-G^{K} 47b. *jaï parakada budhu jidavi* ~ Dhp-G^{K} 47ab.

𐨀𐨐𐨡𐨙𐨆 ***a-kada-ño***, {*akidaña*}, *akṛtajña*, *akataññu*, mfn. ungrateful. *akidaña* nom. sg. Dhp-G^{K} 77a. *kodhaṇa akidaña i drohiṇi pa[rivajaï]* Dhp-G^{K} 77a. knowing the uncreated (=Nirvāṇa) (SWTF *s.v.* p. 4). Nom. sg. Dhp-G^{K} 10d. *sagharaṇa kṣaya ñatva ~ si brammaṇa* Dhp-G^{K} 10cd.

𐨀𐨐𐨤𐨀𐨅 ***akapae***, *see √kḷp.*

𐨀𐨐𐨨 ***akama*** *in dharma~bahoṣuda.*

𐨀𐨐𐨨𐨞𐨀𐨁 ***akamaṇaï***, *see a+√gam.*

𐨀𐨐𐨪 ***akara***, *gāra-*, *ăgāra-*, n. house, dwelling. Acc. sg. Dhp-G^{K} 219a, 220a, 251a; *akare* loc. sg. Dhp-G^{K} 55a. *yadha ~ druchana vuṭhi samadibhinadi* Dhp-G^{K} 219ab.

𐨀𐨐𐨪𐨁𐨯𐨂 ***akarisu***, *see √kṛ.*

𐨀𐨐𐨪𐨅𐨞 ***akareṇa***, *ākāra*, m. gesture. instr. sg. Shāh 12.4; Mān 12.4. *pujetaviya va cu parapraṣa[ṃḍa] tena tena* ~ Shāh 12.3–4.

𐨀𐨐𐨪𐨆𐨡 ***[akaroda]***, *see √kṛ.*

𐨀𐨐𐨫𐨁𐨐𐨎 ***a-kalikaṃ***, *akālika*, mfn. not restricted to time. Nom. sg. Shāh 9.20; *akalike* nom. sg. Mān 9.7. *ida puna dhramamagalaṃ* ~ Shāh 9.20.

𐨀𐨐𐨬𐨂𐨪𐨂𐨮𐨯𐨅𐨬𐨁𐨡 ***akavuruṣa-sevida***, *akāpuruṣasevita*, *akāpurisasevita*, mfn. attended by good men (SWTF *s.v.*, p. 2). Nom. sg. Dhp-G^{K} 71d.

𐨀𐨐𐨭𐨣𐨆 ***aka(*śano)***, *ākāśa*, *ākāsa*, m. sky. Instr. sg. BL 16+25 38. *pracegabudhano pacamatra śada agada ~ cadanakaṭho gina[ta]* BL 16+25 37–8.

𐨀𐨐𐨯𐨁 ***akasi***, *see √kṛ.*

𐨀𐨐𐨁𐨗𐨞 ***a-kijaṇa***, *akiñcana*, mfn. without possessions. Nom. sg. Dhp-G^{K} 167b, d, 168d; acc. sg. Dhp-G^{K} 17e, 34c, 274d. ~ *naṇuvadadi dukhu* Dhp-G^{K} 274d.

𐨀𐨐𐨁𐨡 ***a-kida***, *akṛta*, *akata*, mfn. undone. Nom. sg. Dhp-G^{K} 337a. ~ *kukida ṣehu pacha tavadi drukida* Dhp-G^{K} 337ab.

𐨀𐨐𐨂𐨩𐨞𐨆 ***a-kuyaṇo***, *akūjana*, mfn. not creeking, quiet. Nom. sg. Dhp-G^{K} 97c. *radho ~ namu* Dhp-G^{K} 97c.

𐨀𐨐𐨂𐨬𐨡𐨂 ***a-kuvad[u]***, *akurvat*, *akubbant*, neg. pres. part. not acting (SWTF *s.v.* p. 3). Gen. sg. Dhp-G^{K} 290d. *emu subhaṣida vaya apha[la] (*hodi)* ~ Dhp-G^{K} 290d.

𐨀𐨐𐨂𐨭𐨫 ***a-kuśala***, *akuśala*, *akusala*, mfn. unprofitable (SWTF *s.v.* p. 3). Nom. pl. m. EĀ-G 42‡, 48‡, 52, 55–6‡, 58–9‡. (**abhija do*)*maṇastu pavea ~ dharma ◦ citam arśaveti.* EĀ-G 51–2.

𐨀𐨐𐨆𐨠𐨅𐨞 ***a-kotheṇa***, *akrodha*, *akkodha*, mfn. non-anger, freedom from anger. Instr. sg. Dhp-G^{K} 280a. *jiṇa kodha ~ asadhu sadhuṇa jiṇa* Dhp-G^{K} 280ab.

Figure 1. Sample page from the proposed Gāndhārī Dictionary.

As with the SWTF, the entries can be subdivided into three parts. Items 1 to 8 will form the head of the entry, containing information pertaining to the whole article. Items 9 to 11 will comprise the main part, containing data on specific forms giving citations. Items 12 and 13 when they are needed will form the conclusion.

A list of ghost words should be included as an appendix to the dictionary. This list should include readings that were previously identified and commented upon in modern works, but are now discredited and read differently. The best known example of such is **Bhagamoya* which was read by Bailey in a casket inscription (1982: 150, 152) and identified as a royal name. This reading has now been corrected to *bhagiṇeyeṇa* by Mukherjee (1988) and Falk (1998: 87, 89).

1.0. Entry word(s)

Since the primary purpose of the dictionary is to provide a reference tool for readers of Kharoṣṭhī texts, and this will after all be a *Gāndhārī* dictionary, the headword should, as far as possible, be in Gāndhārī. However, since it is desirable to have finite verb forms and primary derivatives listed in one place, Sanskrit roots must be used as the head words for the verbal forms, owing to the absence of roots in the Gāndhārī tradition. The headword becomes quite artificial when verbs with prefixes are to be listed in the format prefix plus root – i.e., a *Gāndhārī* prefix plus a *Sanskrit* root![7] Nevertheless, the Gāndhārī form of the prefix should be used, since the sorting will otherwise be based on Gāndhārī. When the lemma is a pure Gāndhārī form, the word should be given in Kharoṣṭhī script, and transliteration. Transliteration should be according to the conventions established in Glass (2000).

---

[7] This was not the practice in GBT 2 where, for example, G *avajadi*, *pradivajadi*, and *pracarśoṣu* are found under *ā+√pad*, *prati+√pad*, and *prati+√śru* respectively.

1.1. Sorting

Although a traditional abecedary exists in Kharoṣṭhī, namely the Arapacana (named after the first five akṣaras), it is unsuitable for sorting the dictionary's head words. There are several reasons for this. First, the complete order of the Arapacana is not attested in Kharoṣṭhī, and so we cannot be absolutely certain what the order found in later texts was when applied to the Kharoṣṭhī script. Second, there are variations in the Sanskrit sources such that a definitive ordering cannot be established with certainty (Salomon 1990: 256).

As a member of the Indo-Aryan language family and a close relation to Sanskrit, it makes sense to use the traditional sorting methods of Sanskrit dictionaries, the more so, as it is expected that most users of a Gāndhārī dictionary will also be familiar with Sanskrit. The sort order of the headwords, should therefore, be based on the traditional Indian *varṇamālā,* with some modifications to accommodate Kharoṣṭhī. First, the lack of vowel length notation in most documents removes the need to maintain this distinction in the dictionary. The reader should only need to check one place for a word without being referred to another part of the dictionary in the rare cases where the long vowel mark is attested. Second, the unstandardized use of vowel and consonant modifiers should be leveled when sorting entries. The modifiers are: double ring below (̥̥); line above (̄); cauda (̱); and ring below (̥). Third, the special modified forms *ḱ* and *ṭ́h* should be sorted as the basic signs *k* and *ṭh,* following them when the forms would otherwise be identical, so that *ḱadha* precedes *kama,* but follows *kadha.* For a complete table of the ordering see Glass, Baums & Salomon (2002).

1.2. Completeness

The entry words should, as far as possible, consist of all Gāndhārī words occurring in the corpus. This is, of course, a rather vain hope since the dispersed nature of Kharoṣṭhī materials prevents the compilation of an absolute catalogue. Nevertheless, a great many inscriptions and texts are known and the dictionary should strive to be a complete record of the words occurring in them. As with the SWTF, lexical residues of incomplete words or damaged sequences should not be included when they cannot be reconstructed with reasonable certainty.

1.3. Restored forms

All words with reconstructed and uncertain readings should indicate the questionable elements with appropriate brackets. Words which have been entirely reconstructed should not be included.

1.4. Compounds

Compounds should be decomposed into their component parts, indicated with a hyphen. Otherwise they should be treated as entries in their own right and included in the appropriate place in the sort order. Reference to the complete compound should be included under the non-initial component parts.

1.5. Scribal errors

In cases of suspected scribal error, the resulting form should have no real basis in linguistic usage. However, given the example of Konow's mistaken emendation of *takṣaïlaami* to *takṣa[ś*]ilaami* (see Konow 1929: 90; Salomon forthcoming b), we should be careful about excluding such forms from the dictionary. It is better that, as in the SWTF, they be included and indicated as erroneous. The SWTF indicates such words by "the presence of '[' in front of the entry word" (Schmidt 1994: L). However, this is rather unsuitable as brackets already have another function in transcription and it is easy to imagine an editor seeing an unbalanced bracket and trying to restore the other side – which would either result in an incorrect restoration, or a waste of precious time in the process of confirming the reading, or possibly both. Better that such terms be indicated another way, e.g., *karo⟨*ti⟩*. Reference should be given to the modern edition where the error was first identified.

1.6. Homonyms

Homonyms should be distinguished with a superscript numeral placed before the transliteration of the head word.

1.7. Nouns and adjectives

When multiple forms of a noun occur with the same spelling in the stem, the first occurring form in the order of the cases should be given as the head word. Alternatively oblique forms could be listed under a hypothetical stem form. Variants in the spelling of the stem should be given separate entries with appropriate cross-references.

1.8. Verbs

In keeping with the practice established in the GBT series, verbal forms should be listed under their corresponding roots in Sanskrit. However, unlike the GBT volumes, the Sanskrit roots should be sorted without regard for long vowels. Prefixed verbs should be listed under the prefix plus root. However, unlike Allon (2001), the prefix should be in Gāndhārī. Following the conventions of the SWTF, nonfinite forms should be treated under the root, "with the exception of past participles ending in *-ta* [or *–da* in G] and *-na*, derivations of the latter ending in *-vat* and the *p. nec.*," (Schmidt 1994: L) which should appear as separate entries.

1.9. Proper names, titles

Unlike the SWTF, all names occurring in Gandhari should be included in the dictionary, regardless of whether they are translated or not. Proper names, when they can be distinguished from titles and other appellatives, should be indicated with initial capital. Titles and other appellatives should not be capitalized.

2.0. Deviant spellings

The first item to follow the entry word should be a list of all the variant spellings, in alphabetical order. They should be set in braces ('{}') to distinguish them from the rest of the entry. Owing to the unstandardized nature of Gāndhārī orthography, there will be many terms with a variety of attested spellings and determining a 'standard' spelling among them will inevitably be artificial and arbitrary. However, in a printed dictionary a single standard head word must be identified; otherwise the same entry will be repeated for each variant, unnecessarily swelling the size of the dictionary. Therefore, 'deviants' must be identified and listed independently in alphabetical order giving reference to the 'standard' spelling.

In general, the most common spelling should be treated as the standard. However, it will be necessary to develop another means of determining the standard spelling when frequency alone cannot produce a result. A study of Gāndhārī phonology should be undertaken to produce a hierarchy of phonological changes, so that a given set of variants for a term can be arranged in order of greater or lesser degrees of phonological change, and a 'standard' selected from among them. For example, the reflexes in Gāndhārī of Old Indo-Aryan intervocalic *k* that have been attested so far are: *k, g, gh, Ø*. *Gh* is a secondary development based on intervocalic voicing *k* > *g*, so *g* should rank higher than *gh*. Values should similarly be applied to *k* (typically archaic) and Ø (typically more developed) depending on which stage of Gāndhārī is to be preferred as the 'standard' dialect.[8]

An alternative solution would be to treat the first spelling in alphabetical order as the standard in the absence of a stronger claim.

3.0. Cognate in Sanskrit

Whenever a Gāndhārī word can be connected etymologically to Indo-Aryan, which will be the vast majority of cases, the equivalent Sanskrit term should be given. If the term in question is not attested in Sanskrit a reconstruction of the Sanskrit term may be given and marked with an asterisk, e.g., G *yaṣotoaṇi*, Skt. **yathāvadhikāni*.

[8] The tables charting the phonetic evolution of Gāndhārī given in Fussman 1989: 463-464 make a good starting point for developing such a system.

4.0. Cognate in Pali

Similarly, a Pali cognate should be given wherever possible. When a Pali cognate is identical to the Sanskrit, only one need be given. If a cognate Pali term is not attested and the Sanskrit is, ambiguity could arise since only one term will be given to cover both when they are identical. In this case, the single cognate should be indicated with the abbreviation Skt. preceding the entry.

5.0. Cognates in other languages

When a Gāndhārī term is connected etymologically to a word of non Indo-Aryan origin, a suitable cognate should be given together with an abbreviation for the language in question. When more than one such cognate is listed, they should be arranged in chronological order.

6.0. Grammatical category

The grammatical category should be given following the entry word. The grammatical information will almost invariably be based on the Sanskrit and/or Pali cognates, rather than Gāndhārī. The grammatical category should be indicated by means of abbreviations, numbers, and letters according to the system used in the SWTF, but adapted for English. Verb roots do not need a separate classification to signal that the entry is a verb as this will be self-evident from the heading.

7.0. Definition

Where more than one meaning occurs, definitions should be listed in chronological order according to their source, indicated with an abbreviation. If two different meanings should occur within a single source, the more concrete meaning should be given first. Closely related terms should be separated with a comma, and less closely related ones by a semicolon.

8.0. References to modern works

When the reading, form or meaning of a word has been discussed in modern works other than the published edition of the text concerned, appropriate references should be given.

9.0. Attested forms and grammatical form

Following the references to modern works, all attested inflected forms of the lemma should be listed with their grammatical form.

9.1. Nouns

Substantives, adjectives, pronouns and verbal nouns should be classified according to gender, number, and case. All forms should be identified with appropriate abbreviations.

9.2. Verbs

Verbs should be classified according to tense, mood, number, person, voice, derivative conjugations (causative, intensive, desiderative), and participial forms. All forms should be identified with appropriate abbreviations.

10.0. Reference to sources

Each of the inflected entries listed with grammatical details should be followed by complete references. In the case of indeclinables, references may simply follow the attested form of the entry word. When all attested forms are identical with the entry word, a list of references alone should suffice.

10.1. Completeness

As far as possible, all entries should be given with complete references to every occurrence of the word in Gāndhārī literature. For common words, such as pronouns, conjunctions, and particles it will be impractical to list every occurrence. In such cases the references should cover a selection of sources and the main usages of the word in question. Abbreviated references should be marked 'passim.'

10.2. Conjectures and Reconstructions

When the list of occurrences contains uncertain readings, either in whole or in part, they should be marked with a dagger '†'. Partial reconstructions should be marked with a double dagger '‡'. Total reconstructions should not be included in the dictionary. If a word is both partially uncertain and reconstructed it should be marked as a reconstruction.

10.3. References

References should indicate the occurrences of the word in the published literature. A hyphen should be used when a word occurs in consecutive lines, either as multiple occurrences or when it straddles two lines. When a word occurs more than once in a single line the line number should be followed by an indicator '(2×)', '(3×)' etc. Any words cited from unpublished manuscripts should be cited according to fragment, side, and line number. When the recto and verso of a fragment cannot be determined, the two sides should be cited as 'a' and 'b'. Unpublished inscriptions, secular documents, and coins should be cited according to their abbreviation in the catalogue with appropriate specification.

10.4. Sequence

References should be given in the sequence: Buddhist manuscripts; secular documents; inscriptions; coin legends. Within each category references should be arranged in chronological order or according to a predefined order when the dates are unknown or contemporaneous.

10.5. Cited edition

In general, only the most recent complete edition of a text should be cited. As in the SWTF, older editions may be cited "if they provide documentary evidence for a conjecture, offer a *varia lectio* or in some other respect are of material concern" (Schmidt 1994: LIII).

11. Citation

Citations illustrating the use of the head word should follow the references. The citation should, as a rule, be from the published edition of a document when one is available; any deviation from this should be clearly noted. All parenthetical notation regarding the reading must be preserved. Citations should be as concise as possible, while still preserving clarity. Where the same citation could be used multiple times, as in the case of a list, the full citation should appear under the first term and reference made to it in subsequent entries. The entry word should be replaced by tilde ('~') in citations. The notation '*vs.*' should be used to indicate that a citation is in verse except when the source is a pure verse text (e.g., Khvs-G).

12. Compounds

When an entry word occurs as a middle or final member of a compound, reference to the full compound should be given at the end of the entry.

PART II – AN ELECTRONIC DATABASE

Lexicography involves much drudgery such as collecting and sorting the lemmata. The idea that computers could help with this part of the work has been around for a long time.[9] More recently dictionaries and electronic word databases have come into being entirely as computer files, so that the traditional end product, the printed dictionary, is no longer the only option when publishing a lexicon. Notable examples in the field of Buddhist studies are

---

[9] For an early discussion of this topic see Zgusta 1971: 353-357. On the first electronic Sanskrit dictionary, see Schreiner 1996: 413-426.

Charles Muller's *Digital Dictionary of Buddhism* (http://www.acmuller.net/ddb/index.html) and the *Rangjung Yeshe Tibetan-English Dictionary* (http://www.nitartha.org/dictionary_searchback.html). Indeed the electronic medium offers many advantages over its paper counterpart, particularly when it comes to searching the database. In well designed systems, electronic dictionaries take a fraction of the time taken to look up an entry word that is required by the conventional approach. Furthermore, electronic data stores can be searched for terms other than the head word, so that a Sanskrit-English electronic dictionary is at the same time an English-Sanskrit dictionary. With these benefits in mind, several projects have been formed to digitize existing dictionaries. Notable examples of these are the Cologne Digital Sanskrit Lexicon (http://www.uni-koeln.de/phil-fak/indologie/tamil/mwd_search.html) and the Digital Dictionaries of South Asia Project (http://dsal.uchicago.edu/dictionaries/index.html).

Naturally, the computer's utility at collecting words and sorting entries will be utilized, whatever the final format for the Gāndhārī dictionary may be. The issue here is how the electronic format will affect the way end users access the material in the lexicon — what should be the format for the data?; what are the relative advantages and disadvantages with respect to traditional methods?

In many cases when new technology replaces old, the new methods will maintain much of the format they are replacing. For example, paper, cotton, metal, and even birch bark have all been used to make Indian books in the traditional pothi format which originates from the use of palm leaf as a writing surface (Gaur 1979: 18-19). This should be the case also with electronic dictionaries; the same information is required, and so should be presented in a familiar way. Only the medium is different. A database of Gāndhārī is no exception, and therefore everything that was said above regarding the contents of the dictionary articles also applies to the electronic form. Each entry in the electronic database should arrange the data for the headings listed above in separate fields so it can be retrieved and manipulated automatically. On this basis searches could easily return individual articles that would be visually similar to a printed version, but generated 'on the fly' from the latest version of the data file. The differences that will be discussed here relate to the medium rather than the content, and fall under two categories, scholarly and practical concerns:

An online version of the Gāndhārī dictionary is currently under development. At the time of this writing, already basic searches can be made at: http://depts.washington.edu/ebmp/dictionary.php. The source data was prepared in a Microsoft Excel spreadsheet file because this provides a convenient format to store and import Unicode data. Updates and information about the database will be posted on the EBMP (Early Buddhist Manuscripts Project) website (http://depts.washington.edu/ebmp/).

1.0. Scholarly concerns

1.1. Searching the database

The primary function of most electronic dictionaries is simply as a replacement to a conventional dictionary. As such, the main search requirement is to be able to find the entry words. However, the true value of electronic searching capabilities is found in advanced searches. For instance, the Gāndhārī dictionary as outlined above may be searched for Sanskrit, Pali, Tibetan, and Chinese terms, so that a Gāndhārī term can be identified when it is not readily predictable from the Sanskrit or Pali cognate, for example G *maṇa* = Skt. *punar* in Dhp-GK 65, 272(2×). A conventional dictionary (e.g. Turner 1969) would need a separate index for each cognate in order to match this functionality.

It is also possible to search for any sequence of letters, or even an individual letter. When trying to read a damaged manuscript, the remains of an unusual letter such as *ṭa* or *ḍha* or a sequence of letters could lead the user to a limited set of possibilities and with luck, a likely reading – provided of course the mystery word (or a similar word) appears elsewhere in the corpus. For example, the syllable *ḍha* occurs in 33 of the current database's more than 6,500 entries. If the vowel is not specified, the number for *ḍh* is about 70; in either case, a manageable number for the reader to browse through in search of a match. Since every entry will also be linked to every occurrence of the term in the corpus, this kind of search will be useful for paleographic studies, to locate all instances of a particular akṣara. This kind of search facility far outstrips the capabilities of conventional reverse dictionaries or even the Phonetic Analysis volume of the CDIAL (Turner 1971).

By the same method one could also search for grammatical or any other data recorded in the data tables. It has been suggested, therefore, that all entries should be marked up to indicate phonological as well as morphological data. If this is done, users would be able to perform searches such as finding all Gāndhārī words which show intervocalic voicing, or generating a report of all the attested endings of masculine *-a* stems in the nominative singular together with their frequencies. After the hard work has been done to suitably tag every entry, it would then be a relatively simple matter to compile all the data for a complete descriptive grammar of the Gāndhārī language.

1.2. Sorting the database

Entries in the database can be sorted by any of the fields, e.g., Gāndhārī headword, Sanskrit, English, Chinese. Furthermore, these categories can be sorted in a variety of different ways. For instance: a translation aimed at a general audience might make use of a glossary of key terms, sorted in standard alphabetical order, which could be produced on the basis of a segment of the database; for academic purposes the Gāndhārī, Sanskrit or Pali fields could be sorted according to the traditional arrangement; for those approaching Gāndhārī through Chinese texts, the data could be sorted in one of the ways appropriate to Chinese characters, e.g., by stroke, classifier, or pronunciation; when making a Gāndhārī reader it will also be possible to sort the words according to the order of their occurrence in any particular text.

Multiple sort orders can be arranged in sequence, so that like terms will appear in chronological order, or by type (inscription, manuscript etc.) or any other way of classifying the data. In short, the data exists in a fluid state, ready to take the form of any vessel that may contain it. The possibilities are entirely flexible.

1.3. Hypertext links

Hyperlinks – familiar to anyone who has used the Internet – provide a dynamic means of optionally accessing selected information. Hypertext links can be internal to a document, in which case they may be seen as computerized footnotes, or external, referring to another source of online information, akin to a bibliographic reference. The Gāndhārī database should make use of both. Internal hyperlinks should be constructed so that users can quickly jump to entries referred to within one entry; for example, a word may occur independently and as a second member of a compound. In a printed dictionary, the independent entry would contain a reference to the compound. In the electronic database it should be a simple matter to construct such references as hyperlinks so that the user need not submit a new search under the compound, but simply click on the reference, which will serve as the link.

Of perhaps even greater benefit will be the ability to link entries to the electronic source texts. Since, in the process of compiling the dictionary, all Gāndhārī materials should be entered as electronic texts, it will be possible to link each word in the database to its source text. Rather than quoting a citation in the dictionary, which is still a possibility, the user would be able to simply click on any of the references to see that particular context. With only slightly more work this could also be accomplished for the images of the texts themselves. If a more-or-less complete store of images of the Gāndhārī corpus can be assembled and properly tagged, any reference could also link to the appropriate image.

1.4. Open-endedness

One of the concerns with dictionaries, particularly of modern languages, is that they become out of date almost as soon as they are published. If a dictionary of Gāndhārī is to be published in book format, inevitably new manuscripts or inscriptions will be discovered which will add new words and variant spellings to the lexicon. If numerous new materials should come to light there will be a need to produce supplements to the main volume of the work, requiring the user to check multiple sources. This is not true of an electronic database. Any new material can be added seamlessly to the main data file at any time. Opinions on the readings of words can change, and these too can be corrected.

This flexibility to add and change the contents is one of the issues of concern to scholarship. How can something be authoritative if it will inevitably change? If a publication refers to the dictionary as a source, will the same argument be recoverable in fifty years time if the source has changed? This is a legitimate concern and some means of addressing it should be built into the data-base. One possibility, just as with books, is to publish the database with a version or edition number. In which case, an archive of all previous editions must be kept in some publicly accessible place.[10] Given the ever-increasing storage capacities of computer hardware, creating archives of the data should not prove an unrealistic solution.

2.0. Practical concerns

2.1. Accessibility

Since the advent of the Internet, the World Wide Web has become the natural place to publish shared resources such as electronic dictionaries. Some, such as the Oxford English Dictionary (http://dictionary.oed.com/) provide access for a subscription, while others, such as the Cologne Digital Sanskrit Lexicon (referred to above), provide access free of charge. Whatever the economics of

[10] It should also be quite possible for users to flag particular entries, which, if modified, would automatically notify them of any changes.

the situation, there should be two levels of access. The first should be a limited segment of the data corresponding to those works already published. The second should be the complete set of words both published and unpublished for use by those working directly with the manuscripts and others by invitation.

2.2. Cost of publication

Unfortunately, the costs of publication cannot be ignored by scholars. Here traditional forms of publication and publication via the Internet differ widely. Since the general work of the project will have to involve an electronic database at some level, the database will, in effect, already be there. To publish it over the Internet would simply mean making it accessible. Publishing a dictionary in book format will necessarily involve a far greater commitment of financial resources.

2.3. Shelf life

The fragile birch bark scrolls which form the main subject of the Early Buddhist Manuscript Project's work have already survived almost two millennia. We can only imagine if our books will survive a similar length of time. In stark contrast, our electronic data pose real problems for longevity of just a hundred, or even fifty years. A case in point comes from the phonetic indices to the CDIAL. These were compiled using computers just over thirty years ago (Turner 1971: v), and now these files are no longer accessible by any normal means (J. C. Wright, personal correspondence). If they were to be recovered it would take a specialist, a 'digital archeologist,' to extract anything from them. The problem here is two-fold: first, the actual tapes on which the data was stored are no longer used by current systems; second, even if the data were recovered from the tapes, it is questionable if current systems could process it correctly. The solution to the first problem lies in regularly updating the storage medium so that data is not left marooned on some digital island. The solution to the second problem is much more complex, and is beyond the scope of this paper. Let it suffice to say that if we are to undertake the vast work of compiling all Gāndhārī materials into an electronic data-base, we should do so in close association with librarians and specialists in data archiving and long term preservation of digital data.

CONCLUSIONS

The number of manuscripts now known to exist in Gāndhārī makes some kind of word database an essential requisite for continued study. The advantages of a word database will be that much greater if the corpus can be extended to all linguistically and culturally related materials. Defining Gāndhārī as anything written in the Kharoṣṭhī script makes a convenient and productive touchstone for the corpus that is at the same time largely defensible on linguistic grounds. However, it is entirely possible that future discoveries could necessitate a revision to this definition.

This paper has tried to anticipate many of the issues that need to be addressed in compiling a dictionary of Gāndhārī and has outlined a format by which the data may be presented in both printed and digital media. Whatever the final format, a computer database must underpin the work while it is in progress, owing to the ease with which computers can collect, sort, and manipulate large amounts of data. There are also numerous immediate advantages of the digital format to scholars that make electronic publication desirable. As such, it is natural to think of extending the 'work-in-progress' database to being a web accessible dictionary. However, in the long term, the uncertain life span of our current data makes a strong case for a parallel publication in book format.

REFERENCES

ALLON, Mark 2001. *Three Gāndhārī Ekottarikāgama-Type Sūtras: British Library Kharoṣṭhī Fragments 12 and 14.* (Gandhāran Buddhist Texts, 2.) Seattle: University of Washington Press.

BAILEY, Harold W. 1943. Gāndhārī. *Bulletin of the School of Oriental and African Studies* 11: 765-797.

------ 1982. Two *Kharoṣṭhī* Inscriptions. *Journal of the Royal Asiatic Society*: 142-155.

BECHERT, Heinz (ed.) 1994. *Sanskrit-Wörterbuch der buddhistischen Texte aus den Turfan-Funden und der kanonischen Literatur der Sarvāstivāda-Schule*. 2 vols. to date. Göttingen: Vandenhoeck & Ruprecht.

------ 1998. The Dictionary of the Sinhala Language and the Siṃhala Śabdakoṣaya. In Boris Oguibénine (ed.) 1998, *Lexicography in the Indian and Buddhist Cultural Field*: 21-29. (Studia Tibetica: Quellen und Studien zur tibetischen Lexikographie, 4.) München: Kommission für Zentralasiatische Studien, Bayerische Akademie der Wissenschaften.

BOYER, A. M. & E. J. RAPSON & E. SENART 1918. Une tablette kharoṣṭhī-sanskrite de la collection de Sir Aurel Stein. *Journal asiatique*, sér. 11, vol. 12: 319-327.

------ 1920-1929. *Kharoṣṭhī Inscriptions discovered by Sir Aurel Stein in Chinese Turkestan*. 3 parts (part 3 by E. J. Rapson and P. S. Noble). Oxford: Clarendon Press.

BROUGH, John 1962. *The Gāndhārī Dharmapada*. (London Oriental Series 6.) London.

------ 1996. *Collected Papers*. London: School of Oriental and African Studies.

BURROW, Thomas 1937. *The Language of the Kharoṣṭi Documents from Chinese Turkestan*. Cambridge: Cambridge University Press.

CDIAL = TURNER 1966, 1969, 1971.

DAMSTEEGT, Th. 1978. *Epigraphical Hybrid Sanskrit, Its Rise, Spread, Characteristics and Relationship to Buddhist Hybrid Sanskrit*. (Orientalia Rheno-Trajectina XXIII.) Leiden: E. J. Brill.

FALK, H. 1998. Notes on Some *Apraca* Dedicatory Texts. *Berliner Indologische Studien* 11/12: 85-108.

FUSSMAN, Gérard 1989. Gāndhārī écrite, Gāndhārī parlée. In: Colette Caillat (ed.), *Dialectes dans les Littératures Indo-Aryennes*: 433-501. Paris: Institut de Civilisation Indienne.

GAUR, Albertine 1979. *Writing Materials of the East*. London: The British Library.

GBT = Gandhāran Buddhist Texts series.

GHATAGE, A. M. 1996. *A Comprehensive and Critical Dictionary of the Prakrit Languages with Special Reference to Jain Literature*, Vol. 1. Pune: Bhandarkar Oriental Research Institute.

GLASS, Andrew 2000. A Preliminary Study of *Kharoṣṭhī* Manuscript Paleography. Master's thesis, Department of Asian Languages and Literature, University of Washington.

GLASS, Andrew & Stefan BAUMS & Richard SALOMON 2002. Proposal to Encode Kharoṣṭhī in Plane 1 of ISO/IEC 10646 Proposal submitted to the Unicode Consortium. (http://depts.washington.edu/ebmp/downloads/Kharoshthi.pdf)

HINÜBER, Oskar von 2001. *Das ältere Mittelindisch im Überblick*. Wien: Verlag der Österreichischen Akademie der Wissenschaften.

HULTZSCH, E. 1925. *The Inscriptions of Aśoka*. (Corpus Inscriptionum Indicarum, I.) Oxford: Clarendon Press

JOHNSON, Samuel 1755. *A Dictionary of the English Language*. London: J. & P. Knapton.

KONOW, Sten 1929. *Kharoshṭhī Inscriptions with the Exception of Those of Aśoka*. (Corpus Inscriptionum Indicarum, II.1.) Calcutta: Government of India, Central Publication Branch.

de LANEROLLE, Julius 1950. Sinhalese Dictionary and the Ceylon Branch of the Royal Asiatic Society. *Journal of the Ceylon Branch of the Royal Asiatic Society, Centenary Volume (1845-1945)*. New Series vol. 1: 13-22.

LENZ, Timothy 2002. *A New Version of the Gāndhārī Dharmapada and a Collection of Previous Birth Stories: British Library Kharoṣṭhī Fragments 16 + 25*. (Gandhāran Buddhist Texts, 3.) Seattle: University of Washington Press.

LÜDERS, Heinrich 1936. Textilien in alten Turkistan. *Abhandlungen der Preußischen Akademie der Wissenschaften*: 3-38.

MUKHERJEE, B. N. 1988. A casket inscription of the time of Vijayamitra, the ruler of Avaca. *Indian Museum Bulletin* 23: 7-10.

NORMAN, K. R. 1983. *Pāli Literature, Including the Canonical Literature in Prakrit and Sanskrit of All the Hīnayāna Schools of Buddhism*. (A History of Indian Literature, 7.2.) Wiesbaden: Otto Harrassowitz.

PATKAR, Madhukar Mangesh 1981. *History of Sanskrit Lexicography*. Delhi: Munshiram Manoharlal.

SALOMON, Richard 1990. New evidence for a Gāndhārī origin of the Arapacana syllabary. *Journal of the American Oriental Society* 110.2: 255-273.

------ 1998a. *Indian Epigraphy*. New York: Oxford University Press.

------ 1998b. *Kharoṣṭhī* manuscript fragments in the Pelliot Collection, Bibliothèque Nationale de France. *Bulletin d'Études Indiennes* 16: 123-160.

------ 2000. *A Gāndhārī Version of the Rhinoceros Sūtra: British Library Kharoṣṭhī Fragment 5B.* (Gandhāran Buddhist Texts, 1.) Seattle: University of Washington Press.

------ 2001. 'Gāndhārī Hybrid Sanskrit': New Sources for the Study of the Sanskritization of Buddhist Literature. *Indo-Iranian Journal* 44: 241-252.

------ forthcoming a. A Buddhist anthology in Gāndhārī. In: Jens Braarvig (ed.), *Buddhist Manuscripts,* 3. (Manuscripts in the Schøyen Collection, 4.) Oslo: Hermes Academic Publishing.

------ forthcoming b. The name of Taxila: Greek Τάξιλα, Gāndhārī *Takṣaïla*, Sanskrit *Takṣaśilā,* Pali *Takkasilā.* In: Pierfrancesco Callieri & Anna Filigenzi (eds.), *Studies in the Archaeology and Art History of the Indian Subcontinent and Afghanistan Dedicated to the Memory of Maurizio Taddei.*

SCHMIDT, Michael 1994. The format of the dictionary. In Bechert (ed.) 1994: I.8: xlviii–lvi.

SCHREINER, Peter 1996. On creating, formatting and working with a first electronic Sanskrit dictionary. In: Nalini Balbir & Georges-Jean Pinault (eds.), *Langue, style et structure dans le monde indien, Centenaire de Louis Renou, Actes du Colloque international (Paris, 25-7 janvier 1996)*: 413-426. Paris: Librairie Honoré Champion.

SWTF = BECHERT (ed.) 1994.

TSUKAMOTO, Keisho 1996. *A Comprehensive Study of The Indian Buddhist Inscriptions.* Kyoto: Heirakuji-Shoten.

TURNER, R. L. 1966. *A Comparative Dictionary of the Indo-Aryan Languages.* London: Oxford University Press.

------ 1969. *A Comparative Dictionary of the Indo-Aryan Languages, Indexes.* London: Oxford University Press.

------ 1971. *A Comparative Dictionary of the Indo-Aryan Languages, Phonetic Analysis.* London: Oxford University Press.

ZGUSTA, Ladislav 1971. *Manual of Lexicography.* (Janua Linguarum: Studia Memoriae Nicolai van Wijk Dedicata, 39.) Prague: Academia.

Lexicon-directed segmentation and tagging in Sanskrit

GÉRARD HUET

Abstract

We propose a methodology for Sanskrit processing by computer. The first layer of this software, which analyses the linear structure of a Sanskrit sentence as a set of possible interpretations under sandhi analysis, is operational. Each interpretation proposes a segmentation of the sentence as a list of tagged segments. The method, which is lexicon directed, is complete if the given (stem forms) lexicon is complete for the target corpus. It uses an original design for a finite-state transducers toolkit, based on functional programming principles. Further layers of this computational linguistics architecture are discussed.

1. COMPUTATIONAL LINGUISTICS AND SANSKRIT

Descriptive linguistics is the study of natural language phenomena. Theoretical linguistics strives to provide formal models of linguistic activity. Noam Chomsky initiated modern theoretical linguistics with successive theories (context-free and transformational grammars, government and binding, minimalism). These theories usually provide a *generative grammar* paradigm, by which means any valid sentence in the language may be generated. With the advent of computers a still more formal approach is attempted, where executable programs process a digital representation of natural language into information structures, which provide some degree of understanding of the given text or discourse. In the pioneer days of the fifties, automated translation systems were thus attempted, although difficulties were largely underestimated, leading to doubts about the feasibility of natural language understanding by computers. 50 years later, however, the situation is more promising, due to thorough investigations of linguistic models, the availability of fast processors and large memories, the development of large-scale finite-state methods and the availability of large corpuses where statistical methods could train generic methods by tuning their parameters on real data.

Linguistic studies were part of Indian culture from the early ages. Grammar (*vyākaraṇa*), phonetics (*śikṣā*), prosody (*chandas*), hermeneutics (*nirukta*), were recognised as fields of knowledge (*vedāṅga*). A stream of grammarians set to describe in exact terms the structure of Sanskrit utterances. Thus the grammarian Pāṇini, in the 4th century B.C., wrote a treatise in eight parts (*Aṣṭādhyāyī*) which may be considered a full-fledged generative grammar for classical Sanskrit. Further grammarians of this tradition (Kātyāyana, Patañjali, Bhartṛhari) are basically commentators on Pāṇini. They do not question his basic model, but rather explain it, refine it and complete it. Actually, the existence of this reference generative grammar had a strong influence on the historical development of the language: whereas the common language (*prākṛta*) kept evolving into modern (North Indian) languages, Sanskrit was frozen in a pristine state of preservation, with very regular phonetic, morphological, and syntactic paradigms. On the other hand, the availability of recursive rules in Pāṇini's model allowed poets to develop artificially iterative uses of certain constructs, such as compound formation of unbounded depth, making Sanskrit a quite unique 'natural' language.

However, the availability of Pāṇini's grammar, with its associated lexicons (*dhātupāṭha, gaṇapāṭha*), is not sufficient for the direct implementation of a Sanskrit mechanical analyser. Let us now explain this point.

It is recognized that linguistic modelling proceeds by successive layers, from an external surface form (speech or written text) to an internal informational net of semantic concepts. One traditionally distinguishes these layers as the successive submodels of linguistic activity, from surface speech or text to conceptual structures and plans:

- Phonetics (speech recognition)
- Phonemics (discretization of utterances as streams of phonemes)
- Morphology (structure of words)
- Syntax (structure of sentences)
- Rhetorics (structure of discourse)
- Semantics (structure of concepts and information updating)
- Pragmatics (structure of causality)

A generative grammar such as Pāṇini's gives an account of the generation of correct speech from an intended meaning, going in reverse in the above list, in a deterministic synthesis direction. The process corresponds roughly to the SENS-TEXTE theory of Igor Mel'cuk. On the other hand, a computer program analysing a surface phonetic stream will have to traverse the layers in the opposite direction, leading to an intrinsically non-deterministic analysis. Since the crucial information about semantics and pragmatics is not available in lower layers, ambiguities arise at the various stages, leading to a combinatorial explosion of possible interpretations. The choice between these interpretations depends on knowledge about the subject matter, tradition, and common sense, all processes which are hard to correctly model by computation. Actually, poets and the composers of esoteric treatises took advantage of the inherent ambiguity of the language to compose Sanskrit texts with multiple meanings, which may be deciphered only by separate commentaries. The Indian tradition of frequent metaphorical descriptions adds a supplementary degree of difficulty to an already formidable task. Thus, on one hand Pāṇini's grammar can only be used as a gold standard for any Sanskrit computational processor, and on the other hand we cannot hope, in the current state of knowledge engineering, to provide more than a computer-assisted Sanskrit analyser, usable as a tool for text mark-up assistance by knowledgeable Sanskrit scholars (*paṇḍita*). Still, such a tool would be extremely useful, for facilitating the organisation of critical editions, creating concordance indexes, comparing historical and regional variants of the literary works, organising layers of commentaries, and otherwise computing statistical information which is, in the present state of the art, impossible to achieve rigorously.

2. OVERALL DESIGN OF A LINGUISTICS PLATFORM

The above layer description of linguistics activity determines the overall architectural design of a computational linguistics platform. Of course, the layers are not independent: for instance, agreement and valence constraints from syntax must be consistent with morphological features (gender, number, person); also euphony causes interference between phonemics and morphology. And notions of topic and focus from communicative semantics relate to prosody, which is actually part of phonetics. Nonetheless, this layered architecture gives a first approximation to the structure of informatics processing modules.

In parallel to this sliced cake model of a linguistics flow processor, we find the pervasive *lexicon*, which holds all the word-dependent parameters of the various levels. The lexicon (and its derivatives, such as the inflected forms lexicon, containing conjugated forms of verbs and declined forms of substantives and adjectives) is the central repository of knowledge about words, their phonemic representation, their etymology and morphology analysis, their grammatical role, their semantics, etc.

This general model is fairly generic over language families, but the importance of the various layers, and their mutual interference, vary from language to language. For instance, Sanskrit has a specially complex morphology, compensated by a relatively undemanding syntax. But, first of all, euphony is systematic, with a complex set of morphemic rules, both at the level of morphology derivation of inflected words (internal sandhi) and at the level of shallow syntax for the formation of compounds, as well as for the glueing of words into sentences (external sandhi), leading conversely to a complex segmentation problem. This exposes the first serious difficulty for the mechanical processing of Sanskrit: the problem is to guess the sequence of words which by external sandhi rewriting would yield the given stream of phonemes. This problem occurs either when processing a phoneme stream issued from a speech recognition module or when processing a written sentence. This sandhi decomposition is by no means unique, and actually only semantic considerations will ultimately curb the overgeneration of this non-deterministic analysis.

3. LEXICON

We started by constructing a Sanskrit lexical data base from a Sanskrit to French dictionary which we developed over the years as a glossary of Indian culture. The structure of the lexical data base is explained in (Huet 2000; Huet 2001).

The database comprises 12,500 entries at the time of writing. These include: 520 roots, 7,500 word lemmas, 2,800 compounds, and 1,300 idiomatic expressions. Printable versions of the lexicon are generated in two formats: book PDF format, using a *devanāgarī* font with ligature computation by Velthuis' DEVNAG preprocessor; and HTML hypertext format, as a Web site with search engines.

The lexicon is structured as an inductive datatype rather than as a relational database format. The structure makes explicit the various parameters such as gender, number, etc. in order to facilitate morphology computations. Specific etymological links express the derivation of a word, ultimately to its roots. Various invariants are checked when the lexicon is processed, namely when it is compiled into internal representations. This compilation process is fast, and thus the source form of the database is the reference document which gets corrected and updated as a text file by the lexicographer.

4. SANDHI

External sandhi means euphony transformation of words when they are consecutively uttered. Typically, when a word w_1 is followed by a word w_2, some terminal segment of w_1 merges with some initial segment of w_2 to be replaced by a "smoothed" phonetic interpolation, which corresponds to minimizing the energy necessary to reconfigure the vocal organs at the juncture between the words. Sandhi affects also the morphological derivation of words and their inflected forms, using a more complex *internal sandhi* process - long term usage propagated the smoothing inside the words, for instance by transforming the nasal *n* into the retroflex *ṇ* and similarly the sibilant *s* into the retroflex *ṣ*.

We model sandhi computation by a two-tape transducer. The transducer has two input tapes, one for storing the stream of phonemes issued from w_1 read from right to left, the other for storing the stream of phonemes issued from w_2 read from left to right. According to the interaction between the two boundary phonemes, proper output is generated on the output tape. This process is basically deterministic, although some choices and variants exist. We have two versions of the sandhi automaton, respectively for internal and external sandhi.

The internal sandhi processor is used systematically by the morphological engine described in the next section. External sandhi is iterated over all possible combinations of interactions by phoneme strings of length one or two - no deeper transformations occur in the case of external sandhi. This iteration computes a compiled form of a set of sandhi rules of the form $u|v \rightarrow w$, where u, v and w are words (standing for strings of phonemes). Such a rule represents the regular relation which holds between all pairs of strings $\lambda u|v\rho$ and $\lambda w\rho$, for any strings λ and ρ, where $|$ marks word boundaries. Such rewrite rules are used for constructing the segmentation automaton described below in Section 6. We remark that the set of such rules, owing to their atomic character, is surprisingly large (we generate 2,790 such rules).

5. MORPHOLOGY

First of all, let us emphasize that we do not deal here with derivational morphology, neither primary (*kṛt*) nor secondary (*taddhita*) - we assume that corresponding entries are explicitly listed in the lexicon. We consider only inflexion (*vyaya*), which derives declensions of substantives and conjugation of finite verbal forms. The rationale is that derivational morphology is of interest mostly to semantic layers, that it is far from being as regular as inflexion, and that overgeneration would be hard to control. The price that we have to pay is that the lexicon is cluttered with quality substantives in *-tva* and *-tā*, agents in *-tṛ*, processes in *-na* and so on. On the verbal side, this obliges us to list derived conjugations (causative, desiderative, intensive) and verbal adjectives, nouns and adverbs (participles, infinitives, absolutives). On the other hand, we shall obtain compounds of any depth without the need to list them in the lexicon, since we consider compound analysis as a special case of segmentation.

The second remark is that we *generate* such inflected forms, using internal sandhi generation, as opposed to attempting to analyse them at the morpheme level. We thus avoid stemming, a complex process since it would involve internal sandhi analysis.

We entered the morphological laws for inflexion as paradigm tables. For instance, for nouns, adjectives and pronouns, each table maps a pair (number, case) into a set of possible suffixes. A dispatch switch takes as parameters a word stem and a gender, and determines the corresponding paradigm table. This information may now be used in several ways. First of all, when navigating in the hypertext form of the lexicon, one may click on gender annotations. Each such gender annotation is in the scope of exactly one stem form of the surrounding entry, giving the pair (stem, gender) of parameters of the dispatch switch, yielding a paradigm table. The paradigm table may be filled with the specific declensions, by computing the internal sandhi of the stem and the suffix. The corresponding table of inflected forms may then be displayed in the browser window, as an interactive grammatical aid. We may iterate this computation over all pairs (stem, gender) recorded in the lexicon, and this constructs a static list of all possible inflected forms. We record this list, as a mapping from such forms to the list of all morphological tags (stem, gender, number, case) which yield the given inflected form. From the 12,500 entries of our dictionary (out of which 8,000 are non-compound entries) we produced a total list of 150,000 inflected forms[1], using 88 paradigm tables.

The morphology of verbs is similar, but still more complex, be-

[1]This data is freely available for downloading as an XML resource (given with its validating DTD) at our site `http://sanskrit.inria.fr/`

cause of the many tenses, aspects, voices, and moods. The present system (present, imperfect, optative and imperative, at active, passive and middle voices) has been implemented for the 10 present classes, as well as the future (periphrastic and autonomous), perfect (reduplicating and periphastic), and aorist systems (with the 7 formation schemes of the latter). The derived conjugations (causative, intensive, and desiderative) are not constructed by generative paradigms, but entered in the lexicon on a by need basis. Each root is recorded with the sets of preverb sequences which it allows. These preverb annotations anchor hypertext pointers to the corresponding verb entries.

6. SEGMENTATION OF NOUN PHRASES

The first level of analysis of a Sanskrit written text is segmentation. Words are not separated by blanks and punctuation symbols, but are merged together with external sandhi, in a continuous phonemic stream which faithfully reflects the speech flow. Thus, recognition of written text is actually similar to speech processing, and segmentation must be solved in order to reveal the first level of the linear structure, that is the representation of a sentence as a list of words.

This process is inherently non-deterministic. For instance, in *Bhagavadgītā*, the verse chunk: नासतोविद्यतेभाव: gets interpreted by Śaṅkara as the list of words (*padapāṭha*): *na asataḥ vidyate bhāvaḥ* (the unreal has no existence), while Madhva takes it as: *na asataḥ vidyate abhāvaḥ* (the 'asat' is not inexistent).[2] This is actually a not infrequent situation, since, for instance, long *ā* may be obtained by sandhi from the four mutual combinations of *a* and *ā*. Since *a* is the negation prefix for adjectives and *ā* is the frequent preverb meaning "towards the locutor", one guesses that this leads to many solutions, with possible ambiguities between a notion and its negation as above. Often ambiguities will not be resolved before the verification of syntax and even semantics. And sometimes several interpretations are legitimate, like in the example above, which means that an extra level

[2]Madhav Deshpande, Indology Internet forum communication, 2002.

of interpretation of the text may be necessary to infer its unambiguous meaning. And of course poets took advantage of this feature to write intentional double-entendre works.

We solve the segmentation problem using finite-state technology. A finite state machine expresses the regular relation between streams of words and the streams of phonemes issued from the (external) sandhi rewriting at their mutual junction, and a transducer implements the inverse relation. The precise constructions are documented in (Huet 2005), where we show consistency, completeness and convergence of the algorithm. A general toolkit 'Zen' based on finite state machines described as decorated tries was abstracted from this effort and released as free software (Huet 2002; Huet 2003a; Huet 2003b).

What the completeness property of our algorithm says for our Sanskrit segmentation problem is that a sentence s admits a finite number of decompositions $s_1\ s_2\ ...\ s_n$ where all the words s_i belong to the (inflected forms) lexicon, and (external sandhi) rewrite rules are applied between consecutive words. A segmentation transducer is compiled from the inflected forms lexicon and sandhi rules array which produces exactly this set of solutions.

A crucial requirement is a *non-overlapping* condition, which demands that no word is such that it has a prefix λ participating on its left to sandhi with its predecessor and a suffix ρ participating on its right to sandhi with its successor, with a non-empty overlap of λ and ρ. This is true of external sandhi in the general case, since sandhi contexts are short, if one excludes from the list of words very short particles such as the emphatic u from Vedic Sanskrit, whose occurrence is constrained anyway by prosody (in Vedic hymns, u usually occurs at the end of shlokas).

This segmenter is theoretically complete for any phrase built from words which are inflected forms from the root stems in the dictionary. Note, in particular, that compounds are analysed into their subcomponents using the same segmentation automaton, since external sandhi applies there too, and the inflected form generator also produces the stems used as left components of compounds. This assumes that the inflected forms of a compound $A \cdot B$ are of the form $A \cdot B'$, where B' is an inflected form of B. However, a difficulty appears for *bahuvrīhi* (exocentric) usage of compounds, since this assumption may be violated by compounds where B admits a specific gender, but $A \cdot B$ used as an adjective in some other gender may admit extra forms. For instance, *bīja* (seed) is the stem of a neutral substantive, but *raktabīja*, the monster "whose blood regenerates", admits as nominative form *raktabījaḥ*, not obtainable as compound of *rakta-* with an inflected form of *bīja*. This difficulty is genuine, since we have here a choice between admitting *bahuvrīhi* usage of every compound (and thus opening the way to serious overgeneration problems), or else listing explicitly in the lexicon every *bahuvrīhi* attested usage, a possibly daunting task.

We opted in this segmenter for the second solution, and chose to record in the lexicon such *bahuvrīhi* usage of compounds. Actually, a preprocessing phase on the lexicon identifies all compounds which are irregular, in the sense of not being obtainable by external sandhi of the iic. form of their left component with a regular stem of their right component. This analysis adds 180 'autonomous' compound forms. This list includes *dvandva* compounds with double dual forms, such as *mitrāvaruṇau*, compounds whose left component uses a feminine form, such as *durgāpūjā*, or an inflected form, such as *vasuṃdhara*, irregular external sandhi such as *pṛṣodara*, or internal sandhi such as *rāmāyaṇa*. Their inclusion as autonomous nouns allows the generation of their forms, since our automaton is not able to get their analysis (as compounds) from their components. Besides these exceptional cases, all compounds formed with stems from the lexicon are analysable, down to any nesting level, without the need to have them explicitly listed as lexicon entries.

A kind of reverse difficulty occurs for *avyayībhāva* compounds such as *yathāśakti*, which ought to be recognized as an invariable adverb, although its rightmost component admits inflexion. This is a minor cause of overgeneration.

The main problem with our segmenter is an overgeneration of spurious sandhi solutions with small particle words such as *āt*, *ām*, *upa*, etc. and enclitic agent formation suffixes such as *-ad*, *-ga*, *-da*, *-pa*, *-ya*. Also, a word such as the substantive *āya* clashes badly with dative suffixes. This overgeneration will have to be dealt with either by morphology (so that compounds in say *-ga* are generated on their own, without *ga* appearing by itself) or by prosody considerations.

Here is a simple typical example of segmentation:

```
Chunk: tacchrutvaa
may be segmented as:

 Solution 1 :
[ tat <t|'s -> cch>]
[ 'srutvaa <>]
```

The system indicates that the final *t* of *tat* (this) transforms itself by external sandhi with the initial *ś* of *śrutvā* (having heard) to form the phoneme sequence *cch*, leading to the correct analysis of *tacchrutvā* (having heard this). In *devanāgarī*: तद् | श्रुत्वा = तच्छ्रुत्वा.

7. TAGGING

Since the segmenter is lexicon-directed, it may be easily extended into a tagger. All that is needed is to keep a lemmatization table, recording the generative origin of inflected forms. An economical computer solution for this problem, taking advantage of the regularities of morphology for sharing maximally the inverse morphological map, is provided by the structure of *differential words* (Huet 2005).

Now we obtain a tagging transducer, with two levels of nondeterminism, since a phrase may be segmented into different subwords, and each segment word may be obtained by several morphological constructions. Here is a simple example:

```
Chunk: me.saanajaa.m'sca
may be segmented as:

 Solution 1 :
[  me.saan
   {acc. pl. m.}[me.sa] <>]
[  ajaan
   {acc. pl. m.}[aja#1]|{acc. pl. m.}[aja#2]
```

```
  <n|c -> .m'sc>]
[ ca
  {und.}[ca] <>]

Solution 2 :
[ maa
  {und.}[maa#2]|{acc. sg. *}[aham] <aa|i -> e>]
[ i.saan
  {acc. pl. m.}[i.sa] <>]
[ ajaan
  {acc. pl. m.}[aja#1]|{acc. pl. m.}[aja#2]
  <n|c -> .m'sc>]
[ ca
  {und.}[ca] <>]
```

The first solution is the correct one (sheep and goats), whereas the second one is parasitic. The ambiguity arising from the homonyms aja_1 (goat) and aja_2 (unborn) is duly recorded, so that each segment stem points unambiguously to one of the lexicon entries.

For larger chunks, overgeneration may lead to literally thousands of solutions. This indicates that guidance from further layers (syntax and semantics) will be ultimately needed in order to reduce the set of solutions to manageable sizes.

8. SEGMENTATION OF VERB PHRASES

The next challenge was to analyse verb phrases. This involves several new difficulties. The first one was to build the morphology module for root declensions. In order to have deterministic internal sandhi, the phonemes *j* and *h* had to be partitioned into two variants each. Thus, for instance, *j* | *t* = *kt* (e.g. *yukta*) whereas *j'* | *t* = *ṣṭ* (e.g. *mārṣṭi*). Similarly *h* | *t* = *ḍh* (e.g. *leḍhi*) whereas *h'* | *t* = *gdh* (e.g. *dugdha*). These distinctions exhibit some of the Indo-European substrate of Sanskrit roots.

The second problem concerns the modelling of preverb prefixing. The natural idea would be to affix preverbs to conjugated verb forms, starting at roots, and to store the corresponding inflected forms along with the declined nouns. But this is not the right model for Sanskrit verbal morphology, because preverbs associate to root forms with *external* and not *internal* sandhi (probably owing to their origin as postpositions). And putting preverbs in parallel with root forms and noun forms will not work either, because the non-overlapping condition mentioned above fails for the preverb *ā*. And this overlapping actually makes external sandhi non-associative. For instance, noting sandhi with the vertical bar, we get: (*iha* | *ā*) | *ihi* = *ihā* | *ihi* = *ihehi* (come here). Whereas: *iha* | (*ā* | *ihi*) = *iha* | *ehi* = **ihaihi*, incorrect. This seems to definitely doom the idea of storing conjugated forms such as *ehi*.

The proposed solution to this problem is to prepare special root forms prefixed by *ā* in the case where the root forms starts with *i* or *ī* or *u* or *ū* - cases where a non-associative behaviour of external sandhi obtains. But instead of applying the standard sandhi rule *ā* | *i* = *e* (and similarly for *ī*) we use *ā* | *i* = **e* where **e* is a *phantom* phoneme which obeys special sandhi rules such as: *a* | **e* = *e* and *ā* | **e* = *e*. Through the use of this phantom phoneme, overlapping sandhis with *ā* are dealt with correctly. Symmetrically we introduce another phantom phoneme **o*, obeying e.g. *ā* | *u* = **o* (and similarly for *ū*) and *a* | **o* = *ā* | **o* = *o*. This methodology is explained in (Huet 2003c).

The combination of three automata, one for nouns, one for preverb sequences, and one for root forms (plus the special forms with phantom phonemes) is designed to segment (and tag) simple verbal sentences, where a number of noun phrases is followed by a finite verb form.

It remains to explain what forms are to be entered in the preverbs automaton. We could, of course, just enter individual distinct preverbs, and allow looping in the preverbs phase. But this would be grossly over-generating. At the other extreme, we could record in the lexicon the preverb sequences used with a given root. But then, instead of one roots forms automaton, we would have to use many different automata (at least one for every equivalence class of the relation "admits the same preverb sequences"). We propose a middle way, where we have one preverbs automaton storing all the preverb sequences used for at least one root. Namely: *ati, adhi, adhyava, anu, anuparā, anupra, anuvi, antaḥ, apa, apā, api, abhi, abhini, abhipra, abhivi, abhisam, abhyā, abhyud, abhyupa, ava, ā, ud, udā, upa, upani, upasam, upā, upādhi, ni, niḥ, nirava, parā, pari, parini, parisam, paryupa, pi, pra, prati, pratini, prativi, pratisam, pratyā, pratyud, prani, pravi, pravyā, prā, vi, vini, viniḥ, viparā, vipari, vipra, vyati, vyapa, vyava, vyā, vyud, sa, saṃni, saṃpra, saṃprati, saṃpravi, saṃvi, sam, samava, samā, samud, samudā, samudvi, samupa.*

We remark that preverb *ā* only occurs last in a sequence of preverbs, i.e. it can occur only next to the root form. Thus we do not have to augment the preverbs sequences with phantom phonemes.

Here is an example of tagging the tricky sentence discussed above:

```
Chunk: ihehi
may be segmented as:

 Solution 1 :
[ iha
  {und.}[iha] <a|aa|i -> e>]
[ aa|ihi
  {imp. a. sg. 2}[aa-i] <>]

 Solution 2 :
[ iha
  {und.}[iha] <a|i -> e>]
[ ihi
  {imp. a. sg. 2}[i] <>]
```

The first solution is the correct one ("come here"). The second one is a homophone without the *ā* preverb, corresponding to a non-correct "go here". Also **ihaihi* is righly rejected as having no solution.

Remark 1. This exceptional treatment of the *ā* preverb corresponds to a special case in Pāṇini as well, who uses a similar device with a special mark after the preverb ā. This indicates that our approach is legitimate. The importance of our contribution is to show that this *generative* mechanism is also adequate for *analysis*, since it allows us to regain the nonoverlapping condition needed for correct non-deterministic prediction.

Remark 2. It is easy to adapt the model to special cases and exceptions. For instance, preverb *adhi* combines with middle form *ye* of root *i* to form *adhīye* 'I study', although the usual sandhi rule between final *i* and initial *y* yields *iy*, predicting the wrong form **adhiye*. But our machinery allows to enter a specific sandhi rule *adhi|y→ adhīy*, and then *adhīye* may be correctly analysed:

```
Chunk: adhiiye
may be segmented as:

Solution 1 :
[ adhi <i|y -> iiy>]
[ ye
  {pr. m. sg. 1}[adhi-i] <>]
```

Many more special sandhi cases have to be properly dealt with in our sandhi platform, some of which being dependent on grammatical information (such as special sandhi for dual person forms) or specific to certain words (such as the 3rd person pronoun *sa*). Also, it is expected that the three-automata model will need to be revised with other components, for instance to recognize properly the use of auxiliary verb forms with substantive stems in *ī*, such as *nimittī kṛ* or *sajjī bhū*. Also a finer analysis of the use of preverbs with a given root may avoid generating spurious forms (often only one voice is used with a given preverb sequence for a given root).

Here is a non-pathological typical example of the analysis of a small sentence ("cat drinks milk"):

```
Chunk: maarjaarodugdha.mpibati
may be segmented as:

 Solution 1 :
[ maarjaaras
  {nom. sg. m.}[maarjaara] <as|d -> od>]
[ dugdham
  {acc. sg. m.|acc. sg. n.|nom. sg. n.
  |voc. sg. n.}[dugdha] <m|p -> .mp>]
```

```
[ pibati
  {pr. a. sg. 3}[paa#1] <>]
```

In the Web interface of the lexicon, the above tag sequence anchors hypertext pointers to the dictionary entries of the successive lexemes *mārjāra*, *dugdhā* and *pā*$_1$.

9. TUNING AND LEARNING

At the time of printing, morphology generation has been extended to participles (past passive and active, present active middle and passive, future active middle and passive, the last one having 3 possible forms), and to infinitives and absolutives (in *-tvā* and in *-ya*). From 525 roots, we generate an inflected forms database of 98265 root finite forms, and 204657 participial forms, which in addition to the 128057 noun forms obtained from the lexicon, give a total of about 431 000 forms. The segmentation process uses a total of 9 automata, modelling correctly compound formation, periphrastic forms (in -ī), affixing of preverbs, and forms which may appear only as right component of a compound.

Overgeneration is still problematic, and simple sentences may generate thousands of "solutions", most of them ungrammatical or nonsensical. It is clear that extra syntactic processing will be necessary to filter out most of these candidate solutions, as explained in the next section. Only then shall we be able to start processing a real corpus, as opposed to toy isolated examples. In order to trim spurious solutions, and rank the remaining ones in decreasing order of relevance, before parasitic ones, training of the stochastic automaton will have to take place.

Then a robust version of the segmenter, together with a lemmatizer, should provide a mechanism for lexicon acquisition. This way we may hope to tune our tagger to become a useful preprocessor for scholars, in such a way that fully tagged critical editions may be prepared with computer assistance. We should also allow the automated computation of concordance indexes, as well as various statistical analyses which are unfeasible at present.

10. PARSING

The next step in processing is the verification of government constraints. Verbal valencies (subcategorisation patterns) must be saturated by the available nominal cases of the current phrase (or rather their semantic rôle or *kāraka*). This constraint processing phase will trim out solutions which do not satisfy this requirement. For instance, in the example sentence above, we obtain from the fact that *pā* is a transitive verb the constraint that is requires a subject and an object. The voice being active, this means we need one nominative tag and one accusative tag. The unique solution verifying this constraint is to take *mārjāraḥ* as the subject and *dugdham* as the object.

In the same syntactic process, we shall group compounds, and attempt to unify segments by agreement, in order to refine chunks into a number of concording noun phrases. The interpretation of genitives will distinguish between object genitives which fulfill a genitive role in the verb valency, and between attributive genitives which operate as noun phrase complements.

A difficulty is expected from verbs expecting two accusatives, since the partition of the accusative chunks into the two *kāraka* roles – typically the learning and the learnt in verbs such as *paṭh* (to learn) – is likely to involve semantic features (such as animate versus inanimate). This will involve incorporating into the lexicon an ontology mapping, a standard apparatus in today's natural language treatment platforms. Traditions such as Indian semiotics (*navyanyāya*) may be applied to this semantic modeling.

A major difficulty will be to recognize dislocations and long-distance dependencies, with a penalty cost severe enough to defeat potentially exponential overgeneration. This parsing methodology, in constrast with traditional transformational frameworks, is close to the dependency grammars model. The link between dependency grammars and the Paninian *kāraka* theory was noticed by Bharati, Chaitanya and Sangal (Bharati et al. 1993; Bharati et al. 1995).

We may hope to tune our syntax analyser by using as training data a tree bank constructed over the years by Brendan Gillon (Gillon 1996), who used as corpus a list of typical sentences from Apte's treatise on Sanskrit syntax (Apte 1885). Further layers, dealing with discourse structure (such as anaphora resolution), rhetorics and semantics, are at this point rather remote and speculative, not only for Sanskrit, but for natural languages in general.

11. CONCLUSION

What we have presented in this paper is the state of the art of our Sanskrit reader; it is able to segment and tag simple sentences. The reader will have to be tested on real corpus, firstly on easy texts for which the current lexicon is complete. This will allow statistical training, aiming at listing the possible solutions in decreasing plausibility. A robust version will then be developed, in order to serve as a lexicon acquisition tool, for corpus for which the lexicon may not be complete.

At this point we should be ready to consider doing for Sanskrit what Perseus[3] offers for classical Latin and Greek corpus.

REFERENCES

Abbreviations

ESSLLI = European Summer School in Logic, Language and Information
IEEE = Insitute of Electrical and Electronics Engineers
INRIA = Institut National de Recherche en Informatique et en Automatique

APTE, V. S. 1885. *The Student's Guide to Sanskrit Composition. A Treatise on Sanskrit Syntax for Use of Schools and Colleges.* Poona: Lokasamgraha Press.

BHARATI, Akshar & Vineet CHAITANYA & Rajiv SANGAL 1995. *Natural Language Processing, a Paninian Perspective.* Delhi: Prentice-Hall.

BHARATI, Akshar & Rajiv SANGAL 1993. Parsing Free Word Order Languages in the Paninian Framework. *Proceedings, 31st conference of Association for Computational Linguistics, Columbus, Ohio 1993*: 105-111.

GILLON, Brendan S. 1996. Word Order in Classical Sanskrit. *Indian Linguistics* 57 (1): 1-35.

[3] `http://www.perseus.tufts.edu`

HUET, Gérard 2000. Structure of a Sanskrit Dictionary. Technical report, INRIA. http://pauillac.inria.fr/~huet/PUBLIC/Dicostruct.ps

------ 2001. From an Informal Textual Lexicon to a Well-structured Lexical Database: An Experiment in Data Reverse Engineering. In: *Working Conference on Reverse Engineering (WCRE'2001)*, IEEE: 127-135.

------ 2002. The Zen Computational Linguistics Toolkit. Technical report, ESSLLI Course Notes. http://pauillac.inria.fr/~huet/Zen/esslli.pdf

------ 2003a. Zen and the Art of Symbolic Computing: Light and Fast Applicative Algorithms for Computational Linguistics. In: *Practical Aspects of Declarative Languages (PADL) symposium*. http://pauillac.inria.fr/~huet/PUBLIC/padl.pdf

------ 2003b. Automata Mista. In: N. Dershowitz (ed.), *Festschrift in Honor of Zohar Manna for his 64th anniversary*. Springer-Verlag LNCS vol. 2772: 359-372. http://pauillac.inria.fr/~huet/PUBLIC/zohar.pdf

------ 2003c. Towards Computational Processing of Sanskrit. In: *Proceedings, International Conference on Natural Language Processing (ICON-2003)*: 40-48. Mysore: Central Institute of Indian Languages.

------ 2005. Transducers as Lexicon Morphisms, Phonemic Segmentation by Euphony Analysis, Application to a Sanskrit Tagger. To appear in: *Journal of Functional Programming*. http://pauillac.inria.fr/~huet/PUBLIC/tagger.pdf

Index

(of selected terms, names and words)

absolutive, see *gerund*
accent(uation), 3, 49, 52, 56-58, 60, 70-72, 121, 136, 206, 207, 212, 213
Achaemenian, 143, 144, 157, 256
aṃśú-, 184-189
āṇí-, 170, 175-179, 190-192
Apabhraṃśa, 78-80, 84-85
Arapacana, 283, 285
Asiknī, 200
aspiration throwback, 15
átharvan-, 171-175, 190, 191
áyas-, 186, 187
Bartholomae's Law, 8, 15
bhiṣaj-, 124, 136
cluster simplification, 9, 12, 13
compensatory lengthening, 4, 8, 12, 15
contour segment, 8, 9
dāsa-, *dasyu-*, 36, 181
depalatalized, 7
Ephedra, 169, 184
ergative, ergativity, 68, 86, 87, 90, 115, 116
euphony, see *sandhi*
floating aspiration, 6
Gaṇḍak, 200
gerund(ial)(= absolutive), 24, 41, 90, 99-115, 197-199, 201, 215, 233
Grimm's Law, 14
Haoma, 255, 261, 262, 265
hapax, 27, 49, 51, 52, 55, 57, 58, 61, 263
Hindi, 68, 84-86, 205, 236
hinge(d) compound/participle, 220-232, 242
Hūṇa, 144
hybrid (Sanskrit), 90, 274-278
iṣṭakā-, *iṣṭikā-*, 171
kalaśiyākāḥ, 267
kali-, 177, 178
kalyā́ṇa-, *kalyāṇī́-*, 176, 190
Kankai, 200
Kašmīr, 146
Kṛṣṇa, 200
Kushan, Kuṣāṇa, 144, 145, 152, 170
mayūra, 199
palatalization, palatalized, 7, 8
Pāli, 78, 79, 81, 84, 111, 112
Paṇi, 170, 181-183, 191, 192, 277, 281, 290, 295, 296
Pāṇini, 12, 22, 24, 37, 38, 41, 73, 208-210, 213, 229, 306, 307, 321
Parsi, 255, 257, 258, 263-265
Prakrit(ism), Prakritic, 6, 78-81, 121, 126, 133, 135, 139, 144, 182, 183, 201, 206, 209, 220, 222-224, 229, 232, 238, 241, 242, 244, 245, 274, 275, 277
Pulkasa-, 130
retroflex, 175, 177, 192, 197, 198, 233, 236
rhotazized, 15
RUKI rule/context, 10, 15
Sadānīra, 200
Śaka, 145, 158, 162
saṃprasāraṇa, 124
sandhi (/euphony), 4, 12, 14, 16, 305, 308-319

Sanskritization/-ized/Sanskritic, 85, 126, 147, 156, 157, 159, 162, 200, 232, 276, 277, 280
Śarvá-, 179-181
Sas(s)anian, 255, 256, 267
Soma, 184-189, 191
Sprachbund, 197, 232
syncretism, syncretic, 66, 86
tarśaka, 267
Tolkāppiyam, 209, 210, 213, 214
Túgra-, 122
Tűrghna-, 129
univerbation, univerbated, 70-72, 75, 213, 245
Wackernagel's clitics, 74, 170